C0-AUT-905

DISCARDED

Towards a Well-functioning Economy

To
Salam, Nadya, Nikolai, Natalia and Mikhail

Towards a Well-functioning Economy

The Evolution of Economic Systems and Decision-making

Louis Haddad

Honorary Research Fellow, Department of Economics, University of Sydney, Australia

Edward Elgar
Cheltenham, UK • Northampton, MA, USA

© Louis Haddad 2002

All rights reserved. No part of this publication may be reproduced, stored in a retrieval system or transmitted in any form or by any means, electronic, mechanical or photocopying, recording, or otherwise without the prior permission of the publisher.

Published by
Edward Elgar Publishing Limited
Glensanda House
Montpellier Parade
Cheltenham
Glos GL50 1UA
UK

Edward Elgar Publishing, Inc.
136 West Street
Suite 202
Northampton
Massachusetts 01060
USA

A catalogue record for this book
is available from the British Library

Library of Congress Cataloguing in Publication Data
Haddad, Louis, 1937-
    Towards a well-functioning economy : the evolution of economic systems and decision-making / Louis Haddad.
        p. cm.
    Includes index.
    1. Economic policy–Decision-making. 2. Comparative economics. I. Title.

    HD87 .H337 2002
    330'.01–dc21
                                                            2001018957
ISBN 1 85898 892 6

Printed and bound in Great Britain by Biddles Ltd, *www.biddles.co.uk*

Contents

List of Tables

Preface

Economists are well aware that the economy functions as a system, even as an evolutionary system, and that the behaviour and performance of a particular economy are partly the results of 'systemic' factors. Yet, these factors are rarely systematically studied and remain ill defined and misunderstood. Indeed, the behaviour of the economy as a system is one of the most important assumptions economists habitually make without bothering to investigate it in any detail outside the general equilibrium theory. This theory necessarily omits, among other things, the study of complex organisations and institutions, multi-level decision-making and control, and the process by which knowledge and information are acquired in a social setting. Yet, it is precisely these 'systemic' factors that differentiate economies and explain why some function and perform better than others.

The idea that the economy behaves as a system goes back to the beginning of economics itself in the mid-eighteenth century, to the physiocrats in France, arguably the first school of economists. Their conception of the economy as a system of organised and interdependent activities, as depicted in the famous *tableau* of their doyen, François Quesnay, is one of the early important contributions made to the emergence of economics as a separate albeit not a self-contained discipline. As Schumpeter (1954) noted, it marked the beginning of 'scientific' economics. Until the economy was seen as a system, economics remained in its 'pre-scientific' phase, an unsystematic discipline.

It is no accident that Adam Smith, who was himself inspired by the works of the physiocrats, devoted a good deal of his celebrated book to the study of economic systems across time and space. He took from them the idea that the economy consists of many interdependent parts, each of which sustains and is sustained by the system as a whole. He then made his singular contribution of reconciling the interest of each individual part with that of the whole. In particular, he tried to show how the competitive market mechanism could simultaneously reconcile the interests of all individuals through the resolution of the valuation problem, which is central to a well-functioning economic system.

Much of the history of economics after Adam Smith was centred on the problem of valuation (and distribution). It took about a hundred years and a great deal of intellectual effort to rigorously work out the necessary conditions for reconciling the seemingly conflicting interests of the numerous agents of the economic system. This intellectual effort culminated in the great work of

Léon Walras (1834–1910), his construction of the general equilibrium theory, the core of modern economics. 'It is the only work in economics', to quote Schumpeter again, 'that will stand comparison with the achievement of theoretical physics'. Walras himself had made a similar comparison when he realised the full significance of his 'discovery': 'Thus the system of the economic universe reveals itself, at last, in all its grandeur and complexity: a system at once vast and simple, which, for sheer beauty, resembles the astronomic universe' (Walras 1954).

Walras, it would seem, achieved for economics what Newton had accomplished for physics. For example, the principle of marginal utility plays the same unifying function as the law of gravity in physics. But the marginal utility of a commodity varies a great deal from one individual to another and from one generation to another. Further, the structure and institutions of the economy as well as the behaviour of economic agents vary across time and space. By contrast, the gravitational law is more or less constant in all places and is also the same for us as it was for Newton. It is precisely the lack of constancy in economic matters, the fact of the variability of economic institutions and behaviour across time and space, that provides the methodological foundation and justification for the study of economic systems.

There is, of course, no one right way to study economic systems. Depending on the objectives of the analyst, economic systems can be studied from different perspectives, including property rights, organisational arrangements, levels of development and decision-making processes. These perspectives are not mutually exclusive or inconsistent with one another; they merely focus attention somewhat differently. The focus of this study is on decision-making both because of the common conception of economics as 'the science of (rational) choice' (or decision-making) and because decision-making is a pervasive activity in a modern society as opposed to habit in traditional societies and command in feudal societies. This is not to deny the importance of habits and commands in a modern society. Indeed, we rely a great deal on them, as will be shown in this book. However, choices or decisions make a difference to our lives and affect the operation and performance of the economic system. At the same time, they are constrained by the economic system itself. Economic systems and decisions interact and grow together in an organic fashion, and hence should be studied together.

Economics then is not simply about choices, private and public, rational or otherwise, but also about economic systems. Indeed, the central problem of economics is to understand how the economic system works, which, in turn, depends on the decision-making process. Moreover, the focus on decision-making and economic systems eschews some of the dichotomies and polar extremes found in modern economics, such as individualism versus collectivism, individual rationalism versus institutionalism, and 'decisionism' versus determinism. Economic outcomes, we hope to show in this study, are not merely the product of pure reason or rational decisions, nor of formal and informal institutions, but of all these and more.

Although this book is primarily about economics, non-economic issues, including political and ethical ones, will be brought into the analysis. This is because economics becomes practically useful when it is combined with ethics and politics. There are very few problems in the real world that are purely economic. Certainly, the most important decisions of our lives include choices between economic and non-economic issues. It is, therefore, one of the aims of this book to provide a conceptual framework to cope with such choices. Moreover, since the economic system is a sub-system of a much wider social system, a well-functioning economy is viewed in this study as part and parcel of a 'just society'.

The focus of the book is on 'the big picture', on showing how the elements of the economic system dovetail, and how the various components of the decision-making process and the properties of a well-functioning economy are geared together. Some details are necessarily sacrificed. Hence, the study does not set out to 'prove' anything (not that anything of major practical importance can be 'proven' in economics). Rather it attempts to cast some light on the nature and evolution of economic systems viewed from the decision-making perspective, and to establish some plausible conditions for a well-functioning economy and a just society.

I am deeply grateful to John Purcal, Ihor Gordijew and Maurice Haddad for reading the first draft of this book and for their critical comments. I am also grateful to my colleagues Debesh Bhattacharya, Evan Jones and Flora Gill for helpful suggestions.

No less thanks must go to my wife, Salam, for her patient and persistent struggle with the various versions of the handwritten manuscript, to Mikhail Haddad for assistance with the tables and checking of references, and to Viola Hallahan and Kerry Fairs for their assistance in typesetting the final manuscript.

L.H.
July 2001

1. Introduction

The primary purpose of this book is twofold: to 'see' how and why economic systems work and change across time and space, and to establish some plausible conditions for a well-functioning economy. It is proposed to focus the discussion on the process of decision-making: who makes and implements what decisions, how and why. This focus is suggested by the observation that economic success depends on correct decisions. Correct decisions depend chiefly on the locus of decision-making authority, proper procedures, reliable information flows, rational criteria and effective incentives. Further, deliberate decisions, as opposed to ingrained habit or blind obedience to economic forces, customs and conventions, are the generators of non-deterministic history, discontinuity and novelty. Moreover, much of economics as a science is concerned with decision-making in the public as well as the private sector. Hence, the operation, performance and evolution of economic systems are chiefly the direct and indirect consequences of policies and decisions made and executed by individuals, organisations and governments. Such policies and decisions are never made in a social vacuum. In reality, decision-makers are constrained by their special circumstances, the lack of sufficient information or ignorance, the social, legal, cultural and economic institutions (which are themselves the product of past decisions), the physical environment and 'systemic' factors.

Systemic factors are hard to define precisely. They are often referred to as the 'building blocs', the 'architecture', the institutions or simply the 'rules of the game'. For the purpose of this book, it is best to think of systemic factors as the coordinating and enforcing mechanisms, which link different decision-makers at all levels of the economy and induce or compel them to participate in the preparation, formulation and execution of policies and decisions. There are four principal coordinating mechanisms, which are present in some degree in modern economic systems. They are custom, command, competition and cooperation (the four Cs). Depending on the extent to which each mechanism dominates the economy, the four coordinating mechanisms give rise to four major types of economy: the customary economy, the command economy, the competitive economy and the cooperative economy. In reality economies usually consist of any two or more combinations of the four mechanisms. Indeed, it is the contention of this book that a well-functioning economy is a 'composite economy', consisting of an 'optimal' combination of all four coordinating and enforcing mechanisms.

The decision-making process, as outlined in the next section of this chapter, captures quite adequately the four mechanisms and provides some insights into the performance and evolution of economic systems. Further, the study of decision-making processes across time and space enables us to derive the principles of an integrated decision-making system that will tend to generate the 'right' decisions, and consequently lead to the emergence of a well-functioning economic system. If the decision-making system is fundamentally flawed, the performance of the economy will not only be sub-optimal but the economic system itself might collapse in the long run.

II

Decision-making is an exceedingly complex process of resolution, of choosing a desired course of action from a set of possible alternatives within a deadline. It consists of several steps and involves a number of components or principles. For the purpose of this book, we focus our discussion on five components; each is considered an important determinant of the correctness of economic decisions. A flaw in one will adversely affect the other components and consequently the overall outcome (the correctness of decisions). It is not claimed that the five components of the decision-making process exhaust the possible list; only that when taken together, they tell us what we need to know to make successful decisions. In the rest of this section we briefly discuss each component and show how it affects the quality of decisions. A more detailed discussion will be offered sequentially in the next five chapters.

The first component is the structure of decision-making authority. It tells us who makes what decisions and gives us some idea about the locus of economic authority, and the degree of (de) centralisation and concentration of economic power. It will be shown later that certain types of decision are best made by specialised decision-makers located at different decision-making points and levels in the economy. This implies an 'optimal' structure of decision-making authority, which is necessary both for the formulation and the implementation of 'correct' decisions, correct in the sense of absence of regret. An optimal structure will not eliminate all errors, only systemic ones.

The second component is the procedure of decision-making. It tells us how decisions are reached, whether in an authoritarian or democratic manner. A democratic procedure involving meaningful consultation and participation of people most affected by the decisions may, of course, delay the formulation of decisions but will probably enhance the quality of the decisions by acquiring more and better information and advice from subordinates and experts. An authoritarian procedure, on the other hand, may be more appropriate in certain well-circumscribed cases such as emergency situations when speed is of the utmost consideration.

The third component of a decision-making system is the structure of information flows. It tells us who generates what kind of information and how it is transmitted to decision-making points. The complexity of economic decisions in modern economies necessarily involves a division of labour in the gathering, processing, evaluation and communication of information, as well as in decision-making and decision-implementation. However, this division of labour may create distortions and errors in the process of transmission of information to the decision-makers and of commands from the decision-makers to the 'implementers'. Consequently, there must be a reliable structure of information flows corresponding to the structure and procedure of decision-making. Such a structure will permit the speedy flow of more accurate and timely information necessary for making informed decisions.

The fourth component of the process of decision-making is the choice of criteria on which decisions are based. It tells us something about the rationality of decisions. Decision criteria include the economic calculus (private and social) of costs and benefits, political, social, ethical and administrative considerations. Decision-makers may make their policies and decisions on the basis of a simple criterion, or, more likely, on a combination of two or more criteria. It is our contention that all major decisions, which affect our (total) welfare, involve economic and non-economic considerations, and hence such decisions must be made on the basis of several criteria. They must be 'right' not only from an economic point of view but also from other points of view. In particular, public decisions must be also politically acceptable and ethically desirable.

The fifth component of a decision-making process is the structure of incentives that motivates economic agents. It tells us who gets what. In situations where the decision-makers are separated from the implementers, an appropriate structure, consisting of both positive and negative incentives as well as economic and non-economic ones, is needed to ensure that sound policies and correct decisions are implemented swiftly, efficiently and faithfully. The aim of an effective incentives, structure is not to eliminate 'legitimate' or functional inequalities, but rather to remove unnecessary inequalities resulting from exploitation, rent-seeking activities and shirking.

It will become clearer from further discussion that the five chosen components of a decision-making process are closely interdependent. Accordingly, the entire process of decision-making from the initial stage of preparation and formulation to the final stage of execution and monitoring of decisions must be well integrated. Otherwise, we may end up with three undesirable outcomes: correct and informed decisions that are poorly executed; wrong or ill-informed decisions that are efficiently executed; and wrong decisions that are inefficiently executed.

III

Since the central theme of this book is concerned with the principles of an efficient decision-making system that will minimise systemic errors and generate 'optimal' decisions, which will in turn result in a well-functioning economy, it is worth while before we proceed further to state what we mean by a well-functioning economy and what are its essential properties. A more detailed discussion of these properties is presented in Part III of the book.

The concept of a well-functioning economy is frequently used by economists, but has not been properly defined. We believe different economists will have different notions as to what constitutes a well-functioning economy and will certainly assign different weights to their chosen properties. Indeed, they may not agree on all the properties that constitute a well-functioning economy, let alone on what measures to take to promote such properties. All the same, a well-functioning economy in our view would: (a) allocate resources efficiently; (b) generate an optimal rate of innovation; (c) adapt swiftly and efficiently to external and internal shocks; (d) maintain macroeconomic stability at a high level of employment; and (e) distribute income and wealth equitably. These are usually treated by economists as objectives or desiderata, but in our scheme of things they become properties of the working of the economic system.

Generally, these properties are not mutually exclusive; they overlap and cut across each other. Sometimes compromises have to be made, especially between (a) and (b), between (a) and (e) and between (d) and (e), but, in general, the five properties are interconnected and tend to reinforce one another. Thus, a failure or a setback in one property will adversely affect the other properties and consequently the performance of the whole economy. In what follows we comment very briefly on each property in turn.

Traditionally, economists have focused on allocative efficiency, on the ability of an economic system to allocate resources where they are most needed. It is generally assumed that a competitive market economy provides the necessary conditions for the optimum allocation of resources. However, in practice imperfect and asymmetric information, ignorance, uncertainty and the existence of externalities of one kind or another lead to sub-optimal allocation. Despite these shortcomings, the competitive market remains an important if not an indispensable mechanism for solving the valuation problem and for allocating resources efficiently. The allocative role of the market can be enhanced by 'good' government intervention in cases of 'market failures' such as the prevention of unfavourable externalities and the provision of public goods as well as the formation of an institutional infrastructure required for the efficient functioning of the market.

It has always been recognised that a perfectly competitive economy, which allocates resources efficiently in the short run, may not be viable in the long run, if it fails to generate a rate of innovation sufficient to maintain its competitive advantages in international markets and to offset the law of diminishing returns. The ability to innovate is, arguably, the most important property of a well-functioning economy. However, our knowledge of the innovation and diffusion process is far from adequate. We can specify some but not all of the conditions for successful innovation and diffusion of new technologies. In particular, since innovation is a risk-ridden activity, normally resulting in favourable externalities, the risks should be spread across the community to encourage more investment in research and development (R&D). Indeed, the rate of innovation can be increased and sustained through the development of an 'innovational infrastructure' that has the effect of reducing the risk of innovation for potential innovators.

In a rapidly changing world, where national economies are becoming increasingly open and interdependent, the ability to adjust swiftly and efficiently to external shocks becomes an important and vital property of a well-functioning economy. An economy that fails to adjust quickly to changing circumstances and acquire new comparative advantages will experience a decline in its economic growth. As in the related case of technological change or creative efficiency, we do not know all the necessary conditions for adaptive efficiency. But it seems that a high rate of innovation, flexible institutions and organisations and a commitment on the part of the government to expose domestic enterprises to the rigours of foreign competition play a key role in promoting flexibility and adaptability.

Macroeconomic stability, which is given much attention by financial institutions, such as central banks, the IMF and the World Bank, is regarded by them as a fundamental property of a well-functioning economy, since it is required by the other properties. Thus, without a minimum degree of macroeconomic stability, long-term investment, innovation and economic growth are likely to suffer. An unstable economy will be overly driven by short-term considerations that lead to distortions in the use and allocation of resources. The conditions for macroeconomic stability are many and varied. They include sound monetary, fiscal and (in those countries that do not have a free exchange rate) exchange rate policies, which in turn require developed financial institutions and markets, including an independent, or a semi-independent, central bank to regulate the money supply and keep the monetary system healthy.

The final property of a well-functioning economy is an equitable distribution of income and wealth. Most economists regard equity as belonging to ethics and frequently conflicting with efficiency. In our view, equity is not only an important property of an economic system but is more often than not compatible with efficiency. Indeed, it will be argued later in more detail that equity is good for efficiency and efficiency is good for equity. Here, it is sufficient to say that if the distribution of income and wealth is highly skewed and the wealth of the few has been acquired illegitimately, low-income groups will feel they are not receiving their just rewards. They will only do the minimum amount of work they can get away with. Exploitation of workers by the bosses will encourage shirking. Both acts are unethical and harmful to efficiency. Further, a situation where most workers are dissatisfied can lead to political instability and consequently to economic instability and inefficiency. But if the distribution of income and wealth precludes exploitation, rent-seeking activities and shirking, then the resulting inequalities would be no greater than those strictly warranted by the efficient functioning of the economy. Thus, an equitable distribution of income and wealth is not merely a matter of 'good' ethics but may also be 'good' economics.

IV

This book can be seen as having three parts: conceptual, historical and normative. In Part I we examine in more detail the five selected components of the decision-making process and show how each affects and is affected by the other components. We also attempt a new classification schema for economic systems based on the five components. The first act of any kind of understanding of an economic system is to classify or to group together similar economies. Part I provides a conceptual framework of the decision-making process that will generate new insights into the workings of economic systems.

In Part II the five components of the decision-making process are used to explain and evaluate the functioning of four major historical economies: the customary economy, the command economy, the competitive economy and the composite economy. We would have preferred to devote a chapter to the cooperative economy, but no such economy existed in history except perhaps in small tribal communities. The Soviet-type 'socialist' economy, which was envisaged by its founders to be based primarily on cooperation rather than competition, remained until its collapse in the late 1980s and early 1990s subject to the command principle, which turned out to be hostile to cooperation. Nevertheless, the cooperative principle is present in the modern (market) economy, but it is not sufficiently strong to make it a well-functioning economy, or to refer to it as the cooperative economy. In Part II we also attempt to show how each system is transformed into another while carrying over some features of decision-making from the past. With perhaps the exception of the earliest economic system, the customary economy of the hunter-gatherer and subsistence societies, economic systems are a mixture of some or all the modes of coordination of decision-making. The last chapter of Part II is devoted to the modern economic system, which we call the 'composite economy', consisting of a sub-optimal blend of custom, command, competition and cooperation.

In Part III the five components are brought together in Chapter 11 and transformed into the five principles required for an 'optimal' decision-making system. In Chapter 12 we discuss in more detail the five chosen properties of a well-functioning economy and show how they interact with each other. An attempt is then made in Chapter 13 to link those properties with the principles of a well-designed decision-making system and to explain how each principle of decision-making affects the functioning and performance of the economy. Finally, Chapter 14 concludes the book with a brief discussion of the main transitional problems involved in moving closer towards a well-functioning economy and a just society.

PART ONE

Economic Systems and Decision-making

2. Structures of Decision-making

I

In this chapter we discuss how decision-making authority is dispersed in different economic systems and how this dispersion affects both the process and outcome of decision-making. The structure of decision-making tells us who makes what decisions and indicates the degree of centralisation and concentration of economic power in an economy. It is a fundamental property that influences the other properties of decision-making and consequently the performance of an economy. It is also an important criterion for classifying economic systems. A well-functioning economy will require an 'optimal' decision-making structure that will tell us what is the most desirable way to allocate different decisions and functions to different levels of government, to markets and to organisations. Arguably, the division of decision-making is quite as important as the familiar division of labour. Indeed, one of the most important aspects of the former division is between those making key decisions and those who specialise in implementing them.

The procedure adopted in the rest of the chapter is as follows: Section II examines the nature and types of decision-making structure and discusses the notoriously ambiguous terms 'centralisation' and 'decentralisation'. In Section III an attempt is made to classify economies along the centralisation–decentralisation continuum. Section IV evaluates the comparative advantages and disadvantages of different decision-making structures. Finally, Section V consists of a summary of the key points of the chapter and offers some tentative remarks on the possibility of designing an 'optimal' decision-making structure.

II

Economists have always been interested in decision-making structures, the question of who should be deciding what and the appropriate degree of (de) centralisation. This is reflected in the long-standing debate on the relative merits of *laissez-faire* and government intervention, on individualism and collectivism. The debate is as old as economics itself. It is found as far back as the fourteenth century in the works of Ibn Khaldun (Haddad 1991), in the *Wealth of Nations,* discussed at length by Jeremy Bentham, and popularised by his disciple John Stuart Mill. In his influential *Principles of Political Economy* (first published in 1848) and in his other works dealing with the functions of governments in economic affairs, Mill attempted to draw 'the line of demarcation between the things with which governments should, and those with which they should not directly interfere' (1868, p 479). However, towards the end of the *Principles* it becomes clear that he was unable to draw such a line. Instead, he simply offered five major arguments in favour of the *laissez-faire* principle and six against it. Nevertheless, he concluded 'Let alone' should be the general rule (1868, p 573). Mill's position is paradoxical. Not only did he provide more arguments against the rule of *laissez-faire*, but the exceptions he enumerated seem more important than the rule. Further, in his article 'Centralisation' published in 1862, Mill explicitly acknowledged the difficulty of drawing a demarcation line between the state and the private sector. Given Mill's standing with the neo-liberals and the continuing influence of his authority on the subject, it is worth quoting the whole relevant passage from 'Centralisation':

> State action is regarded as an extreme remedy to be reserved, in general for great purposes; for difficult and critical moments in the course of affairs, or concerns too vital to be trusted to less responsible hands. Few Englishmen, we believe, would grudge the government, for a time, or permanently, the powers necessary to save from serious injury any great national interest; and equally few would claim for it the power of meddling with anything, which it would let alone without touching the public welfare in any vital part. And though the line thus indicated neither is nor can be very definitely drawn, a practical compromise, between the state and the individual, and between central and local authority, is, we believe, the result which must issue for all prolonged and enlightened speculation and discussion on this great subject (*Collected Works* XIX, 1977, pp 609–10).

Because of Mill's failure to draw the line of demarcation, and despite his conclusion that no such line 'can be very definitely drawn', the debate continued unabated and reached something of a peak in the famous 'socialist controversy' of the 1930s, when the idea of 'socialism' and greater government intervention was gaining ground, possibly as a result of the (then) apparent success of Soviet socialism and the failure of *laissez-faire* during the Great Depression. The controversy centred on the question of efficiency and the possibility of economic calculation under various forms and degrees of centralisation. The question was given rigorous treatment first by Enrico Barone in a famous paper, 'The Ministry of Production in the Collective State' (1908). A notable feature of the controversy was the use of the terms 'centralisation' and 'decentralisation' in connection with the problems of disjunction between decision-making and information flows.

The principal protagonists of decentralisation and the market mechanism, von Mises, Hayek and Robbins, raised the fundamental problem of how a central planning (decision-making) authority can acquire complete, accurate and timely information concerning socially owned enterprises to make meaningful decisions relating to their activities. In particular, von Mises (1935) contended that rational economic calculation was impossible under centralised socialism, because of the absence of markets for instruments of production, and also because marginal utilities were subjective entities and, therefore, could not be determined objectively by a central authority. Hayek (1935), however, admitted the theoretical possibility of rational economic calculation but stressed its practical impossibility. As Robbins (1934) argued, by the time the millions of equations representing the activities and preferences of producers and consumers were solved, the information on which they were based would become obsolete and would need to be updated, and the equations themselves would have to be calculated all over again, and so on. Later, Hayek (1945) drew attention to the problem of the fallibility of human communication and the inevitable distortion of information in the process of transmission, especially from enterprises to the central authority. As a member of the Austrian school, he was particularly aware of the problems of aggregation and falsification of information as it passes upwards from one level to another in the administrative hierarchy.

The chief protagonists of centralisation and socialism, Dickinson (1933), Lerner (1934), Dobb (1933) and Lange (1938) saw no real difficulties in the separation of information flows and decision-making. The central decision-making authority (the central planning board), they argued, would, by a process of trial and error, not unlike that of Walras's 'auctioneer', set the prices to which the enterprises would adjust their levels of output until their marginal costs equal marginal revenues. Accordingly, the principle of rational allocation of resources, they concluded, would be more effectively implemented under centralised socialism than under capitalism, where the conditions of perfect competition cannot be obtained. The primary function of the central authority is simply to decide on the set of prices for enterprises. The latter would behave, like their counterparts under perfect competition, as price-takers. Thus, central planning would achieve the same results as perfect competition and, at the same time, would be more feasible.

It is noteworthy that both parties to the debate conducted their arguments in terms of general equilibrium theory, with little or no reference to the momentous events that were taking place in the Soviet Union under Stalin. Socialism was understood to mean simply social or public ownership of the means of production. They focused on the problem of rational allocation of resources and abstracted from questions of power relations and multi-level decision-making and incentives. Information channels were, of course, central to both parties but were treated asymmetrically. For the anti-socialists, the focus was on the upward transmission of information from enterprises to the central authority. For the socialists, it was the other way round. Further, the socialists did not stress the problem of incentives and motivation. They assumed that enterprise managers would have the same objective function as that of the central authority, and would therefore faithfully implement the instructions or commands passed down to them. However, in reality the problem of incentives turned out to be far more serious for the functioning of the socialist economy than that of rational economic calculation, though, as we shall see, the two problems are not unrelated.

Given the emphasis on problems of information flows in the 'socialist controversy', it is not surprising that subsequently information theory and decision theory became almost synonymous. Centralisation and decentralisation were defined in terms of information flows and exchanges. For example, Marschak (1959, pp 399–400) defines an economic system as centralised, if the central authority makes its decisions on information received from peripheral agents, and then sends its decisions (orders or commands) back to the agents; whereas an economic system is decentralised if there is an exchange of information between economic agents. Similarly, Hurwicz (1971, p 96) defines, 'an adjustment process or an economic system as centralised, if…at least one of the participants comes into possession of all relevant information and everyone's prospective actions'; whereas in a decentralised system no such centralisation or concentration of information occurs. In short, according to Marschak and Hurwicz, the degree of (de) centralisation is determined by the direction of information flows.

The definitions of centralisation and decentralisation in terms of information flows seem too narrow and are at odds with those used by other social scientists. As Lynch (1989, p 3) has pointed out, 'for most political scientists, sociologists, organisational theorists, and others, the main concern is not with information flows but with the structure of decision-making authority: how decision-making power is dispersed or delegated'. For political scientists, in particular, 'decentralisation is important, if it offers more opportunities for citizens to influence government or public decisions' (Levy and Truman 1971, p 172). However, since the supply of information is a crucial input in the decision-making process, those who generate the required information necessarily participate in the formulation of decisions, and thus influence the outcomes. Hence, the dispersion of economic power, or the degree of centralisation, cannot be fully assessed without knowing the source of information, or who generates the information on which decisions are based.

Clearly, a distinction has to be drawn between the 'decisional' and 'informational' roles of an agent or principal. Thus, we may define complete or total centralisation as a process in which a central authority decides precisely what each and every subordinate must do in each circumstance on the basis of information collected and processed by the authority itself. Total centralisation thus defined cannot exist. Although the central authority may have the power to make all the decisions required for the functioning of the economy, owing to lack of sufficient time and energy alone, it cannot make all the necessary decisions by itself. It must therefore create lower decision-making organisations, committees and agents to whom it can delegate some, perhaps, the great bulk of decisions. However, the central authority may retain the power to decide on the division of decisions among various echelons in the hierarchy or among different agents. Further, there may be no formal or legal restrictions on the central authority with respect to its decisional role in the affairs of other decision-making agents. Any decision at any time can be made or changed for other agents without warning or consultation. Nevertheless, whatever decision-making power a central authority may possess, in practice it is constrained not only by time and energy but also by a host of other considerations, including its computational capacity, the availability of information, the danger of social unrest resulting from unpopular or harsh decisions and the willingness of subordinate agents to accept and execute its decisions faithfully. Clearly, a totally centralised economy is not feasible except perhaps under an extreme emergency, and even then some decisions must be delegated to other agents.

Total decentralisation implies the absence of a central decision-making authority, or if such an authority exists, it does not interfere directly or indirectly with the economic decisions of autonomous agents. The primary function of the central authority, in a totally decentralised economy, is simply to enforce 'the rules of the game' and to protect the individual against 'force and fraud'. This is the familiar function of the state in the *laissez-faire* system. However, in such a system, decision-making power may be heavily concentrated among few enterprises or corporations. Thus, it is important to distinguish between 'centralisation' and 'concentration' of decision-making authority. Centralisation pertains to hierarchies, which are characterised by vertical relationships, while concentration is associated more with 'polyarchies', which have horizontal relationships (Sah and Stiglitz 1986). In a hierarchy, decision-making power may be both centralised and concentrated; in a polyarchy economic power may be concentrated but not centralised. It is confusing, therefore, to define complete decentralisation as a situation in which 'all agents share equally in decision-making authority'; and 'cannot exist if any agent has more decision-making authority than any other agents' (Lynch 1989, p 5). Clearly, this definition refers more to the degree of concentration and not to the degree of (de) centralisation of economic power. In our view it represents, at best, a special case of decentralisation where there is equality of decision-making power in the decentralised economy.

From the point of view of equity and possibly of human rights, concentration of economic power is the more appropriate measure. The feeling of alienation and powerlessness would persist whether economic power is concentrated in the hands of the state (the centre) or whether it is held by a small group of private citizens. Moreover, as Neuberger and Duffy (1976) observed, theoretically it is easier to measure the degree of concentration of decision-making authority than the degree of (de) centralisation. Such a measure can be obtained by using the Lorenz curve or the Gini ratio in the same way that it is conventionally used to measure the degree of inequality of income and wealth. Neuberger and Duffy (1976 p 43) place all participants in the systems, whether decision-makers or not, on the horizontal axis in order of decision-making authority. The vertical axis measures the total decision-making authority and the percentage of this authority held by a given percentage of the agents. The more skewed the curve the greater the degree of concentration of economic power. If the curve coincides with the vertical axis then one individual possesses all the power; there is complete concentration. The diagonal represents complete equality of decision-making authority.

There are three obvious difficulties with this approach, as Neuberger and Duffy themselves recognise. First, it is hard to get accurate information on the quantity of decision-making power an individual may possess with respect to a large set of decisions that are taken jointly. Second, not all decisions are of equal value and it matters greatly who makes the 'big' decisions and who makes the 'small' ones. Third, the problem of assigning weights to different decisions to reflect their relative importance is far from easy to solve. Given these difficulties, it is impossible to measure accurately the degree of concentration let alone the degree of (de) centralisation.

The decision-making structure, as noted in Section I, refers not only to the degree of (de) centralisation and concentration of decision-making authority within hierarchies (organisations and governments) and polyarchies (markets), but also to the institutional mix of markets, organisations and governments. These are alternative modes of organising economic activity, and in principle there is an 'optimal' mix that leads to a well-functioning economy. However, the existing division of decisions among them is the result of custom and convention, ideology, politics and economics (transaction costs, economies of scale, informational requirements).

Modern economies are too complex to be efficiently organised by markets only, organisations only or governments only. There are many goods and services that are valuable to society, but not profitable to individuals and organisations operating in the market and motivated by profit maximisation or satisfaction. This does not necessarily imply that they must be provided by the state, or that markets for them will not exist. The problem is that we cannot rely on markets or profit-making organisations to supply public goods and services efficiently, or at levels that will be socially optimal. Conversely, there are other goods and services that can be provided by the state, but are best left to economic agents subject to market forces or to organisations, both profit-making and non-profit-making ones.

There are also numerous decisions, especially those concerning complicated production processes, that are more efficiently made and effectively executed within large organisations than by individuals acting alone, or with a small number of people, in the marketplace. According to Arrow (1971) the functional role of organisations is to reduce uncertainty by exploiting the superior productivity of collective action, including the collection and processing of information, and internal economies of scale, which markets do not do well. Indeed, as uncertainty increases, the tendency to shift economic transaction from markets to firms increases. Moreover, markets do not provide full information about the value of specific inputs and assets, as they become more fully specialised to a single use or user (Williamson 1981).

Although markets play a central role in economic theory, modern economies are dominated by organisations. This has led Simon (1991) to suggest that modern economies should be called 'organisational economies' rather than market economies. The great bulk of goods and services are produced within organisations, which are regulated to a limited extent by markets or prices (Stiglitz 1991). Thus, a thorough understanding of how resources are used and allocated in modern economies must include the study of organisations and, in particular, their decision-making structures. As Williamson (1981, p 1550) observed, 'a complete theory of value will recognise that firm structure as well as market structure matters'. The same argument applies also to governments, which are special organisations that have the monopoly of legitimate force.

Returning to the question of (de) centralisation, it is important to emphasise that the *de facto* degree of centralisation cannot be measured or assessed by the formal decision-making structure. Centralisation or decentralisation is not simply a state but also a process that is partly determined by the other aspects of the decision-making system. Thus the procedure of decision-making, how decisions are reached, whether through a process of consultation with subordinates, or through an authoritarian manner, affects the degree of decentralisation. An authoritarian procedure reinforces any existing centralised structure, while a democratic procedure modifies such a structure. Normally, a centralised structure is associated with an authoritarian procedure, but it is quite conceivable that, if a central decision-making authority consults lower decision-making agents and modifies or changes its initial decisions, then the structure is in fact more decentralised than it formally appears.

Second, and as we have already seen, the decision-making structure is influenced by the direction of information flows. To the extent that a central authority depends on subordinate agents for the supply of information needed to reach meaningful decisions, its decision-making power is diminished and the degree of centralisation is correspondingly reduced. A central authority may ignore the information and advice supplied by subordinates, but then its decisions are unlikely to be informed. Similarly, a decentralised structure will become more centralised, if subordinates and independent economic agents act on information supplied by the central authority, as in the case of 'indicative planning' in Western Europe in the 1950s and 1960s. The extent to which information flows influence the degree of decentralisation is discussed at length in Chapter 4.

Third, the decision-making structure, or more specifically the degree of decentralisation, is partly determined by the criteria employed in reaching decisions. If the central authority wishes to make the 'right' decisions to avoid unnecessary waste, then it must rely on the advice and skills of experts and subordinates. This applies particularly to complex decisions, which are beyond its computational capacity. In such cases the central authority acts as the conduit. Moreover, the application of proper (social) economic calculus, as the chief decision criterion, dictates the level of decision-making. If the decisions themselves entail significant externalities, which cannot be internalised at lower levels, as in the case of pure public goods, then they are usually made at the centre. Other types of decision such as the 'when' decisions in agriculture (when to sow, spray or harvest) and micro-decisions that entail no significant externalities are left to decision-making agents on the spot or to private enterprise. Thus, the nature of the decisions and the criteria employed together determine the level of decision-making and consequently the degree of centralisation.

Finally, the decision-making structure is affected by the ability of the centre and higher echelons to secure the compliance of other agents with their decisions, or the ability to achieve the outcomes they desire. For example, a decision-making structure may be highly centralised, in the sense that most decisions are made at the centre, but if the central authority is unable or unwilling to exert its will on subordinates, or if the decisions themselves are modified and sometimes falsified by subordinates, then the structure is more decentralised than it formally appears. Paradoxically, the more decisions a central authority makes the less control it has, and the less it is able to enforce them. Too many decisions taken at the centre create conflict and confusion and encourage falsification at lower levels. Further, peripheral agents responsible for implementation of decisions taken at higher levels invariably make adjustments and changes to suit their interest, and hence participate in decision-making. Furthermore, subordinates often initiate the decisions they are given to implement. The common observation made about the experience of the former Soviet Union and Eastern Europe that the commands (central decisions) were written by the recipients are further explored in Chapter 6.

It is abundantly clear now that the degree of centralisation cannot be determined simply by studying the formal decision-making structure or by asking who decides what, or who has power over certain decisions. This provides only a partial and a superficial view. To obtain a comprehensive view we need to examine more fully the remaining four properties of decision-making, which we attempt to do in the following four chapters. Meanwhile, in the next section an attempt is made to classify economies along the centralised–decentralised continuum, bearing in mind that a comprehensive classification must wait until we discuss the other properties of the decision-making process.

III

If we were to position economies along the centralisation–decentralisation continuum, there would hardly be any that would be placed at the two opposite ends. Indeed, we have already noted that total centralisation cannot exist. In a completely centralised economy all decisions would be made by a single authority (a person or committee) at the centre without consultation, and would be calculated on the basis of information collected by the central authority itself. Further, the decisions would be implemented faithfully by subordinates. Such an economy would be managed chiefly by commands. It would be desirable in times of emergency, when the objectives are simple and clearly defined, and decisions are few, when rational economic calculations are temporarily suspended, and when central decisions or commands are readily obeyed. In such a situation, the aim is to get over the crisis as soon as possible by rapidly mobilising resources without worrying too much about costs. Beyond the emergency period, a complete or even high degree of centralisation would not work for the whole economy. The command principle, however, would still be needed to cope with certain decisions and situations but would have to be supplemented by other modes of decision-making.

Looking at the other end of the continuum, at total decentralisation, where economic relations among agents are purely horizontal (excluding what goes on inside the firm or family) and where the role of the central authority is confined to the enforcement of law and order and the protection of the individual against 'force and fraud', we may be able to find a few small economies, 'the pure *laissez-faire* economies'. Decentralised market economies can be competitive, monopolistic or oligopolistic. Thus decentralisation can be accompanied by concentration of economic power. Indeed, if there are significant economies of scale to be captured, competition may lead to oligopoly and even to monopoly.

While decentralised economies are normally governed or coordinated by competition and market forces, it is quite conceivable to have a highly decentralised administered economy, in which the great bulk of decisions are delegated to committees, subordinates or to state-owned enterprises whose decisions are not constrained by competition and market forces. For example, in the Soviet Union, during the New Economic Policy period and after Stalin's death, serious attempts were made to decentralise the economy as a counter to bureaucratic delays and inefficiencies without introducing the market and without calculating scarcity prices. In a decentralised economy without markets, enterprises would make their decisions and enforce them according to a national plan, which they themselves have drawn up or participated in. The role of the central authority would be largely confined to the coordination of decisions, to correct and reconcile, not to initiate proposals. Sovereignty over the allocation of resources would be transferred from the centre to the periphery. However, in practice a decentralised (administrative) economy would still have to overcome the fundamental problem of valuation, which can only be solved practically by the competitive market. The invention of linear programming and other mathematical devices demonstrated the theoretical possibility of determining scarcity prices without the market mechanism, but their application have been confined to solving few microeconomic problems.

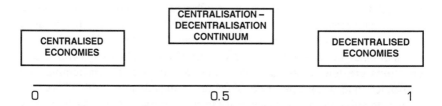

On a scale from 0 to 1 most economies would be located between the two extremes of 'total centralisation' and 'total decentralisation' and would consist of mixtures of hierarchies, polyarchies and associations. Economies that are dominated by hierarchies, as in the former Soviet Union and Eastern and Central Europe, would be located in the centralisation zone of 0–0.5. Other economies that are characterised by polyarchies and associations and whose decisions are dictated mainly by market forces would be located in the decentralisation zone of 0.5–1. In the centralised economies, the chief coordinating mechanism is the command principle; in the decentralised economies it is the competitive principle. However, in both types of economy there are elements of cooperation and custom and convention in their decision-making processes. We would expect the element of cooperation to be much weaker in centralised economies, as the presence of the command principle is somewhat incompatible with the cooperative principle. This is not to say that cooperation does not exist in a command economy. Slaves or serfs who are treated kindly and generously will cooperate with their master or lord.

The classification of traditional economies along the centralisation–decentralisation continuum is rather problematic, as it is not clear where the locus of decision-making authority lies. It may be formally with the chief or tribal elders, but then the authority may be only passing or transmitting decisions taken in the distant past. What is clear, however, is that decisions are frequently made by individuals according to customs and conventions, which have evolved over centuries. This also applies to the decisions of the nominal authority, the chief or council of elders. The whole economy and society is governed by tradition, custom and convention and little else. This system may be viewed as being highly centralised, as individuals do not initiate or make any decisions of their own. If they happen to disagree with the established norms of behaviour and cannot escape them, then the system may be said to be oppressive as well. Indeed, for such individuals restrictive custom or taboos may be more oppressive than commands used by an authoritarian regime or a dictatorship. For one may escape a dictator or an oligarchy, but not custom and convention. If most members of the society feel oppressed by the system but cannot or will not change it, because of the force of taboos, then that society may be located towards the end of the zone of centralisation. In contrast, if most people are content with established norms and feel free to violate them or tolerate the nonconformist minority, then the customary economy would be placed in the decentralised zone of the continuum. However, traditional societies are too varied, too heterogeneous, to permit simple classification. We need to examine the other properties of the decision-making process, particularly the way in which decisions are reached, which influence the degree of centralisation.

Unlike the three main types of decision-making structure discussed so far, there does not appear to be a historical example of a society built entirely on cooperation, enlightened self-interest, or reciprocal altruism, though cooperatives of all kinds have existed in the past and continue to exist in modern economies. We imagine a cooperative economy to be a decentralised economy in which individuals or groups of individuals (committees and associations) would make all or most decisions. Since economic agents would cooperate rather than compete with one another, and would be motivated by reciprocal altruism rather than egoism, there is no need for a central authority to enforce law and order or to protect the individual against 'force and fraud'. The chief coordinating mechanism would be cooperation. Command, authority, competition and selfishness would not feature prominently. Hence, the location of a cooperative economy on the centralisation–decentralisation continuum would be somewhere near the end of the decentralisation zone. Although committees would make most decisions, individuals would participate either directly or indirectly (through the election of committee members) in the decision-making process. In general, a decision is made by a committee only if approved by the number of members equal to or larger than the required level of consensus (Sah and Stiglitz 1988).

So far, we have tried to classify the four pure types of economic system corresponding to four coordinating mechanisms: command, competition, custom and cooperation along the centralisation–decentralisation continuum. Modern economies, and most past economies are too complex to be governed or managed by a single coordinating mechanism. No complex economy can be totally controlled from the centre by commands or orders. Some decisions would have to be delegated to lower or independent decision-making agents, whether the central authority wishes it or not. In some economies the central authority may make some microeconomic decisions but cannot make all the decisions. Thus it is the degree of decentralisation that is relevant for comparing economic systems across time and space.

There are some decisions over which the central authority has complete control; and there are others over which it has partial control, and no control over still other set of decisions. Theoretically, on a scale of 0–1, we can measure the probability of the central authority's power to make decisions, and hence the degree of decentralisation in the entire economy, if we aggregate the authority's inputs in all decisions. However, it must be remembered that what matters for measuring the effective degree of decentralisation is not the number of decisions made directly by the central authority, or the number in which it has participated, but the types of decisions made by it. It is generally the case that in modern economies, the central authority makes the big decisions, the policy or strategic decisions, such as monetary and fiscal policies, in the light of which micro-decisions are taken by other economic agents, by enterprises whether state or privately owned. Further, in polyarchies or 'decentralised economies' the central authority may affect the decisions of autonomous economic agents through the supply of information on the state of the economy and its own programmes. Thus, for meaningful comparisons of the degrees of decentralisation between different economies, we need to assign weights to different decisions. However, other things being equal, when comparing two economies, it is possible to say that if a given decision, or a set of decisions, is made at a lower level in the hierarchy of one country than in another, the former country is said to be more decentralised. Such an inference may be modified after examining the other components of the decision-making process.

For these and other reasons, it is much easier to compare the degree of decentralisation in a particular economy over time, assuming the other properties of decision-making have not changed. Thus, when a central authority loses some of its decision-making power or delegates decisions to subordinates, the economy becomes apparently more decentralised, and vice versa. However, delegating some decisions to lower levels in the administrative hierarchy may increase the effective control of the central authority over lower decision-making units, and the system may in fact become more centralised, or controlled more efficiently by the centre. Moreover, in a hierarchy with several levels of decision-making, it is not always easy to measure the change in the degree of decentralisation if there has been a simultaneous transfer of decision-making authority from both the top and the bottom to the middle level, as was the case in the Soviet Union in the early 1970s (Haddad 1980).

IV

In this section an attempt is made to compare the relative merits and demerits of different types of decision-making structure. This is essential for designing an appropriate structure that will generate the 'right' decisions required for a well-functioning economy. It should be obvious from the above discussion that the advantages and disadvantages associated with different structures and degrees of (de) centralisation depend to a large extent on the other properties of the decision-making process and the nature of the decisions themselves. This conclusion is reinforced by Camacho (1979, p 91) who has shown theoretically that: 'the structure of information, the penalty for lack of local accuracy, the penalty for lack of coordination, and the stringency of the coordinating requirements are the important factors determining whether total decentralisation performs better than total centralisation or vice versa'. Of course, in the real world neither 'total centralisation' nor 'total decentralisation' works at all.

A centralised structure of decision-making enables the central authority to mobilise resources rapidly for the achievement of some specific objectives of national importance, particularly in times of emergency when speed is of the utmost importance. This was recognised and accepted by the champion of decentralisation and liberalism, J.S. Mill, as far back as 1862 in a passage quoted at the beginning of this chapter. Similarly, a centralised structure makes possible the establishment and implementation of a set of priorities, particularly in the early stages of development, or in the process of transition from one system to another, even paradoxically from a centralised to a decentralised system (Haddad 1992). Centralisation of decision-making, when combined with the command principle, is particularly advantageous during periods of emergency and for a short period, because of its ability to get 'great' things done very quickly. It can also promote efficiency by making recalcitrant people participate in socially beneficial activities. The 'executive capacity' of the command principle was demonstrated in the case of the Soviet Union during the industrialisation drive in the 1930s, World War II and post-war reconstruction, and in the construction of major projects in remote and climatically harsh areas of the country. Without the command principle and centralisation, the Soviet government would not have been able to adopt an 'unbalanced growth' strategy, the priority principle, or the 'law of the preferential growth of heavy industry', which laid the foundation for an industrialised economy (Dyker 1983, p 123).

Clearly, centralisation is suitable for rapid, large structural and/or systemic changes. It may also be useful in those decisions that have significant externalities and uncertainties. Thus, the state could directly play a major part in the saving and investment decisions in which there is much uncertainty about the 'rational' allocation of resources over time. In some cultures individuals may be too short-sighted to save for their old age or for their descendants, or they may not possess the capacity to save because of their low income. In this situation the state may assume the role of the 'custodian of future generations' (Dobb 1960). It may also play a useful role in reducing the degree of uncertainty in major investment projects by providing information about the state of the economy and subsidies if these projects entail enormous externalities. Also, the central authority can reduce the type of uncertainty that is endogenous to the system but exogenous to economic agents. Finally, centralisation is needed to coordinate the interdependent activities or decisions of economic agents that cannot be efficiently coordinated by other mechanisms, or cannot be well delegated.

In contrast, the combination of centralisation and command has certain drawbacks in many economic areas or types of decision. For example, growth through central mobilisation of idle resources is likely to be rapid in the short run or in the early stages of development, but once resources are fully employed growth must come from efficiency and innovation. It is then that the organising approach of centralisation and command must give way to the economic approach, which is best served by the market and decentralisation. The competitive market provides proper valuation of renewable resources and encourages efficient allocation and innovation. Centralised choices would still be needed in times of emergency and in those areas mentioned above. Moreover, with the existence of competitive markets, centralised decisions may be better implemented by 'independent' economic agents rather than by commands. This will help reduce administrative costs and delays. Choices, such as the day-to-day micro-decisions, minor technical changes, and the output, cost and prices of products, whose production and consumption do not entail significant externalities, should not be the concern of the central authority.

More importantly, from a long-run perspective, innovative decisions tend to suffer in a centralised structure consisting of several levels of decision-making. The evaluation of innovation-oriented decisions or projects will have to pass through several levels for approval. The unfamiliarity of such decisions makes it more difficult for innovators to prove their merits in order to convince superiors to adopt them. Adequate experience and examples do not exist for such decisions or projects against which higher decision-makers can easily calculate their profitability. The essence of an innovative decision is the high risk element arising from the unknown variables involved in any new ventures. In a centralised decision-making structure, an innovation decision is likely to be rejected, and this will have an adverse effect on the supply of innovators and research scientists, since the acceptance of their ideas is part and parcel of their rewards. Moreover, the rejection of a potentially profitable idea in a centralised structure will be lost for good. In contrast, in a decentralised structure, in which more than one agent can make such decisions, an idea that is rejected by one agent might be taken up and exploited by another (Sah and Stiglitz 1986). Thus, we would expect the rate of innovation to be lower in a centralised than in a decentralised structure of decision-making. This is not to say that a central authority cannot play a useful role in the innovation process (Haddad 1995). However, it is quite clear that centralised choices are more suitable for standard or routine decisions. In such cases, a central authority is able to accumulate enough knowledge and experience to make sound decisions.

A common complaint about centralised decisions is that they cannot adequately adjust to the special circumstances of each case. For example, a wage rate determined by a central authority does not and cannot reflect the supply and demand and other conditions in a particular industry or in a firm and does not change *pari passu* with those conditions. Further, local agents may have private information that affects centralised decisions, but for various reasons they do not pass it on to the central authority, especially if they know it will be used in a decision that adversely affects them. Moreover, as Hayek (1945) has argued, much important information (tacit knowledge) cannot be conveyed to a central authority even if there is a willingness to do so.

Apart from economic arguments, there are socio-political reasons against centralisation. First, no person or a small group of persons possesses the information or wisdom to decide what is best or optimal for society as a whole. Second, a central authority having the access to available resources creates the illusion of power, which may lead to ambitious plans and grandiose projects that exceed the country's capacity to fulfil them, and this could lead to tragic results. Third, as the Soviet and Eastern experience has clearly shown, a high degree of centralisation based on partial ignorance has inhibited the development of mutual trust and cooperation. It has also prevented the development of community-based institutions and voluntary organisations to deal with decisions that cannot be dealt with adequately either through command or competition. Moreover, because the central authority does not trust subordinates or autonomous agents, it is reluctant to delegate important decisions. Hence, centralisation and mistrust mutually reinforce one another. Mutual trust if it exists usually results from the exchange of personal favours extended at personal risk. Finally, under a centralised structure individuals become entirely dependent on the central government and its institutions both formal (bureaucracy) and informal (patronage).

The advantages and disadvantages of decentralisation have already been hinted at; they are the mirror images of those of centralisation. However, it is important to emphasise that the fundamental function of a decentralised (market) economy is its capacity to solve the valuation problem, to generate meaningful prices that are needed for the efficient allocation of scarce resources. In addition, decentralisation of decision-making tends to encourage initiative and innovation. In order to survive and grow autonomous economic agents competing with one another must become more efficient and/or more innovative. However, a decentralised structure with a high degree of concentration of economic power and dominated by monopolies would not necessarily lead to innovation or efficient allocation of resources. The non-economic advantages associated with decentralisation include a greater degree of participation of citizens in the decision-making process and lower concentration of economic power if the degree of competition is high. Finally, decentralisation protects the system from the danger of major errors and blunders of a central authority.

The disadvantages of decentralisation have to do with market failures of one kind or another: the failure to deal with major externalities and inequalities (between regions and persons), to provide public goods, to act in times of emergency and uncertainty, and the failure to coordinate the activities and decisions of economic agents, which result in macroeconomic instability and in unemployment.

The relative advantages and disadvantages of centralisation and decentralisation suggest the need to have both forms or levels of decision-making and to go beyond the conventional centralisation–decentralisation dichotomy. For many decisions two or three levels of government will have to be involved (Sewell 1996). Similarly, there are decisions that require the involvement of both the government (at different levels) and private enterprise as well as voluntary organisations. The problem then is to determine how the different economic agents could and should cooperate. Thus, an 'optimal' structure of decision-making would specify not only at what levels decisions should be made, but how they should be coordinated. Arguably, centralisation would not work without delegation of decision-making authority to lower levels and to private enterprise, and conversely, decentralisation would not function well without the intervention of the central authority. There seems little doubt that the centralised Soviet-type economy would have collapsed long before it did without the *de facto* decentralisation, the 'second economy' or the parallel market (Powell 1977).

The need to combine centralised and decentralised decision-making implies not only the use of the two corresponding coordination mechanisms, command and competition, but also cooperation between government and private enterprise as well as between the different levels of government. The economic literature, particularly games theory, provides numerous examples showing how cooperation can produce better outcomes for all agents. In addition, there are certain decisions or functions, which are best performed by committees or voluntary organisations, which rely heavily on cooperation. Such collective decision-making could avoid some of the worst errors that might occur under decentralisation and centralisation, or under command and competition. The cooperative principle implies the existence of a degree of altruism or enlightened self-interest. However, cooperation and altruism should not be conflated. Frequently, people cooperate with each other out of self-interest, not out of pure altruism. In a society governed chiefly by cooperation and reciprocal altruism, there would be less waste resulting from unnecessary duplication of activities and excessive competition. There would also be more sharing of resources, information and new ideas.

However, a society governed chiefly by committees, associations and collectives making their decisions on the basis of cooperation and altruism, will have some drawbacks. Collective decisions made by committees may take too long to be formulated, and delays in decision-making can be wasteful because of the danger that delayed decisions can become irrelevant and costly. Further, excessive cooperation may speed up the decision-making process but may not provide enough stimulus for change and innovation. A conflict-free society may become too complacent and static for discovering new and better ways of doing things. However, the possibility of having excessive cooperation at the current stage of human evolution is very remote. For the foreseeable future cooperation based on strong altruism will remain a scarce commodity. The experience of socialist countries where altruism was introduced as a motivating principle shows that it is subject to rapidly diminishing returns. Like the command principle, the cooperative principle works for a short period and in times of emergency. However, as we shall see in the normative part of the book, there are appropriate measures that can be introduced to strengthen the spirit of cooperation and reciprocal altruism. Indeed, the cooperative principle must play a significant role in a well-functioning economy.

Not all decisions taken in an economy by governments, business corporations, voluntary organisations and individuals are based on conscious calculation. Some are determined by custom and convention. Customary decisions nominally taken by individuals are in reality more 'centralised' than they seem. Customs and conventions, as we have already noted, can be, and too often are, more effective determinants of behaviour of individuals than the commands of a dictatorial regime. The advantages of customs and conventions for individuals, who do not find them particularly oppressive, are that they provide them with a degree of comfort and save them time and effort in making choices. For the society or economy, they provide stability and continuity. They are part and parcel of the culture of society and play an important role in unifying society. However, if there are too many routine decisions, or if a society is governed chiefly by custom and convention, then that society will not change, except by external shocks, and will not be innovative. Indeed, in the face of external shocks such a society will not be able to adjust quickly and may disintegrate.

V

It should be obvious by now that having an 'optimal' structure of decision-making is a fundamental condition for generating the 'right' decisions and subsequently for a well-functioning economy. The multitude of decisions that have to be made must be assigned to appropriate levels of decision-making or to different economic agents in such a way that the 'right' people will be making the 'right' decisions. Some decisions are made by a central authority, others at lower levels in the hierarchy, and others still by autonomous organisations and individuals either competing or cooperating with one another. In addition, there are many decisions that are 'made' by all economic agents according to customs and conventions. It should be emphasised, however, that having an 'optimal' decision-making structure will not eliminate all errors, but will avoid systemic mistakes that result from an excessive degree of (de) centralisation, or from a sub-optimal mixture of governments, markets and organisations participating in the decision-making process.

In reality, we often find decision-makers in charge of certain decisions and activities, which are best left to others. It seems that ideology, politics, custom and convention rather than economics or ethics determine the choice of decision-makers or the levels of decision-making for a wide variety of decisions. In the former Soviet Union and Eastern Europe there was a preference (by the central authority) for centralisation, for making decisions, even micro-decisions, at the centre. Currently, there is a strong demand for decentralisation throughout the world. In both cases centralisation and decentralisation serve political objectives as much, if not more than economic ones. They become ends in themselves rather than institutional means to achieve economic efficiency, growth and equity. Under ideological commitments either to centralisation or decentralisation, systemic errors are bound to occur.

An optimal decision-making structure will be partly context-specific. It will be optimal for a particular time and place. We would, therefore, expect the 'optimal' degree of centralisation to vary from place to place and over time, to accommodate both differences in culture and history among countries and changes over time in objectives, technology and information in a particular country. However, the ongoing debate about the respective responsibilities of the state and the market and the three levels of government is often conducted in static terms, as if there were fixed demarcation lines that can be drawn between the various functions of markets, organisations and governments. More than 150 years ago, when the economic world was much less complex than it is now, J.S. Mill made such an attempt to present such a demarcation scheme and he failed. Centralisation or decentralisation has many dimensions; it is not a fixed state but a process evolving and taking place over time.

Accordingly, changes in the division of decisions and functions among the levels of government and other economic agents must be encouraged when the social benefits are clear. Such (systemic) changes normally take place gradually in societies that are less constrained by ideology, command and/or custom and convention. They sometimes take place rapidly as a result of social and political revolutions. The current worldwide desire for decentralisation and 'marketisation' is partly ideological, partly logical and pragmatic and partly fashionable — a phase in the historical pendulum, which since the mid 1970s has been swinging towards the right. Nevertheless, in retrospect, one can see that centralisation in the form of state intervention has played a historic role in providing certain essential services that may not have come into existence if they had been 'left alone'. But having set them up and developed them, the state is looking either to local authorities or to private enterprise and voluntary organisations to take them over.

Sometimes, big business and voluntary organizations take on many functions and perform them better than governments. This applies to countries where the private sector is already developed and voluntary organisations are well established. In those countries, one can observe a shift in the mode of government intervention from undertaking and running certain activities to managing and monitoring them indirectly. Indeed, in certain cases, there has been a switch in the functions of the state and the private sector. In the past, when the private sector was underdeveloped, firms were too small to undertake certain activities or services. Now with the growth of big business such activities can be more efficiently undertaken by private firms. The state can then move on and undertake those activities that only it can do, or that are not or could not be performed efficiently either by private profit-making firms or voluntary organisations.

Apart from the desirability of decentralisation *per se*, particularly in democratic countries, where the economic loss of decentralisation is accepted as a kind of premium paid for an insurance against authoritarianism, the appropriate degree of decentralisation is partly a function of the capacity and efficiency of the state bureaucracy. Burdening the state with too many decisions and functions has always been an argument in favour of decentralisation. The ability of the state to cope with many decisions is not simply a matter of organisational structure and division of labour. It is also the result of technology, of the mechanisation, or the 'computerisation' of the government bureaucracy, the information-based technological revolution beginning with the printing press, the typewriter, telephone, copying and fax machines, the Internet revolution and computers. Such developments have given the central government greater capacity to take on many more activities than in the past and this has increased its capacity for monitoring the activities of others – so crucial for higher decision-makers.

Paradoxically, as the capacity of the central government for formulating and monitoring the implementation of decisions has increased, political and economic arguments for decentralisation have been gaining currency. There is a widespread demand for empowering individuals by allowing them to participate in decision-making processes at all levels of government and in the workplace. If decentralisation and democratisation of decision-making lead to a significant economic loss, then it becomes a matter of a trade-off: the benefits of democracy (an insurance against authoritarianism) must be balanced against the economic costs. Such a trade-off may apply only in the short term. In the long run, there may not be any conflicts or contradictions. However, for certain countries, particularly developing countries with corrupt and inefficient central governments and transitional economies with an underdeveloped private sector, the choice of a high degree of decentralisation may not be feasible even though it is most desirable. In these cases, designing an 'optimal' decision-making structure will be a daunting task that could not be implemented over a short period of time. The 'optimal' degree of decentralisation would be constrained by historical factors, customs and convention, the availability of market resources and by international competition and cooperation.

3. Decision-making Procedures

I

The analysis of decision-making structures in the last chapter provided us with a mere skeleton of the decision-making process. To put some flesh on it and breathe some life into it, we need to consider the other components of decision-making. In this chapter we focus on the procedure, the manner and style of decision-making, or on how decisions are reached. Procedures are important not only because they affect the other components and the quality of the decisions taken, but they are very often valued for their own sake. In a well-designed decision-making system, it is not enough that the decisions taken must be 'right'; the procedure for making them must also be right.

Unlike the structure of decision-making, the procedure has not received the attention it deserves from economists, especially from system economists. When it is discussed by the latter, it is usually in passing and under some other aspect of decision-making. More often, the procedure is conflated with structure. Thus, a centralised structure is commonly equated with an authoritarian procedure, and similarly a decentralised one with a democratic procedure.

To redress the balance in the literature and to clarify the confusion between structure and style, we devote Section II of this chapter to an analysis of procedures used in formulating and implementing decisions, and how they interact with the other components of decision-making. In Section III an attempt is made to classify economies first along an authoritarian–democratic continuum and then along a dual continuum of structure and procedure. The latter continuum yields a more complex and realistic classification than either of the two one-dimensional continuums. Section IV evaluates the relative merits of different procedures with a view of determining the most appropriate for generating the 'right' decisions. Finally, Section V consists of a summary of the findings of the chapter and offers some concluding comments about the importance of having proper decision-making procedures.

II

Just as there are different decision-making structures, so there are different procedures and styles of decision-making. In principle, one would expect some correspondence between the two aspects of decision-making. Indeed, as already noted, it is commonly believed that a centralised structure implies an authoritarian procedure, while a decentralised structure is necessarily democratic. However, the correspondence between structures and procedures is not always one to one; different structures can coexist with different procedures. For example, it is perfectly conceivable to have a centralised structure with a democratic procedure and a decentralised one with an authoritarian procedure. Such possibilities are explained in Section III.

Meanwhile, we discuss the various procedures used in reaching and implementing decisions, bearing in mind that different procedures may be used during the various phases of the decision-making process. For example, a democratic procedure may be followed in reaching a decision, while an authoritarian one is used in enforcing the same decision, and vice versa. An authoritarian procedure is characterised by a unidirectional command–obey relationship. Decisions made by superiors are reached without consultation with subordinates. There may be a formal process of consultation that superiors are required to observe, but at the end of the process they do not change their decisions. A distinction must be drawn between formal and effective consultation. The latter occurs when the decision-makers genuinely seek the views of subordinates and others directly affected by the proposed decision and take their view into account. Such consultation usually makes a difference to the final decision. Formal consultation may be little more than a ritual, a convention.

Further, with an authoritarian procedure, subordinates do not question or challenge the decisions of superiors, and superiors do not give reasons for their decisions. Such a procedure lacks transparency and accountability. Decisions are formulated behind closed doors, so to speak. Decision-makers do not wish to reveal their real intentions and objectives underlying their policies and decisions. They have a tendency to rationalise their decisions, particularly unpopular decisions. Such rationalisation is needed to persuade subordinates and others adversely affected by the decisions to accept and implement them and, more generally, to win legitimacy. Secrecy is deemed necessary to defeat opponents and competitors. It may also be used to exclude persons who might want to participate in the decision-making process or to deal quickly and more effectively with more complex decisions. Of course, secrecy is used in decisions affecting national security.

Generally, an authoritarian procedure leads to a speedy formulation of decisions. Consultation takes time and hence fewer decisions are made by a decision-making authority that seeks wide consultation. As Downs (1967, p 77) reminds us, 'if a great many people must be consulted in making a decision, it becomes difficult to communicate to each person the issues involved, the possible alternatives, and the responses and views of other consultants'. If decision-makers are ambitious, having too many plans they must fulfil by a certain deadline, they would adopt an authoritarian procedure. The speed with which decisions must be formulated and implemented may be imposed upon the decision-makers either exogenously, say by the outbreak of a crisis, or deliberately chosen by them to exploit the effects of time pressure and the sense of urgency. If higher decision-makers want to restrict the number of people they consult on a given decision, they can place a very short deadline on it. If they want wide-ranging deliberations, they can take a much longer time. However, in an emergency situation, decision-makers do not have the choice of determining the period of time within which decisions must be reached and implemented. Hence, an authoritarian procedure may be adopted until the crisis has passed.

Another feature of authoritarian procedures is the absence of accountability. Decision-makers are responsive neither to interest groups nor the community at large; they are not accountable for the outcome of their decisions. However, in the long run, if such decisions lead to disastrous consequences, the legitimacy of their authority is undermined, and they may be overthrown. This suggests that 'rational' decision-makers may ignore short-term considerations and make unpopular decisions, which they feel will turn out right in the long run. In particular, since most people are arguably short-sighted and have a tendency to satisfy immediate gratification, long-term decisions, such as saving and investment, may require an authoritarian rather than a democratic procedure.

In general, democratic and consultative procedures involve a larger number of people in decision-making. Such procedures can be seen from two points of view. The first as processes in which all or most citizens participate in various decision-making activities that are taking place in a society. The second as processes in which everybody participates according to certain 'rules of the game', including rules on how the rules of the game can be changed. In the first case, the emphasis is on the participatory aspect of democracy; in the second, the constitutional aspect is stressed. The two aspects are clearly needed to ensure as many people as possible to be genuinely involved in political and economic choices. Political participation of citizens in a representative democracy is not enough for the good life of the citizens. They must be active participants in decision-making processes at all levels: at work, in local government, unions, churches and other social activities. Participation gives them the opportunity for the exercise of initiative, responsibility and self-development. It is also important for the emergence of new ideas and values concerning justice, equity and environmental responsibility. Thus, the ability to participate in decision-making, even over a limited area, is something that is or should be valued by the ordinary citizen. The quality of life of a citizen, who does not or is not allowed to participate in decision-making, is partially impoverished, even though he or she may be economically well-off.

In a centralised economy, it is possible to involve a much greater number of people in the decision-making process through consultation and the establishment of committees to deal especially with complex and technical decisions. However, consultation must be seen to be genuine. It is very easy for a decision-making authority to go through some ritual process of consultation, or adopt pseudo-democratic procedures, without having any intention of changing its initial goals and proposals. Accordingly, transparency is needed to demonstrate that a genuine democratic procedure of consultation has taken place, especially when the initial decisions proposed by the authority are not altered. Interested people affected by the decisions taken have a right to know how the decisions were reached, what criteria were used and who voted for or against the decisions. With a transparent decision-making procedure, outsiders can scrutinise and assess the decisions before they are implemented. A truly democratic procedure provides ample opportunities for interested people to express their opinions; it allows sufficient time for consultation to take place and for participation of as many people as possible when speed is not a top priority. However, prolonged and unnecessary delays can be very costly.

Since accountability is a hallmark of democratic procedures, decision-makers must be accountable: in the political arena to their electorate and in the corporate sector, to their shareholders and other stakeholders including people whose lives are dramatically affected by their decisions. They must be responsible for the consequences of their decisions, rewarded when their decisions turn out to be right and penalised when they are proven to be wrong. Such accountability is necessary to ensure that the decisions taken are right from the point of view of all stakeholders. But to ensure accountability, transparency is needed to know whether or not the interests of the stakeholders are violated. In particular, the transparency of the corporate balance sheet must be demonstrated through independent external accounting, auditing and disclosure, so that the market can monitor corporate performance and investors can make the right decisions. Thus, transparency and accountability are two sides of the same coin.

Decision-making procedures are not always wholly authoritarian or democratic. Often they contain elements of both. Moreover, many decisions are reached through bargaining processes, which cannot be described as simply authoritarian or democratic. Bargaining may be defined as a process of communication, an exchange of information, proposals and (in non-cooperative bargaining) threats. In a hierarchy where the procedure is formally regarded as authoritarian, bargaining and negotiations occur between superiors and subordinates, or between the centre and peripheral agents. Such bargaining may be referred to as 'vertical'. Decisions are usually initiated at the centre and transmitted downwards for feedbacks on their feasibility. Subordinates and peripheral agents responsible for their implementation will, more often than not, inform their superiors that they do not have the capacity or the resources required for implementing them. They will ask for more resources to be given to them or the initial decisions be revised downwards. The top decision-makers know from past experience that this is a bargaining tactic on the part of subordinates to get an 'easy plan' or more resources. Nevertheless, they make some adjustment partly because the initial decisions themselves were deliberately ambitious in anticipation of reports from subordinates, and partly because they cannot be completely certain of the accuracy of the information supplied to them. The final decisions reached will almost certainly be the result of the combined effort of the centre, the periphery and the intermediate agents.

Now the relative influence of participants will depend on their relative bargaining power. In a vertical bargaining situation between superiors and subordinates, the former have by definition more power, but their relative power will vary according to circumstances, their bargaining skill, knowledge and the nature and types of decision. In an emergency, superiors will have a greater say in determining a decision, but if their knowledge is deficient, they will have less influence on the final decision. Also, if the decision refers to a homogeneous product, like electricity, the central authority and the higher orders in the hierarchy rely less on subordinates for information and will therefore have more influence. In contrast, decisions regarding heterogeneous products like machines, whose costs and quality cannot be easily known to superiors, will be more influenced by subordinates. Of course, superiors may refuse to bargain or negotiate with subordinates, as in the command–authoritarian model, but then it is unlikely they would be making meaningful decisions and have them effectively enforced.

In decentralised economies, decision-making is not always simply democratic or autonomous. Economic agents do not always make their decisions independently of other agents, as depicted in the perfect competition model. On the contrary, they often act strategically and engage with other agents in a negotiation or bargaining process. However, bargaining procedures are commonly of the horizontal type, as in the case of bargaining between an employer and an employee (enterprise bargaining), or between organisations and trade unions (collective bargaining). Some vertical bargaining also takes place between governments and various interest groups, when a governmental body makes a decision that requires the approval of an autonomous organisation for implementation, thus giving the organisation a say or even a veto over the decision.

The command model, which implies a downward unidirectional authoritarian procedure, is not an accurate or even an adequate representation of the way in which decisions are reached in centralised economies. It is an extreme procedure that has been used in emergencies and in few countries. Similarly, the perfect competition model, which depicts economic agents making decisions autonomously, is also an inadequate representation of decision-making procedures in decentralised economies. Neither model captures the reality of decision-making processes in both centralised and decentralised economies. There is hardly any decision taken by a central authority, or by an autonomous economic agent, that does not impact on others or require their input. The outcome or pay-off of each decision taken by an agent depends on the decisions taken by other agents. This calls for consultation, negotiation, cooperation and bargaining between economic agents, if the 'right' decisions are to be made.

Indeed, as soon as we move away from the simple command model of a militarised economy, or the perfect competition model of an artisan economy, there is a tendency for decisions to be made in the context of a bargaining process in which two or more agents are involved. There seems little doubt that bargaining has become a pervasive activity in modern economies whether centralised or decentralised. As Johansen (1979, p 498) has pointed out, 'once we go beyond mere accounting and description of production and technology and want or demand to include various aspects of economic behaviour, the bargaining theory or bargaining approach becomes the most appropriate paradigm'. The bargaining model of reaching decisions allows for interaction, negotiation and compromise, and this is more realistic and compelling than either the authoritarian command model or the autonomous–democratic competitive model.

Traditionally, the bargaining approach to decision-making has been confined to, what Wiles (1961) has called, 'primitive hagglers' (such as buyers and sellers in an Oriental bazaar, in peasant markets or any person buying a house, a business and most second-hand articles) and most commonly to the labour market, between workers and employers. However, 'advanced haggling' has become increasingly common in most transactions among corporations, in international agreements, in federal–state relations, in the fixing of prices of public purchasing corporations, in consultation or negotiation with relevant pressure groups such as farmers' cooperatives and other organizations. It also occurs in the provision of welfare services, in consultation or negotiation with all sorts of welfare groups. In particular, the policies of the welfare state demand technical knowledge, which frequently the members of the relevant interest group are best able to supply. Such policies often require the positive cooperation of the group if they are to be effectively carried out. It is, therefore, sensible to give the members of the relevant group some say in both the formulation and administration of decisions.

The growing importance of negotiations and bargaining across the economy is the result of many factors, such as better communication, market failures and the increasing awareness that they can be manipulated so as to serve the interests of various groups. It is also the result of the centralisation and concentration of economic power, which is, in turn, the result of the growth of big business and associations of interest groups as well as the involvement of governments in economic affairs. The increased importance of bargaining and negotiations is reflected in the rapid growth of games theory in the economic literature over the last few decades. Up until then, this aspect of decision-making, especially in the interaction between government bodies and interest groups, was neglected. According to Johansen (1979, p 506), the neglect of bargaining has been responsible for much misunderstanding between economists and policy-makers. In standard economic theory, he argues, the government is seen as a disinterested and omniscient authority making decisions whose underlying objective is to maximise the social welfare function. It takes autonomous decisions (without any consultation and negotiation with interest groups) with respect to various policy instruments that influence the behaviour of economic agents. The economist's advice is usually based on assumptions that governments formulate policies on sound economic principles with little or no pressure from interest groups. However, politicians know too well they are constrained by public opinion and by special interest groups and must consult and negotiate with them on many important issues. Thus, the advice offered by economists may be economically 'right' but the policies and decisions based on that advice might be either politically unacceptable or impracticable.

The problems of decision-making by governments are more satisfactorily addressed by the Virginian school or 'the rent-seeking school' (Buchanan, Tollison and Tulloch 1980), which sees government policies and decisions as a product of negotiation and bargaining with various interest groups seeking 'rent' or special benefits from government intervention. Moreover, the government itself is not simply a disinterested party seeking to maximise the welfare of society as a whole, but one which seeks the support of interest groups in order to win the next election. Obviously, this paradigm applies more to democratic states, where governments must face the electorate every few years, than to authoritarian regimes. Similarly, in centralised economies, bargaining and negotiations still occur at all levels and in all directions (vertical, horizontal and diagonal) in the administrative hierarchies and with autonomous and semi-autonomous economic organisations. An authoritarian regime is subject to pressures and constraints in the longer term. Its power and position will be undermined if it does not deliver on its promises.

Consultations, negotiations and commands are not the only procedures used in reaching decisions. For certain decisions, which are complex and requiring specialised knowledge and skill, a professional approach is needed to enhance the correctness of decisions. An 'amateurish' approach in such decisions is unlikely to yield a satisfactory outcome and may even prove to be disastrous. If the decision-makers do not possess the required knowledge and skill, they must allow certain groups, who possess technical competence in specialised fields, not only to participate in, but also, in some cases, to determine the outcome of the decision-making process. A complex decision may demand, in its formulation or administration, some skill or knowledge over which members of special groups have a monopoly. This is increasingly the case in the age of specialisation. Galbraith (1967) was among the first economists to highlight the importance of 'technocrats' in decision-making in industrial societies. More recently, the growth of the principal–agent literature is a recognition of the critical role of experts in decision-making and the need to adopt a professional approach in reaching sound decisions. Accordingly, we now have three dichotomies in decision-making procedures: authoritarian versus democratic, democratic versus technocratic and authoritarian versus technocratic. A satisfactory procedure must reconcile the trichotomies. This is attempted in Section IV.

In the rest of this section we discuss the interaction and connection between a procedure and the other components of our decision-making schema. We have already seen that a centralised structure is modified by the type of procedure adopted. A democratic procedure, which involves more participants in decision-making, renders the existing structure *de facto* less centralised than it formally appears; and conversely an authoritarian procedure reinforces and strengthens the degree of centralisation. Similarly, a decentralised structure, when combined with an authoritarian procedure, will increase the degree of centralisation, and with a democratic procedure it will increase the existing degree of decentralisation. In turn, the structure will, to some extent, influence the choice of procedure. It is generally the case that a centralised structure tends to foster an authoritarian procedure. Those who possess decision-making authority seldom wish to share it with others, and the more power they have the more authoritarian they become in dealing with subordinates. They become more jealous of their power and less trusting. On the other hand, a totally decentralised structure with no superiors and subordinates will normally be accompanied by a democratic procedure, as there is less opportunity for decision-makers to dictate to others. Autonomous decision-makers can communicate with each other and make agreements (form coalitions) before decisions and actions are taken. Moreover, a decentralised structure encourages negotiations and bargaining, and depending on the relative bargaining power of participants, the final decision will be determined mainly by the party that has more power. In the extreme case where one party has all the power, then the final decision will be equivalent to a decision reached through an authoritarian procedure.

There is interaction also between procedures and the structures of information flows. Democratic procedures tend to generate more and better information, since they involve more consultation and negotiation and more people participate in decision-making. More consultation improves the knowledge on which decisions are based. Accountability and transparency will improve the accuracy of information flows. In turn, information flows will impact on the procedure. For example, if the information is supplied by subordinates, who are also responsible for implementing the decisions handed down to them, an element of bargaining is introduced into what is formally an authoritarian procedure. Subordinates will, most likely, supply the information required by superiors in a distorted manner to serve their own interest. On the other hand, if the information flows are vertical, moving downwards from superiors to subordinates, who are responsible for formulating and implementing decisions, then an authoritarian element is introduced into the decision-making procedure. If the information flows are horizontal, the procedure is likely to be democratic involving negotiations and bargaining.

The connections between decision-making procedures, on one hand, and decision criteria, on the other, are less obvious and more difficult to assess. An authoritarian procedure, which lacks accountability and transparency, encourages arbitrariness and breeds private rent-seeking in the public domain. Decision-makers are not obliged to reveal the reasons and motives underlying their decisions. They make decisions that serve primarily their own interests rather than those of the corporation or of society at large. Often, they may not see any difference between their own interests and those of society. In contrast, democratic procedures encourage the use of 'proper' criteria, which can be defended publicly as serving the interests of those most directly affected by the decisions, or those to whom the decision-makers are ultimately accountable. In turn, the criteria used have some influence on the procedure. If economic criteria are strictly adhered to, then a 'technocratic' procedure is adopted, in which economists would have a say in reaching the 'right' decisions. It must be noted, however, that economic criteria are often used to rationalise decisions taken on less popular grounds, and decision-makers often employ experts to provide them with such rationalisations.

Finally, the decision-making procedure will affect the incentives used to implement decisions and the incentives will impact on the procedure. For example, a thoroughly democratic procedure, in which those affected by the decisions are involved in the decision-making process, will win more support for the decision and will facilitate its implementation. Other things being equal, the implementers will feel morally obliged to execute faithfully the decision in which they have participated. In contrast, an authoritarian procedure is likely to alienate subordinates and to encourage distortions at the implementation stage. Further, an authoritarian procedure will have to rely on external motivation, on force and material incentives to enforce the decisions, whereas a democratic procedure will rely on intrinsic motivation, on moral persuasion and altruism, along with economic incentives. Of course, in times of emergency, when an authoritarian procedure is adopted, decision-makers rely on force and moral incentives such as patriotism and 'altruism' to implement their policies and decisions. On the other hand, the incentives chosen will influence the procedure. If, for example, moral incentives and 'weak altruism' are to be relied upon to any significant degree, the decision-makers will have to adopt more democratic procedures. Economic incentives are consistent with all procedures, but in an authoritarian procedure such incentives have to be supplemented with coercion or the threat of force, when they are inadequate or inappropriate. Authoritarian regimes often resort to moral or non-pecuniary incentives particularly in the early stages of popular revolutions, when there is much optimism and euphoria, but their effectiveness tends to diminish as time goes by.

III

In this section an attempt is made to classify economies on the basis of procedures, mainly along an authoritarian–democratic continuum. As noted in the last section, the authoritarian–democratic approach does not adequately capture all the known procedures, especially the bargaining and technocratic methods of resolving decision problems. Nevertheless, it is of some interest to classify economies along an authoritarian–democratic continuum.

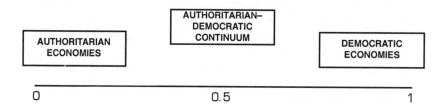

On a scale from 0 to 1 we can rank authoritarian economies in the 0–0.5 zone and democratic economies in the 0.5–1 zone. As in the centralisation–decentralisation continuum very few economies, if any, would occupy the extreme ends. However, a more interesting classification is obtained when we combine both decision-making structures and procedures. The combination of the two components of decision-making yields a more useful and realistic classification than either of the one-dimensional continuums. The combination is also part of our general aim of proceeding from the simple one-dimensional to the more complex multidimensional classification.

As shown in Table 3.1, the juxtaposition of structure and procedure yields four types of economic system.

Table 3.1   Decision-making structure and procedure

Decision-making	Economic systems	
Structure procedure	Centralised–authoritarian	Decentralised–democratic
Structure procedure	Centralised–democratic	Decentralised–authoritarian

The first, a centralised–authoritarian system, is one in which most decisions are unilaterally made by a central authority on the basis of its own preferences and imposed on subordinates for implementation. Decisions flow downwards only. Subordinates play no part in the formulation of decisions. Their task is simply to obey the orders given to them from above. The central authority neither consults with nor seeks advice and information from subordinates. Further, decision-makers are neither accountable nor subject to scrutiny by any authority. This is the familiar command–authoritarian model that has been used, inaccurately in our view, to classify and analyse the former Soviet-type economies. Only a few countries approximate the characteristics of 'authoritarian centralism': the Soviet Union under Stalin, Romania under Ceausescu and Cambodia under Pol Pot. These economies would be located at the left end of the dual continuum.

The second type of economic system, centralised–democratic (or 'democratic centralism') is distinguished from the first by the fact that the proposed decisions flow downwards, then upwards and finally downwards. Decision proposals are initiated by the central authority and sent down the hierarchy for consultation, feedbacks and adjustments. Once the consultation process is completed, the adjusted decisions are sent upwards to the central authority for final adjustments and authorisation, and then the final decisions are sent down again for implementation. If the procedure is transparent and decision-makers are accountable for their decisions, then we have a truly democratic procedure. Those economies that satisfy all these conditions would be located in the centre zone of the continuum. However, it is hard to find centralised economies that satisfy all the characteristics of a democratic procedure, where the central authority takes sufficient time and care to allow for intensive consultation. Most centralised economies allow for some consultation and negotiation, but decision-makers are rarely accountable for their decisions and transparent in their decision-making procedures.

It is of some interest to note here that the idea of 'democratic centralism' was much discussed and debated in the early years of the Soviet Union, and was particularly promoted by Trotsky and Lenin as an attempt to render both subordination and authority democratic. It was meant to be an alternative to the authoritarian centralism, which had resulted in some idiotic decisions, such as when in one of the Urals' districts people were given oats instead of wheat while in a neighbouring district the horses were fed wheat (Day 1988, p 11). Democratic centralism was designed to combine the virtues of centralism particularly for major policy decisions with those of a democratic procedure. It was advocated by Lenin in his *State and Revolution* (1917) as a means for reconciling authority and autonomy. He wanted the central authority to be in charge of the most important decisions ('the commanding heights') and at the same time to be subject to democratic processes. To some extent, democratic states, which are heavily involved in many policy decisions and which manage the economy and intervene in many economic activities, approximate the centralised–democratic system.

The third type, a decentralised–authoritarian system, is one in which most decisions are taken at the periphery and flow upwards through the hierarchy to the central authority, whose principal function is to coordinate and endorse or approve the decisions. There will, of course, be inconsistency in the demands made on resources by various autonomous decision-makers. It is expected that for the system to function, the central authority would have to make the necessary adjustments without consultation and negotiations with those responsible for the decisions. Once the demands are reconciled, the decisions are sent downwards for implementation. The main differences between a decentralised–authoritarian system and a centralised–democratic system are that in the former, decisions flow upwards first and the absence of consultation after the initial decisions are sent to the central decision-makers for authorisation. It is hard to find economies that fit neatly into this system. Perhaps those countries in the 1960s that practised indicative or rather 'persuasive' planning may come close to this system. Decentralised–authoritarian economies would be located to the right of the centre of the continuum.

The fourth economic system, a decentralised–democratic economy, is one in which there are no superiors and no subordinates. Decisions flow horizontally in both directions, unless, of course, in the case of an exercise of extremely uneven bargaining in which one party more or less dictates the terms of a contract or an agreement to the other party. Normally, in a decentralised–democratic system, decisions are made autonomously as in the pure competition model, or cooperatively, or through a process of consultation and negotiation. A central authority exists only to enforce the 'rules of the game' (competition), to protect private property and enforce contracts or decisions reached by autonomous agents. This is the *laissez-faire* model. There are few countries that can be classified neatly under a decentralised–democratic system.

An imaginary cooperative economy may be classified as decentralised–democratic. Decision-making would be made mainly by individuals or associations in cooperation or consultation with other individuals and associations. The role of a central authority, as in the *laissez-faire* model, would be confined to establishing and monitoring the rules of the game (cooperation). The authority may also undertake to provide pure public goods that cannot be provided by other decision-makers. However, such activities would be carried out in cooperation with peripheral agents.

Modern (market) economies usually have strong interventionist states that do not only manage the economy but also intervene directly in specific areas, where the market and other organisations fail to perform satisfactorily or fail to undertake certain activities, which are necessary for the welfare and survival of society. Such economies can be located somewhere between the centralised–authoritarian and the decentralised–democratic zones.

Traditional societies, which are governed by custom, follow all sorts of procedures that are themselves determined by custom and convention. Documented cases of hunter-gatherer societies (Mead 1955; Sahlins 1974; Nash 1966) reveal a variety of procedures that can be ranked on an authoritarian–democratic continuum, or indeed on the dual continuum of structure and procedure of decision-making. For example, in normal emergencies, such as harvest or hunting failures or an attack by a neighbouring tribe, meetings of council of elders would take place to decide on what is to be done, or the chief might announce his decision in accordance with established norms in such circumstances. The chief is generally more like a chairperson of a committee. His function is to give voice to the decisions of the elders. However, if the emergency is new and more serious, an authoritarian procedure might be adopted. Here custom and conventions break down in the face of novelty and upheaval. Of course, routine decisions of when or where to harvest the crop or go hunting would be determined according to well-established procedures, which are neither simply autocratic nor democratic. The procedures adopted in the customary economies are discussed in more detail in Chapter 7.

IV

Like decision-making structures, different procedures have their own strengths and weaknesses, depending on circumstances, attitudes and the types of decision being considered. An authoritarian procedure has the advantage of reaching decisions quickly. This is desirable in times of emergency and when there is general consensus, or when it is quite clear on what is to be done. However, if there is much uncertainty about the outcome of a decision or insufficient information to make a meaningful decision, then an authoritarian procedure that leads to quick decisions may turn out to be very costly indeed. Under these circumstances, the decision-maker is faced with a dilemma. On the one hand, the timeliness of the decision is of the utmost importance, so a decision has to be made quickly to cope with the emergency. On the other hand, decisions made under emergency are usually momentous dealing with unfamiliar circumstances, so they need to be carefully considered. They require much time to collect the necessary information and consult with experts. By then the emergency would have passed or worsened, in which case the proposed decisions would no longer be relevant. Clearly, in times of crisis and emergency, a compromise has to be struck between the timeliness of decisions and the time it takes to reach sound decisions. In other words, a mixture of an authoritarian and a 'technocratic' procedure is required.

Beyond emergency periods and in certain well-circumscribed cases, an authoritarian procedure has very little to commend it. The timeliness of decisions is not a top priority though it remains important. In normal circumstances, or in routine decisions, the emphasis shifts to factors determining the correctness of decisions, such as wider consultation, collection of more and better information, and acceptability. In times of emergency, acceptability by those responsible for implementation and the public at large is not usually a major problem. But once the emergency passes, subordinates and others responsible for implementation of decisions may resent the fact that they have not been consulted and will not put their best effort in carrying out the decisions. Policies or decisions that have not passed through the multiple veto gates do not have the broad-base support they would have acquired had more subordinates signed off on them. Further, since an authoritarian procedure precludes genuine consultation and negotiations and lacks accountability and transparency, the decisions reached will, most likely, be based on imperfect information and on 'arbitrary' criteria. Hence, in the long run authoritarian procedures, particularly in public decisions, tend to create distorted allocation, encourage rent-creating and rent-seeking activities, discourage innovation and exacerbate the existing inequities. Moreover, lack of transparency conceals the extent of the severity of the existing problems so much that corrective action happens too late. This is not to deny that on certain occasions, authoritarian procedures, lack of transparency and secrecy are justified.

It would be improper and unethical to prematurely disclose sensitive statistical information or policy measures that would confer unintended benefits on some groups or weaken the effectiveness of those measures. Certain decisions require confidentiality if they are to be reached by a certain date and this often requires an authoritarian procedure. Another situation in which secrecy in business can be justified concerns scientific invention or discovering and technical knowledge. A period of time is required to reap part of the social gains associated with innovation. The successful maintenance of trade secrets permits the necessary appropriation of economic rents and therefore encourages innovation.

In contrast, democratic procedures first have the advantage of involving a greater number of people in decision-making, an attribute that is politically and ethically desirable. Second, there is strong theoretical and empirical evidence suggesting that, compared with authoritarian work organisations and decision-making, wider participation by workers improves productivity and reduces costs (Blumberg 1968; Vanek 1975; Hodgson 1982–3; Drago 1984–5; Meade 1989). Higher productivity is shown to be the result of increased peer pressure and of less resistance to hierarchical management control, but despite this evidence the principle of participation has not been widely accepted or applied. This is all the more surprising in view of the increasing acknowledgement by executives and businesses of the value of empowered employees, a more democratic workplace and the search for better ways of achieving cooperation of their labour force in reaching higher quality production, process inputs and more generally innovation.

Third, participation in decision-making and profit-sharing could lead to distributional justice, macroeconomic stability and higher employment, by gearing workers' incomes to the economic conditions of firms, thus internalising some of the costs of labour-market adjustments (Weitzman 1984; Meade 1989). The success of workers' participation depends on a number of conditions, perhaps the most important of which is the presence of mutual trust and cooperation between workers and managers or owners. It also depends on the nature and degree of complexity of the production process and the size of firms. There is little doubt that the incentive effects of participation tend to be diluted in large firms, since the difficulty of maintaining a cooperative relationship increases with the number of participants.

Fourth, democratic procedures provide more and better information and, together with transparency and accountability, lead to sound decisions. The criteria on which decisions are based are open to scrutiny by outsiders; and therefore decision-makers, who are accountable for their conduct, have to take much care to make the 'right' decisions, or at least, to avoid major blunders. Finally, democratic procedures, which involve intensive consultation with and participation of those responsible for implementation, are likely to lead to quick and effective implementation of decisions. Decisions will not be unnecessarily delayed because of alienation, indifference or lack of commitment. In short, democratic procedures are likely to lead to sound decisions and effective implementation.

However, democratic decisions can sometimes lead to outcomes that are very costly indeed. In particular, the extension of the principle of participation to workers (industrial democracy) imposes extra costs in the form of time and human resources on the firm. It also creates limitation of freedom of choice in some spheres, while expanding it in others. In Yugoslavia, where enterprise decisions during the 1970s were based on a system of workers' participation, the participatory–democratic decision-making procedures entailed such immense time and resource costs that the self-management system became a drag on the economy (Haddad 1975). Of course, the presence of other incongruent elements may have contributed to the inefficient outcome. Nevertheless, there was a conflict between efficiency and democracy. But the Yugoslav leaders at the time chose industrial democracy as an end to be achieved with minimum costs. For them there was to be no trade-off between efficiency and democracy. However, since in our view both the procedure and outcome matter, the principle of participation should be extended to all stakeholders up to the point, where the delay and extra costs by far outweigh the likely benefits. As in so many things in our choices, a right balance has to be struck between efficiency and democracy.

With those decisions that require the inputs of experts, the proper procedure is neither authoritarian nor democratic, but 'technocratic'. The justification of a technocratic or professional approach is based solely on performance or utilitarianism. In both authoritarian and democratic societies, a compromise has to be made between political objectives, which demand participation of as many people as possible in decision-making, and economic objectives, which may restrict the participation of people to experts. Such a compromise can be reached by devising incentive schemes, which ensure that the experts do the 'right thing' by their constituents, or by the people who employ them. The emergence of the 'principal–agency' literature, which attempts to deal with such problems, is indicative of the increasing importance of decisions being made by technocrats, which is itself a reflection of increasing complexity of decisions and the need for specialisation.

Bargaining procedures can be either authoritarian or democratic in their effects, depending on the relative bargaining power of the participants. If bargaining power is distributed very unevenly, then one party will be dictated to and will have little influence on the outcome. While bargaining procedures are now widely used in resolving decision problems, and often the only means for settling disputes and disagreements, they have some drawbacks. First, they are often time-consuming, especially when one party can afford to wait and see in the hope that the other party will offer more concession, and when bargaining power is evenly distributed so that no party can dictate to the other in order to reach a quick decision. Second, they are not conducive to efficiency and unbiased exchange of information. Economic agents do not reveal their true positions and often give false information in the hope of getting more concession from the other party. Thus the right decisions may not be generated if the information on which an agreement is reached is imperfect. As Johansen (1979, p 520) has concluded: 'bargaining has an inherent tendency to eliminate the potential gain which is the object of bargaining'. In view of the increasing use of bargaining in decision-making processes across the economy, this conclusion raises some serious problems concerning the way in which our societies and institutions are organized; it also raises the ethical issue concerning the misrepresentation of privately held information for strategic purposes.

Our discussion has suggested that the proper procedure depends, to some extent, on circumstances, attitudes and the nature of the decision under deliberation. An authoritarian procedure may be advantageous in times of emergency and when it is fairly clear on what is to be done. Such a procedure may be tolerated in areas of national importance and when secrecy and confidentiality are of the utmost importance. Also, if the decision-makers have a track record of making the right decisions, of serving the interests of their constituents or the community at large, as in the case of 'modernising autocracies', then an authoritarian procedure may be justified for a specific period of time on the basis of performance.

However, apart from the above exceptions, it seems that the general rule is to follow a democratic–participatory procedure. Such a procedure is desirable *per se*, since it recognises the inescapable need for political and economic choices to be made as far as possible by all members of society or, at least, by those most affected. It is also expected in general to lead to better decisions. Transparency and accountability, two important properties of a democratic procedure, will encourage the formulation of correct decisions. But transparency and accountability are not easily enforceable and decision-makers with the 'wrong' attitudes will manipulate these properties to serve their own ends. It is a common observation that certain decision-makers lacking imagination tend to hide behind democratic procedures; they follow the letter rather than the spirit of these procedures. For example, if decision-makers wish for some reason either to delay or speed up decisions, they can manipulate the process of consultation – widen it in the one case and restrict it in the other. Further, in the name of democracy, evil men carry out evil acts – the case of desirable means justifying undesirable ends. Democratic procedures *per se* do not always generate the right decisions.

In the case of many decisions that are complex and difficult, it would be inappropriate to strictly follow a democratic procedure. Decision-makers must have the specialised knowledge and competence to deal with such decisions. In such cases, professional people and technocrats must be allowed to dominate the decision-making process. However, the technocrats must be made accountable to their constituents for their decisions. But again, accountability is especially hard to enforce in highly technical matters. When things go wrong, it is not always clear whether it is the decision-makers themselves who are responsible or whether failures are due to some other factors beyond their control. Nevertheless, some mechanism must be established to make them accountable for their decisions. Professional people and technocrats have their professional ethics and codes of behaviour, but these cannot always be relied upon to force them to do the 'right' thing.

In the case of decisions reached through bargaining processes, to ensure a just outcome or to prevent one party from dictating to another, some mechanism in the form of voluntary or compulsory arbitration must be established, particularly for those decisions, which have far-reaching implications for the welfare of society. Bargaining procedures often break down and involve much delay in reaching a solution to a conflict. Hence, they can be very costly not only to the participants themselves but to society at large. It is then that a third party must step in to resolve the differences of the participants . The third party may be voluntarily chosen by the participants themselves or appointed by the government. In other words, there is a need in certain circumstances for an authoritarian procedure to be adopted when a democratic procedure fails to reach a decision.

In short, in modern societies no simple procedure will suffice. All sorts of procedures, authoritarian, democratic, 'technocratic', bargaining, informal and official procedures, are needed. Obviously, a flexible attitude on the part of the decision-makers is needed to choose the appropriate procedure for a set of given circumstances and decisions. However, it is often the case that procedures that have been developed for one purpose tend to be used for another. They tend to follow a set pattern regardless of the decision and the circumstances. As a result, customs and conventions evolve to deal with many situations, leading to economy of effort, but having a biasing effect on the choice of procedure adopted to deal with decisional problems. Consequently, the decisions reached may be less than optimal, and indeed may turn out to be wrong because they have been decided through inappropriate procedures.

V

This chapter has discussed the importance of procedures in decision-making. A proper procedure will reduce, if not eliminate, systemic errors. Human frailty and fallibility will, more or less, ensure that mistakes will be made, but such mistakes will not be the result of inappropriate procedures of decision-making. We have argued that, as a general rule, democratic procedures should be used in reaching decisions. The values of democratic procedures are not simply 'instrumental' based on performance but also on their desirability as ends in themselves. People should, as far as possible, participate in economic and political decisions that affect the quality of their lives and the character of society in which they live. Such participation is increasingly regarded by many social scientists and philosophers as a component of the bundle of human rights (Rawls 1971; Sen 1992). Fortunately, in many cases, it seems democratic procedures yield better economic results as well. Accountability, transparency, consultation and active participation of a greater number of people in decision-making – all these characteristics of democratic procedures will, in general, generate better decisions.

However, there may be exceptional circumstances where democratic procedures lead to incongruities, or fail to produce, not only the right decisions but any decisions at all. In such cases, an authoritarian or a technocratic procedure would be preferable. For example, major decisions of national importance, which require secrecy and confidentiality, may require an authoritarian procedure. Complex and difficult decisions, beyond the competence of laypeople, requiring the inputs of experts, cannot be meaningfully made through a democratic procedure. At the same time, it must be stressed that democratic procedures are vulnerable to manipulation by self-seeking decision-makers. There is a tendency to accept democratic procedures at their face value, to assume that accountability and transparency will ensure just outcomes. In fact, accountability and transparency are easily evaded by misdemeanours. The inbuilt trust in democratic procedures makes us less vigilant to what is going on, and thus blunders and errors can and do occur, even though democratic procedures are observed. It is important to adopt a healthy degree of scepticism towards democratic procedures precisely because of the inbuilt bias in their favour.

The chapter has also discussed the interaction between the decision-making procedure and the other four aspects of the decision-making process. We have shown that the type of procedure adopted can and does influence and is influenced by the other four components of decision-making. Accordingly, a fully integrated decision-making system must give an important and permanent role for processes and procedures in order to generate the 'correct' decisions. However, it is equally important not to place excessive emphasis on them at the expense of more substantive issues, such as information flows, decision-making criteria and motivations, which are also important for generating the 'right' decisions and desirable outcomes.

Finally, our attempt to classify economies on the basis of decision-making procedures shows that a few can be located at both ends of the authoritarian–democratic continuum, though it seems there are many more economies located in or closer to the democratic zone. However, when we combine structure and procedure into a dual continuum, we get some interesting and indeed more complex cases, such as centralised–democratic and decentralised–authoritarian economies. 'Centralised–authoritarian' and 'decentralised–democratic' economies are even rarer than centralised and decentralised ones. To get a comprehensive classificatory schema, we have to add three other dimensions: information flows, decision criteria and incentives. In the next chapter, we consider the importance of the structure of information flows in the decision-making process.

4. Structures of Information Flows

When we attempt to examine the structure of information flows, it is essential that we recognise that it includes both the mechanisms and channels for the collection, processing and transmission of information. Furthermore, this structure has a crucial effect on the other components of decision-making and on the quality of the decisions. If the information on which decisions are based is imperfect, the decisions themselves will be fallible or sub-optimal. Good decisions require good information; but information is seldom sufficient. Although decisions are frequently made under conditions of uncertainty and partial ignorance, the accumulation of information and learning-by-doing reduce the degree of uncertainty.

Prior to the emergence of the idea of 'bounded rationality' (Simon 1959) and the economics of information (Stigler 1961), it was generally assumed that economic agents were well informed about their circumstances and knew the consequences of their choices. It was also assumed that they possessed in full the required informational capacity (both the computational capacity and the capacity to assimilate and evaluate new and specialised knowledge) to make correct and meaningful decisions. Thus, decision-making became a relatively trivial exercise of balancing the known costs (disutilities) against the known benefits (utilities). The real problems of decision-makers were swept under the carpet, and the fundamental interrelationships between the structure of information flows and other aspects of decision-making were obscured.

However, since the development of the economics of information and bounded rationality, it has become widely recognised that many of the theoretical and practical problems in economics turn on the questions of ignorance, imperfect and asymmetric information. Indeed, informational problems have become the focal point of both theoretical and empirical inquiries. Evidently, a well-functioning economic system depends on, among other things, the quantity and quality of information flows; and in the long run the survival of the system depends on its capacity to generate and exploit new knowledge. Information flows must be as accurate as possible and reliable to facilitate both the correct formulation and effective implementation of decisions as well as to permit proper procedures to be followed and relevant criteria to be chosen.

The rest of the chapter is arranged as follows: Section II discusses the structure and types of information flows and examines their links with other aspects of decision-making. Section III attempts to classify economic systems, along an information continuum. This continuum is then combined with two continuums of structure and procedure of decision-making to yield eight economic systems. Section IV evaluates the various structures and types of information flows, with special reference to the generation and exploitation of new information. Finally, Section V offers some concluding remarks on this fundamental aspect of decision-making.

II

Contrary to a widely held view, first emphasised by Hayek and other opponents of central decision-making, the problems of collecting, processing and transmitting accurate and timely information are not confined to hierarchies and centrally planned economies. The central assumption of Hayek (1945) is that prices in a market economy permit the 'man on the spot' to act rationally on his 'intimate knowledge of the facts of his immediate surroundings' by supplying him with the relevant information about the economy at large, which he requires for making meaningful decisions. Hence, 'knowledge of the particular circumstances of time and place' is crucial. Hayek's view that prices convey the essential information needed for making rational decisions with minimum or zero cost is valid only in the rare and simple world of perfect competition. Outside this model, prices are the result of a bargaining process or simply the last stage of this process in which the exchange of information is crucial. In a way, decision-making is the last round of an iterative information process (Kornai 1971). In modern economies, which are characterised by hierarchical organisations, administered prices, externalities, interdependencies, risks and uncertainties, all types of price and non-price information are needed to prepare, formulate, implement and monitor decisions. Moreover, the complexity of economic decision-making necessarily involves a division of labour in the gathering, processing and communication of information, as well as in the formulation and execution of decisions.

Decision-makers almost everywhere rely on others for all types of information to make their choices. An enormous amount of information flows continuously among them. However, the disjunction between decision-making and information flows is particularly noticeable in large hierarchies with several decision-making levels. Hierarchical organisations range from a small firm operating in a market economy to a centrally planned economy. The latter may be viewed as a single firm. From this perspective, a small firm and a centrally planned economy occupy two extreme points on a continuum of hierarchies and organisations. In large hierarchies, the problem of information flows is addressed by establishing informational channels with a view to minimise costs and distortions as the information passes to decision-making and decision-enforcing points. In small firms no such channels are needed.

Nevertheless, the disjunction between information flows and decision-making in large organisations creates problems of coordination and agency, not unlike those arising from the division of labour in production and the separation of ownership and control. There is some divergence of interests and goals, on the one hand, between the suppliers of information and decision-makers and, on the other, between the decision-makers and implementers. The inevitable distortion of information arising from conflicting interests in hierarchies is compounded if the implementers are themselves the suppliers of information to the decision-makers. Distortions of information or, more generally, problems of information also arise in polyarchies and markets. But first we focus our attention on the problems of information in hierarchies, particularly those of centrally planned economies.

Decision-makers at all levels in a hierarchy depend on information generated by others. Thus, superiors rely on subordinates to supply them with different types of information, primary and feedback, for decision-making and remaking. In turn, subordinates receive command-type information (orders and norms) and 'success indicators' or incentives from above to implement the decisions, which they themselves may have helped to formulate. In addition, there are horizontal information flows among lower decision-making units to work out the details of policies and decisions reached at higher levels.

This broad description of information flows in a hierarchy conceals the enormous difficulty of collecting and transmitting information to decision-makers. The different stages of decision-making, ranging from the preparation and formulation to the implementation and monitoring, require different types of trustworthy information. In particular, sound policies and decisions must take account of their feasibility and acceptability. It is worse than useless to spend time and energy to reach 'optimal' decisions if they have little or no chance of being implemented. There must be adequate information on the feasibility of decisions.

Even in the most centralised and authoritarian system, there are limits on the ability of top decision-makers to enforce their decisions on subordinates and citizens. Central decision-makers need to know the capacity of the economy and available resources to set feasible objectives. They also need to know the limits to which people are prepared to accept further hardship. Such information is necessary for making major decisions such as aggregate investment and saving. This type of information is normally collected by government agencies such as statistical bureaux, which provide what might be called 'non-addressed' or anonymous information for central decision-makers.

If, on the other hand, central decision-makers are heavily involved in micro-decisions, as in the heyday of Soviet-type economies, then they require 'addressed' information from individual enterprises about their productive capacity and resources in their possession. The more accurate the information about such matters, the more likely the decisions made at the centre will turn out to be right, assuming central decision-makers have the computational capacity and the evaluation skills to utilise the primary and feedback information they receive from subordinates. Of course, central decision-makers can employ analysts to assist with information processing. But they must be able to communicate with them and supervise their activities. Those tasks require time and hence central decision-makers can devote only limited attention to them. Clearly, there are limits to the computational capacity of central decision-makers. Such limits compel them to delegate some of their decision-making powers to committees and lower decision-making bodies including enterprises. As Nove (1978, p 53) reminds us, 'it is utterly and totally impossible to collect information at the centre about micro-requirements and then convey the necessary orders to thousands of executant managers... the formulation of the bulk of micro-decisions will not and can not be taken by the centre itself'.

In the former centralised system of the Soviet-type, the required information for making microeconomic decisions at the centre was collected by subordinates, processed, aggregated and transmitted sequentially through the hierarchy. In the course of aggregation and upward communication from one level to the next, some information was destroyed and errors and inevitable distortions were introduced into the information flows. Millions of distinct products were grouped into thousands of categories to be decided on by the central authority. The process of aggregation often entailed incorrect prices and arbitrary judgements. Similar distortions occurred in the downward communication of information (commands) when aggregate targets had to be disaggregated for operational purposes. And since distortion occurred each time the information was transmitted from one level to the next, the more levels the information had to pass, the greater the degree of distortion of the initial information.

Leaving aside the 'technical' distortions arising from the process of aggregation and disaggregation of primary and feedback information, the higher the number of levels of decision-making, the longer it takes for the information to reach the decision-making and decision-enforcing points. By the time the required information has reached its final destination, events on which the initial data are based would have moved on, and the transmitted information would have become less relevant for decision-making and implementation. Deadlines may be set for collecting, processing and transmitting the required information and for enforcing the decisions, with heavy penalty attached to failure to comply with the set date. But such penalties tend to encourage both the suppliers to invent data and falsify the information and for the implementers to distort the spirit of the decisions by lowering the quality of products and services or by incurring avoidable cost and waste. Alternatively, positive incentives may be offered for honest reporting and speedy information flows but, as we shall see, such incentives are seldom effective.

The proclivity of subordinates to provide false and self-serving information to superiors makes it difficult to obtain accurate information both for making meaningful decisions and for measuring the performance of those responsible for implementing the decisions. As Downs (1967, p 27) observed, inside a bureaucracy 'all types of officials tend to exaggerate data that reflect favourably on themselves and to minimise those that reveal their own shortcomings'. In particular, subordinates tend to distort the information they pass upwards to their superiors. In the former Soviet-type economies, misrepresentation to superiors of productive capacity and resources held by peripheral decision-making agents was a familiar problem to central decision-makers (Nove 1978, pp 93–103). Consequently, they responded by allocating fewer resources and by demanding more outputs than suggested by subordinates. However, such response created further problems. The combination of asymmetric information and excessive 'tautness' caused widespread shortages of goods and services (Kornai 1980).

Misrepresentation of information is further encouraged by another characteristic of hierarchies. Typically, subordinates like to please their superiors, and superiors like to be praised by subordinates. In particular, superiors like to be told that their policies and decisions have turned out to be successful. They are often sheltered from the awful reality, which their decisions have brought about. Subordinates withhold unfavourable information and feedback on their superiors' decisions. Central decision-makers are so removed from the action that they are not able to know much of what is happening in the field. As Boulding (1966) states, 'hierarchical organisations tend to produce false images in top decision-makers and the larger and more authoritarian the organisation the more likely that its top decision-makers will be operating in purely imaginary worlds'. Central decision-makers may establish a separate monitory agency to gain reliable information. But monitoring is costly, requiring the use of additional human resources. A more effective way, perhaps, of dealing with this problem would be for the decision-maker at the top to be sceptical of favourable reports and not to penalise reporting of failures, and may indeed reward those who bring him or her 'bad' news.

While the separation of decisional from informational roles in hierarchies is necessary and can lead to satisfactory outcomes in standard and routine decisions, in the case of innovation decisions this separation can produce adverse effects that are not well recognised. If the structure of decision-making consists of many levels, the approval rate of new decisions or innovation-oriented projects is likely to be very low. This is because the unfamiliarity of aspects related to innovation makes it difficult to prove their merits in order to convince superiors to adopt them. The essence of an entrepreneurial function is the high risk element arising from unknown variables and other variables, which cannot be easily factored into the innovation decision. The entrepreneur's vision, like 'tacit knowledge', cannot be easily articulated and communicated to others. It is a kind of inner knowledge or knowledge of the heart (*knosis*). In a highly structured organisation or government bureaucracy, new ideas have more opportunities of being rejected, and once rejected they will most likely be lost for good.

Such an analysis casts doubts on the once popular view held by socialists that in a centralised economy, once a new idea or invention becomes available it can be adopted by other enterprises through command from the centre (Zhou 1991). Thus, wastes associated with duplication of research and development and secrecy are avoided. The common practice in the former Soviet-type economies was to transfer new technology, free of charge, whenever it occurred (which was not very frequent) from the innovating enterprise to other enterprises. This meant that successful enterprises were not rewarded for their innovation, and enterprises, which had failed to innovate, were not penalised. This is obviously not a good recipe for generating and diffusing new information and technology.

Looking at the problem of innovation from the viewpoint of information supplied by higher authorities, either in the form of commands or success indicators, it is not easy to set specific quantitative innovation targets that superiors can transmit to subordinates. Moreover, innovations by order might be effective if they were given freely like 'manna from heaven'. In reality, however, they are produced and their production and reproduction must be stimulated by appropriate incentives. Innovation by order, as the Soviet experience clearly demonstrates, can be effective only in a few industries, where there are few producers and few users, because of difficulties in gathering information, monitoring, coordinating and motivating innovation. Innovative decisions are much harder to coordinate than routine decisions due to their uncertain and targetless nature. If it is hard to communicate existing information in a hierarchy, then transmitting knowledge that has not yet come into existence, or proven to be correct, becomes an extremely difficult and challenging task.

It might be suggested that much of the misrepresentation of information supplied to superiors could be avoided through proper incentives, which can be used to encourage honesty. However, it has been shown that it is far from easy to simultaneously maximise the centre's objective function and honest reporting (Bonin and Marcus 1979; Miller and Murrell 1981). Without fully knowing the utility functions of managers and subordinates, there does not appear to be an effective incentive scheme whereby subordinates can be encouraged to reveal their production functions. The general problem seems to be how to encourage honest reporting without reducing the incentive to maximise production. The resolution of this problem is made more difficult by the fact that input allocation depends on information usually supplied by subordinates. As Miller and Murrell (1984, p 285) have shown, 'there exists no optimal bonus function that would allow the centre to obtain the full-information maximum value of the objective function'.

The difficulties of having a reliable structure of information flows in a centralised structure of decision-making seem at first sight to reinforce Hayek's argument in favour of a decentralised or market system. Hayek's argument is not entirely convincing. First, he places excessive emphasis on the role of prices as conveying the essential information needed by decision-makers operating in the market. This information, he argues, is given in the marketplace free of charge, that is, prices are efficient transmitters of information. However, as Coase (1937) suggested, there is a cost of using the price system. That is why some transactions take place within (hierarchical) organisations or firms rather than between firms or individuals operating in the market. Decision-makers often require other types of information besides prices, which fail to capture all the information about a product. Coase further suggested that it would be too costly to put a price on each of the numerous intermediate and differentiated tasks that are involved in the production process. Hence, considered as information systems, markets are inherently costly and imperfect.

Second, Hayek ignored the fact that some resources are better allocated within hierarchical organisations, which have access to private information about their properties. Such information cannot be easily communicated by agents in the market. Further, as Alchian and Demsetz (1972) argue, organisations have comparative advantages over markets in obtaining certain types of information. Indeed, certain kinds of information cannot be communicated at all in the marketplace (Williamson 1985).

Third, according to Arrow (1994), 'Hayek tends to minimise the role of scientific knowledge and does not really discuss technological knowledge at all, a great deal of which is transmittable to others'. For Hayek, the stock of knowledge (information) is given in a market economy and is dispersed or diffused among economic agents, whereas in a centralised system it is concentrated or rather used at the centre. But he does not discuss the more important question for modern economies, the question of new information (knowledge), of its origins, and how it is generated and diffused. It is argued in Section IV that new information cannot be generated by the market alone or by individual entrepreneurs. Large organisations and the state have comparative advantages in fostering research and development, the main source of new information in modern economies.

Fourth, it is widely recognised that the information generated in the marketplace is distorted by advertising. Indeed, advertising is viewed by many writers as a process of deception aimed at persuading rather than informing consumers. More than 50 years ago Kaldor (1950) argued that advertising is insufficiently informative, because it is provided by those who are interested in selling the product rather than by disinterested and presumably public-spirited agents. Further, advertising and salesmanship create artificial wants and cause misallocation of resources between the private sector and the public sector, generating an over-supply of private goods and services and under-supply of public goods and services (Galbraith 1958, p 753). On the other hand, defenders of advertising argue that in the absence of perfect information advertising is necessary. Individual consumers typically have limited knowledge of the pertinent characteristics of alternative products available to them, and advertising provides information about those products. It is part and parcel of the competitive process, a form of non-price competition, a driving force for both product and process innovation and essential for creating a mass market. Thus, according to Kirzner (1973, p 162), 'the entrepreneur's task is not completed when he makes information available to the consumer. He must also get the consumer to notice and absorb that information'. Of course, in an affluent society as more goods are produced, there are increasing demands on the consumer's attention. Hence, advertising must necessarily make exaggerated claims about the quality of the product, and become more intrusive and jingoistic.

Fifth, Hayek overlooked both the possibility of offering incentives to agents to reveal what they know and the positive role of government in 'indicative planning' as opposed to mandatory planning. Frequently, indicative planning is defined as informing economic agents that something is about to happen, as opposed to forcing them to do something, or as promoting, rather than taking action. The idea of indicative planning is to reduce the uncertainty of the marketplace; to deal with 'market failures that result from failures in the nature or availability of information and in its generally long-term nature' (Brada and Estrin 1990, p 524). Proponents of indicative planning argue that economic agents do not have sufficient knowledge to make important long-term decisions and that governments can provide additional information about the intentions of other agents, and thus help to reduce uncertainty. However, as Estrin and Holmes (1990, p 531) point out, governments can reduce uncertainty 'only when uncertainty is exogenous to the decision-makers but endogenous to the economy'. Moreover, as the purpose of indicative planning is to provide agents with additional information that they themselves cannot acquire, its effectiveness depends on the accuracy of the information it supplies and the willingness of agents to utilise the information. As long as plan projections are based on information provided by economic agents about their future intentions, there will be problems with the accuracy of the information. The participants in indicative planning will be aware that the information they provide is likely to influence the plan targets and so, like their counterparts in central planning, provide misleading information in order to obtain plan targets that are favourable to their own interests. Further, it is not certain that they will disclose fully their real plans, since the latter provide externalities to other agents and therefore undermines their own competitiveness. Thus, the supply of information may not be optimal.

Nevertheless, there is a persuasive case for indicative planning based on the comparative advantages of governments in the gathering and processing of information, due to economies of scale and asymmetrical information. The information provided by governments is generally in the nature of public good and hence cannot be generated efficiently in the marketplace or by private organisations. But, since there are both government and market informational failures, there seems to be no alternative to more dialogue or cooperation between the public sector and the private sector to get better information in order for both governments and markets to work better. This is yet another area, where it is counterproductive to draw a dichotomy or demarcation line between the public and the private sector. The gathering, processing and utilisation of information require the inputs and coordination of information provided by markets, organisations and governments. Such coordination is essential for making decisions that are feasible and consistent with one another.

The structures of information flows in the customary economy and in the emerging cooperative economy will be discussed in the following section. In the remainder of this section we examine the interrelationships between the structure of information flows and other aspects of the decision-making process. We have already seen that the direction of information flows affects the decision-making structure, rendering it less centralised if the information flows upwards and more centralised if information flows downwards. In turn, the decision-making structure has a significant effect on the nature, quality and direction of information flows. A centralised structure with many decision-making levels leads to distortions and falsification of information both in the formulation and implementation of decisions, whereas a decentralised structure minimises distortions and misrepresentations simply because decision-making agents are closer to the source of information. However, the information flows generated in a decentralised (or market) economy, though necessary, are not free from distortions or sufficient for reaching sound decisions. More importantly, perhaps, the decision-making structure has an important influence on the generation and diffusion of new information. A highly centralised structure, through mobilisation of resources for research and development (R&D), can generate new ideas, but bureaucratic tendencies discourage application (use) and diffusion. In contrast, as shown below, a decentralised structure has comparative advantages in innovation and diffusion.

There are also close links between the structure of information flows and decision-making procedure. The upward flow of information tends to make the procedure somewhat more democratic, as the suppliers of information indirectly participate in the formulation of decisions taken at higher levels. Conversely, the downward flow of information tends to reinforce the degree of authoritarianism. In turn, if the procedure is highly authoritarian, it produces false images in the perceptions of decision-makers, as it permits no criticism of decisions that have gone wrong. Errors and mistakes persist from one period to the next. In contrast, a democratic procedure with rigorous standards of accountability and transparency tends to generate more and better information. It also encourages the generation of new information and experiments.

The structures and types of information flows affect the choice of criteria in reaching a decision. A lack of detailed information and proper prices restricts the use of economic criteria and the use of the economic calculus of costs and benefits. In contrast, market-type information permits the use of the economic calculus, though the presence of externalities and other types of market failures place limits on the 'rational' allocation of resources. In turn, decision criteria affect the flow and types of information. For example, economic criteria require the use of scarcity prices, which are practically impossible to obtain in a closed economy that is informationally centralised and without markets. In an open centralised economy, international prices may be used as a short cut to economic rationality but only for tradable goods and services. If decision-makers place more emphasis on non-economic objectives, then they still need the economic information to make meaningful choices, or to achieve the intended outcome with minimum resources.

Finally, there is a close and mutual interaction between information flows and motivational structure. Centralised information flows in the form of obligatory targets and orders are not sufficient to ensure compliance of subordinates with the wishes of central decision-makers. Negative incentives, such as legal sanctions and coercion, need to be supplemented by positive incentives so that subordinates can be motivated to exert more effort and time than the minimum they can get away without being penalised. Information flows in the form of 'success indicators' are needed in cases where decision-makers rely on others to execute their decisions. Success indicators provide signals for subordinates to maximise those targets to which rewards are attached. Much of the distortion and misrepresentation of information generated by subordinates can be traced to the incentives or 'success indicators' set by superiors (Nove 1978, pp 93–9). Subordinates tend to pursue targets and objectives for which they are rewarded and ignore others such as quality, design and innovation, which are not easily quantifiable. The relationship between information structure and incentives is explored in more detail in Chapter 6.

III

As noted in the introduction of this chapter, this section tries to classify economic systems on the basis of the structure of information flows. Economies can be ranked on an information continuum ranging from one extreme, where the stock of knowledge is monopolised by a single authority at the centre and flows downwards, to the other extreme, where information is dispersed more or less evenly among economic agents and flows horizontally. In between these extremes are economies where the stock of knowledge is unequally distributed and flows more or less in all directions.

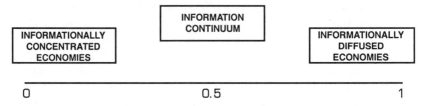

If the information structure completely overlapped with the decision-making structure, then there would be no need to add an information continuum. But since we have already shown in Chapter 2 that the two structures do not always coincide, and that in modern economies there is, in general, a disjunction between decision-making and information flows, it is necessary to introduce an additional dimension to capture those economies that have similar structures and procedures but different information flows. As we did in the last chapter, we simply add the information continuum to the one based on both the structure and procedure of decision-making. As shown in Table 4.1, the three-dimensional classificatory schema yields eight possible types of economic system:

Table 4.1   Decision-making structure, procedure and information flows

	Structure	Decision-making Procedure	Information	Economic systems
1	Centralised	Authoritarian	Concentrated	CAC
2	Centralised	Authoritarian	Diffused	CAD
3	Centralised	Democratic	Concentrated	CDC
4	Centralised	Democratic	Diffused	CDD
5	Decentralised	Authoritarian	Concentrated	DAC
6	Decentralised	Authoritarian	Diffused	DAD
7	Decentralised	Democratic	Concentrated	DDC
8	Decentralised	Democratic	Diffused	DDD

The first, a centralised–authoritarian and informationally concentrated system (CAC), is one in which most decisions are made by a central authority on the basis of non-addressed information provided by national (state) statistical channels. The procedure being authoritarian, there is no consultation with subordinates, whose primary task is the implementation of decisions made by the central authority. Information flows downwards sequentially through the layers of bureaucracy in the form of commands or orders. The system is an extreme form of command, which is rare, but is approximated by totalitarian and militarised economies. Such economies can be located on the left end of the three-dimensional continuum.

The second type is a centralised–authoritarian and informationally diffused system (CAD). This system is distinguished from the first by the fact that central decisions are based on addressed information or on information supplied by subordinates who thereby indirectly participate in decision-making. As we have explained in the previous section, the upward flow of information modifies both the structure and procedure, making them somewhat less centralised and authoritarian. Such economies can be located to the right of CACs. Some of the former Soviet-type economies with partially decentralised information flows can be classified as CADs.

The third possible system in our schema is one, which is centralised–democratic and concentrated information flows (CDC). In this system the central authority combines both the decisional and informational roles. The democratic procedure, which allows more participants in decision-making, will be constrained by the concentration of information at the centre. Hence, participants will probably have less say in determining the final mix of decisions. The precise influence they exert on the final outcome will depend on the freedom they have in interpreting and processing the information supplied to them. Depending on the degree of influence the democratic procedure has on the final decision under an informationally concentrated system, CDCs can be located either to the left or the right of CADs. Naturally, this degree will vary from one set of decisions to another. It will be less in routine and standardised products and more in new and complex decisions.

The fourth type is a centralised–democratic and informationally diffused system (CDD). The difference between CDCs and CDDs is the nature and direction of information flows. Since, in this system, information flows upwards and the procedure is democratic, the influence of the central authority on the final decision is greatly diminished. Indeed, the role of the centre would be largely confined to initiation of decisions. CDDs not only combine the advantages of centralisation and democracy but also have the benefits of diffused information, which is necessary for most microeconomic decisions. Thus, the probability of arriving at informed microeconomic decisions is much higher than in any of the previous three possible systems. CDDs may be positioned to the right of CADs and CDCs and somewhere near the centre of the continuum.

The fifth possible system is decentralised–authoritarian and informationally concentrated (DAC). Decisions are made either by lower decision-making units in a multi-level hierarchy or by 'autonomous' decision-makers on the basis of information supplied by a central authority. The authoritarian character of this system is hard to reconcile with a decentralised decision-making structure. In an administered hierarchy it may be possible to prevent consultation and openness among lower decision-making units, but it is difficult to impose such conditions on autonomous decision-makers. Of course, authoritarianism is not absolute and it is possible, as in the case of an extreme form of indicative planning or 'persuasive' planning, that the central authority through various incentive schemes such as monetary rewards and penalties for lack of compliance or disobedience can succeed in imposing its will on both subordinates and independent decision-makers. The combination of authoritarian procedure with centrally concentrated information may render the formally decentralised decision-making structure more centralised than a centralised system with a democratic procedure and diffused structure of information flows. Thus, DACs may be placed to the left of CDDs.

The sixth system is decentralised–authoritarian and informationally diffused (DAD). The authoritarian element in this system is even more difficult to reconcile with a decentralised decision-making structure than in the previous system where information is supplied by the centre. In DADs there is no separation between informational and decisional roles of agents, and thus the authoritarian element, which entered the system via the centrally concentrated–centralised information would be absent. It is likely that the authoritarian procedure would be eclipsed by the decentralised nature of both the decision-making structure and information flows. Of course, authoritarian procedures would exist within autonomous decision-making units. In any case, DADs may be positioned to the right of the five systems we have so far considered.

The seventh possible economic system is decentralised–democratic and informationally concentrated (DDC). In this system decisions are made either by autonomous economic agents or dependent decision-making agents in a hierarchy on the basis of information supplied by superiors or a central authority. The procedure is nominally democratic; no force is applied and as many people as possible participate in decision-making. The influence of a central authority is confined to the supply of information and some economic incentives to induce decision-makers to operate within guidelines and targets set by the central authority. It is not hard to imagine the existence of such a system. Indeed, it comes close to the indicative planning practised in Western Europe in the 1950s and 1960. DDCs can be placed to the right of DADs and to their right are 'the managing states' where the central authority, in the form of a democratically elected state, manages the economy, but its degree of intervention is less than that of DDCs.

The eighth system is decentralised–democratic and informationally diffused (DDD). This is the familiar *laissez-faire* system, where a central authority plays no role in managing the economy. Unlike agents in DDCs, those in DDDs respond to signals generated by the market rather than by a central authority. The role of the central authority is confined to the enforcement of law and order. DDDs are extreme economies and occupy the right end of our three-dimensional continuum.

It is clear that the introduction of the structure of information flows into our classificatory schema has multiplied the types of economic system from four to eight. The additional four, CAD, CDC, DAD and DDC, were not captured by the classification based on the structure and procedure of decision-making. The other four, CAC, CDD, DAC and DDD, more or less coincide with the four types discussed in the last chapter. In the next chapter, we add another dimension based on decision-making criteria.

Before we attempt to evaluate the different structures of information flows, it is of some interest to consider the structure of information flows in both traditional and cooperative societies and see where they can be located on our continuum. In traditional societies, as economic activities hardly change from year to year very little new information is required to obtain subsistence. People know in their geographical location when and where to hunt, fish and gather food. They may also have detailed botanical knowledge for medicinal purposes. This stock of information, which is handed down from generation to generation, is relatively small and will increase as the diversity of goods increases. In an isolated society an increase in the stock of information comes from a few nonconformists, who are inclined to take exploratory decisions and in the process acquire new information that might be beneficial to the community. New information may also be generated in times of crisis when decision-makers are confronted with a new situation. As noted in the last two chapters, it is not easy to fit traditional societies into our decision-making classification. Depending on their structures and procedures, they may be located along different zones of the continuum. The introduction of information dimension does not appear to alter their existing ranking, except for those economies that are more receptive to new information, which makes them somewhat more decentralised and democratic than those which are hostile to new ideas.

The structure of information flows in cooperative societies would be mostly horizontal. Information is not only diffused among decision-making units, but there would be much cooperation in the gathering, processing and transmission of information and knowledge. Decision-makers in cooperative societies would be eager to consult with other decision-makers that might be affected by their decisions, and to share any new information they generate. If a central authority exists to take care of public decisions or decisions concerning public goods and services, it is assumed there would be cooperation and free exchange of information between the centre and the periphery. Thus, cooperative societies, which are decentralised, democratic and completely transparent, would be located towards the right end of the three-dimensional continuum, and even to the right of DDDs, if the latter follow an authoritarian structure within the decision-making units, namely firms and families.

IV

In the long-standing debate on the advantages and disadvantages of (de) centralisation, the merits of decentralised (market) economies have been emphasised because of the ability of the market to provide a special kind of information that is essential for solving the valuation problem and hence the rational allocation of resources. As Hayek and others pointed out, the task performed by the market cannot be easily simulated by a central authority, which relies on addressed and non-addressed information. In Section II we discussed the difficulties of gathering, processing and transmitting accurate and timely information through multi-level hierarchies. No central authority can cope with the complexity of all relevant information. It seems, therefore, that true decentralisation consists in delegating decisions to those who know more about them.

However, it would be a mistake to think that the structure and type of information flows generated in market economies are sufficient for reaching meaningful decisions. Resource allocation takes place within hierarchical organisations precisely because they sometimes possess superior knowledge of resource characteristics that is difficult or costly to communicate in the marketplace because of bounded rationality and asymmetric information (Coase 1937; Alchian and Demsetz 1972; Williamson 1985). But as Putterman (1995, pp 374–5) points out, the comparative advantage of firms, 'both in recognising and in eliciting differentiation of input characteristics, comes not so much from their hierarchical form of organisation as from their ability to support long-term associations by providing for mutually beneficial sharing of the rents of joint production by supplies of inter-specialised resources'. He goes on to argue that larger hierarchies cannot maintain this advantage both because of the information overload problem and because of the increasing cost of negotiating and sustaining cooperation among themselves. The distortion and misrepresentation of information flows in a multi-tiered hierarchy discussed in Section II imply the existence of diseconomies of scale.

Nevertheless, there are some economies of scale in collecting, processing and communication of information, which cannot be exploited by individuals or small organisations. Such economies will reduce costs and will improve the quantity and quality of information. There may be increasing costs and delays in collecting and processing all the necessary information for reaching a decision. Indeed, if too much time and resources are invested in getting the necessary information, the decision might be outdated. It seems, then, a trade-off has to be made between the increasing costs and delays of acquiring information and the resulting quality of decisions. Clearly, it is not always possible to arrive at error-free decisions, if time and resources are accepted as binding constraints. The wise thing to do is to acquire just enough information to make a satisfactory rather than an optimal decision. Decisions must not be delayed until complete information is available. At the same time, decisions should not be made too hastily. Acquiring more information is a time- and other resource-consuming process. However, information processes exhibit declining complexity; the more information acquired the sooner the decision is made. As in a jigsaw puzzle, the task becomes less complicated as it progresses (Kennedy 1994).

Hierarchical organisations, especially government ones, generate information that cannot be supplied by individuals operating in the market. Individuals left to their own devices and resources are unable to gather, process and interpret all the information they need to make their own decisions. Market prices are normally insufficient for decision-makers to make up their mind. They may need to know the present state of the economy, current trends in particular sectors, or the future plans of the government, these types of information cannot be efficiently generated by individuals; they do not normally have the time, skill and resources to gather and process the required information. Government informational organisations have comparative advantage in providing information about the economic environment within which decision-makers operate. Indeed, such 'macro-information' may be regarded as a public good as it reduces the degree of uncertainty for decision-making agents. However, with the declining role of governments in economic affairs and the growth of organizations specialising in collecting and marketing economic information, there is now comparatively less economic data generated by governments.

Clearly, there are three sources of information, which are necessary for making rational or informed decisions. First, market-type information provides us with information about the relative scarcity of some resources. Without competitive markets the valuation problem cannot be solved satisfactorily. Second, organizations or firms make use of refined information about resources than is readily transmitted across markets. They also exploit any economies of scale in gathering and processing non-price type of information. Third, governments provide 'macro' or sectoral information about the state of the economy. Such information helps to reduce the degree of uncertainty for all decision-makers. Conversely, detailed information about the activities of individuals and organisations cannot be transmitted to central (state) decision-makers without delays, misrepresentation and distortion.

Since the emphasis in the centralisation–decentralisation debate has been on the possibility of transmitting trustworthy information or existing knowledge from subordinates to superiors for the purpose of centralised allocation of resources, the problem of the generation and exploitation of new knowledge has been neglected. How is this knowledge acquired and how does it affect the centralisation–decentralisation debate? More specifically, is there a special role for central decision-makers in the generation of new information? In recent years economists have turned their attention to the problem of the generation and exploitation of new knowledge under the broad heading of 'endogenous' growth theory.

According to this theory new knowledge is generated mainly as a result of the working of the economic system and the behaviour of rational economic agents. More specifically, it is produced by investment in R&D (Romer 1986), or it is acquired either by 'doing' (Arrow 1962) or simply by 'watching' (King and Rebelo 1990). However, the rate of flow of the level of new knowledge depends on past levels of investment in both human and physical capital. Each firm learns from its own experience as well as from the experience of others. In the R&D models of Lucas (1988) and Romer (1990), the focus is on the research sector, the sector specialising in the 'production' of new ideas. In this sector human capital and information, or the existing stock of knowledge, are combined together to produce new information or knowledge, which, in turn, increases the stock of human capital and knowledge. Thus, knowledge feeds upon itself.

It follows that economies with greater stocks of human capital, which are productively utilised to produce physical capital and new information, will experience faster sustainable growth rates. In addition, any country can acquire new ideas from other countries once the ideas have been exploited and transformed into processes or products at relatively low costs through international trade and foreign investment. In other words, knowledge produced anywhere can benefit producers everywhere over time. However, it is hard to use information from others without doing your own R&D that provides spillovers for others. But spillovers reduce the incentives for investment in R&D. Indeed, both theory and empirical data suggest that the amount of research produced by autonomous organisations is below the social optimum level (Nadiri 1993; Grossman and Helpman 1994). Risk and uncertainty discourage investment in R&D. Thus, one of the important implications of endogenous growth theory is that there is a significant role for the state in the innovation process by fostering the accumulation of productive human capital and knowledge.

However, it is not enough to spend money on education and R&D in order to expand the stock of human capital. Physical capital and other complementary factors must also be in place for new ideas to be fully exploited and diffused throughout the economy, so that new products and processes can be produced at internationally competitive prices. There seems to be a dialectical and cumulative process of cause and effect between the development of new ideas and human capital, on the one hand, and other concomitant factors with causation running from scientific research and knowledge, to secure ordinary investment, and then back again through the experience gained, to scientific and engineering knowledge (Scott 1992). Further, there must be an effective patent system to encourage the development of new ideas. Patents are the institutional devices in competitive markets to cope with the peculiarities of knowledge production. The conditions for the generation, development and diffusion of new ideas is further discussed in Chapter 12.

V

The discussion in the present chapter has furnished us with some qualitative insights into the intimate interrelationships between the structure of information flows and other components of decision-making. We have observed that in modern economies there is an increasing tendency for decision-makers to rely on others for information needed to make up their own minds. This disjunction between decision-making and information flows creates problems of communication and coordination especially in multi-tier hierarchies and bureaucracies. The upward and downward transmission of information leads to distortions and misrepresentation, no matter how well subordinates and superiors work together and irrespective of their honesty and communication skills. This is because of the inevitable distortion arising from aggregation and disaggregation of original information and the fallibility of human communication (Sah 1991). The degree of distortion is greater the larger the number of levels through which information flows travel. It is precisely these problems of communication that led Hayek and others to reject the idea of centralised decision-making.

The problems of communication and coordination of information in multi-level hierarchies are compounded in the case of new information (knowledge). It is well known that hierarchies and bureaucracies can cope more easily with standard and routine decisions than with new and exploratory decisions. Even when new ideas pass through the narrow gates of the bureaucracy, there remains the more difficult problems of the implementation and diffusion of new products and processes. Soviet experience has clearly shown that such problems cannot be solved by administrative fiat. The inherent complexity and uncertainty of the innovation process make it extremely difficult to set quantifiable targets that can be implemented and monitored.

Having stressed the problems of information flows in hierarchies and bureaucracies, it is not suggested that decentralised and market economies do not suffer from imperfect information and distortions. Certain types of information about the specific qualities and characteristics of inputs are not revealed in transactions across markets. Hence, the allocation of certain products within firms or hierarchical organisations may be superior to that obtained in markets, albeit, this superiority is not necessarily due to the hierarchical nature of the organisations. Nevertheless, organisations have more resources than individuals to employ specialists and analysts to collect and process more information. Moreover, given that information or knowledge is partly, at least, a public good, government statistical agencies are needed to provide reliable information about the environment and state of the economy within which decision-making units operate. Such information cannot be obtained easily by non-government organisations or individuals. This informational function of central decision-makers is taken for granted and has not been emphasised outside the 'indicative planning' literature.

More importantly, as our discussion of the generation of new information suggests, there is a fundamental role for central decision-makers to play by encouraging R&D and supporting an innovational infrastructure. But as Arrow (1994, p 8) reminds us, 'information may be supplied socially, but to be used it has to be absorbed individually'. Indeed, a central authority has a comparative advantage in focusing on the generation of new information, especially education and basic scientific research, whereas individuals and autonomous organisations have comparative advantage in the application, diffusion and marketing of new ideas.

Accordingly, the traditional dichotomy between centralised and decentralised economies, or between markets and state institutions is false and must be resisted on grounds of information flows. No single optimal information structure exists to meet all the needs of decision-makers in modern societies. It is simply not true that markets provide complete and accurate information for decision-makers. The literature on market economies is littered with examples of imperfect and asymmetric information. It is also not true that central decision-makers or their agents do not possess some specialised knowledge, or that they are incapable of generating useful and trustworthy information. Both markets and governments, as well as organizations, have important and complementary roles to play in the dissemination of existing knowledge and the generation of new knowledge. More specifically, the informational role of central authority is to reduce the degree of uncertainty endogenous to the system but exogenous to autonomous organisations and lower decision-making units. In contrast, the informational role of the market is to provide reliable signals about the relative scarcity of resources, which are necessary for solving the valuation problem. Organisations also play an important role in solving the valuation problem by generating prices of specific inputs that are not valued in the marketplace. With respect to new information, or innovation, markets and organizations have creative roles to play particularly in the application, diffusion and marketing of new products and processes. In short, markets, organisations and governments are complementary rather than alternative means for generating information and knowledge for decision-makers.

Realisation of the significant influence of the structure of information flows on other aspects of decision-making, and in particular on structure and procedure, suggested the need to incorporate the information component into the classification scheme. The result has expanded the number of possible economic systems from four to eight. The expansion has meant that four systems, which were previously subsumed under the four broad classifications obtained in Chapter 3, have become transparent. The four 'new' systems are CAD, CDC, DAD and DAC. In the following chapter we add another continuum based on decision criteria.

5. Decision-making Criteria

I

Theoretically, it is conceivable that different economies may have similar decision-making structures, information flows and procedures, but use a different set of rules of reasoning or criteria for making the same decisions. These criteria may be broadly classified as economic (profit, efficiency, growth, employment and stability) and non-economic (ethics, politics, aesthetics, defence and administrative convenience). More often, various mixtures of economic and non-economic criteria are used in making decisions. Indeed, the most interesting and important choices and decisions involve both economic and non-economic criteria.

The choice of decision criteria is determined by a number of factors, not least by the circumstances and objectives of the decision-makers. Objectives and criteria are sometimes indistinguishable. For example, profit may be used as an objective as well as a criterion for the allocation of resources. Further, since criteria are used as a means of achieving objectives, it is not possible to judge the rationality of the choice of criteria without knowing the objective function of decision-makers. Conventional accounts of rational decision-making identify, among other things, clarification of objectives and values and the alternative means of achieving them. The choice of criteria is also influenced by the other components of the decision-making process and by the nature of the decision being taken.

Since decision-making criteria have a decisive influence on the allocation of resources and consequently the functioning and performance of the economic system, any meaningful classification of economic systems must include the criteria used in making decisions. Arguably, the great divide in economics is not between centralised and decentralised decision-making and information structures, nor between democratic and authoritarian procedures, but between economic and non-economic criteria used for the allocation of resources. For the economist, *qua* economist, decision-making criteria are the decisive factors that distinguish one system from another. This is, of course, not to deny the importance of the other factors in the decision-making process for the allocation of resources and for the classification of economic systems.

The structure of this chapter is as follows: Section II examines the possible criteria used in decision-making and discusses their interaction with other aspects of the decision-making process. Section III attempts to classify economies along an economic–non-economic continuum, which is then added to the classification that we have constructed on the basis of structure, procedure and information flows. Section IV consists of an evaluation of the 'rationality' of different decision-making criteria. Finally, Section V summarises the key points of the chapter and offers some tentative conclusions regarding the use of economic and non-economic criteria in decision-making processes.

II

Before we discuss the possible criteria used in decision-making, it is important to note that there are numerous decisions taken by individuals, organisations and governments, which do not appear to be based on any set of rules of reasoning. In all economies there are many decisions, which are taken at more or less regular intervals, or when some particular circumstances arise, without reference to any criterion or consideration of alternatives. These are habitual or routine decisions. They are governed by customs, conventions and social norms, or acquired by experience and learning, and do not require comparative knowledge of the consequences of alternative choices. Habitual decisions are more or less self-enforcing and often become addictive. Decisions that are determined by social conventions are often accompanied by feelings of embarrassment, guilt and shame by individuals who violate them (Elster 1989). Conventions are transformed into norms by the mechanism, first suggested by David Hume, of the desire for the approval of others (Sugden 1989, p 95). However, a characteristic feature of these types of decision is that they are taken without calculating their costs and benefits, or without considering alternative ways of meeting given objectives and needs. Force of habit, laziness, social conventions and norms, moral beliefs and the scarcity of time and energy discourage us from contemplating alternative choices and identifying the consequences, including side-effects, of each alternative choice. We are truly creatures of habit, fashion and social conventions.

The number of decisions made on the basis of custom and convention and norms varies among individuals, organisations, governments and indeed societies. It is normally higher among older, 'conservative' and lazy persons, monopolistic organisations, authoritarian governments and, of course, traditional societies. The last are governed by little else than habitual decisions. In contrast, the proportion of habitual decisions is lower among dynamic individuals, organisations and modern (democratic) societies. Customs and conventions usually specify the limits of behaviour or fix a certain set of permissible or forbidden decisions and actions. They continue to influence decisions and actions until major disturbances and crises occur, when they tend to give way to a more calculating mode of decision-making, or to a new set of rules of reasoning. It is often the case that when prevailing practices demonstrably fail, the search for alternatives begins in earnest.

Apart from habitual decisions, there are other types of decision that are taken without any consideration of alternatives. Among these are impulsive decisions or acts, which are not taken in any regular way. Suddenly we see or think of something we fancy and our intuition, emotions or passions lead us to act spontaneously on the spot without bothering to calculate the advantages and disadvantages of our decisions. Impulsive decisions based on intuition and emotion may not be as irrational as they appear. Intuition is a process through which people acquire knowledge and swift decision-making skills by storing experience and by recognising situations in which their experience leads them to make the 'right' decisions. Emotion plays a similar role in decision-making. According to Elster (1998, pp 59–63), emotions improve our decision-making capacity in two ways: 'emotional response enhances our capacity to make good decisions not by providing us with the best possible decisions, but by ensuring that we make some decisions in situations where procrastination is likely to be disastrous'; and, 'in some cases emotions help us to make better or even the best decisions, by enabling us to coordinate our behaviour, to respond to crises, or to clarify our priorities'. In short, defective decision-making is often due to a lack of emotion or to indifference.

Since economic decisions are seldom separated from other decisions, economic criteria alone will not be sufficient to understand or resolve decision problems. This is particularly true in traditional societies, where economic decisions are not only habitual but are also closely bound up with other decisions. Economic life is usually organised around a non-economic purpose and people seem to spend less time and energy in the pursuit of economic goods, especially in places where nature is bountiful. Moreover, economic decisions and relations have a collective rather than an individualistic character. Thus, economic decisions are not so much directed at making (private) profits through exchange but rather towards the direct provision of goods and services for both the individual and the community as a whole.

In modern societies economic and non-economic activities are more clearly separated but are not independent of one another. In making important economic decisions, individuals, organisations and governments are influenced by a host of non-economic factors including ideology, ethics and politics. Ideology is commonly defined as a fairly consistent set of ideas and beliefs. It plays an important part in the choice of both the ends and the means as well as in the implementation of decisions. Ideologies, like customs, norms and conventions, are not outcome-oriented. More specifically, an ideology often prohibits or constrains decision-makers from taking certain decisions, which may be beneficial to society as a whole. When ideology precludes certain choices, they become ideological taboos, which mould economic systems. More often, ideology plays an important role in justifying decisions taken either in ignorance or on the basis of a set of reasons that are not acceptable to the authority to which the decision-makers are accountable. In the former Soviet Union, Marxist–Leninist ideology was often used to legitimise decisions taken on some arbitrary or false criteria in order to get them implemented. Similarly, in the USA, the benefit–cost analysis was often used as 'window dressing for projects whose plans have already been formulated with little if any reference to economic criteria' (Marglin 1967, p 16). Indeed, the economic calculus is often used *ex post* as a justification (to win acceptance) not as an *ex ante* criterion for the allocation of resources.

Ideologies may be sincere or consciously deceptive. Gershekron (1971, p 288) contends that 'ideology is essentially deceptive, the product of falsehood rather than false consciousness'. All the same, whether deceptive or honest, ideological biases and taboos create a gap between reality and the official ideology, and in the long run generate conflicts, which react on both ideology and reality. Thus, democratic values and institutions that are at first a mere façade may eventually become real and acquire validity. Similarly, the ideology of 'economic man', which is the cornerstone of modern economics, is increasingly influencing our decisions, as is reflected by the rise of economic rationalism and the spread of economic thinking to non-economic areas (Rowthorn 1996). In this case reality is adjusting to the ruling ideology. But equally, when there is a wide gap between ideology and reality, the ideology is thrown out, as in the case of the Soviet-type economies in the late 1980s when Marxist–Leninist ideology was discarded entirely.

A second major factor that enters the decision-making process of individuals, organisations and governments is ethics or morality. Individuals rarely behave as pure economic creatures: rational, selfish and materialistic. Morality plays a prominent role in the formation of preferences and decisions. People do not cheat as much as they can get away with. They have concern for others and seek to do the 'right' thing. Decisions regarding job choice, how hard to work, where to live, what to consume, and so on, are partly influenced by ethical considerations. Similarly, organisations seem increasingly concerned with social, moral and environmental issues and not simply with the maximisation of their profits (Sen 1993, pp 216–18). They often contribute to worthy and charitable causes. Ethical considerations also influence government policies and decisions (Haddad 1993). Policies regarding the distribution of income and wealth, not only between individuals of the present generation but also between generations, and the provision of welfare services, are influenced to a lesser or greater degree by ethical criteria.

The relevance of ethical criteria for economic decisions (and vice versa) is suggested by the origin of economics, which began as a branch of moral philosophy or applied ethics (normative economics). The founders of economics, David Hume, Frances Hutcheson and Adam Smith, were aware of the real possibility of having two undesirable outcomes: 'bad' ethics and 'good' economics and 'good' ethics and 'bad' economics, but were searching for an 'optimal' combination of 'good' economics and 'good' ethics (Haddad 1996). For Adam Smith, in particular, there was no conflict between good economics and good ethics. Hence, his often quoted statement that: 'the road to virtue and that to fortune are happily in most cases the same'. For him a good society, or a well-functioning economic system, is populated not by 'economic men' but by 'prudent men' who are governed by a judicious mixture of self-interest and altruism. Since the time of Adam Smith, partly as a result of what Sen (1987) has called, 'the distancing of economics from ethics', we have come to approximate the behaviour of 'economic man'. We have moved a long distance from a situation, when economics was a branch of ethics, to what is increasingly becoming one in which ethics is a branch of economics.

Another non-economic factor that enters our decisions, but has not received much analytical attention by economists, is aesthetics. Many of our economic decisions are influenced by consideration of beauty and style and other things that please our senses. Aesthetes or persons with an intense feeling for the beauty or ugliness of goods and physical surroundings endeavour to maximise, what we may call, their 'butility'. For example, decisions regarding the purchase of durable consumer goods are influenced as much by our (subjective) ideas of elegance and beauty as well as by the price. The importance of aesthetics in our decision-making is more directly reflected in the purchase of art works, visits to art galleries, beautiful buildings and places. In general, the more affluent individuals become, the more of their resources are devoted to works of art, 'elegant' buildings and objects of beauty.

As societies become more developed and affluent, the lives of citizens improve with the provision of goods and services that enhance the comforts and conveniences of life, though the physical environment becomes less attractive. This has been a major concern for some economists, environmentalists and aesthetes. One aesthete economist has observed 'two glaring facts' about modern development:

> One is that in this age, much of the richest and most populous the world has known, less public beauty and more of repellent hideousness has been created than any past age in which creation was possible. The other is that of such past beauty, urban and rural, as had survived, more in this age is being destroyed, and faster, than in any other'(Bensusan-Butt 1974, p 179).

These observations are arguably more valid now than when they were made more than 25 years ago. No doubt the neglect of aesthetics is partially the result of the 'rational' approach to doing things. The urban environment is being shaped largely by developers who are naturally more concerned with the rate of return on capital than with aesthetics. Governments, too, are more concerned with balancing their budgets and winning votes than with aesthetics. Further, developers have more political influence and seem all too often willing to bribe politicians to get their way. Aesthetes, on the other hand, being in a minority and less affluent are unable to compete with developers in both the market and the political arena. Nor can they apply rigorously the social economic calculus to persuade opponents of the merit of their cause, when the costs and benefits are thoroughly intangible and not readily given to valuation in the marketplace. Hence, aesthetes have little option but to resort to demonstrations, make noise and mobilise local support against undesirable developments.

Needless to say, political biases influence the formulation of both public policies and private decisions. These biases are not accidental but often flow from existing property or class relations and special interest groups seeking favours from government in exchange for their support. Economic policies and decisions of governments and organisations and even some individuals (the very wealthy) are not made in a political vacuum. Economists may give the right advice for governments on economic matters, but the government in a democratic society must ensure that its decisions are acceptable to the electorate and powerful interest groups. The primacy of political factors is even more evident in authoritarian regimes. In the former Soviet Union, for example, the economy was made subservient to the leadership; hence the notion of planners' priorities or preferences, as opposed to consumers' preferences. In democratic societies the importance of political factors is reflected by the ubiquitous rent-seeking and rent-creating activities and by the replacement of the classical business cycle with 'the political cycle'.

Without going into analytical details, politics and economics are inseparable in major economic policies and decisions of governments, organisations and individuals. Individuals and organisations put pressure on governments to obtain economic gains through legislation favourable to their own interests. They also use their economic wealth to obtain access to political power and influence events. When the very wealthy have satisfied all their material needs, that is, when they have reached the point of economic bliss, or even before that point, they often seek political power and influence over policies and people. Within hierarchical organisations political activities have a great deal to do with policy decisions. The political aspects of business decisions have as much to do with the power and status of subordinates and superiors as with profit maximisation (Pettigrew 1974). Since subordinates have different objectives and interests, they tend to promote their views through political manoeuvring by the formation of alliances, by keeping close to those with the formal decision-making powers, and by the manipulation of information, which they are required to pass on to their superiors. In sum, the intimacy between politics and economics is reflected by the original and more meaningful name of economics, 'political economy'.

Yet another important non-economic criterion that forms a basis for economic decisions in organisations and government bureaucracies is administrative convenience. A frequently encountered conflict is between profitability or efficiency and administrative convenience. It is well known, for example, that one of the criteria for an 'optimal' tax is that it must be easy to administer and to monitor. Also, for much of the history of the Soviet economy, decisions were determined on the basis of administrative convenience rather than on economic criteria. In foreign trade decisions, for example, there was a preference for 'bilateralism' instead of multilateralism, because it is much easier to reach agreements when there are no more than two parties involved. There is a tendency in a bureaucracy or hierarchy to rely on administrative criteria and rules of thumb to coordinate and direct the decisions and activities of their members. Typical rules include 'the average cost plus a mark-up' for price setting, 'the recoupment period' for investment decisions and the monetarist rule that 'the increase in the money supply should not exceed the increase in aggregate output'. Rules are important in all economic systems, but more so in bureaucratic economies.

Before we turn our attention to strictly economic criteria, it is of some relevance to consider two types of economic decision that are taken consciously but not on the basis of the economic calculus. The first are 'exploratory decisions' or acts, whose outcomes are believed by the decider to be uncertain in the sense that they do not have any probability distribution. Innovative decisions fall under this category. The second, which is a sub-category within the class of exploratory decisions, may be called 'experimental' decisions. They are taken with the intention of acquiring new information or knowledge for the purpose of making them in the future if they have turned out to be successful. These types of decision are governed by the principle of learning-by-doing.

Economic criteria are naturally the business of economists, and have been so, at least, since the rise of 'economic man' in the second half of the nineteenth century, when the name 'economics' began to replace 'political economy'. The expanding domain of economics and the economic approach to human behaviour in general has led to the subjection of a wide range of social phenomena including moral issues to the economic calculus. It was the Reverend Philip Wicksteed who was among the first economists to argue that the rational maximising mode covered all human decisions and activities:

> The laws of political economy are but the application to a special set of problems of the universal laws of the distribution and administration of resources in general (whether of money, time, influence, powers of thought or aught else) amongst all the objects that we deliberately pursue or to which we are spontaneously impelled, whether material or spiritual, private or social, wise or foolish (Wicksteed 1933, p 800).

This view led to the famous definition of economics given by his editor, Lionel Robbins (1932, p 16): 'as the science, which studies human behaviour as a relation between ends and scarce means, which have alternative uses'. Perhaps, as a result of Robbins' definition, all human behaviour is viewed by Becker (1976, p 14) as 'involving participants who maximise their utility from a stable set of preferences and accumulate an optimal amount of information and other inputs in a variety of markets'. Accordingly, the economic calculus has been applied to the study of crime, fertility, education, marriage, altruism, violent behaviour, traditions and customs and a host of other social institutions and phenomena.

Economic criteria can be short run or long run: optimum allocation of resources or maximisation of profits at a point in time or over time. They can also be micro or macro, private or social. Typically, microeconomic criteria include profit, efficiency and maximisation of sales. Efficiency and profit dictate that the enterprise should close down if the benefits it produces do not exceed its costs. However, profit can be private or social. Private profit is notoriously an imperfect criterion from the point of view of society. Typical macroeconomic criteria are full employment, growth in output and internal–external stability.

Arguably, market-based decisions tend to be biased in favour of short- or medium-term economic considerations. In particular, profit-making organisations might prefer to take a medium- or a longer-term view, but are constrained by the demands of their shareholders to perform well also in the short term. The issue of whether firms make their decisions on a completely rational basis, or whether they maximise short- or long-term profits, has been debated for a long time. What is clear, however, is that few business decisions, if any, are based on complete rationality. As Simon (1965, p 8) pointed out, 'Rationality requires a choice among all possible alternatives. In actual behaviour only very few of those possible alternatives ever come to mind'. Moreover, complete rationality requires knowledge of all the consequences including by-products of each possible alternative. However, 'bounded rationality' is possible if decision-makers consider all the possible alternatives they can think of and know roughly the likely outcomes of the most profitable course of action. Under these circumstances, they may be said to be maximising their short- and long-term profits. A good many business decisions are made in this way. But there are other decisions, such as large innovative decisions, which are too risky, their outcomes too uncertain, to be rational or to be based on a set of rules of reasoning. As Elster (1998, p 63) points out, 'in most complex decisions people do as a matter of fact consult their gut feelings'. He adds, 'when confronted with novel challenge some people postpone their decisions; others make a snap decision based on some salient feature of the situation'.

Public decisions are more complex than private decisions. Governments have to deal to a greater extent with externalities, long-term economic issues and with non-economic aspects of their decisions. They have a longer-term perspective than the 'representative' consumer or producer. They are concerned not only with the total welfare of the present generation but also with that of future generations. To the neo-liberals this might sound rather paternalistic, if not authoritarian. But it is quite conceivable that the citizens of a democratic society might charge the government with looking after the future on their behalf. It is also 'rational' to do so. Given the short-term bias of market-based private decisions and the strong empirical evidence that not all citizens have the required information and decision-making skills to be rational about their short- and long-term choices (Conlisk 1996, pp 670–72), the government should have a significant role in those decisions that affect the total welfare of present and future generations. Such decisions include the rate of saving and investment, the rate of depletion of vital non-renewable resources, the rate of innovation and the protection of the environment. Since these decisions involve significant externalities, they should not be based on the narrow economic calculus of private costs and benefits, or calculated on the basis of current prices, supply and demand.

Governments are not only concerned with long-run microeconomic criteria or with the allocation of resources over time, but also with macroeconomic and social ones. When they employ the economic calculus in their decision-making processes, they are expected to use social or macro-profit to incorporate the externalities resulting from their decisions. Further, governments in 'managed economies' (as distinct from centrally planned) use macroeconomic criteria such as employment, growth and stability. Governments in centrally planned economies have less need of macroeconomic criteria, since they decide directly and in physical terms the allocation of resources to individual sectors and enterprises. However, they are still required to take account of externalities in their allocation of resources. Indeed, the employment of the social rather than the private calculus constitutes one of the most important arguments for central decision-making in cases where there are substantial externalities, and if it can be shown that such externalities cannot be incorporated at lower levels of decision-making, or by autonomous decision-makers operating in the market.

The decision-making criteria presented above do not exhaust the list of possible ones used by individuals, organisations and governments. Many decisions are made without the use of any apparent criterion or any set of rules of reasoning. Other decisions are based on a mixture of economic and non-economic criteria. This is because decision-makers are rarely single-minded; they normally have more than one objective in mind when they contemplate major decisions, and hence more than one criteria enter into their calculations. The use of multiple criteria in decision-making necessitates the assignment of weights to each one. The relative importance of the objectives and priorities of decision-makers will determine the weights themselves. However, with the rise of economic rationalism, it seems economic criteria are given increasingly more weights in both private and public decisions.

Having considered the important criteria employed in decision-making, we now turn our attention to the relationship of this component to the other components of the decision-making process. First, we have already seen how the structure of decision-making affects the choice of criteria. Central decision-makers, since they deal with major and fundamental decisions, tend to employ macroeconomic and long-term criteria as well as non-economic criteria. In contrast, decentralised decisions are more often than not based on microeconomic and short-term criteria and, to a lesser extent than centralised decisions, on non-economic ones; in turn, decision-making criteria influence the level at which decisions are made. For example, the use of microeconomic criteria tends to favour decentralisation. It is no accident that the rise of economic rationalism has been accompanied by deregulation, marketisation, privatisation and decentralisation. Similarly, the use of macroeconomic criteria encourages centralisation. The rise and fall of Keynesian economics is correspondingly associated with the increased use and decline of macroeconomic criteria.

Second, decision-making criteria are partly determined by procedures. Authoritarian procedures encourage the use of arbitrary or thoughtless criteria and rules of thumb. They also encourage political and administrative criteria as well as long-term criteria. In contrast, democratic procedures favour the use of economic criteria and non-economic criteria that are acceptable to the electorate or shareholders and other stakeholders. In turn, decision-making criteria have some influence on the procedure. Long-term criteria such as the maximisation of consumption in the distant future, and redistribution of income from the majority to a disadvantaged minority, require a degree of authoritarianism for such decisions to be taken. Short-term economic criteria are consistent with democratic procedures, as these criteria are transparent and easily defensible as well as being acceptable to a larger number of people.

Third, the linkage between decision-making criteria and structure of information flows is quite close. The availability of relevant and accurate information influences the choice of economic criteria. Imperfect or incomplete information encourages the use of arbitrary criteria, rules of thumb and short-term criteria. It is difficult to calculate the long-term costs and benefits of economic decisions, as the required information is hard to obtain. In turn, decision-making criteria influence the structure and nature of information flows. The use of economic criteria tends to generate new information. To attain a tolerable level of economic rationality and to reduce the degree of uncertainty, decision-makers seek more and better information. In particular, the use of the social profitability criterion encourages central decision-makers to obtain information on social cost and benefit by employing analysts and environmental experts.

Fourth, there is also a close relationship between incentives and the set of rules of reasoning used in reaching decisions. The motivation structure affects the choice of criteria and vice versa. Economic criteria generally require the use of economic incentives. If outputs or profits are to be maximised then those responsible for production must be rewarded for the extra effort they exert. Indeed, under competitive conditions the optimum allocation of resources requires that the factors of production must receive their marginal contribution. However, non-economic incentives may be used as supplementary motivators in situations where economic incentives are inadequate. Similarly, ethical criteria require moral incentives and altruism. In turn, the motivation structure influences the choice of criteria. Under competitive conditions, the profit motive encourages the use of profit as a criterion. However, there is nothing to stop altruists and others, who are not motivated by economic considerations, to use profit as a criterion for resource allocation and then give away their profits to others. Conversely, governments and non-profit hierarchical organisations can allocate resources on non-economic criteria and then use economic incentives to implement them.

III

It is not easy to classify economies on the basis of decision-making criteria as it is difficult to get information about this component. Different decision-makers use different reasons for their choices and for doing things. These reasons are not always transparent or directly available to the classifier. The problem is compounded by the tendency among decision-makers to rationalise their decisions. More seriously, in many decisions multiple criteria are used, and it is difficult to know their relative weights. Other decisions are devoid of any transparent criteria or rules of reasoning.

Nevertheless, a modest attempt is made in this section to classify economies along a continuum of economic and non-economic criteria, beginning on the left with non-economic and ending on the right with economic. The movement from 0 to 1 measures the degree of economic rationality (the use of the economic calculus) and economic bias present in their activities. The movement also seems to represent a historical trend. We would expect most present-day economies to be located between the two extremes of the continuum; the traditional in the non-economic zone, the developed economies in the economic zone and the developing economies in between.

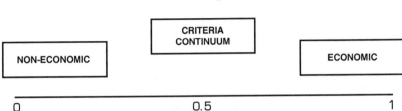

The distinction between economic and non-economic has been variously defined. On the one hand, 'economic' includes every type of decision that could be attempted in a rational maximising way. This is obviously a very wide definition. Equally, a definition in terms of transactions involving the use of money in a market is also too narrow. In modern economies some expenditure is called for in virtually any human activity. However, traditionally the scope of economic decisions and acts has been confined to production, exchange and consumption, but over the last decades nearly all human behaviour seems to have been increasingly subjected to the economic calculus.

At the left end of the continuum, we can place those economies in which decisions are wholly habitual involving little or no conscious calculation of economic costs and benefits, and where economic life is organised around non-economic activities. Also at the extreme left end of the continuum, we can locate the fully centrally planned economies, in which economic decisions regarding the allocation of resources are made in physical terms without calculation of alternative choices. In both economic systems production is directed to satisfy the needs of the population (and/or the goals of their rulers), not to making profits.

At the other end of the continuum are those societies inhabited by 'economic people', who are selfish, calculating and well informed. Decision-makers are economically 'rational' in their choices of both ends and means. No decision is taken if total costs exceed total benefits. Also, there are no habitual or impulsive decisions. Even when they do not have complete information, decision-makers living in 'econopia' will calculate probable outcomes. Such outcomes will not be regretted if they turn out to be unexpected, because they had the best probability distribution when they were taken.

Very few actual economies, if any, would be located at the two extreme ends. Most economies, consisting of innumerable mixtures of habitual decisions, rules of thumb, and consciously calculated choices as well as using both economic and non-economic criteria in their decision-making processes, would be located somewhere between the two extreme points. Thus, a different combination of criteria is used at each point on the continuum.

As Table 5.1 indicates the addition of decision-making criteria to the classification developed in Chapter 14 yields 16 possible systems.

Table 5.1 Decision-making structure, procedure, criteria and information flows

| | Decision-making | | | | Economic systems |
	Structure	Procedure	Information	Criteria	
1	Centralised	Authoritarian	Concentrated	Non-economic	CACN
2	Centralised	Authoritarian	Concentrated	Economic	CACE
3	Centralised	Authoritarian	Diffused	Non-economic	CADN
4	Centralised	Authoritarian	Diffused	Economic	CADE
5	Centralised	Democratic	Concentrated	Non-economic	CDCN
6	Centralised	Democratic	Concentrated	Economic	CDCE
7	Centralised	Democratic	Diffused	Non-economic	CDDN
8	Centralised	Democratic	Diffused	Economic	CDDE
9	Decentralised	Authoritarian	Concentrated	Non-economic	DACN
10	Decentralised	Authoritarian	Concentrated	Economic	DACE
11	Decentralised	Authoritarian	Diffused	Non-economic	DADN
12	Decentralised	Authoritarian	Diffused	Economic	DADE
13	Decentralised	Democratic	Concentrated	Non-economic	DDCN
14	Decentralised	Democratic	Concentrated	Economic	DDCE
15	Decentralised	Democratic	Diffused	Non-economic	DDDN
16	Decentralised	Democratic	Diffused	Economic	DDDE

In the rest of this section we comment briefly on each system:

1. CACN: in this system centralised decisions are reached in an authoritarian manner on information generated by or concentrated at the centre without consideration of alternative choices or calculation of costs and benefits. Under this category we may include command economies, where the allocation of resources is conducted in physical terms without the use of money or 'shadow' prices. Some traditional societies, whose decision-making structures and procedures are centralised and authoritarian, are also included in this category, because their decisions are habitual involving little or no economic calculation and also because of the absence of economic bias in their lives.

2. CACE: this is the same as (1) but with economic calculation. However, the absence of markets makes the valuation problem extremely difficult to solve. 'Shadow' prices generated by linear programming or activity analysis and the use of world prices for comparable commodities and products may be used as guides to rational allocation of resources. Soviet-type economies in the post-Stalin period, when they began to replace administrative criteria with economic ones, fall roughly within this category. Obviously CACEs will be located to the right of CACNs.

3. CADN: this system differs from (1) only in one feature: the information on

the basis of which decisions are reached is supplied by subordinates. This has two main effects: the degree of centralisation–concentration of decision-making authority and authoritarianism will be somewhat reduced, since *de facto* more participants will influence the decisions taken. Also, the quality of microeconomic decisions will improve. CADNs will be located to the right of CACNs and possibly to the left of CACEs, depending on the relative weights given to decentralised–diffused information and economic calculation in the formulation of decisions.

4. CADE: in this system decisions are centralised but calculated on the basis of information supplied by subordinates and according to economic principles. Microeconomic decisions will be economically sound compared with those made under the previous systems. They will be taken on the basis of social profitability. CADEs can be located somewhere near the centre and to the right of the first three systems.

5. CDCN: this system is distinguished from the last four systems in that centralised decisions are reached through democratic processes. However, the democratic element in this system sits uncomfortably with centralised information flows. The effects that participants have on the final decisions are weakened by the fact that information is given to them from above. Economies, which approximate CDCN, would be located somewhere in the left segment of the continuum and to the left of CADEs.

6. CDCE: although this system leads to a better allocation of resources than (5), the tension between its democratic procedure and centralised information remains. CDCEs can be located roughly in the middle of the continuum. Countries that practised some form of indicative planning may be classified under this category.

7. CDDN: this is a more internally consistent system than the previous two systems, as lower decision-making units are able to participate effectively in the decision-making process on the basis of information they themselves have generated. Again, since CDDNs contain two features that place them in the left segment and two in the right, they can be placed somewhere in the centre of the continuum. Their position relative to the other systems that are located in the centre depends on the relative weights of the four features found in each system.

8. CDDE: the probability of reaching sound economic decisions seems quite high under this system. Since CDDEs contain three features that characterise the right segment of the continuum, they can be located somewhere in the middle of the second segment.

9. DACN: this system is internally inconsistent. It is hard to imagine an economy, which is at once decentralised, authoritarian and informationally centralised. Perhaps some traditional societies may have these characteristics. In such societies individuals decide and act according to

information and on the basis of non-economic criteria given to them by customs and conventions. They cannot express their preferences openly or democratically. The effect of custom and convention on the behaviour of individuals is like that of an authoritarian regime. DACNs can be located in the left segment of the continuum, somewhere near the beginning.

10. DACE: this is the same as the last system except that decisions are based on economic criteria and/or the fact that economic activity plays a dominant role in people's lives. However, decentralised decisions are inconsistent with an authoritarian procedure. Economies that practise indicative planning using authoritarian procedures fall within this category. Also reformed Soviet-type economies that became decentralised are also included in this category. Such economies may be located somewhere in the middle of the continuum, or perhaps to the right of its centre.

11. DADN: the authoritarian feature in this system is incongruent with both decentralised decisions and diffused information, and to some extent with non-economic criteria. It is difficult to think of real economies that have those properties. However, the use of non-economic criteria and/or the importance of non-economic activity suggest that some traditional societies may fall within this category. Such economies may be located somewhere in the middle of the continuum, or to the left of its centre.

12. DADE: again the authoritarian element in this system is inconsistent with decentralisation of decisions and diffused information. Market-type economies that follow authoritarian procedures or right-wing dictatorships, which rely on the economic calculus, fall under this category. Such economies may be located somewhere in the third quarter of the continuum.

13. DDCN: this system may be referred to as some kind of indicative planning that gives little or no weight to economic criteria and economic activities. Also, certain traditional societies may be classified under this category. DDCNs will be located somewhere near the left of the centre.

14. DDCE: this system is the classic indicative planning that was extensively practised in Western Europe in the 1950s and 1960. Decisions are made by autonomous economic agents according to economic principles on the basis of information supplied by a central authority. DDCEs can be positioned somewhere in the third quarter of the continuum.

15. DDDN: this system looks very much like a *laissez-faire* economy without economics. A number of economic systems come within this category: full communism where scarcity and the state are abolished; cooperative societies that are based on altruism and basic needs; and many traditional societies whose members feel unconstrained by customs and conventions. All these economies can be located in the third segment of the continuum.

16. DDDE: this is the familiar *laissez-faire* economic system. If all decisions are subjected to the economic calculus then we are in a state of economic

utopia. Such economies will be positioned at the very end of the continuum.

In short, the introduction of decision-making criteria into our classification scheme has resulted in eight economic systems that were subsumed under the eight economic systems of the last chapter. The new systems are CACN, CADN, CDCN, CDDN, DACN, DADN, DDCN and DDDN. These are systems where economic life is dominated by or organised around non-economic activities and where the economic calculus is not used as a basis for making decisions. Such systems range from customary economies, feudalistic economies, fully command economies and 'full communism'. They are, of course, economically inefficient but can survive for a long time as demonstrated by present-day traditional societies, the long period of feudalism in Europe and Asia and, until recently, the Soviet-type economies.

IV

The underlying assumption of economists is that if we want to avoid waste and maximise our profits or utilities we should subject our choices and decisions to the economic calculus. This means that we should calculate all the possible costs and benefits flowing from our decisions. But if we do that we would only manage to make a few decisions of the so many that we are obliged to make within a given period of time. It is impossible to devote equal energy and time to every decision. Even the few decisions that we consciously calculate will probably be sub-optimal or, what Baumol and Quandt (1964, p 23) call 'optimally imperfect decisions', which are completed when the marginal cost of more refined calculation is equal to the expected marginal benefit. It is also clear that the calculating cost of decision-making is an important consideration for rational decision-makers. As Smith and Walker (1993, p 260) show, decision-makers attempt 'to achieve a balance between the benefits of better decision-making and the effort cost of decision'. However, 'computopia', a state of affairs where every decision taken is subjected to conscious calculation of costs and benefits, is not possible beyond a small set of decisions.

Mercifully, many decisions, perhaps the majority, are the product of a complex set of reflex action, impulses, instincts, emotions, habits, fashions, customs, social conventions and norms. Such decisions are taken without going through any deliberate calculation of costs and benefits; they may be called 'ready-made' decisions that enable us to economise on cost of decision-making, intellectual effort and time, and sometimes improve our decision-making capacity. Even if the decisions reached on those bases are sub-optimal, as they are likely to be, the loss of efficiency may be more than offset by the gains that are likely to result from devoting the energy and time saved on habitual and standard decisions to new and complex decisions.

Arguably, decisions guided by emotion and reason are better than can be achieved by pure reason alone or by rational deliberation. Like Simon (1983) and Shackle (1972), Elster (1998, p 62) argues that 'the ideal of impeccable rationality assumes that there are no surprises, no misunderstanding, no irresolvable conflicts... [hence] it cannot guide actions in situations that are characterised by these factors'. Under these conditions attempts by decision-makers to make decisions on reason alone make them unreasonable. On many occasions applying reasons to our circumstances will not be sufficient to reach meaningful decisions. A rational or wise decision-maker would know under certain conditions that it is better to follow a simple rule of thumb, a convention, one's gut feelings, or even to toss a coin. Thus Elster (1998, p 63) contends that 'going by one's gut feelings cuts through the maze of complex decision problems and enables us to make not only swifter decisions but also better ones'. In short, being 'irrational' may even be rational.

Rules of thumb, social conventions and norms, as we have already noted, play an extremely important role in decision-making by individuals, organisations and governments. They acquire validity, which is independent of immediate consequences. It is sometimes argued that they do not necessarily conflict with economic rationality, as they embody the accumulated experience of decision-makers; they are the product of an evolutionary process that jettisons non-rational conventions and rules of decision-making. However, Etzioni (1987, p 509) argues that since these norms and rules were created previously by men, there is no reason to believe that they were any more rational then. In many instances people continue to make the same mistakes because of failure of learning and remembering. Further, Etzioni contends that since human decisions are fallible, simple decision rules in use may seem rational, but it is hard to show that they were chosen out of an alternative set that could have come to be used instead and for the better. Furthermore, he makes the familiar point that 'however rules are originally made, they tend to ossify and lag behind changes in the environment'. Hence, the use of norms and rules or conventions does not always lead to successful, informed and rational decisions, because either they do not change at all or do not adjust quickly enough to changed circumstances to ensure efficient adaptation. Indeed, historically, many developed rules continue long after their usefulness is diminished or lost, and when better alternatives are available. Finally, rules may be rational but may be implemented incorrectly, because they are often too general to take account of particular circumstances.

The loss of efficiency resulting from the use of norms and rules of thumb in decision-making is a serious fault but not a fatal one. 'Irrational' systems exist and flourish for a long time, especially when they are not subjected to frequent external shocks. However, the more they are exposed to external (and internal) shocks the more difficult it becomes for them to function, and the more they need to change and adjust. The longer they take to adjust to changed circumstances, the more painful the adjustment will be, and possibly further adjustment will be needed, as the new circumstances to which they are adjusting would have probably changed by the time the required adjustments have been made. Rational decision-makers would endeavour to anticipate changes and from time to time revise their norms and rules of decision-making. They may even try to be innovative by making exploratory and experimental decisions. This leads us to the evaluation of deliberate decision-making criteria.

Decision-making criteria need not be strictly economic to be considered 'rational'. Individuals, organisations and governments use economic and non-economic criteria in their decision-making processes. Indeed, governments are obliged to take non-economic considerations into account, particularly political and hopefully ethical and aesthetic ones, when formulating their economic policies and decisions. This is because in real life there are hardly any pure economic problems; instead there are problems with economic and non-economic dimensions. Decision-makers must therefore make correctly calculated choices that are both economically and ethically 'right', and at the same time they must be politically acceptable. It may be that in the short run choices between economic and non-economic criteria conflict, as economists are fond of demonstrating, using the example of efficiency and equity. However, in the long run there may be no such conflict. Decisions that are economically 'right' may also be ethically 'right' and politically acceptable. This is explored in Part III of this book, when we come to analyse the conditions for a well-functioning economy.

Turning to economic criteria and taking the economic system as a whole, a combination of micro- and macroeconomic criteria can be used to produce a system of 'mixed rationality'. At the micro-level profit may be used as the dominant criterion for resource allocation, allowing, of course, for externalities, public goods, 'positional' goods and non-renewable resources (Hirsch 1976; Pearce 1976). Central decision-makers may use micro-profit in their 'tactical decisions' or instrumental decisions, or in specific projects. Indeed, 'tactical decisions' are the province of benefit–cost analysis (Marglin 1967). Owing to the rise of economic rationalism, governments everywhere are applying the economic calculus to their tactical decisions. However, there are some difficulties of subjecting public (micro) decisions to the economic calculus. One of these difficulties is defining clearly the government's objective function and the criteria by which benefits and costs are to be measured. Second, the existence of multiple objectives may conflict, at least, in the short term with the emphasis that economists give to economic efficiency. Without wanting to argue against economic efficiency, we believe it should be constrained by other objectives. This belief is based on the fundamental proposition that central decision-makers must be concerned with the total welfare of the population and not simply with their economic welfare. Third, there are certain decisions involving life and death, ethics and aesthetics, whose costs and benefits are intangible. It would not only be absurd to subject such decisions to the economic calculus but to do so would bring more harm than good. Indeed, Keynes (1938) regarded the 'Benthamite tradition' as:

> the worm, which has been gnawing at the insides of modern civilisation and is responsible for its present moral decay. We used to regard the Christians as the enemy because they appeared as the representatives of tradition, convention and hocus pocus. In truth it was the Benthamite calculus, based on over-valuation of the economic criterion, which was destroying the quality of the popular ideal (*Collected Writings*, vol X, pp 445–6).

It is not denied that economic rationality should play a part in those decisions. When two alternative policies are equally desirable aesthetically or ethically, it is obvious that the policy with fewer costs should be chosen. Keynes rejected the 'over-valuation of the economic criterion', not its legitimate but limited role in decision-making.

At the macro-level central decision-makers use 'non-profit' economic criteria (full employment, stability and growth, regional development), and non-economic criteria (environmental protection, and social equality). Most of these criteria can be interpreted as 'macro-profit' or social profit, which generally enhance micro-profits by providing a stable and favourable environment for investment.

It is clear that the multiplicity of objectives in public and private decisions must be explicitly reflected in the choice of criteria that govern the allocation of resources. However, since multiple objectives tend to conflict with one another, decision-makers must make some value judgements about their relative importance. In public choices some guidance about value judgements can be obtained from the electorate through democratic processes and market research that incorporate the views of minorities. Once the objectives are assigned relative weights, the multiple criteria used can be assigned corresponding weights. These weights will go some way to ensure that the decisions taken are wholly 'right' and not partially right. As we explain in Part III, the test of rightness would be the absence of regret at some future date.

V

We have argued in this chapter that decision-making criteria, for better or worse, influence the allocation of resources and the functioning and development of economic systems. They are the underlying reasons for making decisions, for allocating and using resources the way we do. Hence, they are largely responsible for the working of the economic system and constitute the decisive factor for the economists in distinguishing one economic system from another.

The bases for decision-making and the reasons for doing things the way we do them can be customs and conventions, norms, rules of thumb and emotions, all of which are not outcome-oriented and do not involve fresh calculation of costs and benefits or consideration of alternatives. On the other hand, outcome-oriented systematic decisions and judgements are normally based on consciously chosen and well-defined criteria that involve calculation of costs and benefits of alternative choices. Such criteria can be economic and non-economic. Economic criteria can be micro (profit, efficiency) and macro (employment, stability and growth). Non-economic criteria include political, ethical, ideological, aesthetical, defence and so on.

We have shown that economic decisions are seldom taken on the basis of a single criterion. Even at the individual level, economic considerations are not the only ones that enter the decision-making process. Individuals are more complex in their judgements and the choices they make than those suggested by mainstream economic theory. They have both economic and non-economic goals and hence must behave as 'economic men' or 'economic women' up to a point. The mixture of economic and non-economic criteria varies among individuals, organisations and societies across time and space. However, we have observed that there is a trend towards economic bias in our decisions and acts, as depicted in our continuum of economic and non-economic criteria. Indeed, it seems we are heading towards some sort of economic utopia if the rise of economic rationalism and the spread of economic thinking to other disciplines including ethics continue unabated.

This is not to say that the pursuit of economic rationalism is necessarily unethical or undesirable. On the contrary, properly understood and used judiciously, proper economic rationalism, which attempts to get the most out of our scarce resources, is highly ethical. Ethical criteria that ignore economic principles are wasteful and hence immoral. The welfare of current and future generations, or rather the survival of future generations, depends on making the best use of available resources, especially non-renewable ones. However, there is a particular danger associated with the rise of economic rationalism and the expanding domain of economics. This danger does not come simply from the narrow application of economic reasoning, or from ignoring other considerations in major decisions. Rather, the danger comes paradoxically from the very opposite, from using economic rationalism as an ideological tool to mask and legitimise decisions taken either in ignorance or on some unacceptable grounds. Because economic criteria are so widely, if not universally, acceptable as a basis for decision-making, they are often used to defend public decisions, which might have been based on false and self-serving criteria. The temptation to grasp at apparently rational economic evidence is so overwhelming that decision-makers use that evidence as a basis for decision. There may be no harm in this because good decisions that could not be defended otherwise can at least be taken. The danger comes from using economic rationalism to publicly defend bad decisions so that they can be accepted. However, with increasing demands for transparency and accountability and the monitoring of government and corporate decisions by analysts and journalists, this danger might be diminished.

6. Types and Structures of Incentive

So far we have discussed the decision-making process principally up to the point of implementation of decisions. It is one thing to decide on a rational course of action, to formulate optimal plans or to make informed decisions; it is quite another to have them executed or enforced efficiently and effectively. Of course, rationally bounded decision-makers would not build castles in the air; they would consider the feasibility of their plans and decisions and what is required to get them implemented. If decision-makers were to appoint agents to carry out their decisions, they would have to offer them some incentives to ensure that the decisions are faithfully and efficiently executed. Even in an extreme authoritarian regime, coercion and legal sanctions are not sufficient to force people to obey commands. They must also establish performance indicators to reward and penalise agents. Indeed, the essence of agency theory is that incentives need to be designed so as to minimise the scope for agents to distort or violate the interests of principals.

In an integrated decision-making system, we would expect some correspondence between the structure of incentives and other components of the decision-making process. More generally, incentives tend to develop along with the societies, institutions and organisations that engender them. The nature and structure of incentives and the corresponding economic systems grow together in an organic fashion and appear to be designed for one another. Hence, any meaningful classification of economic systems must consider the types of incentive used to motivate people either to make and execute their own decisions or to get others to implement their decisions.

In the interest of clarity, it is useful to point out that in this chapter we are dealing with 'success indicators', not 'criteria'; the two are often conflated. Criteria refer to the *ex ante* allocation of resources and decision-making, and are closely connected with objectives; indicators are concerned with performance after the objectives have been set and decisions made (Wiles 1962, p 76). Success indicators are linked to motivations and incentives. We evaluate criteria by their rationality and indicators by their effectiveness. However, criteria and indicators are closely linked and sometimes overlap. In a hierarchy, profit, for example, may be used as an *ex ante* criterion for making decisions, as an *ex post* indicator of the performance or success of the economic activity resulting from the decisions, and as a motivator for implementing decisions. In a polyarchy or an association, no distinction is required among the three functions of profit if the functions of decision-making and execution are not separated. Thus, in perfect competition and general equilibrium theory, where there is no multi-level decision-making, profit is, at once an objective, a criterion, an indicator and a motivator. Profit maximisation provides both the rationale for making decisions and the incentives to carry them out.

The plan of this chapter is as follows: Section II discusses the types and structures of incentive employed to implement decisions. It also examines the linkages between incentives and other components of the decision-making process. Section III attempts first to classify economies along a continuum of altruistic–egotistic incentives and then combines the continuum with the four continuums to form 32 economic systems. Section IV evaluates the effectiveness of different incentives. Finally, Section V summarises the key points of the chapter and offers some concluding remarks on the possibility of devising an effective incentive scheme.

II

In the absence of extreme affluence and altruism, an economic system requires a structure of motivations consisting of both intrinsic and extrinsic incentives to encourage:

a. workers to join the labour force, work conscientiously, acquire skill, seek promotion, change jobs (not too frequently), do more than the absolute minimum they can get away with, make them feel less alienated, more content and creative;

b. self-employed people, entrepreneurs and managers to undertake and manage new enterprises and projects, to innovate, and to be efficient and socially responsible by minimising any unfavourable externalities resulting from their activities; and

c. subordinates in business organisations and government bureaucracies not only to obey orders but also to take initiative and apply their special skill and knowledge to promote the objectives of their organisation.

More specifically, a well-functioning economic system requires negative as well as positive incentives, 'moral' (non-pecuniary) as well as economic (material) ones. The need for different types of incentive stems basically from the complexity and fallibility of human beings. If we assume that our economic agents behave as if they belong to the *homo economicus* species, then we do not need a theory of incentives, or, at least, a theory of extrinsic incentives. Economic agents would be self-motivated, materialistic, well informed and rational. Indeed, up until the emergence of the economics of organisations and economics of information, there was no explicit theory of incentives. Consequently, all the difficulties stemming from bounded rationality, imperfect and asymmetric information, the exercise of authority and non-economic motivations were ignored. By making 'economic man' the cornerstone of modern economic theory, economists deflected their attention from two important sets of problems that occupy organisational theorists: technical–administration and agency–managerial problems. The resolution of these problems is crucial not only for successful organisations but also for a well-functioning modern economy.

An effective structure of incentives must assume that individuals, whether as workers, self-employed, managers of organizations, or as public servants, are motivated by a mixture of incentives; and further, that this mixture is not uniform but varies among individuals or groups of individuals and also over time and across space. For example, we may be selfish at work where such behaviour is expected or, at least, accepted and cooperative and altruistic outside the workplace. In traditional societies, economic agents appear to behave more altruistically or cooperatively than in modern societies. Arguably, over time, as we become more economically developed, we seem to become more selfish and materialistic.

The distinctions between different types of incentive, though useful and important, are not watertight. For example, self-motivation (an intrinsic incentive) depends on the individual's own environment, on the extrinsic motivations imposed by society, the market, the organisation or the government. Indeed, there is a tendency for extrinsic motivations to drive out intrinsic ones. Nevertheless, intrinsic motivations, the internal drive to excel in one's vocation, the 'instinct of workmanship', the desire to work for others, to be creative and to be useful – all these self-motivated incentives are important for the working of the economic system, and can be exploited by organisations and governments without the need for excessive material rewards. They can also be encouraged or discouraged. Providing proper working conditions for talented people, for scientists and researchers, recognising their contributions through medals and prizes, promotion and allowing them to participate in the decision-making process of the organisation will reinforce their self-motivation. The reverse measures will weaken intrinsic motivations.

The distinction between positive and negative incentives suggests that work is a disutility and needs to be positively rewarded. But for some people work is a pleasure and for most people it is that some of the time. If work is a pleasure in itself, then it does not require an extrinsic set of positive and negative incentives to get it done. However, most tasks require both the stick and the carrot to get them carried out. Depending on individuals' tastes regarding risk-taking averseness and the nature of the work, negative incentives, such as threats to dismiss subordinates or otherwise to punish them, may be more powerful motivations to effort and enterprise than positive incentives. Psychological studies have shown that people have an asymmetric attitude to gains and losses; they dislike losses more than they like gains, or they are 'risk-averse over losses and risk-loving over gains' (Rabin 1998, pp 12–15). They place more value on a marginal drop in income than on a marginal increase. Particularly lazy people, it would seem, need the discipline of the stick more than the incentive of the carrot to get them to work. This has been recognised in the economic literature, including the writings of Marx, in the form of 'those who do not work shall not eat'. More recently, it has been resurrected in the idea of 'workfare' or 'mutual obligation', offering financial support to able workers in exchange for work done. Negative incentives may also be more effective than positive incentives for people who are happy with the status quo and are in some sense in a state of equilibrium, or who have little to gain and everything to lose from a proposed change. It is the fear of losing what they already have, or not surviving that motivates them to work or to innovate. Firms in a competitive market who are not efficient or do not innovate do not normally survive.

The distinction between 'moral' and material incentives is also not watertight. The motivations underlying economic activities, or making money, are not necessarily selfish or materialistic. Philanthropists work hard and make profit to give it away to charitable organisations or to the poor, and some charitable organisations are run on profit-maximisation principles. Other people acquire wealth to buy works of art, to obtain political power or to achieve other non-economic objectives. Typical material or pecuniary incentives include wages, salaries, bonuses, profits, shares, fringe benefits, loss of employment, withdrawal of fringe benefits and bankruptcy. Typical non-pecuniary or 'moral' incentives include prestige, titles, medals, publicity in the media and participation in decision-making. Some incentives, for example, promotion and demotion, are both material and 'moral'. Promotion may be valued in itself without being accompanied by an increase in income as recognition of one's contribution to the organization, or one's standing in society. Alternatively, subordinates might be motivated by the desire to gain status and to be promoted, because of the greater remuneration they expect from higher positions and prestige. Also, higher salaries are valued not only *per se*, but also as symbols of one's status in society, a means to enable one to live a lifestyle appropriate to one's status and aspirations.

Clearly, material and moral incentives are the two extreme ends of a continuum. In between incentives consist of some mixture of both. This mixture is often manipulated by superiors to ensure compliance or to minimise the extent of non-compliance. The monitoring of workers' performance is normally difficult and costly. Superiors rely on moral incentives to build up the subordinates' feeling of loyalty to the organisation, pride in work, to reduce turnover and to maintain teamwork and information-sharing aspects of the work process, which are otherwise difficult to encourage. They are usually stressed when material incentives are weak and fail to adequately motivate people or make them happy. Happy workers are usually more productive not only because they normally work harder but also because they identify more closely with the interests of the organisation. As we shall see in Section IV, the effectiveness of moral and material incentives depends largely on the environment, on the nature of the work and on the information about the motivation of agents.

Egotism and altruism are also two extreme ends of a continuum. Very few people, it would seem, are purely egotistic or purely altruistic. As Adam Smith pointed out in his *Theory of Moral Sentiments* (1976), even the most selfish have some regard or sympathy for others. No reasonable person would deny that man is a social animal with a desire to please and an aversion to offend others. Equally, a saint is not entirely altruistic because, arguably, she wants to save her soul. Similarly, an altruistic–agnostic person presumably gets some psychic reward, a warm-glow feeling, from his altruism. Although the desire to see things done properly is neither selfish nor altruistic, one derives some aesthetic pleasure from having or seeing things being done right. Then, we have the 'kinship models', which deal with 'weak' altruism or kinship solidarity. Arguably, a parent working for his family or community may be a manifestation of the 'selfish gene', or the 'other self', but one cannot deny here the presence of an altruistic element. Kinship provides the minimal conditions under which weak altruism lasts for a long period.

Evidently, altruism in its various manifestations and degrees is almost universal. Several theoretical and empirical studies show the importance of altruism in everyday life (Collard 1978; Menchik and Weisbrod 1987; Andreoni 1988, 1989, 1990; Hodgkinson and Weitzman 1991; Freeman 1996; Rose-Ackerman 1996). However, strong altruism that goes well beyond enlightened self-interest and involves personal sacrifice and hardship has not been developed sufficiently to motivate decisions and actions outside the nuclear family, small rural or religious communities, non-profit and charitable organisations, and emergency situations, such as natural disasters and wars. Also, in periods following the collapse of oppressive and unpopular regimes, or during cultural and political revolutions, altruism is often a strong motivator, until after the revolution the law of diminishing returns starts to set in, owing to false expectations and increasing cynicism among the population. To be effective and long-lasting, altruism and social consciousness must be reinforced by supportive legislation and some sort of public reward system, and by other types of incentive including altruism itself. Indeed, altruism feeds upon itself. That is why 'reciprocal' altruism is quite common. This may be a paradox, but it does suggest that it is possible to increase the degree of altruism in a society by providing a social milieu in which people are given incentives to be less selfish and more cooperative, just as a competitive environment tends to encourage selfishness. The potential for the evolution of altruistic behaviour increases if it is rewarded not necessarily in a materialistic or pecuniary way.

The economic and non-economic considerations that motivate people to work, their decisions on how much to work, what kind of work to do and whether to acquire skills must be incorporated into a coherent structure of incentives in order to get the most out of the available human resources. Moreover, proper incentives are needed for the people themselves to exploit and realise their own potential. This objective is widely considered an important component of the bundle of human rights (Haddad 1998). Thus, the choice of an incentive structure will have important implications not only for the efficient working of the economic system, but also for a happy, good and just society. Such a structure is needed for the total welfare, not simply the economic welfare, of the citizens.

Accordingly, it is important to examine the determinants of the structure of incentives. First, a particular structure is determined by the type of society, by the source of authority and the coordinating mechanism, whether custom, competition, command or cooperation. For example, in a centralised–command society, the ability of central authority to get things done rests partly on negative incentives, on threats and coercion and on its ability to impose certain restrictions on acts and consequences. Such coercion is not feasible in decentralised–democratic societies except in times of emergency. However, coercion and sanctions are not sufficient to ensure compliance, except in certain areas where it is easy to control and monitor the activities of individuals and autonomous agents. In most cases, positive incentives are needed to get more than the minimum degree of compliance from agents. They are especially needed if principals and superiors want their agents and subordinates to take initiative and use their special skill and knowledge to promote the interests of the organisation. Even in the most authoritarian organisation, that is, the military, there are both moral and material incentives (for example medals and promotion) for doing more than the required minimum. Superiors must also appeal to the self-interest and solidarity of subordinates, so that the interests and objectives of the organization or society are served or internalised by the individual member.

In traditional societies there does not seem to be any problems of internalising the objectives of the community by individual members. Customs and taboos will ensure that individuals will carry out their given tasks without extrinsic motivation and monitoring. Unlike in the case of an authoritarian society, the costs of enforcement of decisions are minimal in traditional societies. The latter are relatively free from technical–administration and agency–managerial problems, which plague hierarchical organizations. Also, in cooperatives, we would expect individuals to serve the objective of their organization. In modern societies, habits, social conventions and norms act as intrinsic motivations, and decisions based on them are self-enforcing.

Second, and more specifically, the choice of the incentive structure will be influenced by the decision-making structure. In a highly or totally decentralised structure, where there are no superiors and subordinates, decision-makers will be self-motivated by the expected gains (losses) or utilities (disutilities) in carrying out their plans and decisions (or failing to achieve them). They will be motivated by a variety of factors, but to the extent that there are no agency–managerial problems, there seems little need to differentiate between such factors. In contrast, in a hierarchy or centralised structure, where the functions of decision-making and decision-enforcing are separated, technical-administration and agency–managerial problems are widespread; an appropriate system of success or performance indicators must be devised to ensure that the decisions made by superiors are implemented efficiently and without distortion. In particular, as Montias (1976, pp 200–1) shows, there are, at least, three necessary conditions for an effective structure of incentives in a hierarchy: (i) the individual subject to the given incentives must have a significant influence on the results that are rewarded or penalised; (ii) the superior in charge of distributing the rewards and penalties must be capable of measuring the agent's performance accurately; and (iii) there must be a link between effort and reward. Under conditions of uncertainty and asymmetric information, the principal must be able to discriminate between the contribution of the agent and chance factors. This is particularly relevant in cases of failure where it is important not to penalise the agents for failure due to factors beyond their control. Finally, the structure of incentives must correspond to the objective function of the agent to be influenced. For example, if the agent is motivated primarily by the desire for recognition, or by non-economic factors, then the incentives offered should constitute a strong 'moral' element.

Third, the structure of incentives is influenced by the decision-making procedure. An authoritarian procedure tends to use coercion and legal sanctions to enforce decisions. But since this is not always efficient, additional incentives are introduced such as patriotism, altruism and various types of moral and material incentives. Moral incentives are especially attractive to authoritarian rulers because they cost very little. In general, decision-makers, who adopt authoritarian procedures, rely mainly on their authority and use material and non-pecuniary rewards as supplementary incentives. In democratic procedures, which involve workers and subordinates in decision-making, there is less reliance on coercion and (perhaps) material incentives, and more on moral incentives. This is because agency–managerial problems are minimised under democratic procedures, or because the objectives of the organisation are internalised by the workers and subordinates.

Fourth, the incentive structure is very much influenced by the structure of information flows. In a hierarchy, the ability of superiors to get their decisions implemented by subordinates depends largely on the information they are able to collect about the outcome of subordinates' conduct and on the effectiveness of penalties they may administer to subordinates for failure and deviant behaviour. Further, the effectiveness of incentives depends on information obtained independently of subordinates. If incentives are based primarily on information supplied by subordinates, they create moral hazard problems. By manipulating the information transmitted to superiors, subordinates can influence the rewards and penalties they will receive from their superiors. Furthermore, an effective incentive structure depends on knowing what motivates agents and subordinates so that the relevant incentives can be applied.

Finally, the incentive structure may be partly determined by the choice of criteria for making decisions. It is obvious that habitual decisions and other decisions based on rules, social norms and conventions require no formal incentive mechanism to enforce them. People believe that they ought to keep to these rules and conventions. Indeed, decision-makers often rely on social norms as a supplementary mechanism to enforce their decisions (Elster 1998, p 100). In profit-making polyarchies and associations, where decision-makers are self-motivated, the profit motive is the most important incentive. In non-profit organisations or user-oriented firms, where the emphasis is on the quality of output, decision-makers may use material incentives to motivate their employees or agents. And conversely, profit-making organisations may use a combination of moral and material incentives to get the most out of their agents and employees. The profit-making owner–manager and profit-making associations do not require an explicit extrinsic set of incentives. However, they may require a favourable environment, such as developed institutional and physical infrastructures, within which they can pursue their profit-making activities without 'force or fraud'.

The effects of the incentive structure on the other components of the decision-making system have been discussed in the previous chapters and is further discussed in Chapter 11, when we examine the principles of efficient decision-making design.

III

The classification of economic systems on the basis of incentives can be shown on any of the following three continua: (i) economic and non-economic; (ii) material and moral; and (iii) altruism and egotism. However, the choice of (i) is too broad and does not distinguish between altruism and egotism. Moreover, it would create confusion with the previous classification based on decision criteria and thus would not distinguish between indicators and criteria or between motivation and computation. It would seem that (ii) would be the better choice, but it too would create confusion in the acronyms that we use to identify economic systems. The second best choice is (iii). This is narrower and less ambiguous than the moral material distinction. The term 'moral incentive' is something of a misnomer; it includes prestige, which has a particle of egotism. For our purpose, an altruistic or moral motive will be said to exist when the qualities of 'good' or 'bad' are believed to be attached to a potential act or its consequences; that these qualities are more than pleasant or unpleasant, useful or useless, to the individual. Thus, when subordinates pursue the goals of some authority without any material reward or fear of punishment, we say they are motivated by altruism or ethics. In contrast, persons may be said to be selfish if their decisions or acts have consequences (pleasant or unpleasant) on others, which in no way affect their motives for making or doing them or not doing them.

On a scale from 0 to 1, we include those decisions or actions that do not require any material or personal rewards to be performed, near zero. Economic agents work for others, for society, for God or the party. As we move away from zero we include those decisions or acts that are performed for personal satisfaction, prestige, medals and other moral incentives; then we include enlightened self-interest; material gains, economic and political power solely for one's own benefit, until we finally reach the other end of the continuum; where agents are motivated solely by personal material gains; they are selfish and greedy and have no concern for others. Of course, very few people or countries would occupy the extreme ends of the continuum. As is with other classifications, we would expect the majority of individuals or societies to be located somewhere in the middle, though historically there may be a trend towards the egoistic–materialistic end of the continuum.

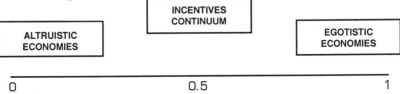

As Table 6.1 indicates, the inclusion of incentives in the classificatory schema of the last chapter increases the number of possible economic systems to 32:

Table 6.1   Decision-making structure, procedure, criteria, information flows and incentives

	Decision-making					Economic systems
	Structure	Procedure	Information	Criteria	Incentives	
1	Centralised	Authoritarian	Concentrated	Non-economic	Altruistic	CACNA
2	Centralised	Authoritarian	Concentrated	Non-economic	Egotistic	CACNE
3	Centralised	Authoritarian	Concentrated	Economic	Altruistic	CACEA
4	Centralised	Authoritarian	Concentrated	Economic	Egotistic	CACEE
5	Centralised	Authoritarian	Diffused	Non-economic	Altruistic	CADNA
6	Centralised	Authoritarian	Diffused	Non-economic	Egotistic	CADNE
7	Centralised	Authoritarian	Diffused	Economic	Altruistic	CADEA
8	Centralised	Authoritarian	Diffused	Economic	Egotistic	CADEE
9	Centralised	Democratic	Concentrated	Non-economic	Altruistic	CDCNA
10	Centralised	Democratic	Concentrated	Non-economic	Egotistic	CDCNE
11	Centralised	Democratic	Concentrated	Economic	Altruistic	CDCEA
12	Centralised	Democratic	Concentrated	Economic	Egotistic	CDCEE
13	Centralised	Democratic	Diffused	Non-economic	Altruistic	CDDNA
14	Centralised	Democratic	Diffused	Non-economic	Egotistic	CDDNE
15	Centralised	Democratic	Diffused	Economic	Altruistic	CDDEA
16	Centralised	Democratic	Diffused	Economic	Egotistic	CDDEE
17	Decentralised	Authoritarian	Concentrated	Non-economic	Altruistic	DACNA
18	Decentralised	Authoritarian	Concentrated	Non-economic	Egotistic	DACNE
19	Decentralised	Authoritarian	Concentrated	Economic	Altruistic	DACEA
20	Decentralised	Authoritarian	Concentrated	Economic	Egotistic	DACEE
21	Decentralised	Authoritarian	Diffused	Non-economic	Altruistic	DADNA
22	Decentralised	Authoritarian	Diffused	Non-economic	Egotistic	DADNE
23	Decentralised	Authoritarian	Diffused	Economic	Altruistic	DADEA
24	Decentralised	Authoritarian	Diffused	Economic	Egotistic	DADEE
25	Decentralised	Democratic	Concentrated	Non-economic	Altruistic	DDCNA
26	Decentralised	Democratic	Concentrated	Non-economic	Egotistic	DDCNE
27	Decentralised	Democratic	Concentrated	Economic	Altruistic	DDCEA
28	Decentralised	Democratic	Concentrated	Economic	Egotistic	DDCEE
29	Decentralised	Democratic	Diffused	Non-economic	Altruistic	DDDNA
30	Decentralised	Democratic	Diffused	Non-economic	Egotistic	DDDNE
31	Decentralised	Democratic	Diffused	Economic	Altruistic	DDDEA
32	Decentralised	Democratic	Diffused	Economic	Egotistic	DDDEE

We comment very briefly on each system:

1. CACNA: this is a pure centralised–command economy devoid of any economic computation and motivation. People are either coerced to work and serve, or work for others – for the community, the party, country or God, out of love or patriotism. Economies that come near this description would be placed on the extreme left of the continuum.

2. CACNE: this is a centralised–command economy with economic motivation but no economic calculation. Resources may be used by the system's directors for prestige projects, for building the physical infrastructure (roads, ports, bridges) or for construction of factories and houses without using the economic calculus. However, workers are provided with material incentives to perform their tasks. Economies that come under this category will be positioned to the right of CACNAs.

3. CACEA: this is a centralised–command economy that uses economic computation for allocating resources but relies on moral incentives to implement the decisions and plans of the central authority. The Chinese economy during the cultural revolution might have come close to this system if the leadership had not violated some basic economic principles such as the division of labour and the opportunity costs of resources. The position of this economic system on the continuum would be somewhere near (2).

4. CACEE: this is a centralised–command economy that uses both economic computation and economic motivation and can be located to the right of the last three systems on the continuum. The reformed Soviet-type economy that had abandoned the forced labour system and began to use economic criteria instead of administrative fiat in resource allocation comes broadly under this economic system.

5. CADNA: this is a centralised–command economy in which a central authority makes its decisions on the basis of information generated from below, but does not use economic computation or material motivation. The location of this system on the continuum is to the right of (1).

6. CADNE: this is the same as (5) except that economic motivation is used. People are selfish and think only of themselves. This system would be worse than (5) if only because the decentralised information that flows to the centre will be distorted and self-serving. But in the absence of economic calculation the economic waste and inefficiencies may not be greater than in (5). In any case, the position of CADNE would be to the right of (5).

7. CADEA: from an economic point of view this is better for a developing economy than (6), because there are economic computations, moral incentives and altruism. This means that the central authority can, if it wishes, increase the rate of accumulation since workers may be paid no more than the subsistence wage. The position of this system is to the right of (6).

8. CADEE: this is a centralised–command system in which the central authority relies on economic computation for making its decisions and on information supplied by subordinates. It also uses economic motivation to get its decisions and plans implemented. Clearly, this system is located on the continuum to the right of the last seven systems.

9. CDCNA: this is a centralised–democratic system in which the central authority supplies the information on the basis of which subordinates or independent economic agents make their decisions without any economic computation and economic motivation. The feasibility of this system is enhanced by the altruistic behaviour of subordinates and economic agents, but at the same time its long-term sustainability is threatened by the absence of economic calculation. The location of this system is to the left of CADEE.

10. CDCNE: this is the same as (9) except that economic agents and subordinates are selfish and motivated mainly by materialistic gains. Hence, the position of this system on the continuum is to the immediate right of (9).

11. CDCEA: this is a centralised–democratic system in which information is supplied by the central authority and subordinates and other economic agents rely on economic computation for the allocation of resources, but are altruistic and will work for a subsistence wage. The position of this system more or less coincides with (10).

12. CDCEE: this is the same as (11) but relies on self-interest and uses material incentives. However, the presence of a democratic procedure may require fewer material incentives at least for some participants. Other participants, who are ruthlessly egotistic and greedy, will demand higher income. CDCEE's position on the continuum is to the right of (11).

13. CDDNA: this is an economic system in which decisions are initiated at the centre on the basis of information supplied by subordinates, who are also consulted and allowed to participate in the decision-making process. However, the system's directors perform no economic calculation and rely on altruism and moral incentives to enforce their decisions, or rather the decisions taken jointly with subordinates. It is hard to position this system on the continuum. It has two elements that would locate it in the right segment and three in the left. Without assigning any weight to the five elements, CDDNA would be somewhere to the left of the centre.

14. CDDNE: this is the same as (13) except that the system's directors rely on material incentives. Clearly, CDDNE's position would be to the right of (13), perhaps to the immediate right of the centre of the continuum.

15. CDDEA: this is again the same as (13) except that economic computations are introduced. This is potentially a desirable system as it combines the advantages of centralism and democratisation, as well as the benefits of altruism. Economies that approximate this system may be positioned just to the right of the centre of the continuum.

16. CDDEE: this is a system in which a central authority initiates decisions on the basis of information supplied from below and uses both economic calculation and incentives to implement its decisions. It contains four elements out of five that appear in the right segment of the continuum. Economies that approximate this system may be placed immediately after CDDEA.

17. DACNA: this is a decentralised system that uses authoritarian procedures and relies on information concentrated at the centre with no economic calculation and motivation. The decentralised elements sit uncomfortably with the authoritarian and informationally centralised elements. However, what makes this system possible is the presence of altruism. On balance, this system would be located in the left segment of the continuum, despite the fact that it is formally decentralised.

18. DACNE: this is the same as (17) except that it relies on self-interest and material incentives. There is a contradiction between the decentralised structure, on one hand, and centralised–concentrated information and authoritarian procedure, on the other. Economies that approximate this system would be located somewhere in the middle of the continuum and to the right of (17).

19. DACEA: this is a decentralised system with an authoritarian procedure and centralised–concentrated information that uses economic criteria for allocating resources but relies on altruism and moral incentives. The latter may counteract the inconsistent elements. This system may be located to the left of the centre of the continuum.

20. DACEE: this is a decentralised system that uses both economic calculation and motivation but also utilises authoritarian procedures and centralised–concentrated information. These characteristics would place it somewhere to the right of the centre of the continuum and after (19).

21. DADNA: this is an economic system with a decentralised structure of decision-making and diffused information. It uses authoritarian procedures but no conscious calculation of costs and benefits and no economic incentives are employed. Again, altruism and moral incentives can coexist with an authoritarian procedure. Without assigning weights to the five elements, economies that come under this category can be located somewhere to the left of the centre.

22. DADNE: this is the same as (21) except for motivations, which are selfish and materialistic. This system will be somewhere near the right of the centre.

23. DADEA: this is a decentralised system of decision-making and diffused information but with an authoritarian procedure. Economic calculations are used for the allocation of resources, and altruism and moral incentives for implementation. The incongruent element in this system is the authoritarian procedure, but the tension is reduced by the presence of

altruism. This system would be located very close to DADNE. Indeed, the two systems may occupy the same position.

24. DADEE: this is the same as (23) with self-interest and material incentives replacing altruism and moral incentives. Again, the authoritarian element is inconsistent with other elements unless agents are given strong material incentives. This system can be located towards the end of the third segment of the continuum.

25. DDCNA: this is an economic system with a decentralised structure and democratic procedure but with centralised–concentrated information and no economic computation or motivation. The odd feature of this system is the centralised–concentrated information, but this can be treated in the same way as the role of prices (as parameters) in a perfect competition model. This system can be located just left of the centre of the continuum.

26. DDCNE: this is the same as (25) with self-interest and material incentives replacing altruism and moral incentives. The position of this system on the continuum is just right of the centre.

27. DDCEA: this is again the same as (25) with conscious economic calculation of costs and benefits in the allocation of resources. Its position on the continuum is close to (26).

28. DDCEE: this resembles the *laissez-faire* system with centralised–concentrated information. From the point of view of decision-makers, this system could be interpreted as perfect competition since the information on which decisions are based is given. Its position on the continuum is towards the end of the third segment.

29. DDDNA: this is a *laissez-faire* economic system without economic calculation or motivation, not unlike Marx's vision of 'full communism'; where both scarcity and the state are eliminated. Also, people are altruistic taking no more from society than what they genuinely need. It may be located in the third segment of the continuum.

30. DDDNE: this is a *laissez-faire* economy without economic calculation but using self-interest and material incentives to get things done. This system may be positioned towards the end of the continuum and to the right of (29).

31. DDDEA: this is a *laissez-faire* economic system with economic computation but relying on altruism and moral incentives to implement decisions. It is, in other words, a cooperative economy. It may be located near the end of the continuum.

32. DDDEE: this is the familiar *laissez-faire* system with democratic procedures, decentralised information, economic computation and material incentives. It occupies the extreme end of the continuum.

Our classificatory schema is now complete. We have identified 32 possible economic systems with somewhat different decision-making processes. As we have already noted, some are purely hypothetical whose existence might be imagined at some distant future, or might in fact turn out to be infeasible, while others will be feasible but obviously not sensible. Some are internally inconsistent and may not be viable, at least, in the long run; others still are the familiar systems but looked at from our decision-making perspective. Nevertheless, the number of potentially viable systems is large and certainly more interesting than the traditional narrow classification of capitalism and socialism, or centralised or decentralised economies. This is precisely what makes the study of economic systems so rich and rewarding.

IV

In this section an attempt is made to evaluate the effectiveness of various types of incentive. First, we consider the broad distinction between 'intrinsic' and 'extrinsic' incentives. As already commented, these are not watertight categories. It is quite obvious that individuals, whether operating independently in the market, or working in private organisations or in government bureau, are motivated by a mixed set of intrinsic and extrinsic incentives. However, it seems that autonomous economic agents rely more on the former than on the latter incentives. Such people are self-motivated and do not require an additional set of external incentives to motivate them. However, to the extent that people have difficulties evaluating their own preferences, or have a strong propensity to pursue immediate gratification, that is inconsistent with their long-term preferences, the state may establish a set of policy incentives, (for example, to encourage savings) that are aimed to correct personal failures and to internalise possible externalities arising from the conduct of individuals in the market. Others, who are not self-motivated, who are lazy or dislike work, require a set of extrinsic incentives including positive and negative ones to motivate them to seek work, to work harder or be more productive and to acquire special skills. However, incentives for skill acquisition appear more difficult since they depend on the authority's ability to calculate potential contribution of the agent or the worker. Nevertheless, since the practice of offering incentives for workers to acquire skill is widespread, the social benefits are assumed to exceed the costs.

Extrinsic incentives are obviously needed for agents and employees in both private and public organisations. Given that employees' objective function tends to differ from that of the organisation, an organisational incentive scheme, consisting of negative and positive as well as moral and material incentives, is needed to internalise the objectives of the organisation. An effective incentive scheme must include penalties as well as rewards to cater for certain people for whom failure and avoidance of pain and losses are more important motivations than success, pleasure and gains. Further, negative incentives are needed for inducing agents to avoid committing the same mistake in the future; they are useful as a learning or corrective mechanism. However, an effective incentive scheme must be 'balanced' in the sense that penalties and rewards must be proportionate to failure and effort. The 'macabre principle' (used in the former Soviet-type economies) of imposing heavy penalties and offering generous rewards for marginal failures and marginal successes, respectively, must be avoided. Extreme penalties may lead to apathy, alienation, rebellion or ingenuous efforts to deceive the motivator. Distortion and deception may also arise from generous positive incentives. If the rewards are too generous, agents might be tempted to distort the 'spirit' of the incentive for their own self-interest. As Lazar (1991) points out, weak incentives may be more effective than strong but 'dysfunctional' incentives.

Turning to moral material incentives, it has already been alluded to that there are limits to both types of incentive. To understand fully what makes managers and employees exert more than the minimum hours and effort, we need to go beyond the economist's standard of incentives, paradigm. As the following examples indicate, there are many situations in which people are not solely or mainly motivated by material rewards, and even some in which economic incentives not only fail to achieve the desired outcome but are counterproductive:

1. People who have a high degree of 'goodwill' and sympathy for others do not need the promise of larger material rewards to work harder. This is borne out by the significant proportion of labour that is done without any non-economic reward at all. Such people work overtime and on weekends. There are also people from all walks of life who do volunteer work (Freeman 1996; Rose-Ackerman 1996).

2. People who have a high degree of creativity would choose to work without receiving strong material incentives. Such people regard excessive material incentives as a distraction from their true vocation. There are quite a few examples in academia where people resigned from positions with higher status and income to pursue their research work.

3. For some artists, poets, writers and musicians, work is not a disutility that needs to be compensated by material rewards. For them work is its own reward, a joy or pleasure. Indeed, the history of many artists, writers and composers reveals a life of poverty and struggle; the material rewards come afterwards, often after their death. Such people would be happy with a guaranteed minimum income to enable them to pursue their vocations.

4. There are even some people who seek work as an escape from boredom, social isolation and idleness (or sin), and as an opportunity to interact socially with other people.

5. People who work by habit, convention or mere compliance, not bothering

much why they do it, do not require much in the way of material incentives. Such people are prevalent in traditional societies, small communities and rural areas, where custom and traditions dictate human behaviour to a greater or lesser degree.

6. People who are given responsibility and decision-making power may work harder without strong material incentives. The increase of their self-esteem (psychic income) more than compensates for extra material rewards. Participation in the decision-making process of the organisation may be an effective means of internalising the objectives of the organisation. Provided the allocation of rewards and sacrifices is fair and perceived to be so, participation in decision-making will be a powerful incentive.

7. People who are already very wealthy, or have reached the point of economic bliss, may not require material rewards to increase the supply of their labour. Under this category we may include exceptionally talented people, who are already receiving high incomes. Offering them more material incentives will not necessarily increase the labour supply simply because of the inelastic nature of their supply curve.

8. We have already mentioned the perverse effect of strong material incentives on agents' behaviour. In some cases material incentives can fail or even be counterproductive. A common example given in the past was blood donation (Collard 1978). Offering material rewards encouraged greedy or needy people with blood disease to sell their blood, though nowadays they are screened before they donate their blood.

The above situations, where moral incentives and altruism are significant motivators, should be more widely recognised and given more emphasis. They affect significantly the elasticity and position of the supply curve for their labour. They should be used not only because they have beneficial effects on output, but also because they are desirable in themselves. They reduce the inequalities in income and wealth in society without reducing productivity or output. This is especially important for developing countries. If moral incentives are effective, then labour productivity would not suffer even if workers are paid less than their marginal productivity. The surplus that would have been consumed by the workers would be reinvested for more consumption in the future, or used for community projects.

It is not obvious that moral incentives or social recognition of expertise and excellence can be an effective long-term motivator, inducing people to carry out their responsibilities without recourse to material incentives. The experience of countries, which emphasised moral incentives in peace time, for example the Soviet Union after the revolution, China during the cultural revolution, and Cuba suggests that they are effective for short periods, for specific projects and campaigns and in emergency situations. After a certain time interval and the passing of the emergency, people become cynical and moral incentives become less effective. However, in many cases moral incentives were not clearly thought out. The system's directors relied on crude propaganda and were themselves corrupt and thus failed to set good examples. They failed to give the workers a say in running the factories that were supposed to be owned by the workers themselves. They also discouraged initiative, trust, cooperation and freedom of expression, which are crucial for creativity. They treated people as if they were homogeneous, pliable and obedient participants motivated by the same set of objectives as those of the leadership. They assumed that under socialism a new morality or a system of social norms would emerge that would encourage people to be disciplined, productive, honest, law-abiding and concerned not merely with the size of their income but with building the good society.

An effective structure of incentives must also depart some way from the economist's presumption that agents are solely self-interested and that rational behaviour necessarily implies selfishness. Not only common observation but also 'experimental research makes clear that preferences depart from pure self-interest in non-trivial ways' (Rabin 1998, p 17). As Adam Smith and others before and after him pointed out, people are not ruthless egotists, thinking only of themselves, but social animals taking delight in the society of their fellows, finding pleasure and happiness in social intercourse with them, realising their own good while promoting that of others. Equally obvious is the fact that, unless we become saints, we cannot be altruistic towards others to the same degree. We tend to be altruistic towards our friends and deserving people, indifferent towards the plight of others, and hostile towards our enemies and rivals. What is even more obvious is that people often react reciprocally in kind. They are generous, reasonable and kind towards those who are also generous, reasonable and kind to them. They may be simultaneously vicious and selfish towards others who possess these qualities. People reciprocate likewise to the presence or absence of public spiritedness in others. Cynics may argue that reciprocal altruism is in the long run enlightened self-interest. However, from the point of view of the functioning of the organisation and the working of the economic system, enlightened self-interest is much better than blind and ruthless selfishness, and under certain conditions may produce better outcomes than pure altruism. Moreover, in situations where the welfare of different persons is interdependent, selfishness may lead to less welfare not only for all persons taken collectively but also for the individual. Hence, Sen's famous article on 'rational fools' (Sen 1977).

The types of incentive available and the imperfect information about the motivation of agents make it difficult to link contributions with contributors. Indeed, as Mirrlees (1997, p 1326) suggests, 'the degree of complexity implied by optimal design of incentive systems is unacceptable and unworkable'. Nevertheless, we can take certain measures to remove some of the causes of distorted incentives. Gibbons (1998, p 115) suggests two main causes: 'those with an objective criterion (sic) that seeks to establish simple quantifiable standards against which to measure real performance and an over emphasis on highly visible behaviour when some tasks are highly visible while others are not'. It is clear that when incentives are attached to outcomes that are both measurable and visible, agents are likely to neglect tasks that are not measurable and visible. Soviet success indicators, which focused on measurable and visible performance, created all sorts of distortions that violated the spirit of the plans. Despite the emphasis on objective indicators, Gibbons points out that subjective evaluations play important roles in many incentives contracts in determining promotion and continued employment.

Even if agents' performance is observable and measurable, the agent knows more than the principal, particularly about the size of the gap between observable effort and performance. Similarly, in a hierarchy, it is often forgotten that subordinates have a countervailing power on their superiors, either through the threat of leaving or the withholding of information. Thus, an effective incentive structure with asymmetric information must have a strong 'moral' incentive to reduce the potential gap between the potential and actual effort of the agent. Relying on strong material incentives alone may lead to unexpected distortions. Agents will try to deceive the monitors and manipulate timing of effort to meet the conditions. However, an appropriate mix of moral and material rewards will likely get the agent to put in more than the minimum requirement. Under a combined scheme, the minimum effort will be guaranteed by negative incentives, the threat of expulsion or loss of benefits, while maximum effort is likely to be achieved by moral incentives. Simultaneously, material incentives will ensure that employers get, at least, what they pay for, and if distortions and falsifications of performance are possible, they may get the opposite.

The bulk of our discussion on the structure of incentives is focused on principal–agent situations, and on hierarchies and authority relations. There are many other motivations, which involve cooperative arrangements or bargaining between people in similar situations. In such cases, most incentives would be considered intrinsic and rely on subjective valuations and motivations. The parties to a contract or agreement must rely on legal enforcement but to be effective the contract must also be fair to both parties. There must be sufficient incentives for both to keep to the terms of the contract. Problems may arise from asymmetric information and expectations, but such horizontal relations are different from typical principal–agent problems. According to Mirrlees (1997, p 1328) 'it is not so much the asymmetry of information that is special about principal/agent relationships, but asymmetry of responsibilities, with the principal moving first the agent following'.

V

The complexity of economic activity and human motivation and the absence of accurate information about what motivates people in certain tasks and situations, what are their preferences and what they are capable of doing, make it extremely difficult to design an effective structure of incentives. The information requirements alone for such a structure cannot be easily fulfilled. Nevertheless, the foregoing discussion suggests some ways of avoiding or minimising systemic errors arising from misaligned incentives. It was shown that an effective incentives' structure must include a set of complementary incentives: intrinsic and extrinsic, positive and negative, moral and material, and self-interest and altruism. Further, the particular structure or mix of incentives must be adapted to individuals, economies and societies and over time.

Accordingly, in a decentralised (market) economy, an intrinsic set of incentives might be adequate provided the necessary physical and institutional infrastructures are already in place. But once we admit organisations with hierarchical decision-making structures, agency–managerial problems emerge, and an extrinsic set of motivations is needed to encourage subordinates to fulfil the goals of the organisation, to identify with or even to adopt the organisation's objective function. The same applies to a centrally planned economy, which may be viewed as an extreme form of hierarchy, even as a single organisation. Customary and cooperative economies do not require an extrinsic set of motivations, because their goals are internalised by all members.

Negative incentives or penalties, which are especially needed for people who dislike work and put a higher value on failure than success, ensure that people do the minimum amount of work they need for their survival. To put in more effort they need positive incentives. However, to avoid distortions and misrepresentations of decisions given to them to implement, the penalties and rewards must be proportional to losses and gains resulting from their effort. That is, people must be paid or penalised according to their positive or negative contributions, assuming there are no problems of measurement.

Even if employees are paid their marginal productivity, and get roughly what they contribute, this may not suffice if their objective function embodies more than material rewards. Indeed, organisations and economies would not function well if such rewards were the only or even the main motivations. We have seen that employees' objective function includes pride in work, loyalty, recognition and having a say in decisions that affect their lives in the workplace. The absence of these motivations makes it difficult to explain why free-riding and shirking are not more widespread, or why employees exert more than the minimum enforceable effort. Moreover, an incentive structure that consists solely of material rewards will not deal effectively with the numerous activities (listed in the previous section), which rely on non-economic incentives.

Another related condition for an effective incentive structure is that rewards and penalties must not be based entirely on the narrow self-interest of agents, nor on pure or simple altruism. Designers of incentives must also take account of 'weak altruism', or enlightened self-interest and reciprocal altruism, which are more common than is generally admitted. It is fairly obvious that if an organisation looks after the welfare of its employees or is generous towards them, they will likely respond by working harder. It is a common observation that high wages generally result in higher productivity.

The importance of incorporating moral incentives and altruism into the incentive structure is not only because they increase output and productivity, but they also have other desirable outcomes such as reducing the inequalities in income and wealth in society, making the labour force more contented and less alienated, and generally rendering work a positive pleasure. Moreover, moral incentives are valued in themselves. They encourage people to be more noble, altruistic, cooperative and caring or, in short, 'good citizens'. However, we should not confuse moral incentives with altruism and altruism with cooperation, or virtue with 'selflessness'. More often we do good not by being selfless or altruistic, but by pursuing our self-interest through willingness to cooperate.

Finally, an effective incentive structure depends on other properties of the decision-making process and on the culture, institutions and values of a given society. This has important implications for a well-functioning economy and a just society. Such a society would require and, in turn, inculcate certain types of incentives and attitudes, and this inculcation will facilitate further its functioning and performance. Thus, an evolutionary process of mutual adjustment and interaction takes place in time between an effective structure of incentives and a well-functioning economy.

PART TWO

The Evolution of Economic Systems

7. The Customary Economy

I

The attempt in Part I to classify and analyse economies using the decision-making approach gave us a partial and rather static view of economic systems. The latter were discussed under each aspect of the decision-making process and no effort was made to deal with the dynamics of systemic change. The focus was on understanding the five components of decision-making taken separately and comparing different economic systems under each component. In this part the focus is reversed; each economic system is analysed in terms of the five components of the decision-making process. The aim is to provide a more coherent view of how economic systems function, perform and change over time.

It is beyond the scope of this book to deal in detail with the 32 possible economic systems we have distinguished in Chapter 6. Instead, the analysis is focused on four major types of economic system that have 'existed' in history. These are: the customary economy, the command economy, the competitive economy and the composite economy.

It is important to note that our account of those economies is primarily abstract rather than concrete, though concrete examples are frequently given to illustrate the underlying principles of decision-making. A major aim of Part II is to show the successive evolution of economic systems, how each system is transformed into another and more complex system while retaining elements of the past. Modern economies are, therefore, mixed, consisting of four coordinating and enforcing mechanisms: custom, command, competition and cooperation. Although no major economic system based primarily on cooperation has existed in the past, cooperative elements have been part and parcel of other historical systems and are present in modern economies; hence, they must be incorporated into the analysis of the modern 'composite' economic system.

This chapter deals with the earliest and, from our perspective, the simplest economic system, the customary economy, whose decision-making system is dominated by habits, customs and traditions. Simplicity, however, often hides sophistication and complexity. Indeed, the customary economy is exceptionally complex when studied in detail as anthropologists do. Under this type of economic system we include the palaeolithic hunter-gatherer, Neolithic agricultural subsistence societies, the isolated tribal communities and self-contained small villages that still exist in various parts of the globe. A common feature of these societies is the dominant influence of the physical environment (geographic location, climate, biology and availability of natural resources). Evidently, this influence is much greater in traditional than in modern societies.

Accordingly, before we begin our analysis of the decision-making process in the customary economy, it is important to consider, if only briefly, the impact of the physical environment on the decisions and behaviour of traditional societies. This is discussed in Section II. Section III analyses the structure of decision-making. Section IV examines the decision-making procedure, Section V discusses the structure of information flows. Section VI examines the decision-making criteria. Section VII deals with the incentive and motivation structure. Finally, Section VIII summarises the key points of the chapter.

II

Hunter-gatherer and subsistence societies have a low capacity to manage, manipulate or damage the environment, primarily because of the small size of population, low levels of physical and human capital and simple technology. Such societies adjust their needs and wants to their natural habitat and live in relative harmony with their surroundings. There are no doubt historical examples of communities, which have failed to adjust to the natural environment through mismanagement and over-exploitation of natural resources. Fertile lands and great forests were destroyed and turned into deserts. Animal species became extinct due to 'overkill'. As a result, the communities moved to new lands and forests, or simply became extinct. The collapse of the Maya civilisation has often been cited as an example of a society, which exploited the environment beyond its possible limits, though other explanations of the disintegration of that civilisation are possible. However, hunter-gatherer communities, which have survived until the present day, must have successfully managed their natural resources and adjusted fully to the environment. The Australian Aborigines, who have a history of more than 40 000 years, lived in relative harmony with the physical environment.

In general, traditional societies are constrained and confined by the physical environment. People living in similar surroundings are astonishingly alike in their manner of life despite differences in language. It is not unreasonable then to assume that in the early stages of development, before the accumulation of human and physical capital on a significant scale, human behaviour is the same except for the influence of the physical environment. We may have started off being equal but the geographical facts have favoured some groups more than others. Thus, of the world's 56 species of large-seeded grains, 32 are found wild in the Mediterranean area, and only four each in North America and sub-Saharan Africa and six in East Asia (Diamond 1997). Wheat and pulses, that grew wild in the fertile crescent, are rich in proteins, whereas, taro and sweet potatoes that are found in the tropics are not. Geography and biology made a difference for the emergence of a rich variety of cultures and modes of living. Where food was plentiful, as in the fertile crescent, close settlement became possible. The availability of large-seeded cereals, sheep and goats, made it worth while for the hunter-gatherer communities to cultivate the cereals and domesticate the animals, and thereby encouraged sedentary culture. In contrast, the relative ease with which the early Americans could obtain their subsistence from hunting large animals prevented the emergence of agriculture. It is only when animals became scarce due to overkill that agriculture became a worthwhile activity (Smith 1975, pp 732–5). Geography and biology also help to explain why other tribal communities, such as the Australian Aborigines and Eskimos, continued to live by hunting, gathering and fishing; and still other communities by a mixture of farming, hunting, herding and gathering.

Perhaps one of the earliest colourful accounts of the influence of the natural environment on the characteristics and behaviour of human beings is that given by Ibn Khaldun, the celebrated fourteenth-century Arab historian, economist and sociologist. He explains how the natural environment, especially the climate, affects their appearance, colour, character, temperament, wants, customs, political life and economic activity. Thus, because of the warm climate:

> The Egyptians are dominated by joyfulness, levity and disregard for the future. They store no provision of food neither for a month nor a year ahead… Fez in the Maghrab, on the other hand, lies inland and is surrounded by cold hills. Its inhabitants can be observed to look sad and gloomy and to be too much concerned for the future. Although a man in Fez might have provisions of wheat stored sufficient to last him for years, he always goes to the market early to buy his food, because he is afraid to consume any of his hoarded food (Ibn Khaldun 1958, p 175).

Where the climate is cold and food is scarce, people are inclined to be more frugal, far-sighted and calculating. They must provide for the long winter and for bad years when food is not so plentiful. The climate has also a significant influence on the size of population and on the supply of labour. In the tropics labour becomes arduous after a few hours of work, though it is possible that physiological adaptation, which is little understood, enables local inhabitants to cope with longer hours of work than new immigrants from colder climates. At the same time natural wants (food, shelter and clothing) are less scarce and are generally obtained with less time and energy. For the Australian Aborigines, shelter and clothing did not appear as major needs. Perhaps physiological adaptation explains the relative absence of such needs even in winter. Although they constructed temporary huts, they saw no need for long-lasting shelter. The

The Evolution of Economic Systems

need for constant movement and the availability of rock shelters in mountainous and coastal areas were adequate in rainy seasons. In the arid areas, of course, there is no need for permanent and elaborate dwellings.

The importance of the physical environment is further illustrated by the intimate relationship between a particular tribe and its land as well as the differences in dialect over short distances. The enormous diversity of languages reflects the self-containment and isolation of tribal communities. In 1980 Papua New Guinea had a population of 2–3 million people who spoke over 1000 different languages representing one-fifth of the world's total (Gregory 1981, p 120). It is widely acknowledged that traditional societies have deep emotional ties and strong attachment to their homelands on which all aspects of their lives, social, ritual and economic depend. Unauthorised entry and trespassing on sacred sights is seldom permitted. Indeed, among some Australian Aboriginal tribes, 'the punishment for trespassing was invariably death' (Reynolds 1996, p 26).

Contrary to common perception, tribal societies have often distinct and clearly defined property rights, which give them protection from other tribes. The variety of land ownership among tribal groups is bewildering and in each case very complex (Schapara 1943). Communal ownership though common is not universal. It does not exist, for example, in the Kamu Valley of Papua New Guinea. In other parts of the country, the ownership of land varies from one extreme, where it is distributed equally among the groups that make up the society, to the other extreme where it is concentrated in one group (Gregory 1982). Property titles are not always thought of as totally exclusive. In arid Australia, where economic life is quasi-nomadic, each tribe had a homeland, but the range over which food could be gathered was not exclusive. Moreover, tribal communities living in arid and desert areas are inclined to be generous and hospitable to strangers and members of other tribes. Perhaps, in areas where nature is so bountiful, there is less need to be generous.

Studies of hunter-gatherer and subsistence societies suggest that in some communities, one person's labour is sufficient to feed four or five people. Accordingly, such societies have much leisure time, and since all their needs are fully satisfied they may be characterised as 'affluent without abundance' or as 'leisured and affluent' (Sahlins 1974). The abundance of leisure not only encourages the development of artistic and religious activities but also makes 'work' more interesting. In many tribal societies there is no distinction between work and leisure. Of course, where nature is not so bountiful, the whole community, including women and children, is occupied with hunting, gathering and processing of food, and is often afflicted by seasonal hunger. The observed leisure the community happens to enjoy may be either seasonal or a necessary recuperation. Nevertheless, Sahlins's characterisation is useful in dealing with the problem of scarcity. Some communities cope with the economic problem not so much through hard work and productivity, but through limited demands or wants.

In summary, environmental factors play a decisive role in traditional economies and societies, but are seldom completely binding. The extent to which environmental constraints can be overcome, managed and exploited depends on the availability of know-how and the attitudes of the inhabitants. Each improvement in human and physical capital will lessen the constraint of the environment on choices, pattern of behaviour and economic development. Thus improvements in insulation materials and heating technology facilitated the movement of populations into colder regions. More recently, the introduction of air cooling systems in tropical countries, such as Singapore and the Philippines, had an enormous influence on labour productivity in manufacturing and services. However, the force of custom and habit in traditional societies makes changes in preferences and technology very slow indeed. Such societies tend to stay in a stationary state for very long periods and will remain in that state until they are disturbed either by external shocks such as foreign invasion and 'acts of God', or by internal forces including population pressure and the spread of the behaviour of a minority of nonconformist individuals.

III

The decision-making structure in the customary economy is primarily predetermined by customs and conventions, by the traditional division of labour, which is based on age and sex, and on caste in large communities consisting of diverse groups. It is customary for men in patriarchal societies to hunt, fish, clear the land, construct buildings and engage in ceremonial activity. Women tend to do the everyday jobs: gather leaves, seeds, fruits and roots, plant and weed crops, fetch wood and water and prepare and process food. It is also customary for older men, who are generally considered wise and knowledgeable, to be in charge of important decisions and to see to it that everyone conforms to them. In some parts of Papua New Guinea leadership is in the hands of elders who acquire their position because of seniority (Gregory 1981). In Aboriginal Australia the burning of grass, an important activity for managing the local environment, is directed by the older men because of their knowledge and experience. The decision-making authority, which 'passes' or 'transmits' decisions, is the chief or the council of elders.

Given the variety of hunter-gatherer and subsistence societies, we would expect the degree of centralisation and concentration of decision-making power to vary accordingly. We would also expect some decision-making structures to be more clearly defined than others. However, it is not easy to position traditional societies along the centralised–decentralised continuum, because the real authority, which regulates the behaviour of people, may not be the tribal chief or the council of elders, and thus it would be inappropriate to describe it as 'centralised'. But looked at from the perspective of individual members, the decision-making structure seems highly 'centralised', since the individuals themselves do not make any significant decisions. Everything, or almost everything, seems to be decided for them by customs and conventions. The difficulty here is that while decision-making authority is exercised, the mechanism is not transparent. Thus, to an outsider of an Australian Aboriginal tribe, there does not seem to be a recognised decision-making authority, but 'there are well-understood customs or tribal laws, which are binding on the individual, and which control him as well as regulate his actions towards others' (Reynolds 1996, p 31).

Since no society can function without leadership or some authority structure, it would be simplistic to suggest that tribal societies always or nearly always decide collectively and spontaneously on what is to be done. There has to be somebody to announce, at least, the routine decisions, the 'when' and 'where' decisions: when and where to hunt or fish or to move to another location. It would be equally simplistic to suggest that such decisions are taken merely by rote. The seasons are seldom the same from year to year. There is always some change to be coped with. Among Australian Aboriginal tribes important issues are generally discussed and resolved separately from others, and each tribe had a chief who directed all its activities (Reynolds 1996, pp 29–30).

Anthropological studies show that the degree of (de) centralised decision-making power varies across groups. There are tribal societies where the central authority exercises absolute or near absolute power and others where decision-making power is much more dispersed and informal. In the former societies the chief is clearly the centre of the customary economy, in charge of goods made available by other members of the tribe, which he allocates in accordance with customary rules for communal purposes. He is also in charge of external relations and trade with other tribes. Moreover, he takes the initiative in the construction of communal projects and in the protection of the local environment. He may declare a taboo on the harvesting, hunting and fishing of threatened trees, animals and fish (Viljoen 1974, p 11). In addition, the central authority decides on the distribution and use of land and determines the seasonal beginning and end of various hunting, gathering and agricultural activities. These functions of the tribal authority have been interpreted as 'the pristine origins of the state' (Gamble 1986) or 'the genesis of centralised political authority' (Sahlins 1958). However, it is important to note that the degree of (de) centralisation also varies within the groups, depending on the importance of the decision or activity for its subsistence and survival. For example, among the Plains Indians of North America during the hunting of bison, an activity that required elaborate preparation and cooperation of all the able-bodied men, centralised control was strictly enforced to prevent premature attacks on the herd. In all other activities, the individual enjoyed complete freedom (Viljoen 1974, p 8).

Since in tribal societies the division and subdivision of decision-making functions are generally less refined than in modern societies, a decision-making authority does not usually limit itself to a particular field of social life. As Pospisil (1971 p 65) points out, 'in most or many cases the headmen or chiefs hand down important political, economic, legal or religious and cultural decisions'. The lack of specialisation within particular areas and the relative absence of a clear distinction between making and enforcing decisions led to the concentration of decision-making powers in some tribal societies. In other societies the division of decision-making activity is more clearly defined. In the traditional Samoan village the head of the governing body was the chief or orator; in certain villages the two titles were combined. According to Davidson (1967, p 19):

> the chief was the titular leader, the ultimate repository of authority; the orator was the executive agent, who performed for the chief a variety of duties which it was contrary to propriety for the chief to perform for himself. The orator was the repository of genealogical knowledge, of history and legend; he made formal speeches on behalf of the village; he organised the ceremonial distribution of food.

The relative power of chiefs and orators differed from village to village, depending upon circumstance and personality, but their functions remained clearly distinct.

As in all societies there is a continuum of formal and informal decision-making authority, and it is important to distinguish between the two. A formal authority is one whose decision-making functions, rights and duties as well as its rules of procedure are defined by law or custom or both. The importance of formal authority is reflected in the publicity given to the ceremonial aspect of the investiture of the ruler, and by the fact that decisions made by others will not be accepted, if they do not go through the formal authority (Pospisil 1971, pp 46–7). Hence, a meaningful and workable concept of authority implies that the decisions and advice of an authority are accepted and implemented by members of the group.

An example of a formal authority without power in tribal societies is the head of the Tiv tribe in Southern Nigeria (Mead 1955, p 90). He is the elected chief, but his function is to announce the decisions of the council of elders consisting of representatives of four or five extended families. Decision-making power is not delegated to him but is incorporated in his person. In none of the decisions passed by the council did he make his own decision; rather he gave voice to the decisions of the elders as the spokesperson of the group authority.

To determine the locus of decision-making authority, it is necessary to look behind the formal structure. In any society or group some members are almost certain to take a more active role than others, to be listened to with more respect than others, and to be dominant over others. This is, perhaps, the beginning of the differentiation of group members into leaders and followers, or into 'decision-makers' and 'decision-implementers', and hence the origin of hierarchical organisations including the state. Members of a society, particularly men who, because of their age, experience, sound judgement, eloquence and superiority gain such moral authority that they become informal headmen. Further, variation in the degree of informal decision-making power is much higher than in the case of formal authority. According to Pospisil (1971, pp 74–5) 'the power and influence of the Eskimo informal power over his followers was often very pronounced approaching at times, that of an autocrat'.

The variability of decision-making structure in tribal societies can also be illustrated in the area of exchange. Stodder (1995, pp 4–5) identified six models of exchange in traditional societies with varying degrees of (de) centralisation. The first is gift exchange, which is 'typically asphalous without a recognised headman, or with a leader picked by consensus'. The second exchange system is 'big-man' exchange, which is centralised. The big-man or chief is the group's 'accountant' as well as its main creditor. He is subject to overthrow in contests of generosity or violence if goods are not distributed properly (Glassman 1986, pp 66–81). The third system is storehouse exchange; it, too, is centralised. The person in charge of the storehouse is appointed by a temple bureaucracy. He keeps the last period's gifts, a kind of tribute or in-kind taxes. The storehouse exchange system is characteristic of the Incas and Aztecs (Pryor 1977, pp 283–7). The fourth system is fixed reciprocity exchange. It is a decentralised system whereby households accept any good as a means of exchange. However, households produce mainly for use rather than for exchange. Another decentralised system is barter. Finally, there is money trade, which uses a single good held by every household. Exchange is short term and impersonal; production and exchange are decentralised.

In summary, the decision-making structure in customary economies is both varied and comparatively static. Variability is determined by the enormous variety of hunter-gatherer and subsistence societies both across time and space. Comparative stability is reinforced by customs and traditions with respect to both the division of labour and the division of decision-making systems. However, as in all systems, there is a gap between formal and informal decision-making power. Within limits this gap may be desirable. Violation of the formal decision-making structure provides flexibility, particularly in times of emergency when overriding decisions by the formal authority have to be made. A decision-making structure that allows no flexibility, no spontaneous decisions, may cause the collapse of the authority in the face of new emergency. Equally, an excessive degree of decentralisation will be inadequate to deal with emergency situations, which call for new and centralised decisions for the mobilisation of the required resources.

IV

The decision-making procedure, like the structure, is largely prescribed by customs and conventions and varies a great deal across cultures. Further, more than one type of procedure may be used within a community depending on the circumstance and the nature of the decision. In some communities decision-making authority is exercised through set patterns of action, or established norms, with no standing officials to enforce them. In other societies decision-making procedures can be very formal and authoritarian. Thus, there is a variety of recognised procedures in hunter-gatherer and subsistence societies that can be ranked along an authoritarian–democratic continuum.

Typically, day-to-day decisions and decisions concerning recurrent emergencies are predetermined and do not have to be made afresh. Other decisions may be reached through meetings of the council of elders, or the chief may make the decision after consultation with representative heads of families. However, in the case of new emergencies, an authoritarian procedure may be adopted, because in such situations speed is of the utmost importance. There may be a quick meeting where each member may be asked to have a say, then a few words from the chief will resolve what is to be done. In traditional Samoan villages, where decisions were normally reached through discussion and consent, 'the individual authority of a dominant chief came to the fore only in times of war, when the slowness of conciliar proceedings made them inappropriate' (Davidson 1967, p 29). Some chiefs would exploit the emergency situation and impose hardship and suffering on the community, but in the long run, when the emergency was over, customs and conventions would reassert themselves.

There are numerous examples of 'customary democratic' procedures in tribal societies. The Navajo Indians decided on important matters through consensus of those present. Although the headman allowed for group discussion until a consensus was reached, in many circumstances he handed down decisions that were agreed to and obeyed by his followers. Similarly, in the Tiv tribe in Southern Nigeria, the decisions made by the kindred council of elders were reached through a process of consensus (Mead 1955, pp 101–2). In the former British protectorate of Bechuanaland bordering South Africa and Southern Rhodesia, the position of the chief was hereditary, but in important matters he took decisions only with the approval of the tribal assembly. Furthermore, custom required him to consult about tribal affairs informally with the notables of the tribe, and more formally with a council formed by the headmen of kinship groups (Sillery 1952, p 200). In the traditional Samoan village, decisions were reached following the consent of the members. However, a multitude of informal discussions often preceded the formal meeting. A practice that was highly developed in Samoan society at every level was 'simple dictation but after consultation' (Davidson

1967, p 17).

One must be careful in interpreting the apparent consensus and conciliatory discussion in tribal societies. The consensus and consultation may be little more than 'customary', a ritual or veneer. People are usually cautious in expressing their views for fear of offending others, particularly those who are more powerful, as open hostilities and disagreement may be used against them in the future. People tend to say whatever the listener wants to hear. Thus, in Palau, Mead (1955, p 150) observed:

> in the traditional meetings of the Council, views were not expressed for open discussion, but were whispered to special messengers who carried the opinions to the proper recipients. The exchange of opinions is often accompanied by the agreement to keep the matter confidential. Many of the crucial conferences are held in closed groups and sometimes secretly.

The decision-making procedure in traditional Samoa was democratic but not egalitarian or open. At the meeting of the governing body of the villages, the members' seating positions reflected the relative importance of members and the order of speaking. Also when a member of higher title expressed an opinion those of lower positions could not with propriety dissent. However, as Davidson (1967, p 21) points out, 'the Samoan conception of a leader as a spokesman for, and representative of, the group had created the habit of informal consultation; and, even where this procedure was not used effectively, the Samoan convention of debate permitted attitudes to be made clear without the open expression of disagreement'. It would appear then that the relative rigidity of the formal decision-making structure was in fact much more flexible. In Davidson's words, 'structural rigidity and operational flexibility were effectively combined'. However, it would be wrong to infer that the decision-making structure and procedure in traditional Samoa resolved all disputes. Sometimes relations between families and villages and districts led to conflicts that were irresolvable by negotiations and consensus. In such situations war was the inevitable outcome.

In some societies where democratic procedures are adopted, the central authority may allow members of the community to select goals, within the limits permitted by custom and convention, and pursue them through interpersonal and horizontal relationships. The authority may also delegate some responsibility for communal decisions to subordinates. Under this procedure, which may be described as 'democratic centralism', lower decision-makers and members of the community are well informed about the goals and standards set by the authority and are accordingly rewarded with praise. At the other extreme is the coercive authoritarian procedure, whereby the decision-making authority relies on commands rather than persuasion and consultation. Under this procedure, the personal ability of the leader seems irrelevant. His followers fear him and comply with his commands only in public. Such a leader 'is supposed to be aloof, determining all policies without discussing with his followers the goals, standards and methods that he employs' (Pospisil 1971, p 58).

In short, tribal societies follow various decision-making procedures that have evolved over time and became customary. However, the extreme procedures of reaching decisions either through democratic, open discussion, negotiations and consensus, or through authoritarian, coercive methods, seem to be rare. The common procedure seems to be a mixture of the two extremes. But, since formal procedures are invariably determined by customs and conventions, actual procedures are far from transparent. As is often the case, we have to look behind the veil of conventions to understand real processes, and decision-making procedures are no exception.

V

Corresponding to the customary decision-making structures and procedures there are routines by which information is obtained and used. Since most decisions are customary and rarely change, no new information is needed as to the time and place for hunting, gathering, sowing and harvesting, or what to do with the temporary surplus, if any. Such decisions are dictated by the seasons and by customs and conventions. Of course, as no two seasons are identical, adjustment with respect to timing would have to be made by the authority. Moreover, acquired skills become partially embedded in customs and routines, which are passed down from one generation to the next. The stock of information required for survival and reproduction gradually grows and seems to be more than adequate, as reflected in the long-term equilibrium of tribal societies. However, the limited capacity to store information, as indicated by the absence of written records, prevents the accumulation of knowledge beyond the mental powers of the current generation.

The importance of local knowledge and information for survival in tribal societies becomes obvious when one is reminded that Aboriginal Australians flourished for thousands of years in places where European explorers died of starvation and thirst. European explorers and settlers, who tried to comprehend the customary economy of Aboriginal Australian communities, came to appreciate that it depended on sophisticated bushcraft and on in-depth knowledge of the physical environment. They observed that in his district the Aboriginal Australian 'knows exactly what it produces, the proper times at which certain articles are in season, and the readiest means of securing them' (Reynolds 1996, p 21). The intimate knowledge of the plants and animals and their management, accumulated by Aboriginal Australians over a period of more than 40 000 years, is being recognised by European-Australian experts who are calling for greater utilisation of this knowledge as a means of coping with environmental problems created by European settlers.

Human capital relative to physical capital tends to be abundant in tribal societies. All the members of the group including children must learn how to make a living whether by hunting, herding, fishing or gathering. They must know intimately the local geography, remedies for illness and much else. That these matters were often taught in a quasi-religious manner, as part of the initiation to adulthood, underlies the seriousness with which they were regarded. The information possessed by women, though often neglected by analysts, is very important. Each woman had to learn the location of, and how and when to harvest, the various fruits and vegetables, and how to process and preserve food. Women even contributed to the hunting effort, often regarded as a male activity, by bringing information about animal tracks and direction of movements. In Aboriginal Australian societies there is certain knowledge over which women have a monopoly, the so-called 'women's business'.

The need for communication of information about non-routine events and activities, which are remote from the decision-makers, is important for the livelihood of the community. The elders in aboriginal Australian societies needed information from all areas of their territory, such that continual reconnaissance of the whole territory became necessary. An example of the need for such communication is the stranding of a whale, which 'was an occasion for local aboriginal people to eat to repletion' (Priddel and Wheeler 1997). The sooner they all knew of events like this, the better; hence, a messenger was dispatched to inform the neighbouring groups.

Arguably, the most important information in tribal societies, besides that relating to the procurement of basic needs such as food, shelter and clothing, concerns matters of religious rituals, kinship relations (genealogy), as well as medicine. Hence, those who possess such information wield significant influence and control over the community. They see themselves, and are regarded by the community, as the guardians of 'the cosmic plan'. As spiritual leaders and medicine men, they are in charge of educational programmes to train and initiate the young and additional 'elders'. The elder initiate is required to know everything necessary to perpetuate the tribe's existence (Anderson 1988). Thus, each generation is a link in the chain of knowledge. Of particular importance to hunter-gatherer societies is the 'science' of tracking, which is developed over years and passed down from one generation to the next.

In any tribal society there would be some individuals who possess certain skills and know-how to deal with a particular problem or conflict. Such people often come to acquire special status and power. In Samoa, the orator was the repository of genealogical knowledge of history and legend, and this knowledge was crucial to an understanding of the balance of power in village politics and of the means to be used in attempting to change it (Davidson 1967, pp 19–21).

As is to be expected, hunter-gatherer and subsistence societies are not subjected to constant technological and cultural change. Nevertheless, it occurred, particularly in those economies, which were not isolated from the outside world, through trade and exchange of gifts. The new technologies had to be incorporated into the traditional way of life and into the educational arrangements. Occasionally new technology and information is generated within communities basically by inquisitive and nonconformist individuals, who are inclined to take exploratory decisions and conduct experiments, and in the process acquire new knowledge and skill that might be beneficial to the whole society. However, the creation of new knowledge is regarded by the leading authority as anti-traditional and anti-authoritarian. Hence, nonconformists and inventors tend to be rare in traditional societies; they are frequently ostracised and persecuted particularly if they break taboos. Nonconformist behaviour is seen as destabilising and threatening the religious and economic life of the community.

VI

In a customary economy, individuals have very limited choices open to them and these are circumscribed by a strictly conformist code of ethics. Economic and non-economic decisions are mostly habitual and are not subjected to conscious calculation of costs and benefits. This is not to deny the existence of purposeful activities or economic 'rationality' in customary economies. Habits or customs may adapt slowly or mutate as the nonconformists discover better ways of doing things. Habitual decisions, which slowly percolate to the rest of the community and have proved beneficial over a long period of time, are not necessarily inconsistent with economic reasoning. This is widely recognised by economists and economic anthropologists. It is often pointed out that although 'primitive' exchange is based on tradition rather than rational calculation, the evolutionary process of natural selection will impose economic rationality upon those traditions that survive. However, this way of thinking may lead to the error that the decisions of traditional societies handed down from generation to generation are always 'rational'.

Economic anthropologists such as Dalton (1971) and Sahlins (1974) have drawn attention to the problem of economic rationality, what it means to be rational in traditional societies. Following Polanyi (1957) they make a distinction between 'substantive rationality' and 'formal rationality' in their analysis of economic activity in traditional societies. However, given the crucial economic and political importance of kinship solidarity, and the fact that economic activity is not clearly differentiated from other activities, nor primarily directed at making personal profits, we need a broader notion of rationality and, perhaps, a 'higher' calculus of costs and benefits to understand the basis on which decisions are made in customary economies.

The question of whether or not economic criteria are used in traditional societies has been much debated under different headings including the 'moral economy' versus the 'political economy' approach (Keyes 1983) and the 'institutional' versus the 'neoclassical economics' school. However, the bewildering diversity of customary economies renders any single approach inadequate. This is clearly shown in the case of exchange relations. Stodder (1995), as already noted, identified no less than six exchange systems, based on a review of anthropological literature and Pryor's (1977) study of 60 primitive and peasant societies that have not been exposed much to influences emanating from developed economies. Stodder shows that some of the exchange systems are more economically efficient than others.

The overwhelming evidence from anthropological studies of hunter-gatherer and subsistence societies suggests that economic reasoning or calculation is deeply embedded in the social, cultural, ritual and political activities. Economic and non-economic processes are mutually determinant. As Dalton (1971, p 11) put it: 'economy and "society" are embedded in each other and that it is impossible to attribute primacy to one over the other, for traditional societies'. Hence, the economic results that economists obtain from constructing economic models that abstract from the non-economic aspects may not be comprehensible in isolation from non-economic issues. Customary economies are highly integrated and neither their means nor their ends are purely economic. Indeed, judged by the amount of time spent in leisure, social and religious activities, particularly in places where the environment is bountiful, traditional societies place less emphasis on economic ends. Of course, where nature is not so bountiful more time and energy is required to earn a living, and thus economic calculation may play a greater role in their decisions. But even in such societies, living on or near the margin of subsistence, and avoiding risks that threaten their basic subsistence, people 'commit themselves to a moral economy predicated on two principles: the norm of reciprocity and the right to subsistence' (Scott 1976, p 4). Since the two principles guarantee the survival of the individual and the community, they must embody, at least, some economic 'calculation'.

The close integration of the economic process into the social process and the implicit existence of multiple decision-making criteria in customary economies can be 'seen' in many activities. In the highlands of Papua New Guinea pigs are so important as objects of gift exchange, they are regarded almost in the same way as people (Gregory 1981, p 175). Certain payments, such as those made for brides, are made only in pigs. As a result, the community produces a surplus of pigs over and above its immediate needs and consumes it later in ceremonial activities. There might be economic calculations underlying such practices but they are not apparent.

The lack of transparency of economic calculation is further indicated by the complexity of exchange. Three of the six exchange systems analysed by Stodder (1995) are not based on 'bilateral mutually improving trade' and hence require debt. However, debt does not usually earn interest, not only because it is often prohibited by religion but is also a form of insurance against future scarcity. Debt without interest is an indicator that the debtor is generous, and generosity is highly valued in traditional societies (Gregory 1982). In such exchange systems economic, political, religious and cultural considerations are closely intertwined. Exchange serves the economic and non-economic needs of both the community and the individual.

The transparency of economic rationality seems to be a characteristic feature of market relations. Economic rationality is more compatible with anonymous relations than with personal and kinship relations. Impersonal market relations solve the valuation problem or relative prices, which is necessary for economic rationality. Traditional societies, which are obviously not based on extensive market relations, have a hierarchical ranking of goods and services but do not know the value of every good in terms of every other good. As Gregory (1981, p 127) points out, the difference between a market exchange relation and a gift exchange relation is the difference between 'rank' and 'value'. Firth (1958, p 69) commenting on the problem of value in a tribal society of south eastern New Guinea stated: 'there is no final measure of value of individual things, and no common medium whereby every type of good and service can be translated into terms of every other'. Similarly, Viljoen (1974, p 7) argues that meetings between tribes to exchange goods 'do not produce the appropriate prices that are adjusted by supply and demand; they rather presuppose that the appropriate rates are already in existence'. There are cases where bargaining between traders determines the 'equilibrium' between supply and demand. However, as Godlier (1971, p 66) points out, bargaining is rare and most frequently each partner knows what he has to give in order to receive. Both parties act as though there were a 'normal' rate, a 'just price' for the items they are exchanging and 'this rate is known to all members of the tribe to which they belong'.

By definition hunter-gatherer and subsistence societies do not in general accumulate material wealth, either because they are too poor to save, or the accumulation of wealth is a hindrance to the need for mobility (in the case of nomadic communities). While it is difficult to define a surplus over the necessities of subsistence, as needs grow with the means to satisfy them, there is a clear distinction between 'daily bread' or 'a daily bowl of rice' and something extra. The need for having a temporary surplus is useful for survival in times of extreme scarcity. Tribal societies generate a surplus above last year's output to sustain a growing population and/or to be consumed or used for ceremonial purposes, but not to reinvest it for the purpose of accumulation of personal wealth. Indeed, in some societies (for example, Trobriand Islanders), if a surplus is produced it is left to rot. In other societies the accumulation of personal wealth is considered unethical or selfish. As a result, customs evolved to check such behaviour. In Rossel Island, the accumulation of personal wealth was held in check by the custom of one man challenging another to give a feast (Robinson 1970, p 27). The competition that followed ended in the dissipation of personal wealth. The person who spent most was declared the winner. A similar system exists among Kapauha Papuans where the highest political status is achieved through generosity. As Gregory (1981, p 120) points out, 'leadership is in the hands of "bigmen" who achieve status according to a "meritocracy system" that involves the competitive giving of gifts'. Rich men who are not generous are ostracised, reprimanded and occasionally killed. Thus, the accumulation and decumulation of personal wealth plays a basic role in economic, political, legal and ethical systems. In particular, emphasis on the accumulation of economic wealth is balanced by the highest value of the culture, namely generosity. Economic rationality and morality are thus integrated systemically.

Economic rationality for the community is often achieved as a by-product of beliefs and emotions in the individual, which have no economic meaning at all. However, there are examples of communities in which the attitude to economic wealth is much more direct. For the Bushong, a tribe in Central Africa, work is the means to accumulate wealth, and wealth is the means to status. But their close neighbours, 'the Lele, have totally opposite notions of dignity and prestige which allow no scope for acquisitiveness' (Robinson 1970, pp 29–31).

In short, economic criteria in customary economies are not separated from non-economic considerations; nor is individual rationality divorced from collective rationality. There is close integration of economic activity with cultural, social, political and religious life. In most cases economic activity is essential both for the survival, and for the cultural and social life of the community. It is not for the purpose of accumulation of personal wealth. Further, there are customary checks on the accumulation of personal wealth. Both these checks and the long-term character of exchange balance or 'delayed reciprocity' are means of binding together communities. In particular, the practice of gift exchanges, which is still observed in modern economies, is a means of binding together families and friends.

VII

The enforcement of decisions in customary economies seems for the most part automatic and internalised by a 'hidden power', which secures scrupulous compliance with customs and norms. Enforcement mechanisms are embedded in cultural and religious taboos rather than provided through economic incentives and legal institutions. People perform their allotted tasks with little resistance. Failure to comply places the individual in an intolerable position. In the Trobriand

Islands, Malinowski (1922, p 40) found 'the honourable citizen is bound to carry out his duties, though his submission is not due to any instinct or intuitive impulse or mysterious "group sentiments", but to the detailed and elaborate working of a system, in which every act has its own place and must be performed without fail'. The psychic power of religion and taboos must not be underestimated in traditional societies. Taboos, decisions, laws and customs are obeyed because individuals have been told from their earliest childhood that disobedience will be followed by some supernatural personal punishment. There are different enforcement mechanisms of taboos. A supernatural sanction usually accompanies a taboo, but its violation in some societies brings secular punishment (Sahlins 1958).

To understand the enforcement of decisions in traditional societies, it is useful to apply the distinction between customary law and authoritarian law. The former is internalised by the majority of the members of the group, while the latter has the support of only a minority (Pospisil 1971, pp 344–5). Consequently, customary law needs little or no external force to enforce it, while the authoritarian law being regarded unjust by most of the people needs for its enforcement the prestige, influence and even physical force of the authority. However, it is possible for one type of law to be transformed into the other. As Pospisil himself explains, 'an authoritarian decision at the beginning may become slowly internalised by more and more people until it becomes customary, and conversely, a customary law may become authoritarian, as it loses more and more supporters until it is accepted only by a very small minority that remains loyal to the authority' (ibid).

There might be deeper motives underlying the acceptance of customs and conventions. Scott (1976) argues that peasant societies are regulated by the norm of reciprocity. Reciprocity implies an enforcement mechanism, but if no such mechanism exists then reciprocal exchange becomes a transfer. Alternatively, when reciprocal obligations have not been fulfilled by one party, relationships break down and then 'political economy' replaces the 'moral economy'. This would suggest that the trust and reciprocity that moral economists stress do not always prevail. Similarly, self-interest is not always the underlying motive and rarely the only motive for accepting customs and conventions. In small communities, there is no inherent conflict between self-interest and altruistic motivation. Self-interest does not overrule collective interest. Individualism and collectivism are merged. Collective action undertaken by the group may be interpreted as aggregated self-interest, particularly if the group is small. Further, tribal societies are regulated by a mixture of unconscious egotism, altruism and material and non-material motivations; this mixture varies from one group to another. Thus it is possible to rank tribal societies on a continuum of egotism and altruism.

We would expect most tribal societies to be nearer the altruistic–collective end of the continuum. This is because individuals in such societies have strong social motivations in their economic activities. They have duties of mutual support and respect going beyond the nuclear family. Kinship relations are very important indeed. Relatives have the right to make demands on the successful individual and in small communities the refusal of such demands is difficult. Viljoen (1974, p 10) reported that 'a Fijian who sets up as a trader is liable to have his goods appropriated by anyone who comes into his store'. Similarly, an African shopkeeper may have his relatives take freely what they want from his shop (Herskovtis 1961, p 132). Thus, although self-interest motivations are present, they are severely constrained by the social and cultural milieu.

The collective character of economic relations is reflected in the provision of the basic necessities of life. Labour, in particular, is often seen as a social service, an obligation to the community. Superficially viewed, this may seem as cooperative or altruistic behaviour. In reality, there may be in addition an egotistic motivation underlying this sort of behaviour. In the short run, it is the impact of social obligation that is observed – the frequent rendering of a service without demanding an immediate equivalent payback. Nevertheless, it is reciprocal and, in the long run, contributions and rewards tend to even out.

As discussed in Chapter 6, the types of incentive depend a good deal on the decision-making structure and procedure. A centralised and an authoritarian system relies on direct control, coercion and negative incentives (the urge to escape from punishment), as well as psychological and 'moral' motivations. Depending on the degree of resistance to or acceptance of these stimuli or incentives, the particular amount of power and influence may be expressed by the effectiveness of an inventory of rewards and penalties available to the decision-maker, or by the limits imposed by a superior, authority, custom, law or public opinion. On the other hand, a decentralised and democratic decision-making system relies on persuasion and self-interest rather than on coercion. A democratic leader obtains both private and public compliance with his decisions, whereas an authoritarian leader achieves only public compliance. In the latter case, there is a tendency to distort the spirit of his decisions through falsification and misrepresentation without legally disobeying him.

A conflict between the self-interest of the head of a family and the community may still arise under democratic procedures. The individual may refuse to carry out the decisions reached, in which case he is punished. If the member of the governing body of a Samoan village refused to carry out the full terms of its decisions, he and his family would be exiled from the village (Davidson 1967, p 21). This punishment, which is intended to avoid continuous dissidence in the village, would be accompanied by some destruction of houses and crops. However, it imposes greater humiliation than physical hardship on those exposed to it. When a serious dispute involves a number of families, it usually leads to the splitting of the village into two factions, each with its own decision-making authority. The village will remain divided until the dispute is healed. Similarly, in Bechuanaland, the tribal authority banished individuals from their village and forced them to live elsewhere (Schapara 1943, p 104). This form of punishment was designed for antisocial behaviour and as a preventative measure against further trouble.

In summary, customary economies do not seem to suffer much from the problem of incentives. The enforcement mechanism in most cases is internalised by customs and conventions, taboos and customary laws. Also, given the small size of the communities, the integration of economic and non-economic aspects of their lives, and the lack of strong incentives for the accumulation of personal wealth, the conflict between the interest of the individual and that of the community seems to be weak. Self-interest and common interest are merged or easily reconciled.

VIII

The enormous variety of hunter-gatherer and subsistence societies across time and space makes it difficult indeed to come up with generalisations about their decision-making processes. Each is to a large extent sui generis. Nevertheless, it is possible to make certain generalisations provided it is borne in mind that they are subject to more than the usual qualification when applied to specific cases.

First, we can safely conclude that the decisions and behaviour of each community are contrived to fit the requirement of its physical environment. As a result, we get a wide variety of modes of living and decision-making, which are governed by the local environment. It is only with the accumulation of human and physical capital and increased contact with other communities that the binding constraints of the environment are relaxed and the uniformity of economic life across cultures is increased. In the course of economic development, it seems geographic determinism is gradually displaced by technological determinism. Indeed, technology increasingly influences and shapes the physical environment.

Second, despite appearances customary economies and societies are exceedingly complex as any anthropologist would confirm. The complexity is derived from highly integrated social, economic, political and religious activities that are more or less compatible with the physical environment. More importantly, from the economist's point of view, customary economies seem to have come nearer than modern economies to solving the 'economic problem'. By having limited wants, tribal communities, particularly those living in favourable environments, live in 'primitive affluence' or in a 'subsistence economy of affluence', with much leisure to pursue artistic, cultural and social activities. In contrast, modern economies partition each human life into a variety of segments, each of which has its own norms and modes of behaviour. Moreover, with their creation and multiplication of factitious wants, they have created a state of 'affluent scarcity', which is increasingly damaging the physical environment (on a much larger scale than the slash and burn practices of some traditional societies) and in which many people are alienated or have 'disequilibrium' lives.

Third, the force of custom and tradition induces a remarkable uniformity of individual behaviour within each community. Habits are so uniform that they become quickly internalised. Deviants and nonconformists evoke the strongest ridicule and resistance. The control exercised by custom and convention is so pervasive that decisions and actions are dictated to the individual. Under certain circumstances one may escape the commands of an authoritarian leader or dictator or, at least, comply with his or her wishes only in public. But one cannot escape those of customs, traditions and taboos. They are internalised by almost all members of the community.

Fourth, the integrated culture of tribal societies together with the force of custom and tradition place no premium on experimental decisions, on trying something new; hence their innate conservatism. People living in such societies accept utterly and unquestionably not only the physical environment but also the institutions including the decision-making process. They regard the decision-making structure and procedure as being 'right' or God-given (hence the notion of 'the divine right of kings'). Accordingly, they would think any attempt on their part to change it as being 'immoral'. Such attitudes underlie not only the inherent stability but also a lack of material progress in the customary economy.

Fifth, and following from the third, there is a positive role to be played by customs and traditions. They provide both continuity and stability, and discourage chaos, anarchy and confusion. In many cases they economise on time and energy in making decisions and spare the individual from agonising about his or her choices. Further, customary decisions may often seem irrational from the point of view of the individual but not from that of the community. They may also seem unjust or irrational when judged from the vantage point of different cultures and time, but are in fact 'rational' having evolved to ensure the continual survival of the community. Thus, in the Bengal famines of 1770 and 1943–7, children were allowed to die of starvation while their parents, especially their fathers, ate what food was available. Similarly, poor peasants starved while the landlords and officials of the state were allowed to obtain sufficient food. What is more remarkable, there was no violent rebellion. In fact, 'there was acceptance that for the moral order to be restored, those who once again could provide subsistence after the famine must be the ones to survive' (Keyes 1983, p 765).

Sixth, against the advantages and benefits of customary decisions, there are certain disadvantages, chiefly those that discourage the creation and use of new information (knowledge), change and adaptation when warranted. Without the capacity to change and adapt to new circumstances, a community will collapse and disintegrate in the face of danger. In contrast, a community that encourages originality and experimentation is more likely to survive and grow. But too much originality and individualism may lead to instability. As Joan Robinson (1970, p 14) reminds us: 'originality and individualism are useful to the group provided there is not too much of them'. In general, however, conformity with the pattern of habits that has proved useful or viable is often imposed on all members.

This leads to the question of how a customary economy breaks out of its long-run equilibrium. Several possibilities have been suggested. Hicks (1977) surmises that if an emergency arises, overriding decisions from the nominal centre would have to be made or a new authority would have to be improvised. This could be a way out of the traditional society into the emergence of a new system. According to Hicks, the attempt to deal with new emergencies or external threats will lead to the emergence of a new leader, who will reorganise the community on a command basis. In its early stage, therefore, the command economy will almost inevitably have a quasi-military character.

Hicks also entertains the possibility of population pressure as the required dynamic force that disturbs the equilibrium of the customary economy. But he dismisses this possibility on the grounds that people who have maintained themselves for long periods must have some ways of containing the population pressure. Indeed, many traditional societies, including Australian Aborigines, had effective birth control methods. Also low fertility of women due to long suckling and high death rates kept the population pressure in check. There were also cycles of famine and disease. However, there may be a failure of such checks and controls, in which case natural resources and suitable land for cultivation will become scarce. This might lead either to territorial wars or the development of more efficient methods of production, or both. A population, which cannot adapt its production techniques as population increases, would either be wiped out or migrate to, or conquer, other lands.

The break up of the customary economy, whether as a result of foreign invasion, population pressure, or the spread of useful ideas and inventions of original and nonconformist individuals, or a combination of all these, leads to the analysis of the next economic system. Historically, this was feudalism, an economic system that lasted for more than four hundred years in Europe and still exists in some countries in the Third World. We may call this system by its chief coordinating and enforcing decision-making mechanism, the command economy, or rather the 'primitive command' system, to distinguish it from the command system of the former Soviet Union and Eastern Europe. Both feudalism and Soviet-type socialism are examples of the command system and are, therefore, discussed together in the next chapter.

8. The Command Economy

Economic systems are never found in reality in pure form. They contain elements of preceding and succeeding systems. We have seen that the customary economy, the first economic system, contained elements of command and cooperation, elements of future systems, though it was the element of custom that permeated both the economy and society. Similarly, the command economy, as shown in this chapter, possesses elements of custom, competition and, to a much lesser extent, cooperation, but it is the command principle that dominates the decision-making process.

The central purpose of this chapter is to show how the command principle works in practice, using two major historical systems: feudalism and Soviet-type socialism. It may seem surprising to treat feudalism and socialism under the same coordinating or organising principle. This is because, following Marx, we are accustomed to think of socialism as an economic system that comes after feudalism and capitalism. Historically, however, Soviet-type socialism was established soon after serfdom had been abolished and well before capitalism had struck deep roots in Russia. Hence, we would expect Soviet-type socialism to contain strong elements of feudalism. From our perspective it may be viewed as a type of feudalism that has been radically modified by a strong and fully developed bureaucracy. Indeed, the Soviet-type economy was often referred to as an administrative or a bureaucratic economy (Greenslade and Schroeder 1977; Wilhelm 1985), and Soviet socialism as bureaucratic socialism or 'bureaucratic collectivism'. Rigby (1977, pp 59–60) described Soviet society as a bureaucratic system in which 'most activities are directly managed by innumerable organizations of bureaucracies, all of which are linked up in a single organisational system'.

The structure of the chapter is as follows: Section II discusses briefly the emergence of feudalism as a prelude to the analysis of its decision-making process in Sections III–VII. Section VIII discusses the decline of the feudal system and why it had to be transformed into a higher system. Sections IX–XIII analyse the decision-making system under Soviet-type socialism. Finally, concluding remarks about the command economy.

II

The historical literature suggests several theories of the origins and development of feudalism. One theory favoured by Hicks (1977, pp 14–18) postulates that feudalism emerged after the displacement of the customary economy by an invasion of a superior military force. In terms of our decision-making approach, the central authority in the early stage makes all the important decisions in an authoritarian manner. Information flows are mainly in the form of commands given to subordinates with little feedback or questioning as befits a military organisation. Since the immediate objective of the central authority is the establishment of its control over the conquered territory, the economic problem of obtaining supplies to feed the army is solved by plunder, with little consideration of the long-term consequences. The decisions and commands of the centre are faithfully carried out by subordinates, generals and their captains. This is clearly a pure command system that works well in times of emergency for a relatively short period and when there are relatively few decisions to be made and people are willing to obey or cooperate with the central authority.

According to Hicks, the next stage comes when the emergency period has passed and the generals and captains are dispersed to govern the provinces and districts. In this stage the decision-making authority of the centre becomes limited, mainly because the decisions themselves have become complex requiring more inputs and feedback information from subordinates. The major decision now is how to obtain supplies on a regular basis. This problem is solved by establishing a new hierarchical structure in which the generals and captains are transformed into landlords to form the most important link between the ruler (the centre) and the cultivators. The landlords provide the essential services to the cultivators: defence and justice. In exchange, the cultivators are obliged to provide an agricultural surplus over and above their own needs. Thus, in Hicks's theory, a physical force or a class system is necessary for the emergence of a surplus, which is needed to sustain the system. Without such a force, the cultivators would have little or no incentive to produce more than what they need, including customary offerings to maintain the small non-labouring class of priests.

An alternative theory, which relies less on military force for the emergence of feudalism, has been suggested in the historical literature. Bensusan-Butt (1962) has provided a theoretical account of how, under a more peaceful transition to a feudal economy, it is the generation of the surplus that results in a class society. Starting from a more or less egalitarian society that has been in a steady state of equilibrium, where there is no increase in income per capita over time, or what he calls 'an expansionary static society', there comes a point when fertile land becomes scarce. To produce more food for the growing population, more land is used per unit of output. When land was plentiful there was no private ownership and no 'rent' – the price of scarcity. But as soon as land becomes scarce, rent emerges in a Ricardian manner. Those who do not own land, the artisans and merchants, experience a fall in their income as the price of food rises. As land becomes more and more scarce and rent rises, there is a transfer of income from the landless to the landowners, and thus an increase in inequality.

More importantly, because rent is rising there is an increasing demand for fertile land, the only income-earning asset, by those who manage to save more, the rich landowners or the rural accumulators. At the same time, the original landowners, who have a low propensity to save, will sell some of their land for the sake of consumption. Even peasants, who have a strong tendency to retain their land, if they are in debt, may be forced to sell land to the rural accumulators. It is very easy to imagine that if this process continues, land ownership will become concentrated. The extravagant owners in each generation will be selling their land, and their descendants facing higher food prices will eventually be forced to work for the wealthy landowners. Thus, we end up in a class society of landless peasants and few landowners. The latter come to rule over the former.

Meanwhile, the third class, the artisans, the handicraft people and merchants still sell their products but their real incomes decline with rising food prices. However, they sell their products less and less to one another and the landless peasants and more and more to the feudal lords, who live in luxury and great mansions. As Brenner (1978, p 126) points out, 'to attract and make coherent a military following, the lord's household had to become a focus of lavish display and conspicuous consumption'. In consequence the artisans produce the increasing amounts of luxury goods and weapons needed by the escalation in size and complexity of armies built into the warfare system of feudalism.

A third theory explains the emergence of feudalism after the collapse of a strong central government, as in the case of the fall of the Roman Empire (Coulborn 1965; Pryor 1980). Starting with a weak central government and a peasant community with weak kinship ties, control by the more economically and politically powerful feudal lords becomes more difficult to resist. The absence of a central government accompanied by the breakdown of law and order and the consequent increase in personal insecurity made a feudal arrangement advantageous both for the peasants (serfs) and the military group (the landlords). The peasants provided the required agricultural surplus for the military group and, in return, the latter offered security and justice.

A fourth theory suggests that feudalism arose with 'the concurrent development of a strong central government, which imposes high taxation on the peasants (Pryor 1980). An increase in taxation economically weakens the peasantry and forces them to acquire loans from the rich landlords. This leads to the accumulation of debt by peasants, sales of their land and eventually to serfdom. Further, the need for reliable military force by the state (king) and the desire of landlords for a more stable labour force are met by the state by giving permission to enserf the peasants on the land. The role of the central government in the development of serfdom is clearly illustrated in the case of Russia in the fifteenth and sixteenth centuries, when the government was engaged in long wars and required large forces that it found impossible to support from tax revenue alone (Domar 1989). The government assigned lands to the military men (servitors) who were expected to use peasant labour for their maintenance and the financing of their weapons. However, because of shortage of labour relative to the supply of land, the government gradually restricted the freedom of peasants by the middle of the seventeenth century. The plentiful supply of land could not yield high rent. The scarce factor was labour. Hence, it was the ownership of peasants not land that could yield a rent or a surplus for the servitors. The Russian experience shows that without strong government intervention serfdom could not have emerged under conditions of scarce labour and plentiful supply of land.

Yet another theory suggests that feudalism emerged from a slave economic system, because it is economically and militarily superior in the long run (Pryor 1980). Proponents of this theory argue that slave economies are static and have low agricultural productivity. In contrast, feudalism first provided greater incentives for greater production to those actively carrying out agricultural work and for the introduction of technological change. Second, feudalism solved the problem of the supply of labour on a long-term basis. It is often argued that in a slave economy increased labour could be obtained only by buying more slaves, overlooking the fact that slaves could be bred like cattle as in the southern states of the USA. Pryor (1980, p 64) maintains that 'the slave population could never be homeostatically stabilised; the economy rested on the possibilities of obtaining more slaves; feudalism did not have this population problem'.

Clearly, there is considerable overlapping and inconsistency in the above theories of the origins and development of feudalism, reflecting the enormous diversity of circumstances in which feudalism emerged across time and space. Nevertheless, the most common feature of all types of feudalism is the extraction of the agricultural surplus on a regular basis for supporting the military establishment and for the maintenance of the upper classes, the king and the landlords. The importance of the agricultural surplus has prompted Hicks (1977, pp 23–4) to describe the feudal economy as the 'Revenue Economy', or rather the 'Primitive Revenue Economy', which has a 'peculiar place in the history of economic thought… in the system of ideas of the Physiocrats'. The importance of the agriculture surplus for the survival of the system raises the questions of who decides on the size of the surplus, how this decision is made, what information and criteria are used for determining the magnitude of the surplus and the methods used for appropriating it. These questions are discussed in the next five sections.

III

The 'classical' feudal decision-making structure was 'hierarchical' but not necessarily centralised. Perhaps, it would be more accurate to describe it as 'polycentric'. Bloch (1962, p 443) argued that because of the rudimentary nature of the hierarchy, feudalism was an 'unequal' rather than a hierarchical society. Hence, it might be more meaningful to talk about the concentration (diffusion) rather than the centralisation (decentralisation) of decision-making power. Indeed, under early or classical feudalism, power became concentrated in the hands of anyone strong enough to defend himself and his dependants and to subjugate other people. Feudalism, according to Bloch (1962, p 443), 'meant the rigorous economic subjugation of a host of humble folks to a few powerful men'. Historically, the degree of (de) centralisation or concentration varied across countries and time. The structure was evidently more centralised in Japan, China and Russia than in Western Europe (Coulborn 1965).

In Japan, for example, the officials regulated private and public lives down to the finest details. This was reinforced by the caste system that ranked and segregated people by codes of dress, the kinds of houses they lived in and even what they ate. Moreover, the decision-making structure was more centralised in some countries in the early stages and more generally in later stages known as 'state feudalism'. At any rate, the ruler or king was formally at the top of the hierarchy, the feudal landlords in the middle, and the peasants, artisans and traders at the bottom. A notable feature of the feudal hierarchy was the network of personal ties of dependence extending from the top to the bottom. Each man 'belonged' to a higher man or was a vassal to another. In this hierarchical organisation of vassalage, 'a vassal was at once a subject and master, a dependent on a more powerful man and protector of humbler ones' (Bloch 1962, pp 220, 1480).

In general, the *de facto* decision-making power was with the local lord. It was local rather than central, though the idea of central government was always present (Strayer 1965, p 17). The feudal lords performed most functions of government. The king had no real power over the country as a whole. His power was largely confined to the domain of his lands, where he was lord over his vassals, like other landlords. However, since the lords were in charge of the military and maintained law and order in their districts, it was in the king's interests to form coalitions with the more powerful lords to keep them on his side and to keep the peace among warring feudal lords. The authority of the centre thus depended on the personal ability of the king to form alliances and on his leadership skills. Decision-making power was decentralised or, rather, diffused among the feudal lords and the king, through a mixed process of cooperation and subordination. In due course, the *de facto* powers of the feudal lords became *de jure* and then inherited by their descendants. Thus, the decision-making structure became customary and thereby feudalism was transformed into a mixed system of custom and command.

It is important to emphasise that the feudal decision-making authority was 'personal' rather than functional. This meant that there was little separation and specialisation of functions. For example, the military leader was usually an administrator and the administrator was usually a judge (Coulborn 1965, p 5). Feudal lords had powers over many decision areas. As in the customary economy, there was no clear distinction between political and economic decision-making power. Political, economic, social and religious institutions and decisions were intertwined. Politically powerful lords were also wealthy landlords. Their wealth was derived from, or more often, maintained by their political power. Similarly, the political dependence of a weak king on the church and the feudal lords had an economic analogue in the form of the way in which the agricultural surplus was extracted from the cultivators. Since the king was remote from the source of the surplus, except his own estate, it was sensible for him to leave this important decision to the local lords who had local knowledge concerning the quantity and quality of the output annually produced. The lords collected the surplus, took their share and then passed the residue to the king. Thus, the most important single decision on which the whole system depended was decided by the feudal lords and not by the king or the centre. For this reason feudalism has been associated for part of its history, at least, with forms of political decentralisation and economic fragmentation.

Under this form of feudalism, with a simple administrative structure of vassalage and personal dependency, the centre was in danger of disappearing or becoming irrelevant from a lack of effective control over the surplus and its source. Naturally, as Hicks points out, an ambitious or determined ruler will try to assert his authority when he sees that his income is diminishing, but lack of information and effective means of enforcing his decisions and wishes will prevent him from extracting the maximum surplus from the cultivators. To do so, he must in the long run, create a line of communication with appropriate feedback mechanism and chain of command to guarantee the income he needs. In Hicks's words, 'the ruler must create a civil administration, a bureaucracy or civil service' (Hicks 1977, p 18). Historically, this was precisely what happened not only in Europe but also in Japan and China, where simple feudalism was transformed into 'state feudalism' or 'bureaucratic feudalism' (Coulborn 1965). The development in Japan is well described by Reischauer (1965, p 33):

> The vast majority [of local warriors] were becoming divorced from the land, receiving their economic support not in terms of local holdings, but as specific quantities of rice produced from the lord's land... they were becoming hereditary salaried officials and officers in the service of the lord. The feudal class was on the way to becoming a hereditary bureaucracy entrusted with the diverse government functions of highly organised and in some ways economically advanced realms.

Clearly, the movement was away from personal ties and dependency and towards more specialised departments with an increasing proportion of the surplus channelled into the hands of the state, which used it to carry out its expanding functions. In this latter stage of feudalism, rights and duties of both lords and vassals were more clearly defined and regulated.

The lord continued to be the government in his own county. He made all the important decisions regarding production, distribution and consumption. He had the power to evict the peasant from his estate if the latter was unfaithful or acted in any way that was deemed harmful to the landlord. As a class, the peasants were not completely powerless, especially in times of labour shortage, but as an individual the peasant was at the mercy of his lord. Thus, the system implied mutual but unequal dependency and patronage between the vassal or peasant and the lord. The peasant was to serve the lord faithfully and provide him with a surplus, and in return the lord was to provide protection and maintenance. Despite their potential collective power, the peasants remained subject to their lord under different forms of feudalism and under different regimes of surplus extraction, whether through direct labour (enserfment) or rents paid either in kind or money. Feudal lords had the right to command and judge the peasants.

IV

Feudalism being a mixed system of custom and command, it is reasonable to deduce that the corresponding procedure would be rather authoritarian with an element of consultation at the higher levels of the hierarchy, between the king and the great lords and between the lords and their vassals. At the lower levels, there would be little consultation between the lord and his peasants. This is consistent with the common conception of feudalism as a hierarchically organised system of peasant subjection and military vassalage. Indeed, given the prominence of military functions and the frequency of warfare in feudal societies, we would expect an authoritarian approach to decision-making.

But the king was no autocrat or dictator, at least, in classical feudalism. The poor communication channels and his dependence on the feudal lords, for financial and military resources, would not have allowed him to dictate to them. Whether he liked it or not, he had to share his powers not only with his great vassals, his junior partners, but also with the clergy. Indeed, in the central Middle Ages the church dominated both the public and private lives of citizens. The distribution of decision-making power between the king and the church, on one hand, and between the king and his 'subordinates' or junior partners, on the other, varied across time and space depending on the ability of the king and circumstances. However, as Herlihy (1970, p 207) points out, 'the principle that power should be shared and decisions based on consultation among those who held it remained central to feudal government'. The king would have consulted at least with the clergy and the more powerful lords on matters that affected them and the country as a whole. Failure to consult with them would be interpreted that the king is growing too strong and this would be a signal for the great lords to check the powers of the monarchy.

In the feudal hierarchy of vassalage, the vassal was obliged to give advice to his lord and, in turn, the lord was expected to consult with his vassal. The obligation of advice and consultation gave rise to courts of justice attended by vassals. According to Strayer (1965, p 23):

important decisions were made by the lord and his vassals, meeting in informal councils which followed no strict rules of procedure. It was easy for an energetic lord to make experiments in governments; for example, there was constant tinkering with the procedure of feudal courts in the eleventh and twelfth centuries in order to find better methods of proof.

Similarly, Ganshof (1952, pp 153–4) has argued that:

the same duty of giving counsel, and the custom which required that the lord should consult his vassals before taking any important decision, played an essential part in the formation of 'estates' and other organisations representing particular classes of society in the course of the three last centuries of the Middle Ages.

Clearly, the basic institution of vassalage, which defined the rights and duties of ruler and ruled, retained the idea that the subject had rights, which he could defend against his feudal lord.

Although there was some consultation process among the higher levels of the feudal hierarchy, there was hardly any at the lower levels. It is unlikely that the lord would have consulted with his serfs or tenants on matters of production and distribution of the output of his estate, though he would have consulted with them on, or even delegated to them, the 'when' decisions: when to sow, plough, weed and harvest the crop. He might have consulted with them on what to produce and how, but would not have delegated such decisions as characterise an independent farmer, not a dependent serf or peasant. Even an independent farmer living in the village community was very much restricted in the rotation of his crops and the time when sowing and harvesting should begin (Viljoen 1974, p 107).

As in the case of the decision-making structure, custom and tradition played an important role in determining procedures and ways of doing things. According to Bloch (1962, p 248) 'the relationships of the lord with the tenants were regulated only by the custom of the manor'. So true was this that 'in France the ordinary name for rents was simply "customs" and that of the person who owned them "customary man"'. The relationship between the lord and the peasant varied across time and place. Indeed, it is useful to think of feudalism as a continuum of lord-and-peasant relationships beginning at one end with strong elements of custom and command, where the serf or peasant is little more than a slave, the relationship then developing into a weak form of bargaining or contract between the lord and the peasant, and finally a market-like relationship emerging where the peasant himself makes the decisions regarding the product mix and consumption, but is still dependent or controlled by the lord – a relationship that may be characterised as a mixture of competition and command.

Historically, there was a major transformation of the procedure or the manner in which the surplus was extracted from the cultivators. In general, there was a reduction of rents, represented by compulsory labour services and an increase in payment of rents in kind, which were finally replaced by money payments. This was a reflection of the more general trend beginning in the central Middle Ages when money came to dominate economic transactions to an ever-increasing extent. In consequence, the form of dependence on the lord changed and eventually disappeared with the decline of feudalism. The process was, however, neither linear nor uniform across countries. According to Bloch (1962 , p 279) 'some serfs while remaining serfs had got their obligations based on a contractual basis'. After the collapse of serfdom in England, the lords had little choice but to enter into new forms of relationship with their tenants characterised by contract. As Brenner (1978, p 133) states, 'the peasants' success in freeing themselves from the landlord controls had allowed them to take advantage of the very high ratio between land and labour from the fourteenth century to establish low rents'. Thus, once the peasant became free he could exploit the conditions of the market to his advantage, to decide, or to have a big say in determining, the size of the surplus to be handed to the landlord. In the absence of freedom of mobility, the peasant could not influence the size of the surplus irrespective of the land–labour ratio. He would simply be commanded to work for the landlord or deliver a fixed amount of the output. However, the size of the surplus that the lord and, more importantly, the centre extracted from the peasants depended, to a large extent, on the information network and communication channels.

V

Communication channels under feudalism were difficult and inadequate; information flows were constantly congested and in many instances did not reach the intended recipients; and when they did they were much delayed and distorted. Thus, decisions were based on imperfect, false and outdated information. Apart from this technical problem, there was the human problem of transmitting accurate information from subordinates to superiors. There would be strong motivation for weak and dishonest vassals to misinform their lords by suppressing unpleasant information and passing on information that the lords would like to hear. A wise king or lord would try to find an independent or an alternative source of gathering information about his subjects.

The main problem, which faced the king or the centre, was how to get accurate information about the number of cultivators and their output in order to extract the required surplus. For this purpose, the centre relied on the information network of protective relationships. Since the lord at every level of the hierarchy was answerable to his superior, he obtained from his subordinate the required information concerning the productive capacity of the estate. Information on the size of the surplus lay chiefly with the local lords. It was the possession of this information that gave them greater decision-making power *vis-à-vis* the king. A great lord who possessed a number of estates would move with his entourage from one of his estates to another not only to inform himself but also, as Bloch (1962, p 63) points out, 'to consume the produce on the spot, for to transport it to a common centre would have been both inconvenient and expensive'. Moreover, the need for the lord to visit his estate and to see for himself the produce may have something to do with the fact that the majority of landlords were incapable of studying personally a report or an account.

The king might not know what was going on in his kingdom or county, but his officials would have some information. It is recorded in the Dialogue concerning the Exchequer, which was written by Richard Fitzreal, Bishop of London, probably in 1177, that 'the officials of the royal household had an accurate knowledge of those counties from what was due, or various types of meat, or fodder for the horses and other necessities' (Herlihy 1970, p 40). The important question is whether or not the officials would have passed on this information accurately to the king. It is also recorded by the Bishop of London that:

> when the peasants protested to the payment of rents in kind, since they had to transport them from their own homes to many parts of the realm, the king heard their complaints and upon the state advice of his barons, he dispatched to the realm men whom he knew to be most prudent and discreet for this task. These men canvassed the individual estates and inspected them with their own eyes; they estimated the value of payments in kind which were paid for them, and they converted it into a sum of money. For the total of all the sums which derived from all the estates in a single county, they made the sheriff of that county responsible before the Exchequer, adding that he should pay according to scale, that is, six pennies over and above each pound of coined money (Herlihy 1970, p 341).

Thus, different ways and means were devised by the centre to acquire information about the conditions of the estates for the purpose of extracting the surplus.

At the lowest level of the hierarchy, the peasants themselves possessed a wealth of information concerning production conditions of the estates. They also knew exactly when to plough, to sow and to harvest. The proper use of this knowledge is important for productivity. A wise and prudent landlord would look after his peasants so that he could benefit from their accumulated knowledge. On the other hand, exploitation and harsh treatment of peasants encouraged them to shirk their duty and conceal their productive capacity. Peasants developed a high degree of cunning whereby they obeyed the letter but not the spirit of the command of their lords.

It is clear that information flows from the local level to the centre were slow, inaccurate and outdated. But, it has to be remembered that 'the regard for accuracy... the respect for figures, remained profoundly alien to the minds even of the leading men of that age' (Bloch 1962, p 75). Under these circumstances the 'rationality' or the quality of decisions suffered, as is made abundantly clear in the next section.

VI

The chief objective of the feudal system, and hence the criterion underlying economic and political decisions, was the maintenance of regular supplies for the upper classes both to maintain themselves and to defend the country or region from foreign invaders or nearby feudal lords. As already noted, the surplus must have been first extracted by force of command and then – with the passage of time – force was replaced by custom. However, neither custom nor command is conducive to rational economic calculation, which requires scarcity prices and other types of information, particularly comparative knowledge. Scarcity prices can be generated through the market mechanism or the competitive principle, or obtained through linear programming, but neither mechanism, or tool, was available under feudalism. In a single commodity world, as in the famous 'corn model' of Ricardo (Hicks 1965), meaningful calculation can take place in physical terms, without the need for a value system or relative prices. There would be no difficulty in calculating the rate of surplus or profit, especially when peasants receive a subsistence 'wage' in the form of the composite commodity 'corn'. Thus, in a simple agricultural output consisting of relatively few products, custom backed by command remained the chief mechanism for determining production levels and distribution (extraction of the surplus). Nevertheless, the lords on occasions could vary the size of the surplus by fiat. As Brenner (1978, p 9) states: 'the lords were able to dictate the outcome according to their needs – deciding to tighten up vis a vis the peasants where labour was scarce, the opposite when it was plentiful'.

In the absence of relative prices to permit conscious calculation of costs and benefits, rules of thumb would be used to determine the size of the surplus. Such rules were usually based on some convention. For example, in Japan, as a rule, roughly half of the produce of the land was collected as taxes for the support of the government. These taxes from the estates of the feudal lords provided the bulk of the central government's income (Reischauer, 1965, p 33). In France in the fourteenth century, according to Bloch (1962, p 207), 'there was a tendency to substitute a fixed scale of tariffs for variable payments, the amount of which was arbitrarily fixed in each case or decided after difficult negotiations'. Moreover, the value of the annual revenue brought in by the estate was adopted as the norm and was uninfluenced by monetary fluctuations. Where, on the contrary, the rates were fixed in terms of cash, as in England, the tax was eventually subjected to progressive devaluation, which affected all payments that were permanently fixed. In fact in the twelfth century in England according to the Dialogue concerning the Exchequer, when payments were made to the royal household 'according to the accustomed measure for each commodity, the royal officials credited the sheriff by converting their values into monetary terms. Thus, for a measure of wheat suitable to make bread for one hundred men, they assigned one shilling; for a ram or for a sheep four pennies' (Herlihy 1970, p 40). These were conventional or customary prices used for the purpose of accounting and control, not for the allocation of resources.

From a long-term perspective, the basic criterion for determining the size of the surplus would have been that enough of the output must be left to the cultivators of the land to survive and reproduce their numbers. Given the force of custom and tradition, the subsistence needs of the individual peasant would not vary from year to year. However, variation in output due to climatic factors and long-term variation in population would have significant effects on the size of the surplus.

The absence of economic calculation and hence the neglect of allocative efficiency had little or no influence on the survival of the lord and his peasants. The landlords were much more interested in the 'prestige' of landholding than in 'profit' or productivity (Pryor 1980, p 60). They were not producing under competitive conditions. So long as production generated a surplus over and above the subsistence of the cultivators, life on the estate would go on. Similarly, there was little or no pressure to increase productivity or to innovate, since survival depended on the availability of the surplus, not on being able to compete in the marketplace. The bottom line was to produce enough to cover the costs (the subsistence of the cultivators) and a minimum level of consumption for the non-labouring class. Nevertheless, there is some evidence that producers were concerned about minimising costs and avoiding unnecessary waste. This is reflected in the development from the mid-thirteenth century of the art of bookkeeping to control and monitor business enterprises and trace cases of embezzlement (Viljoen 1974, p 131).

VII

The enforcement of decisions was effected through a mixture of command or coercive force possessed by the feudal lord and custom backed by some kind of judicial procedure and supernatural sanctions. Coercive force consisted in evicting the tenant off the land and hence subjecting him to loss of livelihood. At the same time, the landlord needed the peasant to produce the required surplus and the peasants relied on the lord for economic and political security and justice. The mutual dependence of interest as well as custom and command ensured that decisions regarding production and distribution of the surplus were implemented. Moreover, the peasants living in a village community had obligations to one another and had to abide by the decisions of the community on many locally important matters.

The command principle is not always coercive or does not always seem so to the recipient. Commands if they are not too harsh come to be accepted as the norm, as in a military organisation. In the feudal system, the peasant delivered a surplus or made a contribution to the landlord provided it was regarded as fair and reasonable. Indeed, as soon as society divides itself by manual labour, there must be a contribution or taxes. As Hicks (1977, p 17) suggested, we should think of taxes paid to the ruler as rights to which he is entitled, as part of some customary system.

More importantly, given the need for protection and security of the peasant, it is not unreasonable to think that the peasant would have been quite content to provide the surplus for the landlord in exchange. It has to be remembered that the need for security was paramount in the feudal period as life was extremely insecure. Plundering raids, highway robbery, theft and injustice were frequent occurrences. This was presumably the result of the decline of kinship ties and clan relations. Consequently, neither the state nor the family provided adequate protection for the individual. The need to be protected and sheltered was an important incentive to work for the lord. The insecure peasant would have been quite content to serve his lord. Indeed, in many present-day developing countries, where the legacy of feudalism is still strong, peasants still offer the best part of their crops or the first fruits to the local 'lord' to obtain favour, or as a prelude to a request for protection and justice.

The problem of providing effective incentives for the lower classes was made easier for the feudal lords by the ruling ideology and religion. The feudal period was an age of religious fervour and of faith. In all types of feudalism religion was a dominant factor that influenced the motivation and behaviour of ordinary people. A specific code of feudal ethics, which emphasised loyalty, obedience and social acceptance of what faith had to offer, was gradually evolved. People were told that their rewards were in heaven and their duties on earth were to pray and work. Moreover, work was viewed as the concrete embodiment of the creative personality of the artisan, a reward in itself, not requiring much incentive.

At the upper levels of the hierarchy, a different incentive system was in operation. The king, in order to obtain the support and services of the great officials, would grant them an estate, on a temporary basis, which, if exploited directly or in the form of taxes levied on the cultivators of the soil, would enable them to provide for their needs. At the lower level of the hierarchy, the small landlord retaining armed followers or farmhands would have to feed and clothe them in return for their services. Incentives for officials were not in the form of salaries. As Bloch (1962, pp 157, 192) points out 'economic conditions precluded the introduction of a vast system of salaried officials... an office was its own salary. The count not only took a third of the fines in his own area, he also received certain estates'. However, in late feudalism, a trend towards salaried officials was beginning to emerge.

It is quite clear that under the feudal system of vassalage, a man's livelihood and survival depended largely on the goodwill of another superior man. This system of personal dependence applied to all social classes. The lord was the man of the king and the peasant was the man of the landlord. In many cases those who commended themselves to new masters sought from them not only protection but also some material rewards. Since the powerful landlord was also a wealthy man, those who sought his protection also expected him to contribute to their support. However, the system of hierarchical personal dependence created much mistrust and dishonesty between lords and vassals, superiors and subordinates. Commands were often evaded, and the appeal to the ruling ideology and divine sanctions was one of the few restraints that compelled men to do their duties and obey their masters. It was precisely this system of personal dependence that was later attacked by Adam Smith for generating all sorts of vice, and against which the virtues of the market system were emphasised.

VIII

Feudalism, as an economic system, was bound to decline or to be transformed into 'higher' and more complex system(s). From our perspective, its decision-making process was inadequate to cope with the growing economic changes, including the need for specialisation, competition, valuation and the maintenance of a regular revenue for the central authority. It is worth while examining these changes and the reasons for the failure of the system to deal with them. This is also important for understanding the historical bifurcation of feudalism into two economic systems. As in the case of the origin of feudalism, the historical literature suggests numerous causes for its decline. For our purpose, however, we focus on four of them.

First, the resumption of European trade with the East, especially after the Crusades, led to a greater volume of internal trade, which, in turn, encouraged greater division of labour and further trade. The growth of trade encouraged landlords to change from labour-service rents to rents in money or produce, which could be sold on the market and thus allow the landlords greater flexibility in consumption of a wider range of luxury items. Further, money or produce rents permitted greater absentee ownership and thus weakened the customary and personal command relations between lord and peasant, and thereby strengthened market-like relations. The peasant gradually came to regard himself as the owner of his holding and to resent any service that he had to render to his landlord. However, the competitive principle was still too weak to have a significant influence on economic decisions, particularly innovative decisions. The landlord and peasants of an estate could still survive without having to innovate or adopt advanced techniques developed in another estate. The long-term result of the failure to innovate led 'to a tendency toward exhausting the means of production, especially soil exhaustion, and ultimately of the labour force itself' (Brenner 1978, p 176).

Second, the developments brought about by the growth of external and internal trade led to the rise of the city state and subsequently the mercantile system. However, the development of commercial activity within the feudal society did not lead to systemic change. As Brenner (1978, pp 129–30) argues, 'the character of town production was largely shaped by the system of needs by the feudal class for weaponry and luxury goods production... a large number of medieval towns were originally established and controlled by the nobility to meet their needs'. Similarly, Dobb (1963, pp 87–90) maintains that 'merchant profits in the long-run tended to become politically based. Thus far from subverting the feudal order, the merchants very often became its bulwark'. Although the development of towns and cities was neither necessary nor sufficient for the decline of feudalism, it provided a market for land-intensive, labour-saving agricultural products, such as wool and meat, and new handicraft goods. The increase in product mix made it necessary to calculate opportunity costs and benefits in order to decide which product is more profitable. This required a proper valuation system or a set of scarcity prices, which could not be generated by custom and command. Incidentally, the idea of 'opportunity costs', which is associated with modern (neoclassical) economics, was not entirely unknown in the age of feudalism (Bernardelli 1961). In any case, the 'commercialisation' of feudal society and the increasing use of money provided greater incentives for peasants, artisans and merchants to increase their income, and thus potentially a greater source of revenue for the central government to tap, thereby weakening the landlords.

Third, the feudal decision-making structure could not cope with the growing expenses of defence resulting from changes in techniques of warfare. This led the state (king) to centralise its finance, to extract the peasant's surplus directly and forcefully by taxation. The growing importance of central government combined with the growth of trade weakened feudal ties and changed the methods of extracting the surplus away from feudal lords and towards village communities, which were made responsible for the collection of royal taxes. Moreover, the greater police power assumed by the state reduced the need for peasants to obtain protection and justice services from the landlord. The rise of a strong state led to the emergence of better organised and more centralised administration supported by mercenary armies and by a salaried bureaucracy.

Fourth, the price revolution of the sixteenth century, caused by the inflow of gold and silver from South America, led to a rise in prices greater than wages. This resulted in a significant increase in the accumulation of merchant capital and subsequent emergence of capital markets and the industrial revolution. As the focus of attention shifted from rural to urban centres, from agricultural to industrial production, the political and economic influence of the landlords declined, and impersonal market relations gradually replaced personal feudal ties and dependence, just as feudal ties had gradually replaced kinship ties.

It is quite clear from the above discussion that towards the end of feudalism two major trends were emerging, or two alternative routes for the transformation of the feudal system into two more complex economic systems. The first is the market or competitive route, which took two or three centuries to evolve in Western Europe, and culminated in the industrial revolution, whose central feature was the development of markets for fixed capital; hence the rise of capitalism. The second is the bureaucratic route, which was followed by Russia after the October revolution. Since the bureaucratic solution depended primarily on the command principle to coordinate and enforce the numerous decisions taken at higher levels of the decision-making structure, it makes sense, as we have already suggested, to analyse the decision-making system of the Soviet-type economy in the rest of this chapter.

IX

By describing the former Soviet-type economy as a command economy, we do not wish to give the impression that all or even the most important decisions were determined at the centre and imposed in an authoritarian manner on subordinates. That would make the Soviet-type system a pure or an absolute command system that would not have functioned at all. An important feature of the Soviet-type decision-making system that is not captured by the pure command model was the wide gap between the *de jure* and *de facto* system. It may be that central decision-makers would have preferred to have had control over all the important decisions, but they had the time, the information and expertise to make only a few decisions. Paradoxically, the more decisions they made the less control they had over them. There had to be some delegation of authority and hence some decentralisation. There is an 'optimal' degree of (de) centralisation that varies across time and space. Indeed, as Grossman (1963, p 107) observed: 'The chief persistent systemic problem of a command economy is the finding of the optimal degree of centralisation (or decentralisation) under given conditions and with reference to given social goods'.

In the following analysis of the Soviet-type decision-making system, we focus on the former Soviet Union both because it was the leading economy of its type and it had the longest history. The Soviet command model was more or less imposed on Eastern Europe after World War II and was adopted in China and other countries. However, with the passage of time important changes were made to it across countries to meet their special needs and circumstances. For example, decision-makers in Eastern Europe gave far more attention to foreign trade than their counterpart in the Soviet Union and China. At any rate, by the time the Soviet 'command' model was abandoned in the late 1980s and early 1990s, the differences in decision-making processes of respective countries were quite significant, almost 'systemic'. Indeed, at that time the Soviet-type economies could be ranked on our decision-making continuum, arguably with Albania to the left of all other economies and Hungary to their right.

The formal Soviet-type decision-making structure was highly but, even under Stalin, not thoroughly centralised. Nevertheless, the degree of centralisation was well above the optimal level. The centre set the economic and non-economic objectives and determined the policy decisions, in the light of which other decisions were made by subordinates. Such policy decisions included the distribution of national income between saving (investment) and consumption, the allocation of investment funds among the key sectors of the economy, the levels of exports and imports, exchange rates and – within limits – the distribution of personal income. To be enforceable these decisions were spelled out in detail by the planners and passed down through the administrative hierarchy to the state-owned enterprises. Subordinate decision-makers and planners spent much of their time performing the day-to-day task of matching the supply and demand for each commodity and the inputs and outputs of enterprises in order to achieve 'material balances' or a minimum degree of coherence without which the economy would not function – a task that seems automatically and effortlessly solved by the market.

Because of the separation of decision-making, planning, information flows and administration, the bulk of detailed decisions were made at lower levels, including the state-owned enterprises. Contrary to popular perception, enterprises were not passive recipients of 'commands' (decisions) from superiors. They often took the initiative in preparing their draft plans by specifying their resource needs and expected outputs. Even when they received labour and equipment utilisation norms, they were allowed to introduce correction factors to take account of local conditions, not known to superiors. In addition, enterprise managers had considerable independence in classifying and grading employees in terms of job professions, skills ability and experience. This had a considerable bearing on the enterprise wage fund, costs of production and prices (Haddad 1972). More importantly, enterprise managers had the right to defend all their proposals through negotiations with higher authorities. They also negotiated with suppliers and customers over specifications of centrally determined input and output targets. Such negotiations were essentially administrative in nature, despite their formal market-type relationships. Any unsolved disputes arising between the participants were dealt with by higher authorities. Finally, since enterprises typically received fewer resources than they asked for, or found themselves short of certain inputs, they were compelled to find the balance on the 'parallel' market if they were to fulfil the plan and avoid heavy penalties, though this market was not integrated into the formal plan.

Higher decision-makers than enterprise managers played a bigger role in the decision-making process. Of particular importance were decision-making agents at the intermediate level, where much of the bargaining between superiors and subordinates took place. The ministries were the analogues of the feudal lords. In an attempt to determine the locus of decision-making power, it has been suggested that the ministry rather than the enterprise should be defined as the basic decision-making unit, because its plans remained unchanged for the entire planning period; whereas the enterprise plans were frequently changed in an *ad hoc* fashion by the ministry (Granick 1980). Moreover, despite the formal hierarchical structure of decision-making, authority over a particular decision varied across countries and over time. In many cases decision-making power rested with several agents. As Berliner (1976, p 61) has pointed out, 'there is no way of knowing how extensive the role of the enterprise is in this respect, but it appears that a great deal of central decision-making turns out to be enterprise-level decision-making'. Similarly, it has been observed that 'the orders received are written by the recipients' (Lane 1985, p 21).

It is far from easy to measure the degree of (de) centralisation in the Soviet command system. This degree is not a simple unidimensional measure of the effective decision-making power along the vertical line of a single hierarchy. The Soviet system consisted of several hierarchies and numerous bureaucracies overlapping and interacting with one another. These included the decision-making (the Party), the planning (Gosplan), the administrative (Government) and the supply (Gosnab) hierarchies. Vertical shifts along one of those bureaucracies were accompanied by either opposite or similar shifts along other bureaucracies. Moreover, the degree of (de) centralisation depended on the other components of the decision-making process. Hence, before we can assess fully the effective degree of (de) centralisation and the *de facto* decision-making structure of the Soviet-type economy, we need to examine the other dimensions of the decision-making system. In the next section attention is focused on the decision-making procedure.

X

The command principle suggests that decisions flow downwards only from superiors to subordinates. The Soviet decision-making procedure, particularly after Stalin, was much more complex than that. Decisions flowed in all directions: vertically (from top to bottom and sometimes vice versa), horizontally and diagonally. Decisions made by the centre were adjusted by subordinates and proposals made by enterprises were adjusted and sometimes rejected by the centre. Thus, the Soviet decision-making procedure resembled more a vertical bargaining process between superiors and subordinates than simply a command one. Superiors had greater bargaining power than subordinates and, to that extent, there was a strong authoritarian or command element. The stronger bargaining power of the centre and higher authorities was not only derived from fiduciary relationships but also from the virtual monopoly over the supply of material inputs. Since the Soviet system was a supply-constrained system, the supply bureaucracy (Gossnab) was more powerful than other bureaucracies (planning and administrative).

Although the centre had the final say and higher authorities approved the basic indices, including inputs, outputs, prices and wages, and altered or rescinded any decision made, enterprises through the exercise of delegated authority and other means, that we have already alluded to, influenced to a significant extent the approved plan and policy decisions. Nevertheless, despite the intention of both Lenin and Trotsky to combine the advantages of centralised decision-making with democratic procedure ('democratic–centralism'), the Soviet decision-making procedure under Stalin became authoritarian. As Nove (1978, p 372) points out, 'a proposal emanating from a higher level could not be queried, even by those who knew that it contained grave errors'. After Stalin business-like decisions based on a limited degree of consultation with subordinates and experts became much more common. However, the greater emphasis given to consultation was primarily aimed at mobilising support for and implementing centrally determined objectives and priorities, rather than at formulating decisions.

Up until Gorbachev's Glasnost (openness) Soviet decision-making procedures remained more or less authoritarian and secretive. The absence of accountability, transparency and criticism – attributes that define democratic procedures – created 'false images' in the top decision-makers, who were fed misleading, inaccurate and wrong information about the real world. Superiors relied heavily on subordinates and sycophants who told them what they wanted to hear. There was no independent criticism of policies and decisions that went wrong. In an authoritarian regime, it takes an exceptionally wise decision-maker to realise the danger of being sheltered by sycophants from the awful consequences of any wrong decision he might have taken. Thus, democratic procedures are more crucial in a centralised than in a decentralised decision-making structure. Such procedures not only favourably influence policies and decisions but allow the flow of more reliable information. Further insights into the Soviet decision-making procedure can be gained by looking at the structure of information flows in the following section.

XI

Decision-makers at all levels of the Soviet hierarchy relied on information generated by others. Superiors relied on subordinates to supply them with all types of information, primary and feedback, for their decision-making and 'remaking'. In turn, subordinates depended on commands and 'success indicators' to implement the policies and decisions that they themselves had helped to formulate. Decisions flowed downwards and information travelled upwards. In addition, there were horizontal information flows (between enterprises and subordinates located at the lower levels of the hierarchy), which were necessary to work out the details of decisions handed down by superiors. Thus, corresponding to the decision-making structure there was a structure of information flows. However, the disjunction between the two structures created serious problems of coordination and distortion (Haddad 1994).

These problems were recognised by Soviet policy makers, with the exception of Stalin. Lenin was fully aware of the need for accurate information and negative feedback for improving the quality of decision-making (Hoffmann 1975). He also stressed the need for political and social information to implement existing policies more effectively rather than to help in the formulation of new policies and decisions. Stalin was particularly hostile to any information, which implied that any of his policies should be adjusted. There was censorship imposed on the flows of information. More seriously, he penalised those who brought him negative feedbacks and even executed those who were critical of his policies. Under Stalin the focus was on downward communication and on 'goal-seeking' rather than 'goal-setting' or 'goal-changing' feedback (Hoffmann 1975). It is the Stalinist model that has been commonly identified with the command model, but no sooner Stalin was interred than the system started to change.

Accordingly, Stalin's successors placed more emphasis on upward and horizontal information flows, albeit, the emphasis on goal-seeking as opposed to goal-setting remained. Primary and feedback information was sought mainly from subordinates to clarify legal and technical aspects of a policy decision but not to change it. The increased reliance on upward information flows and relaxation of censorship was dictated by the growing complexity of the economy and the need to pay greater attention to efficient utilisation of scarce resources. This called for more and better information on the availability of resources, technology and the calculation and application of more precise input–output norms (Bornstein 1985). At the theoretical level the concern for efficiency led to the development of theories of system behaviour or 'cybernetics'. Indeed, in the 1960s and 1970s there was a high degree of optimism concerning the usefulness of cybernetics (Zauberman 1975).

The information required by the central and higher decision-makers was collected from subordinates, processed, aggregated and transmitted through the various levels of the hierarchy. In the course of aggregation (or grouping) and communication inevitable distortions occurred. 'Arbitrary' or accounting prices were used to aggregate heterogeneous products. Similar distortions occurred in the downward flow of information, where aggregate targets or commands had to be disaggregated for operational purposes. In addition, given the large number of decision-making levels, there was much delay for the information flows to reach their destination points. By then events on which the primary data were based would have moved on and the transmitted information would be less relevant to both decision-making and implementation. When deadlines were set and heavy penalties were imposed for failure to comply with the set dates, the suppliers would falsify the information flows by cutting corners and by 'generating' their own information.

More seriously, since subordinates were responsible for the implementation of decisions in which they had participated, they had strong incentives to falsify the information about their productive capacity and available resources in the hope of getting easy plans, which they could fulfil and overfulfil and thus earn high bonuses. The proclivity of subordinates to provide self-serving information to superiors made it extremely difficult for higher decision-makers to obtain accurate information both for making meaningful decisions and for measuring the performance of subordinates, particularly enterprise managers. Higher authorities were very much aware of this problem and responded by establishing tighter plans, demanding more output from and supplying less inputs to subordinates. However, the combination of asymmetric information and excessive 'tautness' of plans led to chronic shortages of goods, waste and low-quality products.

Inaccurate and even false information was further encouraged by sycophancy. Typically, subordinates told their superiors what they wanted to hear. Consequently, achievements were exaggerated and costs were underestimated by 'creative accounting', falsification of the record and by suppressing unfavourable information. There was no rigorous system of accounting and auditing to discourage such tendencies. There was also no alternative or independent source of information on the activities of subordinates. The check and balance system that was established at the enterprise level degenerated into a system of collusion of people who were meant to check on each other, the so-called 'familiness' of the party secretary, the chief engineer, the accountant, the trade union leader and the manager.

In short, the Soviet structure of information flows was fundamentally flawed. The information on which decisions were based was imperfect and outdated. More seriously, the flow of new information, which is necessary for innovation, was even more deficient. Enterprise managers found it difficult to persuade their superiors to accept new ideas. In the nature of the case, they were unable to convince them of their potential merits. Bureaucrats everywhere find it difficult to deal with new or non-standard problems. However, this did not mean that the Soviet system did not generate new ideas. On the contrary, there was no shortage of new ideas coming from research institutions. The main problem was one of innovation (to convince the higher levels of the bureaucracy to apply them) and diffusion. This problem is further explored in Section XIII when we discuss the incentives' structure.

XII

Traditionally, decision-makers relied primarily on political considerations, administrative convenience and rules of thumb to guide their choices. The allocation of resources, which was governed by those choices, was calculated in physical or quantitative terms using accounting prices for aggregation. This method was known as 'material balances', which is a crude version of the input–output technique developed by Leontief who had worked on material balances in the Soviet Union before he migrated to the USA. Planners at all levels from the centre (Gosplan) to the enterprise calculated the inputs and outputs of enterprises and supply and demand for most products. The objective was to achieve a minimum degree of balance, coherence and consistency. A plan was said to be consistent if it had met three conditions: (i) each enterprise should receive the inputs it requires; (ii) no enterprise should be asked to produce more of a good than is possible; and (iii) the output of each good should equal requirements. Although these conditions appear quite simple, in practice they were never achieved. Planners had neither the time nor the necessary information to formulate a consistent plan. Ellman (1973) has shown that even in principle it is very difficult indeed to draw a consistent plan. Nevertheless, the system worked through *ad hoc* adjustments and the use of the 'parallel market', which made it possible for enterprises to obtain sufficient inputs to meet their output plans.

Despite its many shortcomings, the method of material balances continued to be the main allocative mechanism. However, as resources became scarcer and objectives more diversified, Soviet planners and economists began to search for efficiency criteria to guide their choices, particularly in the fields of investment and foreign trade. Investment criteria, however, were confined to the choice of techniques of production, how to produce a given output, not what to produce. The two major investment decisions, the volume of investment (saving) and the pattern of investment or choice of industries continued to be a function of politically determined priorities which, in turn, reflected the relative influence of various pressure groups, regional and ministerial demands. To subject these decisions to objective criteria 'seemed like providing an objective basis for judging whether the decisions of the state and party were right, and under Stalin this would be regarded not as reasonable but treasonable' (Nove 1978, p 149). In any case, the two major investment decisions cannot be resolved purely by economic calculation of costs and benefits. This applies particularly to the saving (investment) decision. It has been suggested that even under *laissez-faire* 'saving is one of the most irrational, conventional, and socially motivated of economic activities and consorts ill with the rational, narrowly mechanical, selfish and sensual behaviour which one can use as the image of normal human nature in examining other kinds of decisions' (Bensusan-Butt 1962, p 35).

At first, the application of investment criteria such as 'the period of recoupment' and 'the coefficient of relative effectiveness' seemed purely technical, designed to produce a planned output with minimum costs, not to determine whether or not the output itself should be produced. This was reinforced by the fact that different sectors and industries were given different periods to recoup their investment, without endangering the conventional 'law of preferential growth of heavy industry', which had been the main determinant of the allocation of investment resources among sectors and industries. In reality, the three investment decisions were interdependent; the distinction between what to produce and how to produce could not be sustained. The choice of techniques had implications for the choice of industries. The most efficient technique used meant that more of the inputs used required their suppliers to produce more. In the long run, the most efficient technique would only be determined by having a single period of recoupment to which all industries were subjected. This meant that all industries would compete on the same terms for the available resources, irrespective of whether or not they were heavy or light industries.

The application of investment criteria to the third investment decision, the choice of technique, introduced an element of efficiency, even though it was relative rather than absolute efficiency, into the decision-making process. Similar 'criteria' were introduced into foreign trade to work out relatively the most efficient volume and composition of exports and imports (Boltho 1971). While these criteria were far from being rigorous, they were better than having no criteria at all. In Hungary, for example, the application of foreign trade efficiency indicators revealed that the exports of aluminium products earned less foreign exchange, which was extremely scarce, than the amount used in their production (Balassa 1959).

The lack of accurate information and scarcity prices restricted the use of economic criteria and the use of the social economic calculus. In particular the type of information needed to make rational choices, knowledge of the opportunity costs of resources was hard to get. The absence of real capital markets, even imperfect ones, deprived the decision-makers of a useful valuation system to assess social policy outcomes, and to calculate the costs and benefits and possible trade-offs. The attempt to solve the problem of valuation through the development of linear programming and 'objectively determined prices', for which Kantorovich won a Nobel prize, did not prove to be very fruitful (except in a few microeconomic decisions) owing to inadequate information and processing constraints.

In summary, in the absence of a meaningful valuation system, economic criteria would have been difficult to incorporate into the primitive (manual) procedure of adjusting the thousands of material balances simultaneously. Further, as Grossman (1963, p 109) pointed out, 'a bias against economic rationality or allocative efficiency was built into the command model via the underlying logic of haste'. As a result Soviet decision-makers were prevented from getting the most out of the available resources, which were becoming increasingly scarce. Much waste occurred both at the production (technical–allocative efficiency) and consumption stage (Pareto–distributive efficiency). The failure to calculate the social costs and benefits of major investment projects contributed to several environmental disasters. Moreover, the absence of proper economic calculation introduced an element of rigidity into the system. Resources continued to flow into the same old industries in the same proportions to produce more of the same with the same techniques.

XIII

Even if the decisions made at higher levels were roughly right, the problem of implementation remained a serious one. Indeed, this is the problem that plagued the Soviet command system from its beginning – the problem of motivating workers, enterprise managers and subordinates to correctly apply the decisions of superiors. Information on what motivates people was not seriously considered. It was assumed that subordinates were motivated by the same factors that motivated their superiors, and that people would in general respond positively to 'moral incentives'. If not then legal sanctions and physical coercion would be sufficient to supply their labour. In fact, moral incentives became less and less effective as people became increasingly cynical about the prospects of establishing socialism in the near future. Coercion or negative incentives merely ensured that individual workers provided the minimum effort they could get away with. Similarly, enterprise managers followed the letter of the plan and violated its spirit in order to avoid heavy penalties for failure to fill their plans.

It became increasingly obvious to the system managers that economic incentives were needed to motivate people to work harder and fulfil and overfulfil the plan. Thus 'success indicators' were introduced to assess the performance of subordinates and reward or punish them accordingly. However, a great deal of distortion and waste resulted from the application of success indicators. These indicators encouraged enterprise managers to focus on those targets that were quantifiable and which decision-makers considered the most important, and to ignore others to which no rewards or penalties were attached. For example, when central decision-makers made gross output the leading success indicator, enterprise managers maximised their output without paying much attention to costs; and when cost minimisation was introduced as a supplementary indicator, they maximised their output and minimised costs simply by neglecting quality, services and other features of production that were not quantifiable.

From a long-run perspective and survival of the system, the emphasis on current output discouraged innovation and diffusion of new technology. Since major innovations usually entail a fall in current output due to installation of new machinery, reorganisation of the production process and retraining of workers, managers were reluctant to engage in innovative activity and preferred to produce more of the same with the same techniques. Even on the rare occasions when managers took the risk of innovation, the resulting benefits in the form of higher productivity and better quality were collectivised. Typically, in the next period, higher decision-makers would raise the output target for the innovating enterprises and thereby made it harder for them to overfulfil the new target and obtained the corresponding bonuses.

Looking at the problem of innovation and diffusion from the higher levels, it is difficult to set specific, quantifiable targets that can be effectively transmitted to subordinates. Innovation by command is not feasible except in a few chosen industries, because of the problems of gathering information, monitoring, motivating and coordinating producers and users. Innovation by order might be effective if it were given freely like 'manna from heaven'. However, innovations are produced and their production and reproduction must be motivated by appropriate incentives. We have already argued that the short-run costs of innovations were real to the enterprises, but their long-term benefits were dissipated by the 'ratchet' principle of planning or planning from the higher level. This discouraged enterprises from introducing major changes in their products and processes. Perhaps the best method to encourage innovation is to collectivise the risk (costs) and privatise the benefits, as in those countries that have a high innovation record. In the Soviet-type economies, risks were privatised and benefits collectivised.

In any case, judged by the Soviet success of innovation in a few key industries, the more serious problem seemed to be one of diffusion. The Soviet command system lacked an efficient diffusion mechanism to spread the new technology developed in the few chosen industries. For this a competitive market is needed to ensure that innovators are followed by imitators who refine and improve on new product or process. Alternatively, diffusion can be encouraged through an effective sales strategy. The experience of the machine-building industry in the West shows that its sales campaign is largely responsible for the diffusion of innovation (Rosenberg 1976). The lack of such campaigns in the Soviet-type economies had the effects of imposing technical conservatism on the industry.

Like all hierarchical organisations the Soviet-type economy was plagued by the twin problems of technical–administration and principal–agent. Both of these problems were compounded by asymmetric information, which made it difficult to formulate rational decisions and to design an effective incentive system so as to enforce those decisions. Since there was usually a discrepancy between the interests and objectives of the centre and the periphery or between superiors and subordinates, there was a need to internalise the objectives of the centre by subordinates. To some extent the gap was narrowed through the use of pecuniary and non-pecuniary incentives. But without knowing what motivated subordinates or what their utility function was, it was not possible to design an effective incentive scheme that encouraged honest reporting and genuine fulfilment of plans and decisions made at higher levels. There are two possible solutions for hierarchical organisations to overcome the twin problems. The first is to decentralise, to delegate more decision-making authority and thereby make the hierarchy flatter. The second is to involve subordinates in decision-making or to democratise the procedure. Both of these solutions go some way towards internalising the objectives of the organisation and the centre by the enterprise. But neither solution was seriously attempted before the collapse of the system, except perhaps in Hungary.

XIV

Looked at from the perspective of our decision-making approach, both feudalism and the Soviet economic system had several common features including some common objectives. Both systems were chiefly governed by the command principle, though the Soviet system was much more hierarchical, centralised and bureaucratised than the feudal system. The decision-making structure of classical or early feudalism was more 'polycentric' or concentrated than centralised, since decision-making authority rested primarily with the feudal lords. They determined the most important decision for the system as a whole, namely the size and distribution of the surplus. However, at the higher stage of feudalism decision-making became more centralised. The centre began to assert its authority by establishing specialised departments or a bureaucracy to collect the surplus on a regular basis in order to finance its growing expenditure without relying on the goodwill of the feudal lords. The Soviet system was a modern version of feudalism that had been 'bureaucratised' and centralised to deal with the more complex problems of industrial production. Like that of its predecessor, the primary concern of the centre in the Soviet system was to collect the surplus from the enterprises and consumers and reinvent it in those sectors, which it considered essential for its survival and for the defence of the country. This was the most important decision that had to be made at the centre. The other decisions were largely derivative and were, therefore, left to lower decision-makers in the hierarchy. The ministries exercised influences on the centre and the distribution of the surplus as the great feudal lords. Like the feudal lords, the ministries derived their power from being closer to the enterprise, the source of the surplus, and from possessing information about its existing capacity and future production possibilities. Thus, the Soviet command system has been referred to as 'centralised pluralism' (Nove 1978, p 63) and 'polycentralism' (Roberts 1971, p 197).

The decision-making procedure in both systems was also similar. Decisions flowed downwards rather than upwards (or horizontal) as befits a command system. Consultation between superiors and subordinates was confined largely to higher levels in the two hierarchies. Under feudalism consultation was between the king and his great vassals, and between the lords and their vassals. In the Soviet system, much of the consultation and negotiation took place between the ministries and the centre and between the ministries and associations of enterprises. In both systems the workers and peasants were hardly consulted on any important matters. Because of the complexity of industrial production, the experts played a relatively more important role under the Soviet system. However, the decision-making procedure in both systems remained authoritarian.

The authoritarian character of the decision-making procedure exerted adverse effects on the structure of information flows in both systems. Poor communication channels and imperfect information rendered the process of sound decision-making very difficult indeed. In the Soviet bureaucracy the large number of levels through which information had to travel inevitably created distortions and falsification of the original information, whether flowing from top to bottom in the form of commands or from bottom to top in the form of demands for inputs. Again, because of the complexity of industrial production, the information required to make meaningful decisions at higher levels in the bureaucracy was much more difficult to collect and process than under feudalism, which was characterised by agricultural production that relied mainly on conventional methods and standard decisions.

Decisions under feudalism were based on rules of thumb, customs and norms as well as political considerations. The same 'criteria' were also used in the Soviet system. In addition, given the importance of bureaucracy in the latter system, administrative convenience played a critical role in the allocation of resources. These criteria worked quite well in the early phases of both systems. However, they became increasingly obsolete as resources became more scarce. In both systems the operation of the law of diminishing returns was becoming increasingly evident. To offset its adverse operation better allocative mechanisms and more innovation were needed to get the most out of existing resources and to create new resources. The best way to achieve allocative and creative efficiency is to create a competitive market, which provides a valuation system and creates new products and processes. Such a market will not only reduce the heavy burden of the central authority and enable it to focus on strategic decisions, decisions that cannot be left to lower levels, but it will also make the bureaucracy more efficient and effective. The existence of markets will enable the decision-makers to arrive at meaningful calculations of costs and benefits and possible trade-offs.

More importantly from the viewpoint of enforcement of decisions, the existence of markets provides the possibility of leaving the enforcement of many decisions to autonomous agents operating in the marketplace. Here the market is used as a tool or a servant to implement the plans of the centre. This would go some way towards solving the problem of incentives, which had undermined the Soviet system. Both the feudal and the Soviet system had to rely on commands or force (negative incentives) and moral incentives (ideology and religion) to get workers and peasants to do their duties. In this area the feudal system was relatively more successful than the Soviet system, thanks to the moral authority of the church that reinforced the feudal values of loyalty, obedience and suffering, in the hope of gaining eternal salvation in the next world. The analogous role of the communist party as a 'vanguard' in instilling and developing 'socialist consciousness' was less effective, due to the fact that it did not possess the psychic power of religion and supernatural sanctions.

9. The Competitive Economy

I

Both the customary and the feudal economy had some form of rudimentary markets and some competitive elements, but these had only a marginal influence on the decision-making process and the working of both types of economic system. Economic activity was dominated respectively by custom and command. Cooperation played a relatively significant role in the customary economy and competition became increasingly important in the later stages of feudalism, before the mercantile economy slipped back into some form of a customary economy.

In this chapter, our analysis is focused on the working of the competitive principle, both as a determinant of the decision-making process of autonomous economic agents and as a coordinating mechanism of the economic system. But before we examine the functioning of the competitive economy from the perspective of decision-making, it is important to have an understanding of how the competitive principle came to dominate economic activity via the development first of commodity and money markets and then of factor markets. This is briefly discussed in Section II. Sections III–VIII analyse the competitive economic system in terms of the five components of the decision-making process. Section IX summarises the key points of the chapter and offers some concluding remarks on the advantages and disadvantages of the competitive principle.

II

Arguably, the best account of the evolution of the market economy, the locus of the competitive principle, is given by Hicks in his important but neglected book, *A Theory of Economic History* (first published in 1969). Hicks himself is reported to have said that 'he would like to be known for this book more than for anything else, and that he would even have preferred that the Nobel prize had been awarded for this book' (Klamer 1989, p 175). In his account of the rise of the market economy, Hicks singles out the role of 'the specialised trader' or 'the shopkeeper' as the systemic difference between feudalism and the modern market economy: 'it is specialisation upon trade, which is the beginning of the new world, not the preliminary stages of trading without specialisation' (Hicks 1977, p 25). This is much clearer than the distinction between 'traders' and 'trading' that anthropologists often make. As soon as there is a class of specialised traders or merchants, they will begin to organise themselves into an association or a community. As a result, the economic system becomes more complex. In addition to custom and command, there is now a new element, the mercantile or commercial principle, which coordinates and determines economic activity. The mercantile principle, which has a strong competitive dimension, is characterised by individualism, economic calculation and impersonal relations, in contrast to custom and command.

To survive and flourish, merchants need certain legal and quasi-legal institutions, which can be provided efficiently only by a central authority. They need protection of property and protection of contract. Under feudalism protection of property was guaranteed by custom. Hicks (1977, p 34) reminds us that, since the dominant form of property was a house or a piece of land, there was no dispute regarding ownership. The property owned by merchants consisted chiefly of 'circulating goods', which needed to be identified and legally protected in order to sell them. Protection of contract arises from the possibility that the agreement or contract may not be kept by one party, or expectations may not be realised when delivery is made. Continuous and profitable trade requires that the terms of the contract be enforced. It makes sense for the state to perform these functions in order to reduce risks; otherwise the market economy, consisting of autonomous and anonymous traders who do not have enough mutual trust, will not flourish. The state will be willing to undertake these functions because it will be able to receive a new source of revenue from the merchant class.

Historically, the market economy flourished first in the city states of Western Europe, in the mercantile economies of Florence, Genoa and Venice, though it originated in the eastern Mediterranean, in Tyre and Sidon in Lebanon. The Mercantile economy is defined by Hicks (1977, p 43) as a 'system of trading centres, trading with one another, but ultimately dependent upon trade with the outside world'. In the course of trading, there were from time to time conflicts and disagreements, which on occasions degenerated into costly wars and caused losses in profits. To offset this tendency, agreements with one's rivals to divide the market became more common. As a result 'the mercantile economy slipped into custom: the merchant is accepting a place in the system of customary rights and duties' (Hicks 1977, p 58). Various crafts and guilds developed, which had the effect of blocking entry and reducing competition from newcomers. For this reason the mercantile economy should be placed at the end of the feudal continuum rather than at the beginning of the 'capitalist' continuum.

For the feudal or the mercantile economy to be transformed into a developed competitive economy, other markets and their institutions had to evolve. There must be money, land, labour and (fixed) capital markets. The development of these markets took a very long time and requires tomes to explain. Hicks devotes the great bulk of his book to this development. For our purpose we give the briefest possible explanation based largely on his theory of economic history.

The evolution of money is intimately connected with the development of the market economy. It started as 'a store of value', with a specialised trader, the goldsmith, who held goods such as gold and silver that are easily storable and easily hidden. Barter still prevailed, but with the expansion of trade it became inconvenient and in due course gold and silver became a 'means of payment', and then a 'standard of value'. It is at this point that the state was called in to perform another function, to provide a standard of weight and quality. Hence the term 'sovereign', a term not used by Hicks, even though he recognises that 'money has appeared to be a creation of the state' (1977, p 63). Sovereigns are permanent, uniform and portable. The state or 'sovereign' was willing to perform this function, because it was much more convenient and efficient to have the taxes collected in money rather than in goods.

Since financial transactions are a natural extension of trade dealings, it is very convenient to switch from one to the other. Thus, goldsmiths probably became financial intermediaries. At first traders deposited their profits, their stock of gold and silver, with a trusted goldsmith in order that he should relend to those whom he trusted at a slightly higher fee than he had paid to depositors. When a goldsmith became specialised in such financial intermediation he was already a banker. The second critical stage in the evolution of money and banking came much later when deposits of gold and silver in banks were made transferable either by cheques or notes. It is at this stage that money was changing its character that the bank started to 'create' money, by lending more than it received in deposits. However, cheques and notes were still backed by gold (the gold standard) and were convertible into gold on demand. The next critical stage in the story of the evolution of money and banking came when the money supply was no longer backed by gold. Money became fiat; it could be increased at will without real costs.

Thus, the evolution of the market economy was mainly the creation of traders and financiers, albeit the state provided a favourable institutional environment, which reduced risks and uncertainty associated with exchanges. But until the development of factor markets, the feudal system, the system of custom and command, remained dominant. The impact of commodity and money markets was confined largely to commercial transactions. Production for the market does not necessarily imply the existence of factor markets. The peasant remained tied to the land, and it was only with difficulty that land could be sold. Normally, land changed hands by inheritance, primarily to the first son or nephew (primogenitor) in Europe.

Hicks (1977, pp 109–10) suggested two possible causes for the development of land market: tenant farming, which consisted of leasing land to the peasant for a long period of time, and employment of peasants for wages. Under a system of wage labour, a shortage of labour will raise the wage rate and rents will decline. Landlords will be more eager to sell their land, and the most likely buyers will be the peasants. Although they do not have the money, they are in a position to give a security for loan. If this takes place on a major scale, as was the case in France, then feudalism would have to give way to the free peasantry, free to buy and sell land. Under a system of tenant farming it is possible, according to Hicks, that landlords may find their rent or income reduced (by the departure or actual death of their peasants), and will be willing to sell their land to overcome their financial difficulties. Again, the most likely buyers will be the peasants themselves.

Turning to the development of the labour market, Hicks (1977, pp 127–31) argues that it was ultimately the mercantile principle, the principle of economic calculation, that encouraged this development. Calculating the rate of return on a serf or a slave is extremely difficult, not unlike calculating the rate of profit on a machine. It was much easier for the landlord or the employer to calculate the value of a hired labourer only for his time at work. In addition, 'a free labourer paid on a piece work will certainly tend to be more efficient than a slave, when the slave is given no such incentive'. Thus, high-paid labour in times of labour scarcity can be very productive if well managed. This gave rise to the argument of 'the economy of high wages', which was quite popular in the seventeenth and eighteenth centuries. From the point of view of the employer, the best labour market is the market for casual labour or piece-rate wage; no wage is paid when the labourer is not working.

The next major development in the evolution of the competitive economy was the rise of the market for fixed capital. Fixed capital in the form of machines was hardly used in the industrial output of the mercantile economy. The increase in the range and variety of machines in production is the characteristic feature of the industrial revolution or, more accurately, the capital revolution. It marked a switch from handicraft (manufacture) to mechanised (machinofacture) techniques, and the rise of a new class of capitalists. According to Hicks (1977, pp 144–8), the availability of finance and lower interest rates encouraged investment in machines. Further, the impact of science on the development of new sources of power and machine tools reduced the costs of machines and made them available for a variety of production processes. In our view, the reduction in the production costs of machines is necessary but not sufficient for the outbreak of the industrial revolution. People would invest in machines only when the rate of return on land, or any other income-yielding asset, falls to the rate of profit, the rate of return on fixed capital. In other words, the industrial–capital revolution would not break out so long as the rate of rent is higher than the rate of profit. Since land before the industrial revolution was the main income-earning asset, potential investors, including landlords, rich peasants and merchants, would compete with one another to buy land. This pushes its price upwards and the rate of rent downwards. There comes a point when the rate of rent is equal to the rate of profit, the rate of return on the most productive machines. Potential investors have a new field of investment open to them, and the industrialisation or mechanisation process takes off.

An excellent analysis of how the mechanisation process spread across the entire economy is given by Bensusan-Butt (1962). He starts with the coexistence of handicraft and mechanised techniques, when capitalists would be earning super profits, as prices under competitive conditions are set by the marginal costs of handicraft producers. With the process of capital accumulation continuing, competition between mechanised and handicraft techniques would push out the inefficient handicraft producers in the first industry that was mechanised, and prices and profits in that industry would fall. Now it becomes profitable to mechanise the next industry that yields the second highest rate of profit, and when this industry is fully mechanised, prices and profits will fall again, and the third industry will begin to be mechanised, and so on until all industries have become more or less mechanised, and handicraft industries have disappeared. But the mechanisation process, which may take place sequentially or simultaneously in some industries, continues under competitive pressures. More capital-intensive techniques are introduced to offset the tendency of the rate of profit to fall by raising labour productivity, and the process of capital accumulation continues with the capital–labour ratio in production processes rising.

The impact of capital accumulation on workers is profound. As a result of falling prices in manufactured goods real wages rise, despite the displacement of some labour by capital. In addition, the mechanisation of agriculture following the capital revolution reduces food prices and raises real wages. If real wages rise sufficiently for workers to start saving, some of them would join the capitalist class and begin to participate in the process of capital accumulation. The possibility of workers' saving may prove crucial for the survival of the capitalist system. In its absence the original capitalists would become so wealthy that they might reach the point of 'economic bliss', when all their natural wants are fully satisfied and would thus lose the motive for further accumulation or investment. If that happens the system will end up in a premature stationary state of zero growth, before natural resources are depleted. Alternatively, if wages do not rise manufactured goods would consist mainly of luxury goods for the rich. Inequalities would be so great and conspicuous that workers would revolt and the capitalist system would be overthrown *à la* Marx. Either scenario confirms the general observation that an economic system, which depends on the decisions and behaviour of a few people, will not survive in the long run.

Apart from transforming some workers into 'capitalists', the competitive capitalist system converted the great bulk of the working class from casual to regular employees. Hicks (1977, pp 154–6) argues that despite the long hours and miserable working conditions during the industrial revolution, the worker was better off in the long run owing to the decisive gains of regular employment, which was the direct result of the introduction of fixed capital in the production process. Fixed capital had to be kept continually in use to yield a maximum rate of return. Moreover, regular employment for workers provided favourable conditions for the formation of trade unions as bargaining organisations and for workers to organise themselves politically. Thus, both trade unions and labour parties are the creatures of capitalism.

Finally, a few words should be said about the spread of the capital–industrial revolution. The search for profits under competitive conditions led to the export of the mechanisation process. It is reasonable to assume that the same process, which had destroyed the handicraft industries in the first industrialised country, would invade and destroy one by one the handicraft industries in other countries. When that happens the first industrialised country would lose its absolute but not relative position. Capital would migrate from the capitalists to the less industrialised countries. This carries the possibility that some of the newly industrialised countries might overtake the country that was the first to be mechanised, as happened in the case of the USA overtaking England, the home of the capital revolution. Historically, however, the great bulk of countries failed to industrialise through trade. The reasons for this are complex and do not concern us here. Perhaps a more effective route towards mechanisation, apart from the Soviet-type forced industrialisation, is through direct foreign investment or international integration effected mainly by transnational corporations competing with one another for markets and profits.

III

The decision-making structure of a competitive economy is naturally decentralised. Economic decisions are made by autonomous economic agents, mainly firms and households constrained by their own circumstances and 'the rules of the competitive game'. However, the competitive principle leads to concentration of decision-making authority among a small number of consumers and producers. Competition is essentially a dynamic process that eliminates small and inefficient firms. The history of industries shows that they start with many firms competing with one another, and end up with a few firms. Thus, there seems to be a movement, both historical and logical, from competition among the many ('perfect competition') to competition among the few (oligopolistic competition). This movement is clearly seen in the rise of mergers and take-overs in the USA in the late nineteenth century, the period when competition became cannibalistic in industries with heavy fixed investments. Companies swallowed up others in the hope of achieving a monopolistic position. In order to stop the strong devouring the weak, the state intervened and regulated the working of the market (Kovacic and Shapiro 2000).

The primary function of the state in a competitive economy is to create a favourable environment for autonomous decision-makers to pursue their own interests without endangering the 'common good'. Besides providing the legal and quasi-legal institutions established to protect property and enforce contract, the state in a competitive economy must enforce the rules of fair competition and prevent anti-competitive practices. Another function of the state is to provide public goods such as roads, ports and bridges without which the decentralised competitive system would not function efficiently. It may also provide such welfare services as health and education, which are not only desired in themselves but also have beneficial effects on the economy and society. Finally, the state may manage the economy through macroeconomic policies without directly controlling the activities of autonomous economic agents. Macroeconomic policies are needed, because the decentralised competitive economy is subject to cyclical fluctuations from time to time, or because of coordination failure. If the state performs its threefold functions intelligently, it becomes the major decision-maker in the entire system influencing other decision-makers without destroying the competitive principle. Historically, the developed (market) economies have evolved from the earlier phase of *laissez-faire* competitive economies, with the state playing a minimal role in establishing and enforcing 'the rules of the game', into managed competitive economies, with the state playing an active role and having a great deal of influence on major decisions, including saving and investment and the distribution of income between and within generations. As a result the decision-making structure became more centralised, *de facto*, if not *de jure*.

Within the macroeconomic environment determined largely by the state, producers and consumers compete for scarce resources to maximise their profits or utilities. Theoretically, it is not very clear whether collectively producers or consumers have more decision-making powers. Conventional economic theory maintains that in a 'perfectly competitive' economy consumers are sovereign; they have the final say in determining the volume and product mix of consumer goods and, indirectly by a process of 'imputation', capital goods. The role of producers is to satisfy the demand of 'sovereign' consumers. In reality, consumers are 'free' to choose from a range of consumer goods, whose production is the result of decisions of producers. This applies particularly to new products. Indeed, producers almost always take the initiative to create new demand and then proceed to satisfy that demand employing various persuasive techniques such as advertising and salesmanship. As a result, consumers tend to become passive and not very autonomous choosers. Nevertheless, the conflation of consumer sovereignty with 'free' choice continues, probably because of the widely held belief that the consumer and no one else knows what is best for herself. At any rate, the idea of consumer sovereignty implies a decentralised, democratic decision-making structure.

In modern economies firms by and large determine what to produce and how much subject to constraints of consumers and the government as well as other producers. The concentration of decision-making authority varies across industries and countries. In monopolistic industries there is obviously a high degree of concentration of economic power. In oligopolistic industries decision-making power is concentrated among few firms, while in (perfectly) competitive industries it is distributed more or less equally. There are various ways of measuring the degree of concentration of economic power in industries. The most common indicators are market shares, the level of employment and the rate of profits. In small economies, the degree of concentration of economic power tends to be high, because of economies of scale and scope that favour monopolistic or oligopolistic market structures.

The decision-making structure of a competitive economy cannot be fully understood and assessed without examining the decision-making process within firms. The degree of centralisation varies a great deal from one firm to another. It varies between large and small firms and between different types of firm. According to Neuberger and Duffy (1976, p 142) the decision-making structures of large firms tend to be relatively more decentralised than those of small firms. This has to do with the span of control. Small firms can be easily managed and controlled from the centre, without the need to delegate decision-making authority. Large firms with diverse lines of manufacture need to delegate some decision-making authority to lower levels in the hierarchy. Moreover, the degree of decentralisation within the firm's hierarchy depends partly on the nature of the product market, whether it is volatile or relatively stable. According to Ben-Ner, Montias and Neuberger (1993, p 227) 'while slowly changing markets can be accommodated through decision-making at higher tiers, in rapidly changing markets decentralisation of decision-making may be necessary'.

The internal structure of modern corporations, which are owned by numerous shareholders and controlled by managers, varies significantly. A general distinction is frequently made between the so-called M-form and U-form of internal organisation. The former is the multidivisional form of organisation where each of its divisions deals with the major functions of the corporation and enjoys considerable autonomy. The latter is a unitary form of organisation where the functional division of activities and coordination is conducted at the centre. Moreover, some firms allow their workers to participate in decision-making and profit sharing. In Germany, for example, many firms are obliged to involve workers in the decision-making process at the managerial level. This gives the workers certain rights that traditionally belong to managers or shareholders, and makes the firms less centralised. In general, however, the decision-making structure of modern corporations is centralised and hierarchical. Decision-making power, particularly over short-term decisions, is held mainly by managers. They control production and workers.

There are some firms that are wholly owned and managed by workers. These are rather rare in competitive economies. The most famous labour-owned and labour-managed firm is Mondragon in Spain (Ben-Ner 1988). In such firms the decision-making structure is highly decentralised. Workers make all the major decisions of the firm such as goal setting, investment, the distribution of profits and hiring and firing decisions. In particular, workers can hire and fire their managers, but managers cannot hire and fire workers. Managers tend to focus their attention more on technical–administration problems and other issues such as reducing the free-rider problem among some workers.

In user-oriented firms, which include non-profit organisations, such as social welfare agencies, charities, clubs and consumer cooperatives, decision-making power is largely decentralised and held by managers and employees. Their hierarchical structures are said to be 'flatter' than in comparable proprietary firms. In addition, their internal structures reflect the interests and objectives of both members and those in charge. The objectives of user-oriented firms are focused on the quantity and quality of output rather than on profits (Ben-Ner, Montias and Neuberger 1993, pp 233–5).

Finally, in government-owned firms in competitive economies, decision-making power tends to be held by managers. In some firms management make decisions without any government intervention; in others management has to operate within relatively narrow constraints of accountability, acceptability and transparency. Indeed, 'the behaviour of top management is regulated through the rules that determine acceptable and unacceptable behaviour, and supplemented by monitoring, in degrees that are likely to exceed those in proprietary firms' (Ben-Ner, Montias and Neuberger 1993, p 237). Rules and the monitoring of behaviour in accord with those rules are the main features of bureaucracy for which government-owned enterprises are renowned.

In summary, the decision-making structure of a competitive economy is formally decentralised. Decision-making authority is dispersed among many economic agents. However, the competitive principle leads to concentration of decision-making power among relatively few producers, with consumers playing a passive role. Further, within hierarchical firms, the decision-making structure tends to be centralised or concentrated at the top of the hierarchy. Moreover, partly as a result of the concentration of decision-making authority and the accompanying externalities, the state has over the years assumed a great deal of decision-making power, making the regulated and managed competitive economy significantly centralised.

IV

The decision-making procedure in competitive economies, like the structure, varies a great deal within and among firms and governments. Some adopt more democratic procedures while others follow an authoritarian approach. In addition, many decisions are reached through negotiation and bargaining, and in the case of complex and technical decisions, decision-makers rely on experts. Despite the variety of procedures used, competitive (market) economies tend to be associated with economic freedom and democratic procedures. However, within firms decision-making procedures tend to be more authoritarian than democratic.

In developed competitive economies, governments are democratically elected and are accountable for their policies to the electorate at large. Their policies and decisions are not always transparent being largely influenced by various interest groups and rent-seekers. Nevertheless, the citizens can and do choose between alternative governments, with somewhat different programmes and policies, competing for their votes. The competitive principle works in the political arena in the same way as it does in the economic sphere. It eliminates the inefficient and incompetent party. An opposition party (a potential government) competes with the government by offering alternative policies. However, a party that rules for a long period, owing to a weak opposition or some other reason, will not be under pressure to innovate, even though its decisions are reached through democratic procedures.

There are special circumstances where authoritarian procedures are acceptable, if not desirable, such as during emergency periods when speed and secrecy are crucial. There may be also a case for modernising governments in less developed countries to perform the task of economic development through authoritarian processes and procedures. Major economic decisions, such as the distribution of national income between saving and consumption and the allocation of investment funds among sectors, would have to be made by the 'developmental state' without having to consult the individual citizen, whose interests are generally more short term than those of the modernising government. Such long-term decisions, which are designed to develop the economy and create a favourable environment for autonomous economic agents, need not and do not conflict with the competitive principle. Within the macroeconomic environment created by the authoritarian government, there would still be room for individual consumers and producers to compete with one another and seek their own goals. Indeed, government decisions imposed on autonomous economic agents generally promote as well undermine competition. As economies become more developed with well-established institutional and physical infrastructures, there is usually a shift to more democratic procedures and a multi-party political system.

Although it is perfectly conceivable to combine authoritarian macroeconomic policies with individual freedom to choose what to consume, and/or produce, where and in which occupation to work, economic freedom is frequently equated with the *laissez-faire* competitive (market) economy. Indeed, since Adam Smith markets and freedom have become so closely linked that the term 'free market' has gained currency and has become something of a cliché. But the so-called 'autonomous decisions', the decisions that individuals make without coercion from others, are more often than not moulded by opinion-makers, advertisers and dictated by the fashion of the moment. It cannot be said with certainty that such decisions represent the self-expression and personal development of the individual. The idea that individuals are free to choose what they desire applies only to some people, who have the resources and special skills to exploit the opportunities presented in the market. Thus, while economic freedom is undoubtedly more common in competitive market economies than in command economies, it remains restricted for the great majority of individuals.

The decision-making procedures of firms vary from one firm to another and across industries, and tend to correspond to the particular firm's internal decision-making structure. According to an empirical study of 55 US and 51 Japanese firms, cited by Ben-Ner, Montias and Neuberger (1993, p 225), 'Japanese manufacturing organisations have taller hierarchies, less functional specialisation, less formal delegation of authority but more de facto participation'. In most firms, however, the decision-making procedure tends to be authoritarian with consultation confined to higher levels in the firm's hierarchy and to experts. At the other extreme, in labour-owned and managed firms and in associations, the procedure tends to be democratic. In between the two extremes some firms consult workers, as in the case of Germany, where workers are represented on the management board and participate in decision-making. Also, in user-oriented firms democratic procedures tend to be adopted; employees tend to have more say in the decision-making process than those in public corporations and state-owned enterprises. Generally, there is a trend among corporations towards greater transparency and accountability to all stakeholders including workers. Workers are demanding and having more say in the decision-making process of their companies.

Negotiations and bargaining processes have become common procedures for reaching decisions and are more consistent with the competitive principle than authoritarian procedures. In some countries and certain markets they are also consistent with custom and convention; the buyer is expected to bargain with the seller. Bargaining, as we have noted in Chapter 3, was originally confined to primitive haggling in oriental bazaars, second-hand markets and in labour markets. Now bargaining is extended to other areas such as government dealings with interest groups and welfare organisations. Bargaining procedures are very much influenced by market forces of supply and demand in reaching a decision. Indeed, bargaining has become a very sophisticated technique, an art, involving a degree of strategic thinking as well as possessing psychological knowledge about one's opponent to influence the outcome.

Finally, in competitive economies, some decisions are reached through cooperation and consensus. Bargaining in good faith implies some consensus and cooperation, or commitment to reach a final decision. There is also much cooperation among competitive firms in reaching decisions that affect them collectively. Associations are formed by firms to promote the interests of their industries. They cooperate for the collective good and compete for their own private good. However, for cooperation and competition to produce a desired outcome, there has to be mutual trust. Without trust the competitive forces of the market would result in short-termism, the maximisation of short-run profits at the expense of long-term gains and, perhaps, even at the cost of one's own interests.

In short, the decision-making procedure in a competitive economy tends to be democratic in the sense that economic agents are by and large free to pursue their interests and decisions subject to budget constraints and the constraints of formal and informal institutions. Public decisions in many or most cases are also reached democratically. Within corporations the procedure tends to be authoritarian. However, there is increased demand for both public and corporate decisions to be more transparent and accountable to their respective constituents.

V

The structure of information flows in a competitive economy corresponds to the decision-making structure. Information flows tend to be predominantly horizontal, decentralised and diffused. Autonomous decision-makers, whether consumers or producers, make their decisions chiefly on the basis of local knowledge and market prices. In the absence of hierarchies there is no separation between information flows and decision-making and hence no distortion of information as it is passed to decision-makers. The division of decisions among agents and the division of knowledge coincide. Thus, one of the major virtues claimed for a decentralised competitive economic system is its information efficiency. According to Hayek (1945) information supplied by the market is costless and accurate. Prices, which are at the centre of a communication system of the competitive economy, are the most important information carriers for 'rational' economic decisions. They are generated by the competitive principle, by the forces of supply and demand. Without competition the relative scarcities of resources and hence the best methods of production and consumer values would not be known.

Moreover, market-based information, such as prices, profits and losses, provides individuals with essential signals to correct bad decisions and to promote mutual accommodation among market participants with minimum information about the circumstances and preferences of others. In particular, market prices resolve peacefully the problem of value for participants competing for the same goods. This is a somewhat tranquil view of competition, which characterises the perfect competition model. But, as Hayek, Schumpeter, Marx and others show, competition is a truly dynamic process, a process of 'discovery', of finding out the best price or the best technique. It is also a turbulent process of 'creative destruction'. In the words of Morgenstern (1972, p 1171):

> Competition means bluff, hiding of information – and precisely that word is used to describe a situation in which no one has any influence on anything, where there is *ni gain, ni perte*, where everyone faces fixed conditions, given prices, and has only to adapt himself to them so as to attain an individual maximum.

Despite Hayek's view that the division of knowledge in a competitive economy is more important than the division of labour, it is the latter division that gives rise to specialised knowledge and asymmetric information, between buyers and sellers and between principals and agents. Each agent or participant in the market possesses certain knowledge about his specialties or circumstances that others do not know. This means, as Scitovsky (1990, p 137) points out, that 'market relevant information is biased in favour of one or the other side: those on the better-informed side can exploit the people on the other'.

In the real world of 'workable' competition, as distinct from perfect competition, where decision-makers do not have sufficient information to make their decisions, they often rely on agents to gather, process and interpret the information they require for making informed decisions. More importantly, they require more, much more information than prices to make up their minds. Consumers need to know the quality, durability and other characteristics of the goods and services they wish to acquire that are most often not reflected in prices. Competitive advertisements, which provide non-price information, are inevitably biased, notwithstanding consumer protection laws against misleading information. Similarly, producers, who are not price-takers, need to know the possible reaction of their competitors to any change in their prices, output and investment decisions. Market prices do not cover all goods. They are the outcome of individual decision-making in a competitive setting and are ill-suited for collective goods that require cooperation as well as competition. Also they do not reflect the real value of specific goods. The inadequacy of the market to provide valuation of specific goods is one of the reasons for having firms and organisations. The importance of non-price information in competitive (oligopolistic) markets is reflected by the importance of non-price competition, which takes the form of product differentiation and innovation. Oligopolistic or 'asymmetric monopolistic' markets generate, in addition to prices, new information relevant to investment decisions (Scitovsky 1990, p 142).

The information structure within firms, like the decision-making structure and procedure, varies from one firm to another. It depends on the type and size of the firm, on both the nature of technology and product, and its organisational structure. All these factors affect the degree to which subordinates have access to information generated by members of the same or higher levels in the firm's hierarchy. In most firms, especially the U-form, the structure of information flows is relatively centralised with vertical communication channels mainly from top to lower levels. In contrast, in the M-form with separate profit centres designed to encourage a more independent use of local information, there is a reduction in information flows across the divisions. In these firms the structure of information flows is decentralised. Also the direction of information flows depends on the nature of the information itself or the technology. In general, simple technical information moves up the communication channels, while complex, scientific information flows downwards. In most high-tech firms the know-how needed to make a compact or finished product is so sophisticated that the average worker would not be able to propose any useful innovation. The only way to manage such firms is by using a top-down approach with manuals prepared by specialists that spell out in minute detail all the individual steps to be taken.

In worker-owned managed firms, workers are more likely to be much better informed about the decisions of management, at least in the production area, than typical non-managing shareholders. To that extent the information asymmetries between workers and managers are less serious than those between shareholders and managers. At the other extreme, in government-owned firms, information flows in both directions from top to bottom and vice versa. As in all hierarchies, information tends to be distorted as it flows from one level to another. Moreover, since managers of state-owned enterprises are generally not constrained by market forces, information processing tends to be delayed. However, they may be required by law to provide more information about their activities than private corporations.

Since competitive markets and organisations do not provide all the necessary information required to make informed decisions, whether by individuals, organisations or governments, there is a role for the state, or a central authority, to collect information about the state of the economy, which would improve the quality of decisions. Such centralised information is in the nature of a public good, which is too costly to collect by individuals and organisations. In addition, centralised information is necessary for the state to carry out the functions of enforcing the rules of competition, providing welfare services and managing the economy.

It is fairly obvious that except in the special case of perfect competition, the structure of information flows in a real competitive economy is much more complex and less efficient than is suggested by traditional economic theory. To meet the information requirement of the whole economy, we need different types of information generated by markets, organisations and governments. Market-type information is necessary but not sufficient. Indeed, for markets to function efficiently they have to rely on, to a significant extent, information generated by governments and organisations, and vice-versa. The competitive economy needs all types of information, price and non-price, which are both centralised–concentrated and decentralised–dispersed. However, it does not seem to have any serious problems generating new information and ideas.

VI

The rise of the competitive principle made possible economic calculation on the basis of market-based prices. As the method of economic calculation improved, a transformation of people's attitude occurred not only towards economic but non-economic activities as well. The competitive principle encouraged individualism, materialism and 'economic rationalism'. Economic and non-economic ends from now on were to be achieved with minimum resources or even abandoned if the costs exceeded the expected benefits. Thus, highly irrational ends (particularly from the point of view of society) can now be accomplished by rationally allocated resources and rational ends (again from the point of view of society) are abandoned because (private) costs exceed (private) benefits, or the 'ends' in question are not profitable.

In a competitive economy, the chief decision-making criterion is the maximisation of profit for producers and maximisation of utility for consumers. Producers will continue to produce up to the point where the marginal revenue is equal to the marginal cost, and consumers will continue to consume until the marginal utility is equal to the market price, or when the marginal utilities of all commodities are equalised. As a result, resources will flow where the rate of return is the highest and where they are most valued by consumers. Competition among producers and consumers ensures that we get the most out of scarce resources, or that allocative and distributive (Pareto) efficiency is maximised. Of course, these results apply to the world of 'perfect competition' and of price-takers.

In the real world of imperfect competition, where there is much rivalry and interdependence, the conditions for maximisation of profits and utilities are the same, but with different social outcomes. Prices are normally above marginal costs and consequently profits are high. This may not be altogether undesirable if the excessive profit is invested or is used to develop new products or new processes. Under perfect competition, on the other hand, with normal (zero) profit, the producer is in no position to undertake risky investment, for which he may not be able to raise funds on the money markets. In any case, the capacity to borrow depends on both accumulated profits and the expected rate of profit.

As in the last three components of the decision-making process, decision-making criteria vary across firms. Even in the case of the profit criterion, there are major differences among firms. Some firms maximise either their short-run or long-run profits, while others maximise both. Others still are content with covering their costs and making enough profits to satisfy their shareholders. This applies to corporations where managers have other objectives besides making enough profits, objectives that include maximisation of output and employment, better working conditions for employees and environmental and ethical considerations. Such non-profit considerations can never be allowed, under competitive conditions, to dominate the reasons for making decisions. They act as constraints on the economic calculus of private costs and benefits. Still, other firms may for strategic reasons sell below marginal costs in order to capture a greater share of the market, particularly in industries subject to substantial economies of scale and scope. In this case, the firm is making short-term losses in order to maximise long-term profits.

In labour-owned firms, the main decision-making criterion seems to be a dual one: the maximisation of profit and security of employment for members. In a sense this type of firm is similar to the owner-manager, where profit-making is a means of economic survival. It is generally argued that workers are shortsighted and would tend to choose higher wages instead of reinvestment. However, this assumes that workers continue to behave as workers rather than as entrepreneurs or capitalists. The evidence suggests that once workers are given the responsibility of making decisions, they begin to take a long-term view of their own interest (Haddad 1975).

In the user-oriented firms the owners are mainly concerned with the output of the organisation, its quantity and quality, rather than with profits. Owners, however, are not always identified formally, and frequently assume their ownership role through voluntary action. They may or may not pay for their membership; as in the case of charitable organisations, which rely on donations. According to Ben-Ner, Montias and Neuberger (1993, p 234) 'many user-oriented firms adopt a nondistribution-of-profit constraint, mostly by incorporating as non-profit organisations which are compelled by law to obey this constraint'. In many countries the law forbids user-oriented firms from distributing profits to their members. Instead, they are obliged to 'distribute' them in a different guise through greater quantity and quality, or lower prices of output. However, the legal constraint on the distribution of profit does not exclude the expenditure of funds for improving working conditions or as benefits to members.

In competitive market economies most government enterprises are established to provide goods and services that have favourable externalities. The principal criterion of these firms is not the maximisation of profit or some other rule of economic reasoning, but some complex set of rules of reasoning including education, public health and employment. Many of the goods and services provided by state enterprises are not sold on the market and hence their profitability cannot be readily measured. Even government firms that produce private goods are expected to promote public policies such as regional development or better environment. In the past, government-owned enterprises were not expected to maximise profits, but with the rise of 'economic rationalism', government activities and policies are increasingly subjected to rigorous economic calculations.

Public choice criteria are seemingly more complex than private ones. Governments in democratic, competitive societies cannot ignore various interest groups, if only because they cannot implement their policies or programmes without their support and cooperation. Hence, political criteria are important determinants of public policies and decisions. In a 'competitive democracy', where political parties compete with one another for votes, political considerations are part and parcel of economic policies. Only a strong government or an authoritarian regime can afford to ignore the demands of various pressure groups. In addition, ethical criteria are often taken into consideration in public choices. The state has the responsibility to protect the weak and disadvantaged citizens. In the interest of equity and long-term efficiency of the economy, the state is involved in the redistribution of income and wealth from the relatively rich to the poor.

VII

The motivation structure of a competitive economic system seems at first sight quite simple. Economic agents are motivated mainly, if not wholly, by self-interest and materialism. Self-interest is generally regarded as a characteristic of economic rationality, a defining element of *homo-economicus*. It was one of Adam Smith's great achievements to have demonstrated that in a competitive economy the pursuit of self-interest will lead to outcomes that are socially desirable. However, Adam Smith was careful to distinguish between enlightened self-interest and selfishness. The former is a virtue, the latter a vice. In any case, the complexity of humans prevents us from attributing a single motive for their behaviours except, perhaps, in abstract theorising. As we have argued in

Chapter 6, individuals, organisations and governments are motivated by a complex mixture of extrinsic and intrinsic, positive and negative, non-pecuniary and material incentives, as well as egotism and altruism. This mixture, as we have repeatedly stressed, varies across individuals, organisations, governments and more importantly across systems.

Indeed, incentives tend to be sustained by the system and they sustain the system. Thus, the competitive economic system tends to rely more on intrinsic than extrinsic incentives. Freedom to choose, or economic liberty, implies that individuals are self-motivated and do not require an authority to motivate them. Extrinsic motivations are needed in hierarchies, where individuals are not the decision-makers. They are also used by governments to encourage certain activities that are deemed socially desirable. For example, governments provide incentives for firms to innovate because innovation is considered to have favourable externalities for the economy. They also impose taxes on certain activities (for example, smoking) that are considered harmful.

The competitive system relies on both positive and negative incentives. Although the pursuit of profit or income acts as a strong incentive for people, it is the negative incentives (the fear of failure, loss of profit and employment) that seem to characterise the competitive system. The survival of the firm depends on its ability to compete. The competitive principle acts as a process of natural selection. Successful innovators survive and grow; unsuccessful ones decline and disappear. In the absence of competition, there is no effective mechanism to force producers to be efficient. As noted in Chapter 6, empirical evidence suggests that negative incentives are more effective than positive incentives. People tend to place more value on marginal losses than marginal gains.

Material incentives tend to be more dominant than 'moral' ones in a competitive economy. In general, the producer is motivated by profits and the consumer by maximising the satisfaction of his or her material wants. No distinction is drawn between economic welfare and total welfare; the two are usually conflated. However, the distinction between 'moral' and material incentives is not always clear. Promotion, for example, is partly material (pecuniary) and partly moral (non-pecuniary). Work for many people is an end in itself and not just a means of earning an income. This applies to those people who do creative work and are proud of their workmanship. Nevertheless, material incentives remain the dominant consideration in economic activity.

Similarly, egotism or self-interest is far more effective than altruism in a competitive system. Indeed, an altruistic person may not be able to survive in such a system, though enlightened self-interest or weak altruism can give groups, with a sufficient number of individuals who are governed by it, a competitive advantage. Altruism is present to a lesser or greater extent in all of us, but the competitive environment does not encourage us to develop our altruistic tendencies. When everybody is striving for more material goods, competition becomes so intense that even the most successful are compelled to fight for survival and to be indifferent to the welfare of others. Indeed, it has been shown on many occasions that the rational pursuit of self-interest leads to everyone ending up worse off (Sen 1977). However, conventions and customs make us altruistic in times of emergency, in natural disasters, and in dealing with our friends and relatives.

Turning to organisations, the motivation structure varies a great deal from one firm to another. In the classic owner/manager firm, profit is clearly the main motivator. In this type of organisation, intrinsic incentives tend to be dominant. The entrepreneur is motivated by his or her role as claimant of residual rewards. In hierarchical firms, where there is separation of ownership and control, the problem of motivation becomes more complex as reflected in the vast principal–agency literature. Here intrinsic incentives are inadequate. The decision-maker or principal provides a set of extrinsic incentives consisting of: (a) material benefits in the form of salaries, bonuses, stock options and other fringe benefits; (b) non-material benefits, such as the creation of a sense of identification between the goals of the organisation and the goals of the individual member; and (c) the extremely important incentive of promotion, which combines both pecuniary and non-pecuniary incentives. The managers themselves are motivated by a mixture of income maximisation and security. Hence, they tend to pursue profits high enough to satisfy shareholders and prevent takeovers. Moreover, because of the problem of asymmetric information, managers are often given profit shares or stock options in order to maximise net worth for the shareholders.

In labour-owned and managed firms the motivation structure is similar to that of the owner–manager firm. It consists of profit and security of employment or survival. The objectives of the firm are internalised by the workers. Since they monitor each other, workers have fewer opportunities as well as weaker incentives to shirk, hence there is no need for a set of extrinsic incentives.

In user-oriented firms, the problems of incentives differ from those of other firms. Since owners rely on managers to carry out most functions in their organisation, the agency–management problem may allow the managers greater freedom to follow their own objectives. Thus as Ben-Ner, Montias and Neuberger (1993, p 235) point out, 'in order to reduce the incentives of managers to act against the wishes of their owners, the former are selected not only on the basis of competence but also for their demonstrated pre-commitment to the objectives of the controllers'.

Finally, in government-owned firms the agency–managerial problems are more serious than those of other types of organisations. Since top managers cannot be motivated through pecuniary incentives' schemes such as profit-sharing or stock options, the agency–management problem is dealt with through selection methods which place considerable weight on the moral commitment of candidates to the objectives of the organisation. In turn, managers, acting as quasi-principals in relation to employees, also confront severe motivation problems. Their behaviour is regulated primarily through rules and monitoring that are used in all bureaucracies.

In sum, the incentives' structure of a competitive economy reflects the characteristics of the other components of the decision-making process. Incentives are intrinsic except within hierarchical organisations, which have serious agency problems and thus agents must be motivated by a set of extrinsic incentives. Further, the competitive principle acts as a carrot and stick, and hence is valued as a disciplinarian tool. Successful competitors are handsomely rewarded and failed ones are heavily penalised or eliminated by this impersonal societal device. It is, however, the stick, the fear of failure that seems to be the more effective incentive of the competitive principle.

VIII

The preceding discussion has shown that the rise and operation of the competitive principle solved'two fundamental problems for a well-functioning economy: valuation and innovation. Neither custom nor command deals adequately with these problems, though as we shall see in the next chapter, they can be useful as supplementary mechanisms when the competitive principle is inadequate, or when it fails. The competitive principle encourages resources to move where they are most valued. It compels producers to search for the most efficient methods of producing goods and services and to develop new products. But they can do this if they know the relative prices or values of resources. These values are generated in the market as consumers and producers compete for resources to maximise their profits and utilities. The competitive principle reconciles the different subjective valuations of economic agents, and in doing so, it elicits from all agents taken together a certain kind of consensus as to what should be produced and by what means. Thus, through the competitive process of the market, the private and subjective valuations of goods and services are transformed into public and objective 'facts' on which economic agents tend to agree. This applies, at least, to goods for immediate consumption. The valuation of producer goods is much more complicated, as it involves expectations and uncertainty regarding their profitability.

More importantly from the point of view of the long-term survival of the economic system, the competitive principle generates new products and processes. However, it is the 'competition among the few', or oligopoly that produces a high rate of innovation and diffusion (Sylos-Labini 1962). Indeed, the main form of competition among oligopolistic firms is product differentiation. Such firms cannot survive and grow without innovation. Further, it is the fear of failure among existing firms, rather than the prospect of success, that motivates them to innovate or emulate innovators, and in doing so spread the new technology or product across the entire economy. Firms operating under perfect competition have neither the resources nor the motivation to invest in new products and processes. They can survive through price competition.

The two types of price and non-price competition have both benefits and costs. Non-price competition is associated with process innovation and its diffusion across the economy. It is therefore essential for long-run economic growth and adaptation of the economy to external shocks. However, the notion of (non-price) competition as a process of 'destructive creation' involves some waste of resources. Indeed, non-price competition is equated with product differentiation, which can be wasteful as in the proliferation of the same variety of consumer goods with different brands. On the other hand, price competition tends to make existing products cheaper and thus leads to a more efficient use of resources. But it is 'static'; it does not increase the variety of goods available to the consumer. According to Scitovsky (1990, pp 141–2) non-price competition is to be preferred, not only because it is good for economic growth and adaptability, but also because it has important side-effects on equity. In his words: 'market-oriented innovation consists largely of means of production methods for cheapening and making generally available an ever increasing number of goods and services that were the privilege of the rich... although the market economy tolerates substantial inequalities in income distribution, it nevertheless increases equity'. One must agree with Scitovsky on the vital importance of the creative role of the competitive market, but there remains the suspicion that it is 'too' creative; it creates too many factitious wants, goods and services that we do not really need. It also generates both inequality (by meeting the trivial wants of a few before the urgent needs of the many) and disutility for others.

The successful resolution of the valuation and innovation problems depends a good deal on a decentralised, if not a concentrated, decision-making structure. Most microeconomic decisions have to be left to autonomous economic agents competing with one another in the market, subject to rules enforced by a central authority. Some of the micro-decisions involve significant externalities, which have to be incorporated or taken into account in order to avoid misallocation of resources and to encourage innovation. The central authority has also the task of ensuring that public goods are provided for the community at large. The competitive principle cannot deal adequately with such goods. Another area where this principle fails or is inadequate is the coordination of aggregate supply and demand; such coordination is needed to ensure macroeconomic stability at high levels of employment. Macroeconomic decisions and policies must be taken by the state.

The decision-making procedure of a competitive economy largely corresponds to the structure of decision-making. Autonomous economic agents are left more or less free to pursue their goals and implement their decisions. Decisions are reached either independently or through cooperation, negotiation and bargaining. These procedures are consistent with the democratic principle, since they involve little or no coercion. However, within firms there are various procedures that can be ranked on an authoritarian–democratic continuum. For most firms an authoritarian procedure seems to dominate. Democratic procedures are largely confined to labour-managed firms and user-oriented or non-profit-making firms. There is also a wide variety of procedures adopted at the macro-level by the central decision-makers. Authoritarian procedures, particularly in developing countries, are quite compatible with the competitive principle, and are often used in times of emergency and in decisions of national security in developed economies.

The structure of information flows is predominantly decentralised and diffused. Many decisions are made by individual consumers and producers on the basis of market prices and local knowledge. However, for complex decisions market prices are inadequate and have to be supplemented by information generated by experts, organisations and governments. Individuals acting in the marketplace do not have the time or the capacity to collect all the information they need to make informed decisions. Organisations have more resources to gather and process existing information and to generate new information. But even then there are certain data, which are too costly for private organisations to collect and process and/or have favourable externalities. Such information is usually generated by the state, as it is in the nature of public good. Hence, a competitive economy requires for its efficient functioning much more than prices and decentralised or local knowledge. It also requires a variety of non-price information as well as centralised data collected by the state.

The leading decision-making criterion of a competitive economy is the maximisation of profit or income. Resources tend to flow where the rate of profit is the highest and where they are most valued. The profit criterion may be supplemented or qualified by other criteria such as maximisation of output or sales, or by employment and ethical considerations, but it remains in the long run the dominant one. It is indeed one of the major systemic features, if not the major one, of a competitive economy. At the macroeconomic level, the central decision-makers rely on 'macro-profitability', political and ethical considerations. Public decisions, as we have already mentioned, must be economically sound, politically acceptable and ethically desirable.

Finally, the motivation structure of a competitive economy is primarily intrinsic, egotistic, materialistic and incorporates both negative and positive incentives. Individual consumers and producers operating in the market have inbuilt incentives and generally do not rely on external incentives in their decision-making processes. The government may establish a set of external incentives to influence autonomous decision-makers to act in a way that is beneficial for the common good. External incentives are used widely in all hierarchies within private organisations and government bureaucracies. Other characteristics of the incentives' structure of a competitive economy are the heavy reliance on self-interest and pecuniary motivation, though altruism and non-pecuniary incentives are sometimes used as supplementary incentives. But perhaps the most effective incentive feature of a competitive economy is the dual carrot and stick method. The competitive principle produces successes and failures; it rewards the efficient and successful innovator and punishes the inefficient and unsuccessful one. However, in the interest of social cohesion, losers – especially if they are major players – must be taken care of by the government. They cannot be allowed to perish. This is yet another area where the competitive principle has to be constrained, supplemented and encapsulated by the state and moral norms. This is further discussed in the next chapter.

10. The Composite Economy

I

Modern economies are 'composite' or 'additive' consisting of several coordinating and enforcing mechanisms inherited from the past. These elements coexist in various degrees in different economies, and are modified by local physical and social conditions. All modern economies rely on a mixture of custom, command, competition and cooperation to formulate, coordinate and implement policies and decisions.

In the last three chapters we focused on three principles, which had dominated the decision-making process of three major historical economies: the customary economy, the command economy and the competitive economy. The fourth principle, cooperation, has never been dominant except in small communities. It was meant to be the leading coordinating and enforcing principle, replacing competition, in socialist countries. However, Soviet-type socialism, as we have seen in Chapter 8, relied increasingly on command, and command is generally incompatible with cooperation. In contrast, developed competitive economies contain a significant degree of cooperation, which enables them to function satisfactorily, but this degree is not developed enough to make them well functioning.

In this chapter we examine the relevance and importance of the four principles or pillars of the current composite economy from the perspective of our decision-making approach. We also show how they impact on one another. In particular, Section II discusses the role of customs and conventions and how they affect the decision-making process of the composite economy. Section III explains the function and importance of command and its effects on the decision-making process. Section IV discusses the value and limitation of competition and how it influences the decision-making process. Section IV analyses the role of cooperation in the modern composite economy and how it impacts on all aspects of the decision-making process. Finally, Section V summarises the key points of the chapter and discusses the main shortcomings of current composite economies.

II

The important functions of customs and conventions in modern economies are underestimated by economists and ignored by most theorists. Yet, they permeate much of contemporary economic life, and influence (and in some cases dictate) many of our decisions. The great bulk of our day-to-day decisions and decisions taken at regular intervals are habitual, being determined by custom and requiring little or no conscious calculation. Examples of customary decisions and behaviour include the exchange of gifts and reciprocal invitation to dinners. But customs and conventions go beyond such obvious cases. Many economic decisions, such as consumption, the fixing of prices, including wages and salaries, and the profit margin, are often determined by convention. Indeed, prices have been referred to as 'social conventions, reinforced by habits' (Hodgson 1998, p 169). A conventional price is constant but it is not an equilibrium or a 'necessary' price. An oligopolistic price, as Shackle (1972, p 222) points out, 'is conventional since its constancy depends on a mutual recognition between our supplier and his rivals that there shall be immobility on both sides for fear of worse consequences for all'. Further, he states that conventional prices or

> Prices which have stood at particular levels for some time acquire thereby some sanction and authority. They are the 'right' and even the 'just' prices. But also they are the prices which the society has adapted its ways and habits, they are prices which mutually cohere in an established frame of social life. To upset one of them would be to upset all of them in an exercise of general unsettlement and general groping for readjustment, which would promise no advantages commensurate with the work, expense and uncertainty which it would entail (Schackle 1972, p 227).

It is not hard to see that customs and conventions provide stability and continuity as well as economy of time and effort in our decision-making processes. Stability is important for efficiency and without continuity and economy, we would not be able to cope with more than relatively few decisions among the many that we are obliged to make both at the micro- and macro-levels. Moreover, customs and conventions provide some protection of the weak against the strong, particularly in areas where there are no laws adequate for this purpose. However, if customs and conventions dominate the decision-making process, as in the customary economy, they hinder 'progress' and prevent efficient adaptation to new circumstances.

To understand more clearly the function of customs and conventions in the modern composite economy, we need to examine their effects on the five components of the decision-making process. First, it would seem that differences in decision-making structures of modern developed economies are partly shaped by custom and convention. It is generally believed that the degree of centralisation in France is greater than that in the UK, that certain decisions such as those relating to education are made by the central authority in Paris, whereas the same decisions are made at regional or local levels in the UK. Similarly, the existence of a class system in Europe, which is customary and a legacy of the past feudal system, has an important influence, both direct and indirect, on the decision-making structure. This is obvious in the case of the UK, which has a hereditary head of state. In contrast, the US political decision-making structure is unhampered by a feudal heritage and rigid social stratification. Its political pluralism has often been attributed precisely to the absence of a feudal background.

Decision-making structures are usually subject to marginal changes, unless there is a political or cultural revolution, or a systemic collapse, as witnessed in the former Soviet Union and Eastern Europe in the late 1980s and early 1990s. But even in such systemic changes, customs and conventions continue to exert an important influence on the *de facto* decision-making structure. By and large the new élites, the decision-makers, in the post-socialist economies, were the old élites, who managed the former Soviet system. In any case, the decision 'who should be deciding what' is at least influenced by and often based on custom and convention.

Second, the influence of customs and conventions is more apparent in the decision-making procedures of a composite economy. Indeed, conventions frequently dictate procedures, and precisely for this reason, it is often difficult to change procedures. The importance of conventions in procedures is fairly obvious. They save time and effort and thus facilitate the decision-making process. Once procedural matters are settled, the participants in decision-making can turn to more substantial issues. On the other hand, if there were no agreed procedures in ongoing decision-making processes, there would be delays in reaching decisions. Such delays can lead to sub-optimal decisions. Again, customs and conventions promote economy, stability and continuity.

Third, the effects of customs and conventions on the structure of information flows in a composite economy are fairly obvious. We inherit a lot of information from the past that affects our economic activity. Customs and conventions, which embody the stock of accumulated knowledge and wisdom of past generations, affect the way we interpret new information. They provide the individual with cognitive means to interpret and comprehend new knowledge. The perception of new information is not possible without past knowledge. However, inherited knowledge can and does prevent us from readily accepting new ideas. If a new idea is revolutionary and out of step with the prevailing perception, it is generally rejected.

As in other related matters, the effect of customs and conventions on the structure of information flows is a double-edged sword. On one hand, the accumulation of wisdom, the transmission of invaluable information from one generation to another, provides stability, continuity and economy. Customs and conventions facilitate the communication of information by providing shared concepts, rules and norms. On the other hand, they can prevent us from accepting new knowledge. Alternatively, the accumulation of past knowledge can result in information overload as a result of which important items go unnoticed. Relevant information tends to be lost in the avalanche of information. However, in the absence of customs and conventions, old ideas and values tend to be rejected too quickly and replaced by new ones, before their merits have been demonstrated. Thus we often end up with new ideas, which are inferior to old ideas. This is chiefly the result of fashion, which emphasises innovation or novelty as something that is valued in itself. New ideas may soon become conventions to be replaced by 'newer' ideas, which again become conventions and so on. The effect of customs and conventions is to slow down this endless cycle of novelty and convention.

Fourth, many decisions in a modern composite economy are dictated by customs and conventions, or are based on some rules of thumb, which may be referred to as 'thoughtless' criteria (Etzioni 1987). Such decisions are habitually made without a thought about their correctness. In routine or standard decisions no conscious calculations of costs and benefits are made. Such decisions have demonstrated their usefulness over some period of time; their makers are content and have no regrets. They may be sub-optimal in the sense that they do not produce the best outcome, but decision-makers are satisfied with this state of affairs and do not think it worth while to expend time and energy on changing their habits. They feel no impulse to change them. Moreover, they know if they were to subject all their decisions to conscious calculations, then only relatively few decisions would be made. Given the scarcity of time and energy, custom-based decisions, which may not be optimal in themselves, permit us to devote more time and energy to other decisions, particularly to new decisions. Consequently custom-based decisions impart a greater degree of rationality to all the decisions we are required to make. They free individuals from the necessity of deliberating on every facet of life in which they must act. Rational individuals rely on habits and rules for the making of their decisions, particularly in situations of extreme uncertainty.

As with other aspects of the decision-making process, the effects of customs and conventions on decision-making criteria can be stifling. Attempts to make 'rational' decisions can be weighed down by the shackles of the past. The conventions or rules on which some decisions are made normally change inadequately or fail to change when circumstances change, and thus they cease to be 'rational'. In such cases there is a waste of resources. Moreover, customs and conventions tend to discourage new ideas and thus reduce the rate of innovation and creative efficiency. Decisions based on customs and conventions are likely to prevent adaptation to external and internal shocks. To follow customs and conventions is to be indifferent to the changing circumstances of each choice situation.

In short, custom-based decisions serve a useful and necessary purpose in modern economies, but we need to revise them from time to time to avoid unnecessary waste and to permit progress to take place. However, it is important not to enforce changes in customs and conventions too quickly, without knowing all the important consequences, some of which may turn out to be disastrous. But there has to be a safeguard against the stagnation and tyranny of customs and conventions. In the composite economy such a safeguard is provided by the competitive principle, by the freedom of individuals to disregard conventions according to their costs and benefits. Indeed, the presence of competition tends to ensure that customs and conventions that have become too costly will not survive.

Fifth, the motivation structure of a composite economy is partly based on customs and conventions. The existing distribution of income and wealth, which is both the cause and effect of the incentive system, cannot be explained purely in economic terms without reference to historical factors, to customs and conventions. In particular, wage relativities are determined by custom and adjusted from time to time to take account of market forces. Many of the incomes and wages people earn cannot be justified in terms of marginal productivity or the contribution they make to the product of industry. It is customary for certain groups in society to receive an income commensurate with their status rather than with their contribution. Also customs and conventions affect the types of incentive used in a society. In Japan, for example, 'moral' incentives, or what Morishima (1982) has called 'the Japanese ethos', seem to play a relatively bigger role than in other developed market economies, and may explain why the distribution of income in that country is less skewed than that of the USA.

The value of custom in the area of incentives is that it reduces conflict over the determination of wages and salaries, through the maintenance of relativities. This has the additional effect of increasing stability. Against such advantages, the effect of customs and conventions on incentives is increased resistance to changes in relativities, when warranted by changes in supply and demand in the labour market. If relativities are strictly adhered to, the incentives' system would cease to be effective. On the other hand, if customs and conventions were completely discarded, it becomes difficult to establish appropriate remuneration, particularly in industries whose outputs are not sold on the market. It seems the sensible solution is to keep traditional relativities and adjust them from time to time to stay in touch with market forces. Again, the stifling effects of customs are modified by the presence of competition. But without customs and conventions there might not be agreements on who should get what, since the marginal productivities are seldom known. Even when they are known they do not necessarily lead to a satisfactory resolution.

Clearly, customs and conventions play a significant role in modern composite economies. They influence all aspects of the decision-making process and behaviour of economic agents, without becoming binding constraints as in traditional societies. They provide us with economy of time and effort, stability, protection and continuity. Indeed, without customs and conventions, we would not be able to cope with the numerous decisions that have to be made everyday by individuals, organisations and governments. We would have to start from scratch and then the solutions to many of our problems might be indeterminate. Customs and conventions provide us with a starting point from which we can move on to make marginal adjustments in accordance with new circumstances. Of course, if not revised from time to time, or if they are allowed to dominate our decision-making process, customs and conventions can lead to stagnation, inefficiency and prevent swift adjustment to external and internal changes. Such an eventuality is unlikely in the presence of the competitive principle. The danger is likely to come from having too much competition, which has a tendency to displace useful customs and conventions. Indeed, competition replaces the basic bonds of custom and religion that hold traditional societies together.

III

Like custom and convention, command plays a more important role in the modern composite economy than is generally recognised. It is used extensively within households, corporations and by governments to enforce 'the rules of the game', to mobilise resources in times of emergency and to implement national priorities. Ultimately, the command principle relies on force and coercion to implement decisions, but in modern societies force is a monopoly of the state. The state sets boundaries of permissible action and in doing so it substitutes force for freedom in those areas where freedom would be too costly in terms of social order foregone. Heads of households and corporations are not permitted to use physical force, though they may command their subordinates to carry out their wishes subject to heavy penalty if they refuse. However, the use of command has been modified by the 'values' of modern democratic societies, such as the rule of law, openness, transparency and accountability. More importantly, in economic affairs, the command principle has been transformed and rendered more effective and efficient by modern management techniques, the information revolution and by the valuation of resources generated by competitive markets. The command principle operates very differently in a modern composite economy from its traditional and dominant role in the feudal and Soviet-type economies.

First, in terms of the decision-making structure, the presence of command imparts and, in turn, requires a degree of centralisation to mobilise resources quickly in times of emergency, to set and enforce national objectives and priorities and to provide public goods and services that would not be provided by custom and convention, competition and by the existing degree of cooperation in society. In particular, the command principle is needed to tax and redistribute income from the rich to the poor, primarily because the degree of altruism and cooperation is not sufficiently developed in society to rely on voluntary contributions to meet the urgent needs of disadvantaged groups. Without a degree of centralisation and command, the modern economy would not function satisfactorily or may even not function at all. There would be enormous inequalities and much chaos and confusion. That is why in all modern economies, the state plays an important role; indeed, it is the main player. However, an excessive degree of centralisation and command, as obtained in the former Soviet-type economies, leads to misallocation of resources, stagnation and rigidity.

Second, the presence of command in modern economies affects the decision-making procedure. In times of emergency, when decisions have to be reached quickly and resources have to be mobilised rapidly, an authoritarian procedure is adopted. A similar procedure is often adopted in determining national priorities, when a democratic procedure fails to reach a consensus on such matters. Arrow's impossibility theorem shows that the objective function of a society cannot be reached through democratic procedures. Also, in decisions affecting national security, transparency is suspended in favour of secrecy, and governments resort to security in denying basic freedoms. Although authoritarian procedures are justified under certain circumstances, the decision-makers ultimately remain accountable to the electorate, and are removed from office if their policies turn out to be disastrous. Where speed and secrecy are not required, a democratic procedure is compatible with centralisation, at least in the formulation of decisions and policies. However, democratic procedures in conflicting situations can paralyse the decision-making process, or render the decisions unsound, as they embody the inputs of various interest groups that are not in the national interest. A command element or an authoritarian procedure may be needed to overcome the pressures exerted by such groups.

Within corporations authoritarian procedures are extensively used particularly in organisations, where processes and products can be easily controlled from the centre. Decisions are made by top managers and given to workers or subordinates to execute without consulting them. Although modern corporations adopting principles of effective and efficient corporate governance tend to be somewhat more transparent and accountable, a significant degree of command remains a feature of their *modus operandi*.

Third, the presence of command in a composite economy permits the collection, processing and dissemination of certain information pertaining to the state of the economy and public goods and services that might not otherwise be available for use by individuals and private corporations. The state has the legal power to compel individuals and corporations to provide its statistical agency with information it requires for its primary functions of enforcing the rule of law, regulation, redistribution and management of the economy. Information provision requirements about firms' environmental performance, occupational safety and health record, and other matters are increasingly incorporated into federal, state and local environmental laws. In addition, the state requires private corporations to provide information to the public concerning their activities, so that their shareholders and potential investors can monitor them. Finally, the state forces individuals to provide information about their financial assets and incomes for taxation purposes and for the provision of welfare services for those people who have little or no income. As a result, the command principle generates enormous amounts of information about the activities of individuals, organisations and governments. Such information is necessary for formulating sound decisions and policies at all levels of the economy.

As the record of the Soviet-type economies shows, the command principle generates a great deal of new information through the channelling of resources into education, research and development. Since scientific research and development is a semi-public good, the state plays an important role in diverting resources to the research sector, either directly through the establishment of research organisations or indirectly through subsidies to the private sector. The mobilisation of such resources is ultimately effected through taxation or forced saving. There is little doubt that in the absence of command in a modern composite economy, the amount of basic research would suffer. More importantly, since education is compulsory, the use of public knowledge generated by the state is diffused throughout the economy, as skilled people move from one occupation to another.

Fourth, with respect to decision-making criteria, the command element in the composite economy enables certain decisions to be made by a central authority on the basis of any chosen criterion, or a mixture of criteria, it thinks appropriate. We have noted in Chapter 8 that in a pure command economy, it is difficult to solve the valuation problem, and consequently the decisions may not be economically rational. But in a composite economy the values of many goods and services are solved basically by competitive markets; the central authority can use those values or relative prices to make meaningful economic decisions. However, since the valuation of the market is ill-suited for determining the quantity of collective goods to be produced, their values have to be generated by some form of command to incorporate externalities. Thus, the command principle is necessary in the composite economy to enable better allocation of resources through the enforcement of the social economic calculus.

Since the command principle at the national level in the composite economy is usually confined to public goods or to major decisions of national importance and security, the pure economic calculus is inappropriate in certain situations, particularly in times of emergency, when haste acquires its own logic. However, where speed and national security are not relevant and important, the central authority can employ the social economic calculus, incorporating all types of externality. Further, the command principle in the hands of a strong elected government permits certain decisions to be made on the basis of national interest rather than on the aggregated interests of some pressure groups. It permits the central authority to employ ethical criteria and to adopt a long-term perspective in its decision-making processes, especially on environmental issues and the use of non-renewable resources. Thus, in a composite economy the command principle can lead to a better allocation of resources in the long run, where the competitive market is likely to fail by adopting a short-term perspective.

Fifth, with respect to incentives and the execution of decisions, the command principle plays a special role in the composite economy as the enforcer of the rule of law, collecting taxes and ensuring national security. Not all decisions are implemented through custom and convention, the pecuniary incentives of competitive markets, or through altruism and cooperation. Where material and 'moral' incentives are ineffective motivators, coercion is used by the state to force individuals and private organisations to do the 'right' thing or more often to prevent them from doing harm. Also, the use of force is often a more effective deterrence against violating the rule of law than fines. But, as we have maintained, command or force cannot be used arbitrarily by the democratic state. The command principle is at once an enforcer and a subject of the rule of law. Another limitation of the command principle, as an enforcer of decisions and policies of the state, is that it guarantees only minimum compliance and effort. Economic agents do the minimum amount of work or provide the minimum amount of information they can get away with, without incurring penalties. To get the most out of people, pecuniary and non-pecuniary incentives are needed. However, the presence of asymmetric information makes it extremely difficult to devise optimal incentives' structures to get people to act not only within the law. This is clearly seen in the taxation area, where people pay the minimum tax they can get away with, and not the maximum tax they ought to pay. It is only when the degree of altruism and cooperation is sufficiently developed that the command principle becomes redundant as an enforcing mechanism.

In short, the command principle has an important place in the composite economy to deal with certain decisions that must be taken at the centre, particularly in times of emergency and for purpose of national security, when an authoritarian procedure is appropriate and the economic calculus is suspended in the interest of speed of action. However, where speed and national security are not of major concern, transparency, accountability and economic calculation are compatible with command. Indeed, under certain circumstances the command principle, through the use of the social economic calculus, can produce a better economic outcome, or a more efficient allocation of resources. In addition, the command principle generates a great deal of information used by individuals, organisations and governments to make informed decisions. Finally, the command principle is an important enforcer of the rule of law, and public policies and decisions.

IV

The competitive principle in the modern composite economy is the major coordinating and enforcing mechanism. Its primary function is twofold: to solve the valuation problem and to generate and diffuse new products and production processes. Both functions are necessary for efficient allocation of resources and economic growth. The operation of the competitive principle has been modified and enhanced by the other coordinating and enforcing mechanisms. In particular, customs and conventions, as we have already seen, are often the starting point and regulators of competition. They are particularly reflected in the informal rules of competition. Competition is also enhanced by the command principle, through the enforcement of laws banning anti-competitive trade practices. At the same time, the command principle may inhibit competition, when it leads to rent-creating and rent-seeking activity. Finally, competitors often cooperate with one another to promote their common interest. Competition and cooperation are frequently seen as two sides of the same coin.

To see more clearly the effects of the competitive principle on the workings of the composite economy, we need to examine its role in the decision-making process. First, the competitive principle requires for its operation a decentralised structure of decision-making. Rivalry, which is another name for competition, cannot exist unless there is at least one other economic agent competing for resources and/or customers. However, if there are too many competitors, as in the perfect competition model, then paradoxically the element of rivalry evaporates. In that sense, there is no 'competition' in perfect competition. Individual decisions are made in isolation from other participants in the market and as if in response to impersonal, elemental forces. In contrast, real competition or rivalry takes place in oligopolistic markets, where competitors are relatively few and known to one another. Their decisions are mutually determined and they are keen to know one another's strategies and plans. Moreover, since firms in oligopolistic markets compete mainly through product innovation and differentiation, such markets are crucial for the generation and diffusion of innovation (Sylos-Labini 1962).

In a modern economy, where numerous decisions have to be made regarding prices and outputs, a high but not an excessive degree of decentralisation is needed to ensure that most of the microeconomic decisions are made by individuals and organisations in pursuit of their own goals and in accordance with their own circumstances, tastes and preferences. A central authority has neither the time and energy nor the information and capability to make the bulk of microeconomic decisions. An excessive degree of centralisation of microeconomic decisions leads to unnecessary waste and misallocation of resources without satisfying consumers' tastes and preferences.

Second, the competitive principle in a composite economy has a significant effect on the decision-making procedure. Provided they keep within the rule of law, competitors make their decisions in the manner they see fit. Competition relies on freedom of individuals and organisations to use their resources and opportunities to achieve their goals and preferences. They are generally free to collect information, acquire skills and consult with others before they make their final decisions. Thus, the decision-making procedure implicit in the competitive principle is basically democratic. People are 'free' to choose what to produce or consume and where to work. Of course, they are constrained in their choices by their own circumstances, resources, the rule of law and customs and conventions.

In many areas, the final decision is not reached by individuals, organisations and governments acting autonomously on the basis of their own knowledge and preferences, but rather through a process of bargaining and negotiation. Although bargaining, which often takes place between one seller (or a group of sellers) facing one buyer (or a group of buyers), may be described as bilateral monopoly, the process remains part and parcel of the competitive principle, reflecting the supply and demand forces in the market. However, where relative bargaining powers are unequal, the outcome or the final decision is likely to be dictated by one party. In such cases, the decision-making procedure is *de facto* authoritarian. One party is being coerced within the rule of law to accept the terms of the stronger party. The weaker party may refuse to negotiate with or accept the terms of the stronger party, but this may leave the weaker party in a worse position. For example, a worker who refuses to accept the terms of the employer may end up being unemployed.

Authoritarian procedures are quite common within organisations competing with other organisations. An authoritarian procedure, which relies on secrecy and speed in reaching decisions, may enhance one's competitive advantages. We have seen in Chapter 3 that the advantages of an authoritarian procedure, as opposed to a democratic one, depend on the nature of the product, technology and industry. Other things being equal, democratic procedures, which involve consultation with subordinates and workers, are likely to improve productivity both through the supply of more reliable information and the internalisation of the goals of the firm by all its employees.

Decision-making procedures of public corporations have been increasingly influenced by the rule of law, which is enforced by the command principle. Firms are required to be transparent, to disclose information to the public and shareholders, and to the government for taxation and regulation purposes. In some countries they are required to have workers represented on their management boards. There are also firms managed by their workers and competing with other firms. Such firms seem to have competitive advantages, particularly in times of recession when workers are willing to accept lower incomes in order to survive. Clearly, the competitive principle in a composite economy coexists with different procedures.

Third, with respect to the structure of information flows, the competitive principle plays a crucial role in both the dissemination of the existing stock of knowledge and the generation of new information. According to Hayek (1978, p 179) competition is a process of discovery, 'a procedure for the discovery of such facts, as without resort to it, would not be known to anyone, or at least would not be utilised'. It is an efficient means for solving the knowledge problem. In particular, competitive prices summarise in an abstract manner all sorts of information about supply and demand conditions, the knowledge of individuals about their tastes, values, preferences and cost of production. They enable individuals to make informed choices; they provide information to producers about the value to society of the existing resource allocation. Without competition knowledge about relative scarcities, least cost methods of production, and the subjective values consumers place on commodities, would not be known, or would be obtained only at an enormous cost of resources. However, the competitive principle is necessary but not sufficient for solving the information problem. There are externalities, uncertainties and asymmetric information, which cannot be dealt with satisfactorily by competition.

In short, the competitive principle is essential for generating and indeed for diffusing new knowledge. While the command principle can generate quite adequately new knowledge through the channelling of resources into education, research and development, it is inadequate for the spread of new ideas. On the other hand, the competitive principle contains an inbuilt diffusion mechanism. When a firm introduces a profitable invention, it is generally imitated by its competitors. Indeed, firms in oligopolistic markets compete mainly through the generation and application of new ideas. Also, in a competitive market when a potentially profitable new idea is rejected by one firm, it may be taken up by another firm with different expectations and vision and made profitable. The competitive principle is indispensable for the utilisation and dissemination of new knowledge.

Fourth, we have already noted that one of the primary functions of the competitive principle is to solve the valuation problem, which is fundamental for an efficient economic system. The lack of effective competition in domestic markets distorts the informational content of price and output signals, which, in turn, results in wrong investment and output decisions. Without knowing the relative scarcities of resources, it is impossible to make rational economic calculation. Competition enables resources to be used where they are most valued, or where the rate of return is the highest, since the main decision-making criterion is the maximisation of profit and/or the minimisation of costs. To survive and grow under competitive conditions, firms must be efficient and creative; they must minimise costs and maximise profits, or innovate. Again, the competitive principle is indispensable for both allocative and creative efficiencies.

It is possible, however, that if the degree of competition is excessive, it could result in inefficiencies, duplication of effort and wasted resources that might have been more profitably employed. Capital goods are rendered prematurely obsolete before their costs are recouped. Product differentiation is multiplied and factitious wants are created. This is the negative side of the creative process of competition. Further, competition often encourages short-termism; the pursuit of short-term profits at the expense of long-term gains, particularly in the exploitation of non-renewable resources and environmental issues. There is no certainty that competition will provide substitutes for non-renewable resources if they are depleted prematurely. The allocation of non-renewable resources and other resources whose supply cannot be readily increased as well as the provision of public goods and services, if left to the competitive principle and the narrow economic calculus of private costs and profits, will not result in efficiency. In such cases we have to rely on some form of command or cooperation.

Finally, the competitive principle has profound effects on the motivation structure of a composite economy. It provides an intrinsic set of positive and negative incentives based on self-interest and materialism. The competitive principle embodies, at once, both the carrot and the stick. Failure to compete, to be efficient or innovative, can be disastrous, leading to loss of profits or employment and threat to livelihood. Arguably, it is the negative incentives of competition, which compel individuals and organisations to work harder, to be more efficient and creative in order to survive, while its positive incentives handsomely reward successful competitors. In the risk-ridden area of innovation, the rewards and penalties are very high, though the penalties for failure seem much higher than the rewards for success. Thus, competition is distressing; to relax in the struggle for survival can be very dangerous.

Within competitive firms, management relies on extrinsic incentives, both pecuniary and non-pecuniary, to get employees to work harder and to acquire new skills. While the owners are motivated by a set of intrinsic incentives, their agents (managers and workers) are given a set of extrinsic incentives. The dominant form of incentives favoured by the competitive principle is monetary or material gains. The competitive principle relies primarily on self-interest. There is little room for altruism under competition, although it is quite conceivable for individuals and cooperative organisations to maximise their income through competition in order to give it away to charitable causes, or for a small group of individuals to be altruistic towards one another in order to compete more effectively with other groups.

In summary, the competitive principle plays a central role in the modern composite economy. It is essential for solving the four major problems of an economy or society: information, valuation, innovation and motivation. The efficiency and simplicity of the competitive principle in dealing with these problems is best illustrated by the way it unifies the four dimensions of profit. Under competitive conditions profit is, at once, an objective, a criterion for the allocation of resources, an indicator of the efficiency of the enterprise and a motivator. In addition, there is a general belief in the moral virtue of competition, as a process of natural selection and builder of character. Here, it is worth quoting J.S. Mill:

> But if competition has its evils, it prevents greater evils...It is the common error of Socialists to overlook the natural indolence of mankind; their tendency to be passive; to be the slaves of habit, to persist indefinitely in a course once chosen...To be protected against competition is to be protected in idleness, in mental dullness; to be saved the necessity of being as active and as intelligent as other people (Mill 1868, p 477).

However, there are several areas of the composite economy where the competitive principle is either inadequate or breaks down. We have already discussed the areas where custom and command are more appropriate than competition. In the next section we explore those areas where cooperation is more effective than competition, custom and command.

V

The cooperative principle plays an important role in the modern composite economy. It makes the economic system work more smoothly and efficiently by reducing conflict, or by resolving conflict more quickly, by disclosing more accurate information, by encouraging the use of rational decision-making criteria and by reducing the problem of asymmetric information and motivation. Indeed, the cooperative principle affects favourably all aspects of the decision-making process.

First, it renders the decision-making structure more decentralised. We have already noted that the command principle inhibits cooperation. In a composite economy, where command plays an important but restricted role, there is room for the cooperative principle to flourish in certain areas, such as the provision of welfare services and communal activities, and other non-profit activities. The decisions involved in such areas are better made by cooperative organisations rather than through custom, command and competition. Like the competitive principle, the cooperative principle works better in a decentralised decision-making structure. Cooperative decisions are made at local or regional levels where individual members can participate in the decision-making process. Decision-making structures of cooperative and non-profit organisation are usually horizontal. There are neither superiors nor subordinates, though somebody must provide leadership. Decisions are made collectively by members of the organisation. This is not to deny the possibility of cooperation in a hierarchy, between superiors and subordinates.

Second, the cooperative principle has a favourable impact on decision-making procedures. This is clearly seen when centralised decisions are reached through cooperation rather than command. Indeed, the impact of the cooperative principle is more clearly felt on the decision-making procedure than on the decision-making structure. In many organisations, including government and international ones, decisions are reached through a spirit of cooperation. The parties involved are usually aware of one another's needs and try to meet those needs through voluntary compromise and consensus. Negotiation or bargaining takes place within a consensual rather than confrontational, competitive or adversarial environment. Even when one party is stronger than the other, the stronger party tends to refrain from dictating its terms if the other party is unhappy with the outcome. Decisions reached through cooperation would be agreeable to all parties, and hence there would be no need to renegotiate the terms when relative bargaining powers change. Another effect of the cooperative principle on the decision-making procedure is increased openness and transparency. Decision-makers would have little or no reason to be secretive or use delaying tactics to acquire some advantage for themselves. The cooperative principle would speed up the decision-making process or, at least, it would not lead to unnecessary delays that serve the interest of the individual at the expense of the interest of the group as a whole.

Third, there is little doubt that the cooperative principle has a favourable effect on the structure of information flows in the composite economy. The transmission of information from one person to another or from one level to another in a hierarchy is less distorted by self-interest. Since there is cooperation between superiors and subordinates, the problem of asymmetric information is reduced. Also, information channels are not blocked for reasons of narrow self-interest. The cooperative principle improves the accuracy and speed of information flows. Moreover, cooperation encourages the diffusion of new information. Useful ideas are not held back from other users by patent laws; unnecessary duplication of research effort is avoided. Researchers exchange their new ideas without fear of losing out. Their rewards consist in seeing their ideas or inventions put into useful purposes for the community, while their effort and contribution would not go unrecognised and unrewarded. Finally, information collected by government organisations from individuals and corporations would be more accurate in a climate of cooperation. Individuals and corporations would provide accurate information about the real income and costs for taxation and subsidy purposes. There would be more honest reporting and information about the state of the economy. Thus, the cooperative principle reduces the cost of monitoring, accounting, auditing and litigation. Decisions made by governments, corporations and individuals would be based on accurate and reliable information.

Fourth, the cooperative principle influences favourably the basis on which decisions are reached. Where decisions are reached through cooperation, the narrow economic calculus of private costs and benefits is replaced by a wider calculus that serves the interest of the group, the organisation or the wider community. Further, the cooperative principle allows non-economic considerations to be taken into account in decision-making, when it is appropriate to do so. Cooperative organisations have usually wider objectives than making profits, and thus their decisions are based on a mixture of economic and non-economic criteria. These criteria may include profits, output maximisation, higher employment and ethical considerations, such as a more equitable distribution of income and provision of welfare services. There is no irreconcilable incompatibility between the cooperative principle and economic criteria, or rational economic calculation. Under competition, profit is the main criterion and the satisfaction of the community is the means or the by-product. Under Cooperation it is the other way round. Satisfaction of the needs of the population is the basic criterion and profit is the means. Indeed, cooperation encourages the use of the social economic calculus in decisions that have significant externalities. With intelligent cooperation such externalities are or can be internalised. There are numerous cases of the 'prisoner's dilemma', which demonstrate the superiority of cooperation over competition in producing a better outcome and more efficient allocation of resources.

The cooperative principle also affects the quality of public decisions. Not only are the information flows rendered more reliable by cooperation between the central authority, on the one hand, and individuals and organisations, on the other, the criteria on which the decisions are based are likely to be more rational. cooperation reduces the level of rent-creating and rent-seeking activities, and hence it leads to better allocation of resources. Often, cooperation between competing parties can and does take place at the expense of the third party, as in the case of restrictive trade practices. However, the cooperative principle encourages participants to take a long-run view with respect to the allocation and use of non-renewable resources and protection of the environment. Finally, the presence of cooperation and consensus in the formulation of public policies and decisions enables the central authority to make its decisions on the basis of a mixture of economic and ethical grounds resulting in better outcomes.

Fifth, the most decisive influence of the cooperative principle on the decision-making process in a composite economy is on motivation. Without confusing cooperation with altruism, cooperation implies a degree of reciprocal altruism and enlightened self-interest. Altruism is present in a smaller or greater degree in all human beings, but for most of the time it is dormant. Altruistic behaviour is most visible in times of crisis and war (paradoxically), in small communities and among friends and relations. There are many activities that are performed by individuals and organisations not out of self-interest or material gains. The degree of cooperation and altruism in society is partly reflected by the amount of voluntary work, particularly in the education, health and welfare areas. Studies of voluntary work show that it is much more significant in the modern composite economy than is commonly acknowledged (Arrow 1972; Andreoni 1988; Rose-Ackerman 1996).

The presence of cooperation and altruism reduces enforcement costs, free-rider problems and shirking. More importantly, the cooperative principle makes it easier to reconcile the trichotomy of efficiency, equity and stability. Factors of production are rewarded by dividing up in agreed proportions the actual output of their cooperative efforts, and thus instability would not be caused by conflicts over distributive shares. People motivated by altruism work harder, or give their maximum effort towards achieving the objectives of the organisation or the community, without expecting commensurate remuneration. Many people, who contribute significantly to the welfare of the community, are satisfied with incomes less than their marginal productivities, and this makes the distribution of income and wealth less skewed.

In sum, the cooperative principle plays a useful role in motivating people to do their civic duties, to help others and to do the right thing without expecting excessive material rewards. It is particularly important in the welfare sector where other enforcing mechanisms fail or are inappropriate. Moreover, cooperation based on altruism or enlightened self-interest is desirable in itself. It makes society function more smoothly by reconciling its economic, political and ethical objectives. Adverse cooperation or collusion violates the spirit of the competitive principle and is therefore harmful to the welfare of society. As Adam Smith observed, cooperation among competitors is highly suspect. But there are circumstances when cooperation among competitors promotes competition and diversity. For example, if small firms are to compete in the highly competitive external market, they may need to cooperate with one another on matters that collectively enhance their capacity to compete. Further, as Jorde and Teese (1990, pp 81–2) point out, successful innovators often require 'horizontal, lateral as well as vertical cooperation'. In the research area cooperation is beneficial, because it reduces unnecessary duplication of effort without necessarily harming diversity.

VI

The discussion in this chapter has shown that the modern composite economy is based on four major principles that coordinate and enforce the numerous decisions made by individuals, organisations and governments. No modern economy can function effectively without the presence of custom, command, competition and cooperation. The absence of one will adversely affect the other three, and consequently the performance of the economy. And conversely, the dominance of one principle will lead to a similar outcome. This does not imply that the four elements must be given equal weights in a well-functioning economy. But there is little doubt that the present combination of the four elements is far from optimal. In particular, the modern composite economy suffers from a low degree of cooperation and (perhaps) command to be able to deal with some of the major economic and social problems, such as the persistence of poverty and inequitable distribution of incomes and wealth that are found even in the most developed economies.

We have shown that the presence of customs, habits and conventions in the composite economy enables us to cope with the numerous decisions that are required to be made, by saving time and effort, which are then directed at making new and complex decisions. They also provide stability, continuity and cohesion to the economy and society. Without customs and conventions there would be much chaos and confusion and, in turn, inefficiency and waste. Customs and conventions are also necessary for the functioning of command, competition and cooperation. They provide the starting point for the decision-making process. However, an excessive degree of customs and conventions will be hostile to change and this may lead to stagnation and decline. But this danger is likely to be checked by the presence of the competitive principle.

The command principle is needed in a modern composite economy to deal with certain decisions that have to be made and enforced by a central authority. Such decisions include the enforcement of the rule of law, macroeconomic policies, the provision of public goods and services, redistribution of income and wealth and decisions that have to be made quickly in times of emergency. Without the presence of command and legal coercion, a segment of the population would not respect the rule of law, the weaker members of society would be subject to force by the stronger members. Moreover, activities that are beneficial to the society as a whole but too costly to be undertaken by individuals or organisations operating under the competitive principle would not come into existence. In short, there would be inefficiencies, instability and chaos. But, if there is too much command and force, private initiative would be stifled, innovation reduced and stagnation would follow.

The competitive principle is needed in the composite economy to solve especially the problems of valuation and innovation and, to a lesser extent, information and motivation that custom and command cannot solve. Competition is essential for allocative efficiency, creative efficiency and adaptive efficiency. However, there are several areas in the economy where competition fails and needs to be supplemented by custom, command and cooperation. In particular, the command principle is needed to regulate but not to undermine the competitive process. An excessive degree of competition can be wasteful and needs to be subject to the rules of law. If the competitive principle is not 'encapsulated' it will destroy all customs and conventions that are economically inefficient but are socially desirable and necessary for decent living, for civilisation. In the words of Etzioni (1985, pp 296–7):

> The model of encapsulated competition requires some governmental activities, while it defines some other governmental activities as undermining the proper balance between activities organized by the rules of competition and those that constitute the capsule. Government is required to sustain the capsule because conflicts are assumed to be endemic to the system, and gaining resolutions cannot rely only upon voluntary ethical commitments and social bonds because an actor can violate them at will. It follows that an institution that commands coercive power must be the ultimate arbiter of conflicts (e.g. by jailing violators of a court decree to force compliance).

Finally, the cooperative principle plays an important role in the modern composite economy by having favourable effects on the five components of the decision-making process. It deals with a number of decisions, particularly in the welfare sector, which cannot be dealt with adequately by custom, command and competition. In addition, it makes the other three coordinating mechanisms function more smoothly, and thus reduces waste and inefficiency. Of course, too much altruism and cooperation might destroy competition and the economy will lose its dynamism. However, this is an unlikely event in the foreseeable future. The degree of cooperation and altruism present in the modern composite economy is insufficient to deal with some of the problems created by custom, command and competition. In Part III an attempt is made to show where and how the principle of cooperation can be strengthened in order to generate a well-functioning economy and a just society.

PART THREE

Towards a Well-functioning Economic System

11. The Principles of a Well-designed Decision-making System

The primary purpose of this chapter is to gear together the five components, which we now call principles, of an integrated decision-making system required for a well-functioning economy. These principles, which are in the main complementary and mutually reinforcing, have been discussed more or less separately in Part I. In this chapter we attempt to integrate them with the benefit of insights gained from the discussion in Part II. Their integration permits a far fuller and more precise understanding of a well-designed decision-making system.

We would expect a well-designed decision-making system to generate correctly calculated private and public choices and decisions and, at the same time, to show the objectivity of decision-making and the transparency of the procedure. In our view, correctly calculated choices must satisfy economic and non-economic criteria. Otherwise, our decisions may turn out to be 'good' economics but 'bad' politics or 'bad' ethics; or the other way around. In either case, our choices and decisions are almost certain to be, at best, partially right or, at worst, simply wrong.

Given that the most important decisions in life involve economic and non-economic considerations, it is quite clear that we need a conceptual framework to deal with those decisions. A good starting point for such a framework is to discard the traditional notion of *homo economicus*, the foundation stone of modern economic theory, in favour of a composite construction of '*homo ethicus-politicus economicus*' (HEPE), which takes a more realistic and comprehensive view of human nature and aspiration. Our representative HEPE is a well-integrated person, concerned not just with economic matters and material satisfaction but with a wider range of satisfactions, a being who is neither entirely selfish nor entirely altruistic, but composed of a mixture of both. Further, our HEPE means well and wants to do the 'right' thing, but he or she is not always well informed about the consequences of his or her choices or may not possess the capacity to make complex calculations of costs and benefits. There is much empirical evidence suggesting that 'people are capable of a wide variety of substantial and systemic reasoning errors', and further that these errors are 'related to economic conditions, such as deliberation costs, incentives and experience' (Conlisk 1996, pp 669–72). Finally, our representative HEPE is a creature of habit and circumstances, emotions and passions as well as reason. He or she is fallible and subject to learning and forgetting, and hence can be provided with appropriate institutions, incentives and information to do the 'right' thing and to eliminate or minimise systemic errors.

Given the characteristics of HEPE, our proposed conceptual framework makes no sharp separation between material and non-material satisfaction, or between 'economic' and 'total' welfare. Obviously, the construction of such a framework is too ambitious a task to be undertaken by a single individual or a specialist group. It must ultimately involve experts from all the social sciences including economists, sociologists, political scientists and moral philosophers. However, our aim in this chapter is a very modest one, of providing the skeletal outlines of how correctly calculated choices and decisions might be reached.

The structure of the rest of this chapter is as follows. Section II examines the general characteristics of an 'optimal' decision-making structure. Section III discusses the appropriate procedure(s) consistent with other properties of decision-making. Section IV explores the structure of information flows required for correctly calculated choices. Section V discusses the choice of criteria for making rational decisions. Section VI examines the motivation and incentive structure required for an effective decision-making system. Finally, Section VII offers some concluding remarks about the prospects of designing an integrated decision-making system.

II

The first task of designing an integrated decision-making system is to specify the 'optimal' structure of decision-making, the division of decision-making authority, or, who should be deciding what. Arguably, this is the most fundamental aspect of an economic system. An 'optimal' decision-making structure would ensure that the set of decisions that have to be made in the modern composite economy would be allocated in such a way that the 'right' people would be making the 'right' decisions. The 'right people' in this context refers primarily to those who possess the knowledge and qualifications to make certain decisions. Alternatively, the set of decisions would be allocated rationally within and among markets, organisations and governments. An 'optimal' decision-making structure would minimise the possibility of having the 'wrong' people, institutions and organisations in charge of decisions that should be made by others. Such a structure constitutes a necessary condition for making the 'right' decisions and, in turn, for maximising the greatest 'good' of society.

There are obviously enormous conceptual and practical difficulties in determining the 'optimal' structure of decision-making, or in drawing demarcation lines between markets, organisations and governments (at all levels), especially when non-economic considerations are taken into account, as they must be, if the proposed structure is to be politically acceptable and morally defensible, in the sense of giving as many people as possible some decision-making autonomy. As John Rawls (1971, p 65) has argued, 'every rational man is presumed to want powers, and prerogatives of offices and positions of responsibility'. Despite the difficulties, it is both necessary and desirable to specify some of the conditions for an 'optimal' structure, in order to avoid certain systemic errors arising from an excessive degree of (de) centralisation and/or concentration of decision-making authority; or from an inappropriate mix of markets, organisations and governments.

Although there is no single optimal decision-making structure appropriate for all times and places, there are many decisions on which there is a general agreement as to who should make them or at what level in a hierarchy they should be made. Also, in the modern composite economy many, if not most, decisions seem to be made by the right people at the appropriate level in the economy, but there is room for improvement and marginal adjustments. It is precisely in the area of marginal adjustments that endless arguments arise in deciding who should be in charge of those decisions.

Accordingly, our proposed division of decisions may not satisfy either the conservative neo-liberal or the radical collectivist, but it is defensible on both economic and non-economic grounds. There are good reasons for both centralisation and decentralisation of decision-making. In what follows, we first consider the set of decisions that belongs to the domain of the state and thus should be made either at the centre or at the regional and local levels. It is convenient to classify this set of decisions under three distinct functions of the state in a developed composite economy.

First, we look at the role of the interventionist state. Here we consider those decisions which are needed to: (a) enforce the rule of law, to protect the individual against 'force and fraud'; (b) correct market failures arising from significant externalities, restrictive trade practices and environmental degradation; and (c) provide institutional and physical infrastructures and other public goods and services. All these decisions are traditionally considered necessary for the efficient functioning of a decentralised (market) economy. The state intervenes in specific areas of the economy and makes some major microeconomic decisions. Such intervention usually improves the performance of the economy if the costs of regulation are less than the expected benefits. Without such intervention the economy would not function or, at least, would not function well. The role of the interventionist state is subject to marginal adjustments over time. Over the past two or three decades, as a result of the rise of liberal economics in both thought and deed as well as the growth of big business, state-owned enterprises have been privatised and public utilities and other industries deregulated. The provision of some public goods and services, particularly in the area of the physical infrastructure, is being undertaken by the private sector. Nevertheless, it remains the primary duty of the state to see that such goods and services are provided adequately to the community, without necessarily itself having to carry them out.

Second, we examine the role of the welfare state: the functions of the welfare state are not clearly defined and vary from one developed economy to another. In recent years, the welfare state has come under heavy attack by neo-liberals and reformers on grounds of paternalism, economic waste and disincentive to work or to save. By attacking the paternalistic aspect of welfare, the critics want the state to encourage individuals to look after themselves, to save for their future and to take up private insurance and private pensions. Given our emphasis on the need for people to participate in decisions that affect their life, a welfare system that gives people the opportunity to decide for themselves how much to spend on education and health, and how much to save for their retirement is desirable in itself. But such a system applies only to those people who already have the capacity to save and to take private insurance. It does very little for those who want to help themselves but do not have the capacity to do so. In any case, encouraging people to look after their own welfare still has a ring of paternalism.

Despite the criticism of the 'paternalistic model' of welfare, there is a wide consensus that the state should provide a guaranteed minimum income or a 'safety net' for those people who for some reasons cannot provide for themselves the essentials of life. Under the welfare functions of the state, we include those decisions affecting social security benefits, health, education and, to a lesser extent, housing and transport. There are complex economic, political and ethical arguments about the level of those services that should be provided by the state. It has been suggested that 'the welfare state is fundamentally about political and ethical values' (Dilnot 1995, p 4). Yet, political and ethical objectives and values cannot be realised without resources, and resources are scarce. Hence, economic considerations cannot be ignored. It may be better economically and morally to hand over to private enterprise and voluntary organisations some of the traditional functions of the welfare state. However, the function of forced redistribution of income and wealth from the better to the worse off cannot be left to the private sector. That function remains the monopoly of the state, until such time as the degree of altruism in society is sufficiently high to leave it to the rich to voluntarily hand over part of their earned wealth to their chosen charitable organisations.

Third, the managing state: like the welfare state, the managing or Keynesian state has been under attack for generating stagflation in the 1970s. While there is some evidence for the validity of this belief, the fact remains that an industrial economy left entirely to the forces of the market will not lead to macroeconomic stability at high levels of employment. Hence, it must be managed by a central authority, chiefly through monetary and fiscal policies, which can be intelligently designed to correct coordination failures of matching aggregate demand and supply. There may be disagreements about the extent and timing of such policies, and whether such policies are sufficient to bring about the desired outcome. But such disagreements do not alter the basic assumption that the modern industrial economy must be managed by a central authority if we are to avoid the heavy human and economic costs resulting from high rates of unemployment and inflation. There must be a central authority to take an overview or a macro-view of the economy and to set long-term priorities and objectives.

The sets of decisions discussed under the three functions of the state must not all be viewed as belonging exclusively and permanently to the domain of the central authority. Some of the decisions that are exclusive to the state can be made or enforced at lower levels of government, at the regional and local levels (Sewell 1996). Other state decisions, if they are to be operational, require the participation of private individuals and autonomous organisations. Participation may take the form of providing information, expert advice and cooperation to enforce the set policies and decisions. In short, centralisation to be successful and effective must depend, to a significant extent, on decentralisation and cooperation of subordinates and autonomous decision-makers.

Looking at the decentralised zone of the centralisation–decentralisation continuum, we list those decisions that should be made at the local level by individuals, committees and organisations. Provided these micro-decisions do not have major externalities, the central authority should not intervene. There are several sets of decisions that belong to the domain of the market, to non-government organisations such as profit-making corporations and voluntary organisations. The sets of microeconomic decisions include:

1. Consumption decisions: decisions as to what goods to consume and how much to spend on them belong to the domain of the individual, as suggested by the notion of 'consumer sovereignty'; though the state may prohibit or discourage the consumption of socially harmful products such as tobacco and alcohol and promote the consumption of cultural goods such as books, the arts and sports. In any case, the average consumer tends to rely partly on prices and other information (advertisement) provided by the producer to decide what to consume and how much. However, in an optimal decision-making structure, the notion of consumer sovereignty must be amended by including a specification of a set of 'basic needs' that are determined by 'society' on 'objective' grounds. In our view the welfare of society as a whole depends on satisfying basic needs before satisfying luxury wants.

2. Production decisions: these include investments, choice of technique, prices, costs and outputs. Such decisions are made mainly by firms, committees or individuals subject to state regulation or the rules of law. However, there is no a priori reason why production decisions cannot be made by some or all workers either directly or through appointed managers, as in the former Yugoslav system of workers' control or self-management, or in worker cooperatives. Indeed, on democratic and ethical grounds, workers should be encouraged to participate in the decision-making process of their enterprise.

3. Labour supply decisions: these include the choice of occupation, acquisition of skills, the number of hours worked and place of work. Such decisions should be left to the individual worker, though the employer may wish to impose a minimum number of hours of work for the efficient operation of the enterprise. The state ought to set minimum wage rates and regulate working conditions to ensure safety at work and to prevent exploitation. It must also partly determine the long-run supply of labour, through its decisions on immigration and education.

4. Within hierarchies, corporations and government bureaucracies, routine day-to-day decisions should not, in general, be interfered with by higher authorities. Similarly, the 'when' decisions, particularly in agriculture, and other decisions that require swift response to changes are best made by individuals on the spot. On the other hand, the geographical location of enterprises and activities, the 'where' decisions, should not be left entirely to individuals and organisations as they normally entail externalities.

As in the case of centralised decisions, decentralised decisions on their own do not produce optimal outcomes. They require some inputs from the state and regional authorities. In general, the state, as we have seen, must provide a favourable and stable environment, institutional and physical infrastructures, to ensure the viability and profitability of private enterprise and to encourage both individuals and organisations to make informed decisions and to enforce them.

Quite apart from the above 'centralised' and 'decentralised' decisions, which belong respectively though not exclusively to the domain of the state, on the one hand, and the market and organisations, on the other, there are other decisions that must be made jointly and cooperatively by the state, individuals and organisations. The function of the central authority in such decisions goes beyond providing a favourable environment, information and financial assistance; and similarly the role of individuals and private organisations goes beyond providing information, advice and implementation of decisions. Both parties must be directly involved in the formulation of decisions. In other words, in this type of decisions, the state, the individuals or the organisations are partners. Examples of joint centralised–decentralised decisions include infrastructural projects, welfare provisions and environmental issues. In such examples, the structure of decision-making may be referred to as 'centralised–decentralised'. The participants cooperate together to achieve the same objectives.

Now formulating rules about who should decide or do what is fraught with difficulties and may, as in the case of the attempt by J.S. Mill to draw a demarcation line between the state and private enterprise, lead to exceptions that are more numerous than the rule. Nevertheless, it is better to have some rules than no rules. Our general rule is that decisions or functions should be assigned to a central authority when individuals, private organisations and local governments cannot correctly formulate them or cannot make them efficiently. However, given the desirability of decentralisation on both political and ethical grounds, when differences in costs and benefits of centralisation and decentralisation are marginal, decisions should be allocated to lower levels of governments or to autonomous economic agents. The real difficulty arises when the costs of decentralisation are substantial. It is then that a trade-off has to be made between the economic benefits of centralisation and the non-economic benefits of decentralisation. Depending on general preferences of the community, the trade-off will vary across countries. In countries where economic benefits are highly appreciated in relation to non-economic benefits, the trade-off will be in favour of centralisation, if considerations of efficiency require greater centralisation.

In short, an optimal decision-making structure must specify not only the optimal mix of governments, organisations and markets but also, as Sah and Stiglitz (1988) show, the optimal number of levels for hierarchies and the optimal number of units in polyarchies as well as the optimal size of committees. Given that many, if not most, of the important decisions require inputs from governments, organisations, committees and individuals, an integrated decision-making system must specify not only who should decide what but also how their respective roles should be coordinated. The discussion in the next section sheds light on the appropriate procedure of reaching decisions that involve more than one party or decision-making authority.

III

An optimal decision-making structure is just one prerequisite for the formulation of sound policies and decisions. Decision-makers must also follow proper procedures. The choice of the appropriate procedure depends on the circumstances and the nature of the decision as well as on other properties of the decision-making system. An authoritarian procedure is more appropriate in times of emergency, when speed is of the utmost importance, or when it is fairly clear what is to be done. Another circumstance when an authoritarian procedure may be deemed desirable is when there is a rational reason for secrecy as in matters of national security or tactical necessity in a broader strategy. But as Stiglitz (1998, p 16) points out 'all too often secrecy serves as a cloak behind which special interest groups can most effectively advance their interests outside of public scrutiny'. Further, an authoritarian procedure that relies on secrecy protects government officials who are corrupt or incompetent and stay in office longer than they could under a democratic procedure.

Accordingly, a well-designed decision-making system would allow authoritarian procedures only in exceptional circumstances and recommend democratic procedures as a general rule. Democratic procedures make decision-makers accountable and responsible for their actions; they force them to provide reasons for their actions, and hence such procedures reduce the level of rent-seeking and rent-creating activities. Democratic procedures also generate and increase the flow of reliable information. Moreover, decisions reached through proper democratic procedures are more likely to be acceptable and quickly implemented, because those in charge of implementation would have been consulted or participated in the decision-making process, and hence they would feel morally obliged to carry them out. Such consultation makes them feel important and gives them a sense of belonging.

Aside from improving the quality of the decision-making process and the correctness of the decisions, democratic procedures are valuable in their own right. They are indeed desirable on political and ethical grounds. Participating in decisions that affect us directly and indirectly, through their effects on society, is a basic human right. It is good for our well-being, self-esteem and personal development; it satisfies our political and moral aspirations. However, democratic procedures would have to be compromised in the case of complex and technical decisions that require the inputs of experts. Such decisions cannot be adequately evaluated by ordinary people or by those who are most directly affected by them. In the case of complex public decisions, independent agencies may be established to evaluate and monitor the decisions of experts. Such agencies can be made politically responsible and accountable. In any case, attempts must be made to explain in non-technical terms the reasons for and importance of those decisions. Those who are affected by the decisions have a legitimate interest in knowing what is going on and they are rightly, in the last resort, the judges.

As in determining the optimal decision-making structure, so there is a need to examine the consequential merits of different decision-making procedures in order to choose the most appropriate one. Consideration of efficiency, which is important for reaching both economic and non-economic objectives, may require a more authoritarian procedure. Letting all members of the organisation or society share in the decision-making process is bound to be inefficient, because it violates the division of labour principle. A trade-off may have to be made between a better outcome and less desirable procedure or vice versa. In situations where democratic procedures are highly valued, the decision-makers will sacrifice some efficiency in order to give people some responsibility and decision-making powers. However, if the costs of democratic procedures are too high, authoritarian procedures may be adopted to reach better outcomes.

In modern economies many decisions are reached through bargaining and negotiation. A bargaining process is not usually transparent and well understood by all parties. There will be asymmetric information and exchange of false information. But if the relative bargaining powers of the participants are evenly matched, the final decision will be a compromise. If not, the stronger party will have a greater influence on the final decision and, in the extreme case, will dictate the outcome. The result is not much different from that of an authoritarian procedure. Moreover, if the bargaining process takes place in a conflict situation, as in industrial disputes between employers and workers, the final decision will, in all probability, be based on imperfect information. Each party will deliberately suppress its true position in the hope of achieving tactical advantages, and will make false claims, mainly for public consumption in order to win public support for its claim and thus put pressure on the other party to make more concessions. Such bargaining procedures can be costly and time-consuming not only to the parties involved but also to society.

In recognition of this problem, a system of conciliation and arbitration must be established to ensure a better outcome in situations where bargaining breaks down or results in unsatisfactory outcomes. A conciliator may be able to persuade the parties to agree by suggesting a compromise that either has not occurred to the parties or would not appear as a sign of weakness to both of them, if they were to accept it. If conciliation fails in cases of serious and costly disputes, there is a case for compulsory arbitration, where the two parties are compelled to accept the decisions of the arbitrator. However, compulsory arbitration may turn out to be only a temporary solution to the problem if one or both parties are unhappy with the decision, in which case the conflict will resurface at some future date.

Ideally, negotiation should take place in a spirit of cooperation, consultation and consensus-seeking. There must be transparency and open dialogue to encourage the parties involved to understand and sympathise with the position of one another. However, consensus procedures should not prevent constructive debate when there is a genuine conflict. Such debate is necessary in order to resolve the conflict. It generates information that might be suppressed by the desire not to offend the other party. Stiglitz (1998, p 19) correctly states that 'reaching a consensus is an outcome that is valued in its own right, and reaching consensus in a democratic and open way is a process valued its own right'. Further, he writes, 'because the process in which a decision is made is seen to be fair, even the "losers" feel committed to upholding it, and because the consensus process typically provides some accommodation to all parties, there is a sense in which no one feels defined as a loser'. As a result, once an issue has been decided or settled it is likely that it will stay closed, at least, until a major change occurs. Clearly, there must be incentives and institutions to encourage cooperation, consultation and consensus in resolving conflicts.

In an economy where consultation and democratic processes take place at all levels of decision-making, participants or stakeholders try to achieve a harmony of interests. In such a consultative, cooperative and consensus-seeking economy, each participant would be in a position to reach the correct decision not only from his or her own point of view but also from the point of view of the organisation or society. Cooperation or consensus is possible when participants have identical interests and information. It is more feasible when there is genuine consultation, which encourages the formation of identical interest and information. Cooperation is also more feasible in a small group precisely because members have identical interests and information. If the interests, objectives and information differ among participants and cannot be reconciled through consultation, the costs of achieving consensus and cooperation will be high, and the value of cooperation and consultation as a mode of decision-making procedure diminishes relative to other procedures.

In summary, a well-designed decision-making system must have appropriate procedures to ensure not only that the right decisions are made, but they also must be seen to be fair and right. The outcome as well as the process must be right and just. Like an optimal decision-making structure, an appropriate procedure must satisfy not only economic but also non-economic (chiefly political and ethical) objectives and criteria. Democratic and open procedures, which encourage participation, consultation, consensus and cooperation, are valued both in their own right and for reinforcing other desirable features of an integrated decision-making system, and hence for generating better decisions. In general, democratic procedures result in decisions that are economically efficient, politically acceptable and morally desirable. Authoritarian procedures may achieve such outcomes only in special circumstances. However, it should not be assumed that democratically reached decisions are best at promoting the welfare of all citizens, or that they are necessarily correct. Democratic procedures may fail to achieve all the expected outcomes, especially in complex decisions where experts play a large role. If the objective is to choose a better economic outcome and 'not just better feelings' as Stiglitz puts it, then the decision-making process must rely heavily on technical and professional expertise. In any case, appropriate procedures, like optimal structures, are necessary but not sufficient to generate the 'right' decisions; they must be accompanied by efficient channels of communication and reliable information flows.

IV

Since decisions are dependent on information, a well-designed decision-making system must have reliable information flows to enable the formulation of informed decisions. Such a system must encourage all economic and social institutions, including markets, organisations and governments to generate and transmit information necessary for making meaningful choices. It must also encourage the generation and diffusion of new knowledge, so that the innovation process becomes part and parcel of the working of the economic system. One of the conditions for making correct choices is that decisions should be made as close as possible to the source of information. Alternatively, the dual function of information-gathering and decision-making should be located in a single authority in order to avoid distortion and manipulation of original information.

In modern economies, however, this is not always possible. The complexity of economic decisions and the ubiquity of hierarchical organisations and bureaucracies necessarily involve the separation of decisional and informational functions. Decision-makers normally rely on others, subordinates, experts and professional people for making informed and meaningful decisions. However, the disjunction between decision-making and information flows creates problems of coordination, distortions and misrepresentation. Such problems usually arise from the divergent interests of the suppliers of information and decision-makers. There are also technical–administration problems not related to self-interested behaviour; they are the consequences of the inability to transmit accurately timely information from local levels to top decision-makers and vice versa. Distortions, delays and misrepresentation of information can be reduced, to some extent, by designing an effective system of incentives. In particular, unnecessary delays can be dealt with by imposing deadlines with progressive penalties attached to failure to meet the set date. Positive incentives can be used to speed up the process of information flows and encourage honest reporting. In addition, 'moral' incentives and other means can be used to reconcile the interests of the suppliers of information with those of the decision-makers. Such measures have the effect of internalising the objectives of the organisation by the suppliers of the information.

As shown in Chapter 4, decision-makers, in general, require three types of information to make meaningful decisions: (i) market-type or price information to solve the valuation and scarcity problems; (ii) organisational information to deal with the valuation of specific inputs not transacted across markets, and whose values are therefore unknown to outsiders; and (iii) government information relating to its own activities and the state of the economy is needed to reduce uncertainties faced by individuals and organisations. The three types of information are complementary, reflecting both the complementary nature of markets, organisations and governments and the corresponding 'rational' allocation of decisions.

More specifically, market signals and prices are needed by individuals, organisations and governments at all levels to allocate their resources rationally. However, market prices are necessary but not sufficient, except in simple decisions; most decisions require more than market prices. Market signals are frequently defective, misleading and asymmetrical. They cannot be relied on in cases of market failures. In such cases, the consequences of decisions based on market signals can cause much waste of capital and environmental damage resulting from the pursuit of short-term profits. Further, market-based information often favours some groups at the expense of others. For example, large fortunes have been made quickly on the stock market as a result of privileged access to information denied to others. Clearly, market-generated information flows need to be supplemented with other types of information generated by organisations and governments.

Organisations know more precisely the value of specific inputs, their quality and performance. Such information cannot be obtained in the marketplace. Compared to individuals, organisations have more capacity and resources to gather, process and utilise information. They also have more resources to invest in R&D activities, to employ researchers in order to develop and exploit new ideas. However, the information generated by corporations can also be misleading, self-serving, defective and asymmetrical. For example, the 'administered prices' of corporations cannot always be relied upon to reflect the relative scarcities of resources, as such prices may be the result of 'tacit collusion'. Also, the information they provide to consumers about the quality of their products is often defective, misleading and asymmetrical; hence, the need for antitrust laws and laws to protect the consumer against misleading advertising. There is also a need for rules governing the disclosure of certain information for the purpose of capturing social benefits, in order to promote socially responsible business behaviour and improve the efficiency of the market.

The informational role of the state or a central authority is primarily to encourage the free flow of information about the state of the economy and its own policies and activities. State-generated information should be seen as a public good to be used by individuals, organisations and governments. It must be objective, timely and as accurate as possible. These conditions are not always satisfied, and sometimes trade-offs have to be made, especially between timeliness and accuracy. Also, accuracy and relevance conflict when a cental decision is made to produce data for regional and local areas at the expense of reducing the reliability of national statistics. In any case, the information generated by a central authority must be checked by an autonomous agency to eliminate political biases and self-serving information. The maintenance and improvement of the quality of government statistical data is a critical responsibility. There must be more openness and less secrecy in matters that are not directly related to national security issues, more and better information to evaluate public choices. Moreover, since in the 'knowledge economy' wealth is generated by human capital and new knowledge, it is important for the government to focus on the generation of new information by establishing and subsidising educational and scientific organisations. A central authority has a comparative advantage in encouraging and supporting basic scientific research and general education that can be used by individuals and organisations.

In short, a well-designed decision-making system must have reliable information flows for both the formulation and implementation of decisions. Accurate and timely information is also needed to enable people to participate in and monitor those decisions that affect them directly. Information flows must be as accurate and reliable as possible to permit proper calculation of costs and benefits. Whatever criteria are used for making decisions, they must be based on relevant and adequate information. Since in the real world the full information required to make correct decisions is seldom available, making decisions under uncertainty is one of the most valued skills.

V

A well-designed decision-making system must above all encourage decision-makers to make correctly calculated choices. The need for this can be ultimately traced to the fact of scarcity of resources – a predicament of the human condition. Scarcity makes efficiency a matter of concern not only for the economist but also for the moralist. It is simply immoral to waste resources, especially non-renewable ones. The well-being of current generations and the survival of future generations depend on the prudent management of scarce resources. Further, the achievement of non-economic objectives depends on the availability of resources; hence the need for efficiency. Correct choices or decisions must not be calculated on the narrow economic consideration of private costs and benefits, but rather on a broader calculation and definition of social costs and social benefits. The costs must include the cost of calculation itself. As Conlisk (1996, p 669) states, 'deliberation about an economic decision is a costly activity, and good economics requires that we entertain all costs'. The private pursuit of profit will remain the chief economic criterion, but will have to be constrained through public regulation when the costs to society exceed the benefits. Again, the cost of regulation would have to be included.

In economics, the notion of correctly calculated decisions is depicted by the idea of equilibrium. If decision-makers are happy with their choices they would not retrospectively regret them. They are in a state of equilibrium. Confronted with the same circumstance again and equipped with the same information, they would repeat the same set of decisions. Of course, if their circumstances and preferences change and new information comes to light, they would change their decisions but would not regret their past choices. They could not have chosen better. If things turn out to be wrong, they would not blame themselves but resign themselves to another facet of the human condition: imperfect knowledge and uncertainty of the future. However, if they had miscalculated or made an avoidable error, they would be in a state of disequilibrium; they could have chosen better.

The idea of equilibrium can be extended to a whole set of interrelated decisions involving economic and non-economic considerations. It can be extended not only to the life of an individual but to society as a whole and over time. In a series of equilibria, there is first the equilibrium of the person in a single short period. Such a person may be in equilibrium even if other persons are not, provided, however, that their state of disequilibrium does not cause him or her to regret the decisions taken. Second, there is the equilibrium of a person over time. This does not imply that the person makes the same set of decisions. Rather, to stay in equilibrium, the person must change his or her decisions according to changing circumstances, information and preferences. The third conception of equilibrium is the equilibrium of a society in a very short period. This is a situation in which all members are equally content with their past decisions. They could not have done better by choosing otherwise. Finally, there is the 'social dynamic' equilibrium, in which everyone is retrospectively satisfied with each successive interval outcome. In this last equilibrium, there are many individuals, or generations of them, adjusting their plans and preferences and changing their decisions in order to remain in a state of contentment as things change over time. In short, it seems plausible to equate the characteristics of 'right' decisions, or correctly calculated choices, with those of equilibrium. If people are happy with their decisions and if they are in equilibrium, they feel they are doing the 'right' thing, even though they allow for unforeseeable discrepancies between forecasts or intentions and outcomes.

Many decisions, as we have already observed, are habitual governed by customs and conventions, norms and rules of thumb, and hence do not normally require any conscious calculation, probably because they appeal to intuition, and do not incur deliberation costs. Although they may be in some sense 'rational', it is wise to revise them from time to time to keep up with changing circumstances and to accommodate the increasing costs that may be associated with them. At the other polar end, there are decisions, which have to be based on conscious calculation of economic costs and benefits. Given the fact of uncertainty, decision-makers will calculate probable outcomes, and although the expected outcomes may not be realised, they will not regret their choices *ex post*. They will simply lament their bad luck. If the economic calculus is extended to public choices, as seems to be the current practice, the activities of the state are brought into the economic sphere. In the extreme case, where economic criteria are decisive, society is ruled by 'economic rationalism'. However, since most decisions involve economic and non-economic considerations, they should be based on a mixture of criteria in order to satisfy the various constraints and objectives faced by decision-makers. The 'right' (equilibrium) decisions will not be based on a single criterion. In situations where there are conflicts among the chosen criteria, compromises must be made by assigning them weights. Such weights can be derived from the set of objectives, priorities and circumstances of decision-makers. But we must not be too ambitious or too complacent.

Too ambitious, if we think we can attach exact weight to each criterion. What we can do is to rank the relevant criteria in order of importance. The relative importance and mix of different decision criteria, and the exact nature of the trade-off will vary according to circumstances and objectives of decision-makers. For example, an affluent person or society may put less weight on economic criteria and more on non-economic ones. Alternatively, in situations where political and ethical criteria are already satisfied, more weight might be given to economic ones. Similarly, a poor person or society may put more emphasis on economic criteria and less on non-economic ones. In the long run it is expected that a harmonious balance is achieved among the chosen criteria and objectives, though as a matter of tactics, an 'imbalance development' might be chosen in the short run.

Too complacent, if we assume we can say nothing about the relative weights of the chosen decision criteria, or if we assume that economists should refrain from passing judgement about the political and ethical implications of their decisions. If we adhere to this attitude, then equally, moralists and political scientists should also ignore the economic implications of their decisions or advice. Under these circumstances, the multiple criteria that are relevant to a given decision would have little or no chance of being harmoniously combined. Consequently, the advice given to public decision-makers by economists would, at best, be 'good' economics, but may turn out to be 'bad' ethics or 'bad' politics and conversely, the advice given by moralists or political scientists may turn out to be 'good' ethics, or 'good' politics, but 'bad' economics. Such a disjointed approach will at best achieve a tolerable degree of rationality in decision-making. Clearly, a well-designed decision-making system must allow for the integration of the multiple criteria that are necessarily involved in major decisions if we are to ensure that the decisions are economically rational, politically feasible and ethically desirable. From the point of view of the economist, the integration of the multiple decision criteria will dictate the degree of economic rationality, consistent with non-economic criteria.

VI

A final feature of a well-designed decision-making system is an effective incentives' structure needed to motivate people to do the 'right' thing, to expose or punish errors and to follow through their choices, or to implement decisions made by their superiors. Since people are motivated by a mixture of economic and non-economic incentives and since this mixture varies across individuals and societies and over time, different incentives are needed for different people and systems. In designing an effective incentive structure, allowance must be made for the fact that incentives tend to develop in an organic fashion with the development of the economy and society: they sustain and are sustained by the economy and society. Thus, the types of incentives and economic systems and societies must be designed for each other. A well-functioning economy and a just society will have a different incentive structure from an ill-functioning economy and an unjust society.

In Chapter 6 we have shown that people are motivated by a mixture of extrinsic and intrinsic incentives, positive and negative incentives, pecuniary and non-pecuniary incentives, and a moderate degree of altruism or enlightened self-interest. Accordingly, in designing an effective incentive structure, we assume that most people would prefer to work given sufficient incentives to compensate them for the presence of disutilities associated with the type of work they have chosen or have been asked to do. We leave out those people who are extremely lazy since no reasonable amount of positive and negative incentives would move them to work. In a well-functioning economy, which is a sub-set of a just society, those lazy individuals would constitute a very small minority, in which case the community can afford to support them by giving them a minimum income rather than allow them to starve.

Nevertheless, there remain serious concerns about incentives to work and the possible negative effects of a guaranteed minimum income. If individuals derive no benefits of any kind other than money from doing paid work, which is likely to be the case in low-paid and unpleasant jobs, and further if there is no stigma attached to benefit receipt, then a guaranteed minimum income will discourage able-bodied people from seeking work. This raises the possibility of imposing some penalties as a deterrent against shirking. A more constructive response would be to educate those people or to make the tedious tasks more attractive through mechanisation, higher wages, better working conditions, including participation in decision-making, and 'moral' incentives.

Given our assumptions about human nature, if we want to get more out of available resources, or if we want to increase them, then there must be sufficient economic and non-economic incentives for people to join the labour force, work harder, acquire new skills, save more and take the risks associated with innovation. They must be rewarded and penalised proportionately for their services and disservices to society. This raises the conceptual and practical problems of how to calculate the relative contributions of different people to society. In many institutions, particularly in government and non-profit-making organisations whose outputs are not sold on the market, there is no independent measure of employees' contributions other than the salaries and wages they get, or they could get if they were to seek employment in profit-making organisations. But such people may have specialised skills, which are best employed in their current jobs and hence those skills are not transferable.

In any case, market values do not always reflect accurately the real contributions of individual employees and employers. The prevalence of imperfections in the market such as monopolies, rent-seeking activities, exploitation, shirking, moral hazards and externalities of one kind or another does not give us much confidence in the belief that people who participate in the labour market or sell their products get what they deserve or what they contribute to society. If markets were perfect or near perfect the distribution of income in society would not be highly skewed.

Even if, for argument's sake, markets were perfect, there remains a fundamental objection to market distribution. The value placed on the labour of the individual is seldom generated by the individual alone and hence he or she is not entitled to the whole value of the product or the service. A person on a desert island would not be in a position to earn the sort of income that a corporate manager nowadays earns in a modern society. Arguably, society has given the individual both the capacity and the opportunity to earn the income that she or he is currently receiving. Unless the distribution of income is fairly equitable and there are no people in absolute need, society has a demand on her or his income. The individual has a moral responsibility to surrender part of his or her income, either voluntarily or in the form of taxes to society, for redistribution purposes and the provision of public goods. This is consistent with Rawl's first principle of justice that members of society as a whole have rights over the income from the labour of other members.

Notwithstanding the difficulties of measurement and our objection to some productivity-based rewards at the extreme points, commutative justice implies that people who work longer or harder, or who do more unpleasant, dangerous and skilled work should obviously get more. Failure to link reward to effort and output may lead to a fall in productivity and hence fewer resources to redistribute to the less well-off members of society. By linking the personal accumulation of wealth strictly to the efficient functioning of the economic system, we are in a better position to eliminate or minimise exploitation, rent-seeking activities and shirking. The resulting inequalities would not only lead to greater efficiency, but would also be consistent with Rawl's second welfare principle that the greater well-being of those who are well-off is justified only if it is required to improve the welfare of the less or least well-off people.

Rewarding people according to their relative contribution to society is justified, particularly if work is seen as a pure means, a pain not a pleasure, a disutility not a utility. Hence, the need for profits, bonuses, piece-rate incentives, fringe benefits, promotion, demotion, firing and hiring. In general, economists assume that these incentives are the only ones or the most effective. But, as discussed at some length in Chapter 6, there are non-pecuniary incentives and other work situations, which make it possible to reduce the degree of inequality without violating the efficiency criterion. Such incentives are important motivators; they affect significantly the elasticity and position of the supply curve for labour. They should be used more widely not only because they have beneficial effects on output, but also because they are desirable in themselves. Their use reduces the possible conflict between efficiency and equity. They make it easier to have a more egalitarian society or a just society without reducing efficiency.

Further, the degree of inequality can be reduced without endangering efficiency by reducing the incomes of highly paid people who enjoy more decision-making powers and do more interesting, creative, challenging and psychologically rewarding work and who have a high social status. In contrast, those who are in low-paid jobs, do menial and boring work and exercise little or no decision-making power, and have low status in the community should be offered more material rewards to compensate them for the low 'psychic incomes' attached to such jobs. This is not only necessary to promote equity but also to improve their productivity (the 'economy' of high wages) and to discourage them from choosing to be on unemployment benefits. Contrary to common belief, the market-determined incomes do not reflect accurately the economic and non-economic characteristics of various occupations. Many of the existing wage differentials can be explained by custom and convention, arbitrary or political decisions, and not by all the characteristics of the corresponding work.

In the corporate sector, which is only partially subject to market forces, those at the top set their own salaries and 'design their own golden parachutes' (Brockway 1984–5, p 175). Their salaries and stock options are calculated in millions (even hundreds of millions of dollars). Such astronomical remuneration packages are frequently justified in terms of responsibilities, difficulties of decision-making, experience, and fear that top executives may defect taking with them their contacts and even their colleagues to competing firms. There may be something in these justifications but they are not convincing. First, since the decisions of top executives are not transparent, it is very difficult to judge the degree of difficulty attaching to particular types of decisions. But it seems that really important decisions, 'decisions that do make a difference are often blindingly obvious' (Brockway 1984–5, p 175). Second, and as far as their experience is concerned, 'they happen to be in the right place at the right time and not uncommonly they inherited the right place' (ibid). Third, with regard to defection or 'decamping', an increase in pay alone rarely stops people from moving to other firms.

Clearly, there is no way that the fabulous executive salaries can be explained, let alone justified, in terms of the amount of effort or work, the difficulty of decision-making, contribution to the success of the firm or to the general welfare. Very often executives are rewarded whether they make profits or losses. Certainly, many of them are getting far more than would be needed to persuade them to do their job. Their salaries have become part of the corporate culture or the customary corporate practice that has little economic and ethical justification.

Arguably, the excessive financial rewards the top executives receive may prove to be counterproductive. Since the decision-making process is a collective activity, in the course of which the chief executives merely approve and coordinate decisions that flow up to them from subordinates, their enormous pay packets arouse envy and a feeling of injustice among subordinates, thereby undermining teamwork and cooperation, leading to a reduction in efficiency of the corporation. Moreover, given that cooperation is a prominent attribute of 'meaningful work', it should be encouraged by directing incentives at team rather than at individual effort and performance. In any case, pay is not the top priority of most executives, so why offer them, or rather allow them to give themselves excessive salaries?

In summary, an effective incentive structure consistent with a well-designed decision-making system is one in which people would, as far as possible, be rewarded according to their effort and contribution, as judged not only by market valuation of their contributions, but also by the 'needs' of society, which are not always reflected in the market. Further, the incentive structure must have a strong component of non-economic motivation in order to increase efficiency without increasing inequalities. Finally, the incentive system can encourage people to be more altruistic and cooperative by recognising their work through offering them individual 'moral' incentives, such as trust and respect, and pecuniary team incentives. The resulting inequalities in such a society would be 'optimal' or, at least, 'functional', and the potential conflict between ethics and economics is reduced. There would also be greater social mobility and harmony. A more gradual gradation of pay allows the lower-income groups to rise up on the social ladder, because the steps are not so far apart. However, when the rungs on the ladder of career are too far apart, only a few can climb up and many are left out. Such a state of affairs is incongruent with a just society and a well-functioning economy.

VII

In this chapter we have tried to bring together the five chosen principles of a well-designed decision-making system, and to show how they interact and reinforce one another to generate the 'right' decisions. In such a system there will be discrepancies from time to time between expectations and outcomes, but decision-makers will not, in general, regret their choices. They will be in a state of equilibrium convinced of the rightness of their decisions. The idea of a well-designed decision-making system is not to eliminate or minimise all errors, but only to attend to the systemic ones. It seems inevitable that wrong decisions will be taken in any economic system, but if the errors are not systemic, the economic system will allow reversals of policies and decisions that have turned out to be wrong.

The first task in designing such a system is to specify the optimal structure of decision-making, or who should be deciding which decision. This will ensure that the 'right' decisions will be taken by the 'right' people. The second task is to ensure that proper procedures are followed in reaching decisions. This is important not only because the decisions will more likely turn out to be right, but they will be seen to be right. The third task is to make sure that the structure of information flows is reliable. If the information flows are flawed, then the decisions will not turn out to be correct. The fourth task is to ensure that 'rational' criteria are used for deciding on a course of action. This requires proper calculation of costs and benefits. Such criteria are designed to ensure the efficient use of scarce resources and to avoid unnecessary waste. They are not designed to avoid taking decisions in the face of uncertainty. It seems likely that no major decision will be taken and not much investment will take place as a result of what Keynes called 'cold calculation'. The fifth and final task is to design an effective motivation structure to ensure that the right decisions are implemented efficiently.

A well-designed decision-making system will ensure that the set of decisions prescribed for individuals, organisations and governments will differ from one period to the next, as their respective makers and their circumstances change. Moreover, the whole set of decisions will be in equilibrium in the sense of being retrospectively approved, an assessment that the decision-makers did the right thing at the time of decision-making. In order to make sure that the outcomes or decisions are right economically and non-economically, we have extended the notion of economic equilibrium of an individual to the 'equilibrium life' of the individual, and that of macroeconomic equilibrium to 'social equilibrium'. The equilibrium life might be referred to as the 'good life', a life free from remorse and regret.

12. The Properties of a Well-functioning Economy

I

Although different economists may have different conceptions of a well-functioning economy and disagree strenuously on how to achieve the desired properties, we believe most economists would agree that a well-functioning economy would: (i) allocate resources efficiently both at a point in time and over time; (ii) generate and diffuse a satisfactory rate of innovation; (iii) adapt swiftly and efficiently to external and internal shocks; (iv) maintain macroeconomic stability at a high level of employment; and (v) produce an equitable distribution of income and wealth. As noted in the Introduction, these are normally treated by economists as objectives of an economic system. We refer to them as properties, because in a well-functioning economy they cease to be objectives and become 'internalised'. They become part and parcel of the working of the economic system.

The five properties do not exhaust the relevant set, but taken together they define adequately a well-functioning economy. They suffice to show that there are stringent requirements that a well-functioning economy must satisfy. In a less than well-functioning economy, the five properties adversely affect and contradict each other and thus short-term trade-offs would have to be made especially between (i) and (ii) and between (v) and the rest. But in a well-functioning economy, the five properties would be mutually consistent and would sustain and reinforce one another. Nevertheless, a flaw in one property would have adverse consequences for the other properties and consequently for the performance of the economy.

The structure of the chapter is as follows: Sections II–VI discuss the five properties and show how they affect one another. Section VII summarises the chapter and offers some concluding remarks about a well-functioning economy.

II

Since the rise of modern economics in the last quarter of the nineteenth century, economic theory has focused mainly on the problem of value or relative prices for the purpose of allocating resources efficiently. Much time and intellectual effort went into the specification of conditions for the best allocation of resources. These conditions constitute the set of welfare equations, which demonstrate that, given the best available technology and the existing distribution of income and wealth, no movement of resources can yield greater production and social utility. The resulting allocation is the best; no waste occurs at both the production and consumption stages. The conditions for this state of affairs are:

1. marginal social cost = marginal private cost;
2. marginal private cost = marginal private revenue;
3. marginal private revenue = price;
4. price = marginal private utility;
5. marginal private utility = marginal social utility; and
6. marginal social cost of the given product = marginal social utility of the next product that could be produced by the factors entering into the marginal social cost.

These equations can be taken normatively as a suitable guide to microeconomic policy. They are important in dealing with market failures such as the presence of significant externalities, which cause discrepancies between private and social costs and benefits.

Allocative or distributive efficiency refers to both efficiency, at a point in time and efficiency over time (inter-temporal efficiency). It is possible to achieve efficient allocation of resources in the short run at the expense of a longer time period, particularly when non-renewable resources are involved. The presence of non-renewable resources makes inter-temporal efficiency a more relevant and desirable notion of allocative efficiency. Inter-temporal efficiency is also relevant for choosing the optimal size and structure of investment. However, it is much more difficult to achieve than efficiency at a point in time, because of the inherent unpredictability of changes in technology, preferences and distribution of income over time. Moreover, as Koopmans and Montias (1971, p 45) argue, single period efficiency implies maximum consumption in that period, whereas inter-temporal efficiency is compatible with high or low growth, stationary, declining or fluctuating per capita consumption.

In mainstream economics allocative efficiency is normally considered an economic concept, but in our view it also has an ethical dimension. Given the inescapable fact of scarcity, our moral intuition suggests we ought not waste scarce resources. Our welfare and indeed the survival of future generations depend on how efficiently we use the available resources. Hence, inter-temporal efficiency is the more important and relevant notion of efficiency for achieving intergenerational equity. The ethical dimension of efficiency casts doubt on the validity of the efficiency-equity trade-off so popular among many economists.

In addition to the set of welfare equations, allocative efficiency depends partly on the other properties of a well-functioning economy. Creative efficiency in the form of product and process innovation can improve the allocation of available resources, through finding alternative and better uses for them. Similarly, adaptive efficiency has a favourable effect on allocative efficiency through the removal of impediments to the mobility of resources. Also, more reliable and accurate information flows can improve allocative efficiency by telling us where the available resources are most productive and where they are most valued. Macroeconomic stability at full employment reduces the degree of uncertainty and encourages the use of idle resources. Finally, equity, fairness and justice have an additional positive effect on efficiency through providing 'moral' incentives and elimination of alienation. A contented labour force that is satisfied with the distribution of income and wealth will be more cooperative and will exert more effort than one, which believes that the distribution is inequitable. Thus allocative efficiency is enhanced by the other properties of a well-functioning economy.

III

An economy that allocates resources efficiently, both in a single period and over several periods, may not generate an adequate rate of innovation, which is needed to offset the law of diminishing returns, maintain international competitiveness and expand the range of choices available to consumers. The welfare equations, which ensure the optimum allocation of resources at a point in time, may not promote innovation, as there would be no surplus to invest in R&D activities. The economy would be getting the most out of its available resources but there may not be much growth in the long run. As Schumpeter (1950, p 83) observed:

> A system – any system, economic or other – that at every point of time fully utilises its possibilities to the best advantage may yet in the long-run be inferior to a system that does so at no given point of time, because the latter's failure to do so may be a condition for the level or speed of its long-run performance.

The primary function of innovation or creative efficiency is to offset the law of diminishing returns and prevent stagnation. In a closed economy technological change is the only factor in the long run that can sustain economic prosperity in the context of population growth. Even globally, given that some of the resources are non-renewable, innovation is still needed to offset the law of diminishing returns. Further, innovation is needed to maintain one's ability to compete. This applies both to the individual firm and the nation at large. In a dynamic world, where competitive advantages are largely acquired rather than given by nature and are continuously changing, a country must innovate in order to make the required structural adjustments forced upon it largely by external disturbances. Failure to do so will lead to a loss of its competitive advantages. Furthermore, innovation is required to expand the range of consumer goods available to the population. This applies particularly to a closed or relatively closed economy, where imports of new products are restricted for one reason or another, as in the former Soviet-type economies. Within limits, expanding the range of consumer goods enhances welfare, especially if the new products serve a genuine need and not an artificial want.

Arguably, then, the ability to innovate and diffuse innovation across the economy is the most important property of a well-functioning economy. However, we know less about the innovation and diffusion process than about allocative efficiency. Despite the rise of endogenous growth theory, which purports to explain technological progress, there remains an element of mystery surrounding the innovation process. The innovation 'equation' contains many variables including some unknown ones. Unlike in the case of rational allocation of scarce resources, we can specify some but not all the necessary conditions for successful innovation and diffusion of new products and processes.

First, there must be a congenial social, cultural and political environment for indigenous entrepreneurship to flourish. The importance of such an environment is demonstrated by the experience of the former Soviet-type economies, which failed to produce a dynamic group of entrepreneurs to take the risks of innovation. The bureaucratisation of economic life led to attitudes and behaviours that were hostile to change, risk-taking and money making. Individuals became too dependent on the state and, in turn, the state did not trust its citizens to take initiatives and make innovatory decisions. There is evidence to suggest that innovation is partly a function of trust (Casson 1993). In societies where there is 'high trust', entrepreneurship flourishes, and conversely there is scarcity of entrepreneurship in 'low-trust' cultures.

Second, there must also be an 'innovational' infrastructure to support potential innovators to develop and exploit their ideas and inventions commercially. The innovational infrastructure includes the provision of public resources for R&D, especially for the development of basic scientific knowledge and for training of scientists, engineers and technicians. Since R&D is generally viewed as a semi-public good, it seems that the state must spread the risks and costs of innovation across society. The state has a creative role to play in the early phase of the research-product cycle. Government funding of basic research is essential for broadening the economy-wide scientific knowledge base. One of the policy implications of the new growth theory is that there is a special role for the state to develop human capital, the most important single factor in the long run for innovation and diffusion of new products and processes.

Another feature of an innovational infrastructure is a patent system designed to protect intellectual property rights by giving temporary monopoly rights to inventors to give them enough time to reap the fruits of their original ideas, before they are copied and exploited by others. Innovation has well-known free-rider and public good characteristics; hence the need for patents, copyrights and trade secrets. In addition, the government can promote innovation by enacting laws to ensure high quality, safety and health standards, and to promote products and processes that are environmentally sound. Trust in product is fundamental both for the efficient operation of the market and for international competition. However, the task of maintaining high product standards cannot be performed by the government alone; firms in an industry must, and often do, get together to form an association, which ensures that members adhere to the guidelines set for the industry. There is sufficient evidence, which shows that in countries with a high innovation record, industry associations mainly for small member firms play a key role in maintaining, targeting and performing several functions required to transfer a technical innovation into a commercially viable line of products and services (Van de Ven 1993). Within these associations a network of competitive and cooperative relationships is established by key entrepreneurs and firms.

Yet, another crucial feature of an effective innovational infrastructure is an efficient financial mechanism. In the Schumpeterian innovation process, banks play a critical role in financing new projects. For new entrepreneurs start-up funding for a venture enables them to develop and commercialise their inventions. In particular, it reduces the risks of terminating the innovation process during the early stages, when difficulties are likely to arise and when prospects appear unfavourable. Since the innovation process is time-consuming, requiring continuous commitment and interest on the part of innovators, the availability of credits and subsidies increases the survival rate of innovators during their uncertain journey from the initial conception to the final stage of completion and marketing.

It may be argued that an open economy, which encourages trade and direct foreign investment, does not have to develop a world-class research sector for domestic innovation. Instead, it can rely on transnational corporations for the transfer of new technologies and direct investment of technology-intensive industries. However, no country, even the most developed, can either afford to ignore or escape the impact of multinational firms. Since the diffusion of new technology is more rapid among the more developed market economies, this suggests that such economies have the required innovational infrastructure to absorb and participate in the growing international division of labour in R&D.

Moreover, when the multinational firms relocate their activities to more favourable countries, the losing country must be able to attract new investment or substitute domestic investment. This adjustment is made easier if the country has a developed innovational infrastructure.

Third, and perhaps the most important condition for innovation, is competition. Competition is a dynamic process, a process of discovery, or in Schumpeter's phrase, 'a disequilibrium process of creative destruction'. Without competition there would be little innovation and, more importantly, as Soviet experience demonstrates, there would be no diffusion across the economy. Under competitive conditions the threat of survival stimulates firms to innovate, to find more efficient methods of producing a given level of output or to develop new products. Thus in competitive markets, especially those with few competitors, the main form of competition is through product and/or process innovation.

The ability to generate and diffuse new products and processes is affected by the other properties of a well-functioning economy. If scarce resources are allocated efficiently and their prices reflect accurately their opportunity costs, then those prices provide reliable signals for entrepreneurs to find ways of reducing costs or develop substitutes for products that are scarce or are becoming more scarce. Inventions and innovations require adaptation, flexible and social structures that respond quickly to change. The effect of adaptive efficiency on innovation is through the removal of physical and institutional barriers. The resulting innovation would be part and parcel of adaptive efficiency. As already hinted, reliable information flows in the form of scarcity prices are important for creative efficiency. More importantly, perhaps, the ability of the economy to generate new ideas and scientific information is a precondition for inventions and innovations. Similarly, macroeconomic stability is conducive to innovation. It reduces the degree of uncertainty and encourages potential innovators to make long-term calculations regarding the profitability of their inventions. Finally, equity is more likely to be beneficial than harmful for innovation. If innovators are remunerated according to their contribution, the supply of innovation will increase. Given the fact that innovation is a risk-ridden activity, an activity that has generally positive externalities, potential innovations must be given pecuniary and non-pecuniary incentives to pursue their innovations.

IV

In a rapidly changing world, where national economies are becoming more and more open and integrated, the ability to adjust swiftly and smoothly to shocks becomes an increasingly important property of a well-functioning economy. Long ago Hayek (1945, pp 52–4) observed: 'the economic problem of society is mainly one of adaptation to changes in particular circumstances of time and place'. Further, given the growth of globalisation of production, the ability of the economy to be versatile and to integrate successfully its productive capacity with the rest of the world, or with a particular regional market, is also an important feature of a well-functioning economy. Needless to say, an economy that fails to adjust quickly to unforeseen and unforeseeable circumstances will experience a decline in its economic growth.

As in the closely related property of creative efficiency, we do not know all the necessary conditions for adaptive efficiency. According to North (1990, p 80) 'adaptive efficiency is concerned with the kinds of rules that shape the way an economy evolves through time. It is also concerned with the willingness of a society to acquire knowledge and learning, to induce innovation, to undertake risk and creative activity of all sorts, as well as to resolve problems and bottlenecks of the society through time'. Clearly, this view of adaptive efficiency has to do with innovation and institutional change. With a high rate of innovation the economy is able to make structural adjustment by shifting resources from the declining to the growing industries. If innovation takes the form of process innovation, or more efficient methods of producing an existing product, the country will be able to maintain its competitive advantages. If, on the other hand, innovation takes the form of product innovation, the economy would acquire a new competitive advantage until a new competitor is able to produce the new product more efficiently.

More importantly, perhaps, adaptive efficiency implies learning from failures, the elimination of errors, organisational and institutional rigidities, customs and conventions and ideologies that are hostile to change or not oriented to adaptive efficiency. Adaptive efficiency depends on flexible institutions, which are needed to take advantage of the opportunities and challenges presented by the changing world. Both formal and informal institutions influence the quality of the decision-making process and the behaviour of economic agents, and through their effects on the costs of exchange and production, the performance of the economy

Institutional changes are usually slow-moving and incremental processes, except in the case of revolutions or foreign conquests. In times of rapid external and internal economic changes, there is the possibility that both formal and informal institutions may not change sufficiently to keep in step with the economic changes. Decentralised decision-making and spontaneous adaptation by the market will not be generally sufficient and must be supplemented by public policy to strengthen the incentives for change in technology and preferences. Governments can do something to change the formal institutions, or 'the rules of the game', by repealing outdated legislation, and/or introducing new rules and regulations more suited to current economic conditions. Examples of formal institutional changes include tariffs, labour markets, financial and fiscal reforms.

Reforming the formal institutions that have become obsolete is necessary but not sufficient for adaptive efficiency. Informal institutional constraints persist and survive long after the formal institutional reforms have been effected. They include attitudes, conventions, norms and codes of behaviour. These are often more difficult to change and require both positive and negative incentives to force people to shed their habitual decisions and behaviour. Exposing economic agents to the rigours of international competition can be an effective method of promoting flexibility and adaptability. Such competition forces firms to innovate and change their traditional ways of doing things, or find new ways of reducing costs. However, openness to international competition is at best necessary but not sufficient for adaptive efficiency. As North (1990, p 24) points out, 'competition may be so muted and the signals so confused that adjustment may be slow or misguided and the classic evolutionary consequences may not be obtained for very long periods of time'. On the other hand, if international competition is too strong then domestic firms will not be able to survive without some assistance from the government.

Then there is the problem of rent-seekers. Formal institutions are often created to serve the interests of particular groups rather than those of society. If relatively efficient institutions are created, it is because the two kinds of interests coincide. But if the formal institutions serve particular interest groups, the latter will continue to resist institutional reforms until the time is reached when the gains from existing institutions are assessed to be less than those expected from the proposed institutional reforms. Clearly, public policy should be directed at promoting rivalry and removing economic privileges throughout the economy. This should be backed by adequate resources to enable agencies concerned with promoting competition to enforce such a policy.

There seems little doubt that the institutional structure of a society affects the degree of innovation and the encouragement of experiments, which, in turn, affect adaptive efficiency. More specifically, as North (1990, p 83) argues, 'the incentives included in the institutional framework direct the process of learning-by-doing, learning from one's own mistakes and the development of new (tacit) knowledge and attitudes that will lead individuals in decision-making processes to value systems gradually that are different from the ones they had to begin with'. The society that permits the generation of new ideas, experiments and flexible institutions will be the one most likely to solve its problems over time and adapt quickly to changing environments.

Different institutional rules or arrangements will produce different incentives for people to change and adapt. In the corporate sector, the particular institutions will shape the adaptive efficiency of the internal structures of organisations. For example, freeing entry and exit by means of anti-monopoly and trade practices' legislation, bankruptcy laws and laws dealing with transparency and accountability is crucial for effective and flexible organisations and consequently for the adaptive efficiency of the economy. However, as we have already noted, it is much harder to deal with informal institutions, simply because they are part of habitual behaviour, custom and conventions, which allow people to go through routine processes of decision-making without having to think out the reasons for doing things. To quote North (1990, p 87) once more, 'the persistence of cultural traits in the face of changes in relative prices, formal rules, or political status make informal constraints change at a different rate from formal rules'. This is clearly seen after political revolutions, when most people continue to behave more or less in the same way as they did before the revolution. Perhaps this is one reason why the Chinese had to have a 'cultural revolution' some two decades after the political revolution that changed the formal rules and institutions.

The adaptability of an economic system is generally understood as its ability to change in a favourable direction in response to changes in its environment, particularly as to international changes. But a high propensity to change does not lead to only positive and lasting benefits. Adaptation is often accompanied by significant human and economic costs such as maldistribution of income, dislocation of entire communities and the break-up of customs and traditions that make life worth living. Everywhere towns and cities are losing their unique character and are beginning to resemble one another. A well-functioning economy, in our view, must consist of an optimal mix of adaptive efficiency and equity. It must be humane as well as internationally competitive, or else it must combine the best of technological innovation with customs and traditions.

It was noted earlier that allocative efficiency and adaptive efficiency may not always be consistent. The conditions for allocative efficiency, as depicted in the welfare equations, would get the most out of available resources in the short run, but prevent economic agents from adapting to changing circumstances, mainly through the Schumpeterian process of 'creative destruction'. On the other hand, if resources are used efficiently, their prices would reflect changes in supply and demand and thus provide signals for economic agents to change their plans and adapt. On balance, it would seem that allocative efficiency helps rather than hinders adaptive efficiency. The effects of creative efficiency on adaptive efficiency have already been discussed and shown to be very favourable. Indeed, the two types of efficiency reinforce one another. Reliable and speedy information flows are, of course, necessary for adaptive efficiency. They enable economic agents to take timely decisions and adjust their plans accordingly. Delay in reactions to external shocks can be very costly indeed. Macroeconomic stability at full or near full employment provides a favourable environment for long-term decisions that could anticipate some changes in the external environment, and thus make the required adjustment efficiently. Further, a favourable macroeconomic environment reduces resistance to structural adjustments by those whose jobs are made redundant. Finally, equity seems to have dual effects on adaptive efficiency. The property of adaptive efficiency implies some costs to a section of the community or industry in the form of loss of employment and shutdown. A just society would ensure that the losers are compensated or helped to adjust to new circumstances. On the other hand, workers and interest groups will not resist the change if they know their livelihood will not be threatened or that they will receive fair compensation. Thus, equity will facilitate change and promote adaptive efficiency.

V

Macroeconomic stability has received much attention from both domestic and international financial institutions. It is regarded by them as a fundamental property of a well-functioning economy, in the sense that it is required by other properties. Without a degree of macroeconomic stability, long-term investment, innovation and growth, and efficient allocation of resources, particularly over time, would suffer. An unstable economy would be driven by 'short-termism' and would distribute income and wealth in favour of small groups who are in a position to exploit the existing instability at the expense of others. Like allocative efficiency, much time and intellectual effort has gone into specifying the conditions for macroeconomic stability. Macroeconomics is a highly developed and controversial branch of economics. However, in this section we can only provide a brief summary of the conditions for macroeconomic stability at near full employment.

We emphasise macroeconomic stability at near full employment as a property of a well-functioning economy to highlight the importance of full employment as a desideratum and to distinguish it from the Keynesian unemployment equilibrium or macroeconomic stability at a high level of unemployment. By a high level of employment, we mean the capacity of the economy to generate employment for all those who want or seek employment. In other words, a well-functioning economy would eliminate involuntary unemployment. At the same time, macroeconomic stability implies price stability or a very low rate of inflation. As a result of the fall in the inflation rate in the 1990s, a number of developed economies have managed to achieve macroeconomic stability with relatively high growth rates and a lower but still significant rate of involuntary unemployment. It may be argued that it is better to accept the resulting unemployment as the necessary price for stability and growth, and to compensate the unemployed by giving them a minimum income rather than employment, which may result in a loss of stability and productivity. Society as a whole would be economically better off in preference to the removal of involuntary unemployment. It is often argued that unemployment is necessary for efficiency and productivity, as a stick to discipline the work force.

However, from an equity point of view, the existence of involuntary unemployment implies a dilemma of inequality; either the unemployed workers will receive a minimum income well below current wage levels (inequality of income) or they receive benefits close to the wage (inequality of effort). To this must be added the harmful social, political and above all personal consequences of enforced idleness. A guaranteed minimum income (GMI) is necessary but not sufficient for self-development and well-being; it tends to make people dependent on society and encourages them to be mere consumers of goods and services. Such people often suffer from loss of self-esteem, a feeling of failure, because the income they receive is contingent on being unable to secure employment. More importantly, the elimination of involuntary unemployment is a more effective and lasting solution to the problem of poverty. As Sen (1992, p 151) argues, 'the re-orientation from an income-centred to a capability centred view gives us a better understanding of what is involved in the challenge of poverty'. Finally, a GMI does not satisfy our psychological need for work and 'the instinct of workmanship'. The purpose of work is not simply to satisfy wants, but is a basic source of human well-being, satisfaction and utility. In general, people with jobs are very much happier than the unemployed. Here we can take a leaf from Marx's writing about his future socialist society in which 'work becomes not only the means of living but the first need of the living person' (Marx 1875, p 26).

Now macroeconomic stability at full or near full employment depends on a number of things including an appropriate mix of monetary, fiscal and exchange rate policies. There has been much debate about the place and relative importance of these policies in achieving stability. In recent years the burden of achieving this objective has fallen mainly on monetary policy, with fiscal and (for some countries) exchange rate policies having supporting roles. It is widely believed that monetary policy has a comparative advantage in achieving price stability. An effective monetary policy depends on developed financial institutions and capital markets, especially on a sound banking system with an independent or semi-independent central bank to manage the money supply and avoid high inflation and unemployment rates. There is some debate as to whether or not the central bank should be politically 'independent' or autonomous in determining a monetary policy, whose priorities might be at variance with those of the community, or whether too much power should be given to non-elected officials. On the other hand, by leaving monetary policy to the preferences of political authorities, there is a danger that it might be used for short-term expediency of the electoral cycle. Clearly, given the importance that monetary policy has assumed, the degree of independence given to the central bank must be balanced by greater accountability and transparency. This is consistent with our view that complex decisions, which require the inputs of experts, should not be reached through democratic processes if we want them to be sound. However, the experts must be made accountable, in this case directly to the government and indirectly to the electorate.

There is also some debate as to whether the central bank should follow a rule, such as keeping the money supply in line with potential output growth, or allow it to use its discretion to increase the money supply and reduce the rate of interest in times of low economic activity and conversely in terms of high economic activity and inflation. Time inconsistency is generally acknowledged to be a problem with discretionary policy. There is a presumption on the part of those who advocate a monetary rule that the economic 'credibility' of central banks is enhanced by rules-based regimes over policy discretion, that central banks in the absence of such rules necessarily behave in a discretionary fashion that implies an inflationary bias. Some writers have been sceptical about discretionary policy when the outcome depends on the expectations of private decision-makers, who discount announced policies of low inflation (Fischer 1980; Calvo 1978; Barro and Gordon 1983). According to these writers policy-makers can sometimes achieve macroeconomic stability by having their discretion taken away from them. However, there is no functional connection between discretionary monetary policy responses and inflation. It is entirely feasible for the bias to be avoided by central banks.

In any case, the central bank is able to perform its task of keeping the money supply scarce only if there is a developed and transparent banking system and efficient capital markets, so that it can carry out its open market operations of selling and buying government bonds, or changing the rate of interest on deposits and loans. It can promote stability by lowering the interest rate in times when people wish to add too much to their deposits (savings); raising them when they wish to reduce them. However, because of the uncertainties of real life central bankers do not know precisely when and by how much to change interest rates, and so are able to achieve only approximate stability.

Traditionally, monetary policy was reserved for short-term instability and fiscal policy for medium- and long-term growth. This is partly because the time lags involved in monetary policies are shorter than in fiscal policies, and partly because money is generally thought to be 'neutral' in the long run, apart from changes in the growth rate of the money stock effected by fiscal policy, through lump sum taxes or subsidies. Such changes are bound to affect the long-run real interest rate paid on cash balances. Since fiscal policy has a comparative advantage in dealing with structural issues, it should be directed at long-term growth and employment. To be effective the channels through which fiscal policy affect growth and employment must be identified. The economic growth literature, particularly endogenous growth theory, sheds some light on those channels. First, policies can affect the incentives to invest in R&D and human capital, which have a lasting impact on the long-run rate of growth of output and employment. Second, government expenditure on education and health has positive effects on growth and output. Educated and healthy workers are generally more productive and better able to adjust to technical and other changes in the workplace than uneducated and unhealthy workers. Third, government expenditure on welfare can have growth-enhancing effects by maintaining the social fabric and by contributing to political stability. Finally, the provision of public sector infrastructure can affect positively the viability and productivity of private investment.

Monetary and fiscal policies have important effects on foreign exchange and on the current account. As a result of financial liberalisation, monetary policy now works increasingly through the exchange rate. When an economy expands and interest rates are expected to rise, the exchange rate quickly appreciates helping to keep inflation in check. On the other hand, a fiscal deficit designed to increase the level of employment might be interpreted as an indication of loss of fiscal discipline, in which case it would be followed by capital flight and depreciation of the exchange rate. Exchange rate movements have a significant impact on other economic variables such as real GDP and inflation. Hence, it is desirable to maintain exchange rate stability, or at least avoid violent fluctuations. Under floating exchange regimes, exchange rate policy has a limited role in avoiding such fluctuations. There is much scepticism about the ability of central banks and/or governments to intervene in foreign exchange markets and move the exchange rate in the desired direction. Interventions can, at best, smooth the fluctuations of exchange rate movement along the long-run path, and only marginally affect that path.

Attempts to change the long-run path can be counterproductive and may conflict with the domestic objectives of price stability and full employment. For this reason it is generally preferable to pursue price stability and full employment through monetary and fiscal policies and let the market assume the burden of external adjustment. A flexible exchange rate regime is widely believed to be necessary for national macroeconomic autonomy, to free national economic policy from the balance of payments constraint. Interventions to correct misalignment of foreign exchange rates tend to have limited short-run successes. They are particularly helpful in situations where exchange rates are moving slowly in the right direction, but need a push to speed up the process.

Clearly, macroeconomic stability at full or near full employment depends on the coordination of monetary, fiscal and exchange rate policies as well as other instruments available to the government. While each instrument has its own comparative advantage, it is the function of other instruments to achieve or maintain that advantage. Thus monetary policy is best for pursuing price stability, and price stability is favourable for sustained high employment; but it cannot achieve price stability on its own. Similarly, fiscal policy has a comparative advantage in promoting growth and employment, but it depends on monetary policy, or price stability, to do what it is best at doing. Also, exchange rate policy, except for occasional smoothing out, cannot maintain external stability without monetary and fiscal discipline. In short, monetary, fiscal and (for some countries) exchange rate policies have to be geared together to achieve and sustain macroeconomic stability. This will not be an easy matter, as each of these policies has its own limitations. As De Long (2000, p 84) has observed: 'Any sound approach to stabilisation policy must recognise the limits of stabilisation policy, including the long lags and low multipliers associated with fiscal policy and the long and variable lags and uncertain magnitude of the effects of monetary policy'. Moreover, there is the unresolved question of the best way to deal with the formation of expectations in macroeconomic theory (Solow 2000).

Although we have stated that macroeconomic stability is a fundamental property of a well-functioning economy, it is also true that other properties impact on macroeconomic stability. If the economy allocates resources efficiently, operating near the production feasibility frontier, adapting quickly to external shocks, and generating a satisfactory rate of innovation, it is much easier for the monetary and fiscal authorities to achieve macroeconomic stability at full or near full employment. Indeed, sustainable growth in income and employment relies on a continuous shift of resources from declining, to expanding industries in a process of 'creative destruction'. Finally, equity has favourable effects on macroeconomic stability, both indirectly through its effects on the three kinds of efficiency, and directly through redistribution policies, which keep the level of effective demand in times of low economic activity from falling below a certain level. Also, an equitable distribution of income and wealth reduces social conflicts and major disruptions of economic life. Our view of equity, which places more emphasis on employment rather than on a guaranteed minimum income, is more likely to achieve stability at or near full employment.

VI

The final property in our conception of a well-functioning economy is equity, a multidimensional concept encompassing equality of opportunity and access as well as the redistribution of consumption and wealth (Sen 1992). Given the multidimensional nature of equity, the key to addressing extreme inequality is not simply redistribution but improvement. Improvements in health, education, access to credit and public services and elimination of artificial barriers to entry can enable individuals to participate more fully and more productively in the economy and hence reduce inequalities.

Generally, economists tend to view equity as an ethical criterion, often conflicting with efficiency. But the close connection between economics and ethics suggests the possibility of treating them as mutually reinforcing. It is not hard to see why equity is good for efficiency and growth and vice versa. If the distribution of income and wealth is highly skewed, or if the wealth of the few is seen by the rest of the population to have been acquired illegitimately, low-income groups will feel that they are not receiving their just rewards; they will only do the minimum amount of work they can get away with. A society where many workers are dissatisfied and poorly motivated will tend to be socially and politically unstable and, in turn, economically unstable and wasteful. In contrast a society that has an equitable distribution of income and wealth, which is free from exploitation, rent-seeking activities and shirking, and which strictly links rewards with effort and contribution, will be economically efficient, politically stable and ethically desirable. A just society must first ensure that the basic needs of every member of that society are satisfied. Welfare alone will not help people to live decently. Our view of equity suggests that they should be equipped with skills and guaranteed employment. Work fosters personal development, deepens skills and makes people independent and creative. In particular, a highly subsidised and targeted work support system is needed for those people who are willing to work but who are not very attractive to private employers. A guaranteed minimum income and/or hours of work are not merely a matter of 'good' ethics but also of 'good' economics and politics.

Public policy should aim to eliminate not only poverty and unemployment but also all inequalities that are not necessary for the three kinds of efficiency and for macroeconomic stability, so that the inequality of income and wealth distribution is no greater than that strictly warranted by the efficient working of the system. Attempts to reduce inequalities below this level will harm efficiency and productivity, and hence the amount of goods and services available for redistribution in subsequent periods. On the other hand, there should be limits to inequalities. This raises the difficult question of whether or not a ceiling should be placed on personal income and wealth. While there is general consensus on the need for economic security or a guaranteed minimum income and, to a lesser extent, a guaranteed minimum hours of work, there does not seem to be any agreement on the need for imposing a ceiling on personal income and wealth beyond what is necessary to secure a minimum income for everyone in society and to finance the activities of the state. In our view, a just society is characterised not simply by the absence of absolute poverty, but also by the absence of extreme affluence. We believe a reasonable person living in a just society would regard extreme personal wealth just as offensive as abject poverty.

The case for imposing a ceiling on personal income and wealth can be made on several grounds. First, many moral philosophers and perfectionists claim that, past a point, additional wealth is not important for increasing one's excellence and well-being and will probably decrease a person's well-being

(Hurka 1993). This suggests the possibility of deriving not only diminishing marginal utility but also negative marginal utility from having very high incomes. Extreme wealth is likely to corrupt a person's values, turning that person from true goods, from the pursuit of the finer things in life and personal development to the pursuit of material acquisition and conspicuous consumption. According to the perfectionist school, wealth does not always buy happiness; beyond the satisfaction of basic needs and a life of simple but comfortable living, there is no certainty that more income and consumption will promote happiness or welfare.

In a competitive society, where new wants are continually being created by corporations, a growth of consumption does not guarantee a growth of satisfaction. The things that contribute most to a sense of well-being cannot be bought with money. They include a good family life, genuine friendship, work satisfaction and satisfaction with the uses of one's leisure. It is of some interest to note that the great economists did not identify increased consumption with increased happiness. But as economics drifted away from ethics, economic welfare came to be equated with total welfare. Adam Smith, J.S. Mill and J.M. Keynes, to name but a few, warned against mindless materialism, the increased consumption of unnecessary and luxury goods, but their warning has not been heeded. Indeed, modern society is in a grip of luxury fever. Excessive consumption has become a kind of competition to display more and more of the symbols of success. It is preventing us from solving the problem of scarcity.

Second, distributional justice demands the transfer of resources from the super rich to the poor. Most people would accept a 'ceiling' on this ground, if only because a ceiling would not apply to them. However, the argument goes beyond that and implies a further lowering of the ceiling. There are unfavourable externalities associated with ostentatious wealth and consumption. It often leads to envy and jealousy and hence loss of welfare. No doubt many people derive vicarious pleasure from the wealth and consumption of the rich, and admire their lifestyle as a model to follow. Moralists who object to an imposition of a ceiling would say that the problem of externality is not a problem for the rich but for the poor and not so poor. The poor, they argue, should not be jealous – envy is one of the seven deadly sins. However, the spending habits of the super rich are drawing an increasing number of people into debt and bankruptcy. As they spend more, the people just below them also spend more, and gradually the new spending levels spread all the way down the income ladder. Some spend more than they earn in order to keep up appearances. Moreover, if more and more people in the developing countries continue to adopt the lifestyle of the rich in the developed countries, as they are doing under the spread of globalisation, the resulting impact on the physical environment, especially the ozone layer, would of itself make the world uninhabitable. Clearly, prudence and justice require moderation in the consumption of wealth. Moderation in consumption is a virtue and has 'a justice dimension' (Danner 1980, p 108). Hence, in a just society, personal consumption beyond a certain level should be strongly discouraged.

Third, a persuasive argument for imposing a ceiling on personal wealth and income has to do with the effects of wealth on political power. There is often a direct and close link between economic wealth and political power. Well-off people have disproportionate political influence and power. When people reach the bliss point of consumption or even before this point, when all their wants are satisfied, they tend to use their wealth to obtain privileges and power over other people. They form powerful lobby groups to acquire and maintain special privileges. Hence, the concentration of wealth in the hands of the few may conflict with the democratic rights of other people. A truly democratic society cannot have a totally free market that allows unlimited accumulation of personal wealth. Moreover, the concentration of wealth tends to persist from one generation to the next. Increasing inequality creates the political and economic conditions that lead to even more inequality.

Fourth, there is a more fundamental and compelling reason why we should be economical and prudent in the use of wealth, and why there should be a ceiling. The fact of scarcity compels us to be efficient both in production by avoiding unnecessary waste and in consumption by minimising unnecessary consumption. Excessive consumption may not lead to a serious economic problem for society as a whole if all our resources were renewable, or if we consume no more of the non-renewable resources than what we produce or put back through recycling. While technical progress may provide substitutes for non-renewable resources, there can be no certainty that it, or some other *deus ex machina*, will provide suitable substitutes for all the non-renewable resources that are needed for the welfare and perhaps the survival of future generations. Already, we have experienced several environmental disasters. Our supplies of some minerals, forests, fertile soil, clean water and air are disappearing too quickly or replaced by inferior substitutes. If we comprehend fully the economics of non-renewable resources, we might come to realise that not only the economic but the total welfare of the human race and, perhaps, its very survival on this planet ultimately depend on the proper management and sustainable use of these resources.

Accordingly, unless we are certain that technological progress or change in taste will make some non-renewable resources redundant, we should strongly discourage and even prohibit their consumption beyond what we absolutely need to alleviate abject poverty. It has to be remembered that the marginal wants of the rich or the relatively rich are not given or determined by the facts of physiological needs but are created by advertising, marketing techniques and all kinds of social pressure. It is, therefore, no longer certain that economic policy and market forces should seek to satisfy those wants any more than they should try to prevent them from arising in the first place. Perhaps a variable tax on advertising and some limitation on tax deductibility in respect of advertising expenditure would do something to remedy the situation.

By placing a ceiling on the income and hence the consumption of the mega rich we can reduce but not eliminate the social differences that exist in affluent societies. Such differences are generally manifested by ostentatious consumption, and hence a ceiling might go some way to reduce unnecessary consumption and check that endless process of the creation and multiplication of factitious wants. It may be argued, however, that such a ceiling would make little difference to the total volume of consumption. The traditional view is that if we want to discourage consumption, we should distribute income from the relatively poor, who have a high propensity to consume, to the relatively rich who have a low propensity. But this view ignores the fact that the consumption habits of the rich have a powerful demonstration effect on lower-income groups in society. Thus, a policy that aims to reduce the level of consumption should start at the very top, where the dynamic process of creating and satisfying new and unnecessary wants mainly originates. This is not to deny that a great deal of factitious goods are consumed by the lower-income groups, who are perhaps more vulnerable to the pressures of the advertising industry.

The arguments advanced in favour of a ceiling are based on the assumption that incentives for work and enterprise would not be affected and hence the ceiling would not violate the efficiency conditions. On the contrary, it is assumed that between the floor and ceiling there would still be a significant degree of inequality of income and wealth needed for incentives and equity considerations. Both the floor and the ceiling are needed to enhance efficiency and productivity in the long run as well as being desirable in themselves. The degree of inequality would be no greater than that dictated by the efficient working of the system. While it is possible that the ceiling would act as a disincentive for a minority who might thus be induced to work less or to move to other countries with no ceiling on personal income, it provides incentives for the majority by virtue of the fact that people living in a just society would behave more responsibly and would not shirk their duties.

Within the floor and ceiling the resulting inequalities would represent and reflect relative performance and contributions as well as needs. Such inequalities would be consistent with Nozick's 'entitlement theory', according to which 'individuals have rights or entitlement of benefits that derive from their own production' (Nozick 1974). Further, such inequalities would be readily acceptable. Most people will not object to the fact of inequality but rather to the fact that differences in rewards do not correspond to any recognisable differences in the merit or performance of those who receive them. Wide income disparities are more readily tolerated if wealth is perceived as the product of talent and effort.

The principle of matching rewards with performance and contribution is fraught with conceptual and practical difficulties that were discussed in Chapter 6. There are also serious difficulties with defining the ceiling, much more serious than those encountered with defining the floor or guaranteed minimum income. This is not the place to determine what the level of the ceiling should be. It would require a great deal of research and inputs from different sections of the community, especially from those who are or likely to be affected by the ceiling. But it has to be remembered that there are always transitional difficulties involved in moving from the present state of affairs to a more desirable state. It is precisely because we live in an unjust society, which has its own incentive system and social behaviour, that the idea of a ceiling may not be accepted. However, people living in a just society would readily accept a ceiling and look upon it as the norm. In any case, the idea of placing a limit on personal wealth has a long history going back to Plato and Aristotle. Perhaps the best statement on placing a ceiling on personal wealth is that given by John Stuart Mill (1868, pp 453–4):

> I know not why it should be a matter of congratulation that persons who are already richer than any one needs to be, should have doubled their means of consuming things which give little or no pleasure except as representations of wealth; or that numbers of individuals should pass over, every year, from the middle classes into a richer class...But the best state of human nature is that in which, while no one is poor, no one desires to be richer, nor has any reason to fear being thrust back, by any efforts of others to push themselves forward.

What J.S. Mill was hinting at is that an 'equilibrium' state of economic development is not about maximising economic growth and consumption per capita year after year. Rather it is about better distribution, and the pursuit of the finer things of life such as having time for reflection and for one's friends or even for one's family. Mill did not want people to overwork and over-consume. Like Adam Smith, he regarded economic growth as a means for establishing the foundation of a liberal and just society (Prash 1991).

As with any other property of a well-functioning economy, equity is generally reinforced by the other four properties. Allocative efficiency can promote equity by reducing waste and rewarding factors of production according to their marginal contributions (computative justice). Similarly, creative efficiency through its effects on growth can also promote equity. In a growing and dynamic economy, there would be less resistance to distributive policies aimed at supporting the disadvantaged groups in society. Adaptive efficiency is good for equity. Removal of institutional barriers and improved human capital development, which are necessary for adaptive efficiency, help the poor to improve their opportunity to succeed. Finally, sustainable macroeconomic stability at full employment is a necessary condition for promoting equity, directly through more access to employment and indirectly through its effect on other properties.

VII

To summarise the discussion of the chapter, the first point that needs to be made is that the five chosen properties of a well-functioning economy, as a sub-set of a just society, are mutually interdependent and reinforcing. An economy that possesses the five properties will be free from involuntary unemployment and waste; it will get the most out of available resources; it will be growing at a steady rate, adapting smoothly and rapidly to changing circumstances; and, most importantly, it will have an equitable distribution of income and wealth that reflects relative contributions and needs. It will also be free from abject poverty and extreme affluence. Indeed, the absence of extreme wealth and poverty is traditionally accepted as an indicator of a just society. Further, a society in which 'no one is poor and no one desires to be richer' will be more cheerful and contented. It is also a society that manages its non-renewable resources in such a way that the welfare and survival of future generations are not compromised. In short, such a society will be the best of all possible worlds.

At present, no economy or society has those properties. But with a well-designed decision-making system and favourable institutions, errors are minimised and confined to human fallibility. It then becomes feasible to move nearer to each property. But this may take several years or even decades, since some of the conditions involve attitudinal and institutional changes, which are slow-moving processes. In the next chapter an attempt is made to show how a well-designed decision-making system can promote the five desirable properties.

13. The Decision-making Process of a Well-functioning Economy

I

This chapter attempts to link the principles of a well-designed decision-making system with the properties of a well-functioning economy. Thus far, we have argued that the performance of an economy depends directly and indirectly on the quality of the decision-making system. The central aim of this chapter is to show more precisely how each principle of the decision-making system affects the five properties of a well-functioning economy. It is important to establish the link because we can then pinpoint the causes of the weakness of the economic system and suggest possible changes in the specific components of the decision-making process. There are, of course, some feedback effects from the performance of the economy on the decision-making system itself, which will need to be considered.

It should be noted that in this chapter we are discussing the prerequisites, not suggesting any guarantees of a well-functioning economy. Our aim is to show that an appropriately designed decision-making system will go a long way towards establishing a well-functioning economy as defined in Chapter 12. We have already hinted at the possible links between the five principles of a well-designed decision-making system and the five properties of a well-functioning economy in other chapters, but we need to discuss them here in more detail and greater depth.

Sections II–VII discuss, in turn, the effects of the five principles of the decision-making process on the five properties of a well-functioning economy. Section VIII examines very briefly the possible feedback effects of the five properties of a well-functioning economy on the five principles of the decision-making system. Section IX offers some concluding remarks on the connection between a well-integrated decision-making system and a well-functioning economy.

II

It should be clear by now that the decision-making structure is a crucial determinant of the 'correctness' of decisions and hence the performance of the economy. A sub-optimal structure, or an excessive degree of (de) centralisation, will result in too many market, organisational and government failures, in which case none of the properties of a well-functioning economy would be fully achieved. First, an optimal decision-making structure, or an appropriate mix of markets, organisations and governments, is necessary for achieving allocative and distributive efficiency. To get the most out of available resources, there has to be a proper division of all the sets of decisions, which have to be made in an economy, among individuals operating in the marketplace, organisations and governments. This will ensure that the right people or agencies will be in charge of those decisions that are more appropriate to make by the particular entity on economic, political and ethical grounds. Of course, the optimal division of decisions changes over time in a particular economy, depending on development in technology, cultural and institutional changes. It also differs across countries depending on the existing institutional and physical infrastructure as well as customs and conventions.

Allowing for differences across space and time, which influence the optimal degree of decentralisation, there must be a decentralised market system or a competitive process to generate scarcity prices for allocative and distributive efficiency. Theoretically, it is possible to have a decentralised system without a market, but then the problem of valuation would have to be solved by some other mechanism such as linear programming, and this may turn out to be too costly and impracticable. Rational allocation and efficient use of resources depend on reliable information concerning the relative scarcity of resources. Much of this information is readily generated by the market and by organisations competing with one another. At the same time there must be a central decision-making authority to regulate the market system and encapsulate the competitive process. Such an authority is also necessary to provide the required institutional and physical infrastructure for a well-functioning market system, and to make certain decisions that are not made by the interaction of market force and organisations. An excessive degree of decentralisation would not lead to allocative efficiency, as externalities would not be incorporated into the decision-making process, and indeed certain decisions and corresponding activities would not be undertaken at all.

Second, the decision-making structure has a major impact on creative efficiency. An excessive degree of centralisation inhibits the development of new ideas, and further, whatever new ideas and inventions a central authority may generate through the channelling of resources into education and research, such inventions would be confined to the industries where they were developed, or simply they would not be applied. A centralised decision-making structure may generate a lot of inventions and new ideas, but they may not translate into innovations, or may not spread across the economy. The central authority can focus on a few industries but not on all industries at once. Accordingly, a decentralised system with a significant degree of concentration of decision-making power, or an oligopolistic market structure, is needed for innovation and diffusion. Oligopolistic firms have the resources to invest in R&D activities. They compete chiefly in product differentiation by a process of imitation, and thereby the generated innovations are diffused quickly throughout the economy. Frequently, small firms develop new ideas, but it is the large firms that commercialise the inventions and market them. Thus, there seems to be an 'optimal' structure of sizes of firms and by implication an optimal degree of concentration of decision-making authority.

The government, or a central authority, has a complementary role in the innovation process through the development of an 'innovational infrastructure'. More precisely, its role is to encourage basic research and general education, which neither the market nor private organisations provide in sufficient quantity, because of the high risks and uncertainty. The primary function of the central authority in promoting creative efficiency is to spread the risks and collectivise the costs of inventions and innovations. Clearly, an optimal decision-making structure, consisting of individuals operating in the market, organisations competing with one another, and governments, is needed to ensure an adequate rate of innovation and diffusion.

Third, an optimal decision-making structure is needed for adaptive efficiency. Except in emergency situations, an excessive degree of centralisation–concentration of decision-making power encourages rigidity and inflexibility as well as delays in reaching and implementing decisions that are needed for adjustment. The more concentrated the decision-making power, the greater the likelihood the decision-makers will use their power to ensure that the system, which safeguards their position, remains unchanged. Systems with concentrated political and economic powers tend to obstruct evolutionary changes, and when changes come about they are usually abrupt and violent. Centralised economies are notorious for their failures to adjust to changing economic and social conditions. Even when there is a will to change, central decision-makers can cope only with a few decisions at a time. That is why they are needed in an emergency when they can channel resources to deal with the problem at hand. In addition, a central authority is needed to change from time to time the formal institutions that have become obsolete and an obstacle to change. Governments should do everything possible to encourage adjustment, while easing the pains for those hit by the change. They also need to ensure, by improving the skills of the work force, that more people are able to take advantage of new opportunities. Both international competition and globalisation favour the highly skilled.

More importantly, perhaps, adaptive efficiency depends on informal institutions, on attitudes and behaviour of individuals. A centralised structure tends to discourage initiative and innovation, which are necessary for adaptive efficiency. In contrast, a decentralised competitive structure is more flexible and has the capacity to adjust and adapt to new ideas more readily than a centralised structure. A high, though not an excessive, degree of decentralisation is necessary for continuous adjustment of ideas and attitudes in response to external and internal shocks. At the same time, a central authority is needed to offer incentives for people to shed their outmoded attitudes and behaviour and adopt new ones that are more in tune with the changing needs of society. Thus, adaptive efficiency requires both elements of centralisation and decentralisation of decision-making.

Fourth, the decision-making structure has a profound effect on macroeconomic stability. A *laissez-faire* system is inherently unstable, though not necessarily violently unstable. It is subject to coordination failure. This was clearly demonstrated by Keynes for a 'static' economy and more convincingly by Harrod (1948) for a dynamic economy in his famous 'instability theorem', which generated a vast literature in the 1950s and 1960s on the possibility of steady state growth. The outcome of this literature is that the conditions for a *laissez-faire* steady growth rate are so far-fetched, they could not be obtained in the real world; hence Joan Robinson (1965) dubbed the steady state growth at full employment, 'the golden age'. At the other extreme, in a centrally controlled economy, it is easy to achieve macroeconomic stability at full employment, because there is no coordination failure, no discrepancy between aggregate supply and demand, or between planned saving and investment. But this outcome is likely to be achieved, as in the case of the Soviet-type economies, at the cost of the three kinds of efficiency and hidden unemployment (unemployment within factories) and inflation (long queues). The unsatisfactory outcomes of the two extremes of centralisation and decentralisation suggest the need for an optimal decision-making structure to achieve macroeconomic stability at or near full employment. The state must play a critical role by adopting an appropriate mix of macroeconomic policies, while leaving most microeconomic decisions to the private sector. It must manage rather than control the economy from the centre. A degree of centralisation is, therefore, required to achieve macroeconomic stability.

Finally, the decision-making structure is important for equity. An excessive degree of decentralisation will lead to extreme inequalities of income and wealth. Even if markets were perfect, which they are very seldom, and the resulting inequalities are legitimate reflecting the relative contributions of economic agents, distributive justice demands redistribution of income from the rich to the poor. A central authority in the form of a welfare state is needed to guarantee a minimum income for those who are unable to fend for themselves in the marketplace, namely the aged, the disabled and the involuntarily unemployed (if any). The state is also needed, as we have argued in the last chapter, to provide a minimum hours of work and to place a ceiling on personal income and wealth if there is unemployment and if an equitable distribution of income and wealth is not generated by the system. An excessive degree of centralisation can in the long run be damaging to equity. It would lead to inefficiency, stagnation and instability, and the economy would lack the required resources to achieve equity in all its dimensions (Sen 1992). At best, an excessive degree of centralisation might achieve equity in the short run at the expense of efficiency and personal freedom. In short, an optimal decision-making structure is a precondition for an equitable distribution of income and wealth.

III

Appropriate decision-making procedures are required both because they affect the quality of decisions and the properties of a well-functioning economy. Except in special circumstances, where authoritarian procedures are needed and in complex decisions that require the inputs of experts, democratic procedures should be the general rule, not simply because they have favourable outcomes but also because they are valued in their own right. Decisions and procedures must not be merely right but they must be seen to be right. Accordingly, the decision-making procedure must be transparent and decision-makers must be accountable to those who are most affected by the decisions. In this section an attempt is made to link the decision-making procedure with the five properties of a well-functioning economy.

First, an authoritarian procedure is unlikely to lead to an efficient allocation of resources except in certain cases where there are major externalities that could not be internalised through democratic procedures. Further, an authoritarian procedure is appropriate when decisions involving allocation of resources and national security have to be made either quickly or secretly, in which case there is no room for consultation and consensus.

On the other hand, in order to satisfy the allocative efficiency equations (Section II, Chapter 12), a central authority would have to know both the private and social costs and benefits. It must, therefore, consult individual firms and consumers. Without their inputs it is simply not possible for such an authority to allocate resources efficiently. Hence, a democratic procedure is needed as a general rule to enable the efficient allocation and use of resources. However, a democratic agreement about detailed allocation of resources is almost impossible, as suggested by Arrow's 'general possibility theorem' (Arrow 1951). Nevertheless, allocative efficiency cannot be achieved without some democratic procedures that would reveal the marginal private costs and utilities. It is in exceptional cases that rational allocation of resources requires an authoritarian procedure. Authoritarian procedures, however, should not be confused with centralised decision-making. There are many more decisions requiring the input of a centralised authority than those requiring an authoritarian procedure to meet the conditions of allocative and distributive efficiency. Centralised decisions need not be reached through an authoritarian procedure. Indeed, very often they require democratic procedures.

Second, creative efficiency is also affected by the decision-making procedure. An authoritarian procedure is not conducive to innovation and experimentation. Democratic procedures are needed to foster trust, initiative, new ideas and to encourage subordinates in large corporations and government agencies to internalise the objectives of the organisation and search for alternative and better ways of performing their task. Subordinates are often more familiar with the nature of their jobs than their superiors. However, innovative efficiency often depends on experts, scientists and engineers, and this requirement may conflict with democratic procedures. Within limits, experts can be made accountable for their action but asymmetric information and tacit knowledge as well as technical knowledge, which cannot be understood or appreciated by non-experts, make it hard to enforce the requirements of transparency and accountability.

Third, adaptive efficiency requires democratic rather than authoritarian procedures. However, in major systemic–institutional and structural changes an authoritarian approach is often needed, particularly if speed is of the utmost importance. But the kind of institutional changes required for adaptive efficiency are usually incremental and can therefore be more easily effected through democratic procedures. Further, informal institutional changes, changes in attitudes and habitual ways of doing things, can also be effected through open and persuasive discussions and through changes in incentives. People must be convinced or persuaded of the importance of the proposed changes rather than forced by some authoritarian ways to accept them.

Fourth, the impact of the decision-making procedure on macroeconomic stability is not as clear or strong as on other properties of a well-functioning economy. On the one hand, there is reason to believe that democratic procedures are conducive to macroeconomic stability. In the so-called consultative economy, government, employers' organisations and trade unions consult each other about economic goals and on the policy instruments to be used. These participants in decision-making try to achieve a harmony of interests. In such an economy the primary objective is sustainable, stable and continuous growth in output and employment. Further, the cooperative and consensus mode of economic policy formulation reduces industrial conflict and allows governments to make the 'right' decisions. As a result of the consultative process, it is expected that governments' proposals would be modified, before decisions are made. No government possesses a monopoly on knowledge. On the other hand, there may be a conflict between macroeconomic stability in the long run and democratic procedures, as suggested by the existence of political cycles in developed market economies. Policy-makers in the short run have to satisfy the demands of the electorate in order to be re-elected. They formulate policies that may be harmful to economic stability in the long run. However, in recent years the burden of macroeconomic stability has fallen on monetary policy and that is arguably the task of the central bank, which usually has a high degree of independence, and thus somewhat removed from the democratic process. The rationale for an independent central bank is that monetary policy is so crucial to the health of the economy; it must be the outcome of professional conscious calculations of what the money supply should be to maintain macroeconomic stability. It is too important to be left to politicians who are subject to pressure from special interest groups. However, the independence or autonomy of the central bank must be balanced by a greater degree of accountability and transparency.

Finally, an important effect of the decision-making procedure is on equity. An authoritarian procedure violates the freedom dimension of equity and opportunity to participate in the decision-making process. The 'sting of command' or authoritarianism is the humiliation of having to take orders from somebody else. However, an authoritarian procedure is generally necessary to redistribute income and wealth from the rich to the poor. Democratic procedures can promote equity if the majority of the population are worse off than the wealthy minority and can benefit from any redistribution. If the majority are likely to lose from a redistribution then equity may not be achieved through democratic processes. However, since democratic procedures imply equal opportunity and access to public services and education, they can promote equity. But equality of opportunity is necessary though not sufficient for equity. An equitable system must be judged by both the outcome and the provision of equal opportunity.

As we have argued in the last chapter, an imposition of a floor and a ceiling on personal income and wealth may require an authoritarian procedure, at least in the short run, until the majority of the population come to accept the wisdom of such an equitable policy. Ideally, it is much more desirable that the better-off should voluntarily surrender part of their personal wealth for the benefit of others who are worse-off. In a just society they will probably accept this as the norm, or as the price for living in such a society. Accordingly, an equitable distribution would be quite consistent with democratic procedures. People would more or less accept a limit on the accumulation of personal wealth as part and parcel of living in an economic and political democracy. They may not need an authoritarian state to impose an equitable distribution upon society. By definition, in a well-functioning economy and a just society, there would be no need for redistribution, or for an imposition of a floor and a ceiling on personal income and wealth.

IV

Needless to say, the structure of information flows has a profound impact on all properties of a well-functioning economy. First, the efficient allocation of resources depends on reliable and accurate information about scarcity prices, marginal costs and marginal utilities, both private and public. Decisions involving externalities are not easy to deal with. Without knowing the social benefits and costs, it is difficult to fulfil the conditions for the efficient allocation of resources. Further, the attainment of allocative efficiency requires both centralised and decentralised information flows. Decentralised information and market-based prices are needed for allocating scarce resources efficiently. But market-type information does not include the valuation of specific inputs, which are not transacted in the marketplace, or if they are the market does not give accurate information about their real values. Such information is obtained within organisations that know the value of specific inputs by their actual contribution to production. Centralised information provided by the government is in the nature of public goods and is used by individuals, organisations and governments in their decision-making processes.

Second, the structure of information flows has an important effect on creative efficiency or innovation. The generation, application and diffusion of new ideas require both centralised and decentralised information flows. As the 'new' endogenous growth theory suggests, centralised information generated by governments through investment in the information sector, in R&D and education, is an important determinant of the rate of innovation. New information cannot be sufficiently generated by the market alone or by profit-making organisations. The types of information provided by individuals, small firms, large organisations and governments are complementary in the generation and diffusion of new products and processes. An excessive degree of concentration of information will inhibit the rate of innovation and diffusion, and hence creative efficiency. Investment in the information sector by organisations and governments to produce more information is necessary but not sufficient for creative efficiency. Other conditions must be met for the application and diffusion of new information. Nevertheless, the more information is generated and applied, the more it will generate new information. The new information technology, which is partly the product of past knowledge, improves the speed and credibility of information. It is the information technology that is driving the modern economy and is behind the increase in creative efficiency.

Third, the structure of information flows is crucial for adaptive efficiency, and in several ways. First, indirectly through its effect on the rate of innovation and diffusion that encourages structural change and adaptability. Second, and more directly, reliable and accurate information flows are needed by the government and the corporate sector to make the required changes in policies and institutions that are more suitable to new circumstances. In the corporate sector, the easy accessibility of timely information offered by the new information technology has allowed substantial improvements in efficiency, production planning, delivery and reduction of inventories. All these factors increase the flexibility of capital goods, making investment more profitable. Third, to the extent that adaptive efficiency is a function of attitudinal and cultural changes, centralised and decentralised information flows in the form of education, advertisement and persuasion are needed to encourage people to shed their habitual ways of thinking and behaving and to acquire new attitudes and skills. As in the case of creative efficiency, an excessive degree of concentration of information will inhibit adaptive efficiency.

Fourth, the importance of centralised information flows for macroeconomic stability is so crucial that before the development of national accounts, which provided information about the state of the economy, including the level of prices, aggregate supply and demand and employment, it was not possible to formulate strict, sustainable macroeconomic policies. Even after several decades of collection and refinement of national statistics, governments and central banks do not have adequate and timely information for formulating sound macroeconomic policies. It is widely accepted that economic information and knowledge is not secure enough to support 'fine tuning'. Nevertheless, a more modest goal for stabilisation policies is sensible and feasible. For example, a government need not have detailed information to adopt an expansionary monetary policy when the unemployment rate is very high. In the macroeconomic sphere, the government is knowledgeable and capable enough to improve on free market outcomes. This is not to deny that there are serious time lags involved in both the formulation and implementation of stabilisation policies, which prevent macroeconomic policies from immediately affecting an unexpected shift in the demand for commodities or money. Policy-makers do not know what is going on in the economy the moment it happens. It may take up to three months before they become aware of the changes. There is also a time interval between the policy decision and the subsequent change in the policy instruments. Moreover, there is the effectiveness lag, or the length of time required for a policy to have the desired outcome. All these time lags make macroeconomic stabilisation less effective. The removal or minimisation of such lags will improve the speed and accuracy of information flows both for the formulation and implementation of national economic policies.

Finally, both centralised and decentralised information flows are needed for equity. The welfare state must have decentralised information flows about the special needs of different groups. Such needs must be made known to the authority to compensate them. An equitable distribution must also be based on reliable information about people's efforts and contributions or marginal productivities. Without having accurate information about the relative needs and contributions of different people, it becomes very difficult indeed to achieve equity. More importantly, information is needed to identify inequalities that are not needed for productivity or efficiency, in order to reduce or even eliminate them. In a well-functioning economy and a just society, where people get their just rewards, there would be a tendency to transmit information about needs and contributions more honestly.

V

The choice of decision criteria affects all the properties of a well-functioning economy. First, the importance of the choice of criteria is obvious for allocative efficiency. If the economic calculus of social costs and benefits is applied to all decisions, there would be no waste from miscalculation and misallocation of available resources. No activity would be undertaken if the expected marginal social costs exceed the marginal social benefits. If we subject all our choices and acts to the economic calculus, we would end up in an economic utopia. However, allocative decisions based on pure economic criteria may not be politically acceptable or ethically desirable. In these circumstances, a compromise has to be reached where economic and non-economic criteria are considered. A tolerable level of rationality is possible and desirable when the decision-making process is viewed as a whole in its economic, political and ethical context. Further, even if it is politically acceptable and ethically desirable to base our decisions on the social economic calculus, the information required for the calculation may not be adequate, or it may take too much time and energy to collect. And, since time and energy are scarce commodities, it would be irrational to subject all decisions to the economic calculus. Nevertheless, on both economic and ethical grounds, we should not tolerate unnecessary waste at both the production and consumption stages.

Second, the choice of criteria also affects creative efficiency. Creative efficiency can be maximised by channelling enough resources into the research sector. This is a necessary but not a sufficient condition. Other requirements, which we have specified in Chapter 4, are needed. However, for creative efficiency, it is useful to distinguish between product and process innovation, though it is not always possible to separate them. Much of the product innovation takes the form of product differentiation and creation of new products that are not really needed. Advertising techniques and social pressure are then used to convince people to buy them. While this process continues, it is not possible to solve the problem of scarcity and prevent environmental degradation. In contrast, process innovation provides us with bigger quantities of existing products with fewer resources. Product innovation requires some of the available resources to go into the satisfaction of new wants, and this makes resources even scarcer. Of course, if the new products replace the old ones and require no more resources or even less, then product differentiation is equally desirable. Arguably, the multiplication of new wants is the real enemy of a just society. With less product differentiation it is possible to satisfy the legitimate needs of everyone and avoid excessive consumption. Our innovation criterion suggests that resources should be directed more towards process rather than product innovation.

Third, the choice of criteria has a similar effect on adaptive efficiency as on creative efficiency. First, it has indirect effects through creative efficiency, by channelling resources into education, retraining and acquisition of new skills. These make the system more flexible and facilitate the process of change and adaptability. More directly, decision-making criteria affect institutional changes. They tell us whether existing institutions are still relevant to current conditions or whether they need to be reformed to allow the system to change and adapt. Institutions and formal rules need to change from time to time to cope with new circumstances.

Fourth, macroeconomic stability is affected by the decision-making criteria employed by the government in its capacity as manager of the economy. Economists have a pretty good idea of the conditions required for macroeconomic stability such as keeping the money supply in line with the potential growth of output, though it is allowed to deviate from this rule in times of contraction and expansion. Further, policy-makers have to meet other criteria besides macroeconomic stability and 'the general interest'. They have to ensure their own re-election and hence they must satisfy the short-term demands of the electorate, which may compromise the long-term stability of the economy. On the other hand, if the government takes only a short-term perspective, it may put the economy in such a mess that beyond the next election it would be voted out. Also the state, in its capacity as the provider of welfare, must take care of the unemployed if its macroeconomic stabilisation policies fail to achieve full or near full employment, and meet the needs of disadvantaged groups who cannot provide for themselves. These welfare activities tend to reinforce stability rather than undermine it. Indeed, they are known as 'automatic stabilisers'. In times of recession they prevent effective demand from falling, thereby establishing a floor for the trade cycle. Similarly, a progressive income tax designed to finance the welfare budget and redistribute income from the rich to the poor places a ceiling on inflation.

Finally, the effects of decision-making criteria on equity are crucial. We have argued that since economics and ethics are closely intertwined, we should aim to maximise total welfare, not simply economic welfare. The distribution of income and wealth must satisfy simultaneously the two criteria: desert and needs.

The first is primarily economic, based on contribution or effort. If society wants more goods and services, it must reward those who contribute more to the common good. The second is more fundamental and should take precedence when the two criteria clash (Sen 1973). However, as we have argued in more than one place in this book, there is no fundamental conflict between ethics and economics. The conflict arises only if we take a narrow view of economics and ethics and if we assume that people are motivated solely by self-interest and material rewards. Our contention is that a well-functioning economy is a necessary condition for a just society, and a just society is necessary for a well-functioning economy. An equitable distribution based on needs must incorporate to some extent, economic and political criteria if it is to be economically feasible and politically acceptable. Equity or justice implies that scarce resources are directed towards meeting the basic needs of the population before the trivial wants of a few, and that the use of non-renewable resources by the present generation must take into consideration the welfare of future generations.

VI

The incentive structure, which effectively determines who gets what, has a far-reaching effect on the functioning and performance of the economy. It affects all properties of a well-functioning economy. Incentive structures, as we have already argued, tend to develop in an organic fashion along with the societies they serve. They seem to be designed for each other. Thus, a well-functioning economy would require and, in turn, inculcate certain types of incentives and attitudes, and this inculcation will facilitate its functioning further.

First, the efficient allocation of resources depends on the existence of an effective motivation structure consisting of extrinsic and intrinsic incentives, positive and negative incentives, and economic and non-economic as well as a mixture of egotism and altruism. Such incentives will enable a society to get the most out of its scarce resources. Economic or pecuniary incentives alone will not ensure efficient allocation and use of resources. The emphasis on self-interest, typical of a competitive system, makes it difficult to secure collective goods and cooperation, which are increasingly needed for the proper functioning of the economic system. Non-pecuniary incentives are also required especially in dealing with human resources. As a general rule, people should get what they contribute, or rather their rewards should be commensurate with their effort and contribution.

Second, creative efficiency depends also on an effective motivation structure. Since innovation is a high-risk activity, entrepreneurs need to be encouraged to overcome the uncertainty involved in the innovation process. This is best done through the establishment of an innovational infrastructure, which spreads the risks of innovation across the economy. Some creative efficiency will result from scientific curiosity, instinct of workmanship and learning-by-doing, but these are not normally strong enough to enable an adequate rate of innovation and diffusion. Successful innovations tend to feed on themselves. They provide moral and material incentives to continue with innovative activity. Creative efficiency, as shown in Chapter 6, depends on a mixture of extrinsic and intrinsic, positive and negative as well as pecuniary and non-pecuniary incentives.

Third, an effective incentives' structure is needed for adaptive efficiency and flexibility. There must be sufficient incentives for people not to resist the required institutional changes for adaptive efficiency. In addition, adequate incentives must be provided for workers, managers, entrepreneurs and others to change their habits of thinking and attitudes that are out of step with the demands of the moment. As with the other two types of efficiency, a mixture of motivations consisting of material and moral, extrinsic and intrinsic, positive and negative incentives is required to promote adaptive efficiency. Since adaptive efficiency usually leads to some participants being losers and others gainers, the gains resulting from institutional changes can be used to compensate the losers. This is not only equitable but also politically desirable. It reduces the degree of resistance by those who feel they will be made worse off.

Fourth, the link between macroeconomic stability and the incentives' structure is mainly indirect through the effects of incentives on the other properties of a well-functioning economy. Since macroeconomic stability is achieved through government policies, the relevant incentives are the political ones. The desire to be elected and re-elected acts as an incentive for the government to do the 'right' thing, by managing the economy sensibly and avoiding recessions and inflations. However, the government must provide proper incentives for individuals and organisations to implement its macroeconomic stabilisation policies.

Finally, there is an intimate connection between the incentive structure and equity. An effective incentive structure will lead to inequalities that are no greater than those strictly warranted by the efficient working of the economic system. Equity can be achieved through the use of non-pecuniary incentives where appropriate, through the elimination of anti-competitive practices of rent-seeking and rent-creating activities, and exploitation, through higher taxes on 'unearned' incomes, and through an 'optimal' ceiling on personal income and wealth. The level of the ceiling would be partly determined by the possible negative effects on incentives, at the point where the marginal revenue of income tax is equal to the value of marginal output produced. To lower the ceiling below this point would be counterproductive. Arguably, when people feel they are getting a just reward for their effort, they will work harder than what they can get away with. A just distribution will encourage people to be less greedy and less envious, to give their best effort without necessarily expecting higher income. In a just society people would, in general, be less selfish and more cooperative.

VII

Clearly, a well-functioning economy is largely the product of a well-designed decision-making system, consisting of an optimal decision-making structure, appropriate procedures, reliable information flows, rational decision-making criteria and an effective incentive structure. Of course, as the economy changes and develops, the decision-making system itself will also change. In other words, there are some feedbacks from the five properties of a well-functioning economy to the five principles of a well-designed decision-making system. It is of some interest to note these feedbacks very briefly.

First, the feedback effects on the decision-making structure seem to come mainly from creative efficiency or technological progress. New technology and products alter to some extent the optimal degree of centralisation and concentration of decision-making authority. For example, the new information technology has made it easier for central governments to make and monitor their decisions more effectively, and thereby increase the *de facto* degree of centralisation. At the same time, the growth of big business, itself the product of technology and other factors, meant that many tasks, which were previously performed by the state, can now be left to the private sector, in which case this increases the degree of decentralisation and perhaps the concentration of decision-making authority. There are also feedback effects of adaptive efficiency on the degree of decentralisation. As North (1990, p 81) points out, 'adaptive efficiency provides the incentives to encourage the development of decentralised decision-making processes that will allow societies to maximise the efforts required to explore alternative ways of solving problems'.

Second, decision-making procedures are also affected by creative efficiency or technological progress. The other properties of a well-functioning economy seem to have marginal effects on procedures. The new information technology makes it relatively more difficult for decision-makers to maintain secrecy and conceal their motivation and reasoning underlying their decisions. More positively, the new information technology enables a greater number of people to participate in decision-making processes. The greater speed of communication encourages the diffusion of knowledge as new ideas are quickly disseminated and absorbed. All this suggests the encouragement of democratic procedures that are transparent and involving a larger number of participants. On the other hand, the increasing complexity of decisions and technology encourages technocratic and authoritarian procedures, or the flow of decisions from top to bottom.

Third, the feedback effects of the properties of a well-functioning economy on the information flows seem much stronger than on the structure and procedure of decision-making. The effect of allocative efficiency is an improvement of market-based information. In particular, prices would reflect more accurately the relative scarcity of resources or their opportunity costs. Creative efficiency or technological progress increases the flow of new information or knowledge. Adaptive efficiency increases the speed of information flows and encourages people to shed their old ideas and attitudes. The effect of macroeconomic stability is to provide economic agents operating in the money and foreign exchange markets with more reliable information about the state of the economy. Finally, equity has a positive effect on the flow of information. When people are getting their just rewards, they will transmit information about their needs and contributions more accurately. Subordinates will be more honest in reporting to their superiors and will not distort the information passed down to them.

Fourth, the feedback effects on decision-making criteria seem, in general, to be weak and indirect. For example, the effect of allocative efficiency is through the generation of proper price signals, which make it possible to make rational economic calculations. The effects of other properties appear negligible. Thus, if the economy is adjusting smoothly to shocks, if it is generating a satisfactory rate of innovation, if it is growing steadily with little or no unemployment, and if the distribution of income and wealth is fair and equitable, then there is no need to change the way in which decisions are formulated and implemented, no need to change the decision criteria.

Fifth, the feedback effects on incentives appear to be quite significant. Allocative efficiency implies that factors of production are rewarded according to their marginal contribution. Adaptive and creative efficiencies have positive effects on incentives as they reward successful economic agents and penalise failed ones. Macroeconomic stability provides incentives for investors and innovators to make sound, long-term decisions. Equally, the effect of equity on incentives is quite strong. An equitable distribution of income and wealth encourages people to work harder, cooperate with one another, avoid shirking and sabotage and internalise the objectives of their organisation.

VIII

This chapter has discussed the likely effects of each of the five principles of our normative decision-making system on the five selected properties of a well-functioning economy. It has also discussed some possible feedback effects of the properties of a well-functioning economy on the decision-making system itself. We have sought to show that each principle of the decision-making process is a necessary condition for one or more and, in some cases, for all of the five properties of a well-functioning economy. This is important for policy-making.

A poor performance in one property can be traced to the flawed component(s) of the decision-making system.

More specifically, we have shown that an 'optimal' decision-making structure, which avoids both an excessive degree of (de) centralisation and concentration of decision-making authority and an inappropriate mix of markets, organisations and governments, is a necessary condition for all the five properties of a well-functioning economy. A sub-optimal structure will result in misallocation of resources, a slow rate of innovation, a low degree of versatility and adaptability, macroeconomic instability, unemployment and inequitable distribution of wealth and incomes. Clearly, an optimal decision-making structure is a prerequisite condition for a well-functioning economy.

Proper decision-making procedures were shown to have favourable effects on the quality of decisions and hence on the performance of the economy. In particular, democratic procedures are important for creative and adaptive efficiencies and for equity. However, under certain conditions and depending on the nature of the decision, authoritarian procedures can be more appropriate. Apart from their favourable effects on outcomes in most cases, democratic procedures are valued in themselves. Decisions must not only be right, but they must appear to be so, or the procedure must be right; hence the need for transparency. A genuine economic democracy must allow people to participate in decision-making in proportion to the degree they are affected by the outcome of an economic decision. This applies particularly to the workplace, local government and voluntary organisations. Of course, participation in decision-making can be costly and time-consuming, and may not produce the desired outcomes. Where there is a conflict between procedures and outcomes, a trade-off would have to be made. However, it is expected that if the other principles of our normative decision-making system are applied correctly, there would be little conflict between democratic procedures, which are both transparent and participatory, on the one hand, and desired economic outcomes on the other.

Like an 'optimal' decision-making structure, so a reliable structure of information flows, which facilitates the generation and transmission of accurate and timely information to the decision-making points in the system, is also a necessary condition for the five properties of a well-functioning economy. If the information flows are flawed, decision-makers will not be able to make informed or meaningful decisions and each property of a well-functioning economy will suffer. In the real world, decisions have to be made under conditions of uncertainty and imperfect information, and only imaginative decision-makers would have the experience or wisdom to make correct decisions under those conditions.

A well-functioning economy implies that the decisions taken are based on sound economic criteria tempered by political and ethical considerations. Such criteria avoid unnecessary wastes arising from miscalculation and misallocation of resources. In particular, a well-functioning economy that allocates and distributes resources efficiently must use the social economic calculus to incorporate all the economic and non-economic costs and benefits. An economic activity should not be undertaken if the total economic and non-economic costs exceed the economic and non-economic benefits to society. While it is not possible to subject all or many decisions to such calculations, we should avoid the use of false criteria and thoughtless rules of thumb in making important decisions. We should also revise from time to time our habitual decisions that might prevent us from using scarce resources more efficiently. This is not to deny a role for emotions and passions in making decisions. Indeed, they are often necessary to make up our minds or to reach some decisions, which may be better than not making any decisions.

An effective incentive structure, like an optimal decision-making structure and reliable information flows, affects all the properties of a well-functioning economy. Effective incentives consisting of pecuniary and non-pecuniary rewards and penalties are necessary for the efficient allocation of labour and capital resources. Incentives are also needed for entrepreneurs to take risk and innovate and to adjust to changing circumstances. Policy-makers in charge of managing the economy must be well-motivated to ensure macroeconomic stability at or near full employment. Above all, an effective incentives' system is needed to reward people according to their effort and contribution and to penalise them for failing to do their duties. Such a system would go a long way to reduce unnecessary inequalities that have little to do with marginal productivities or relative contributions. It will also minimise the role of the state in redistributing income from the rich to the poor, and eliminate the need for imposing a ceiling on personal income and wealth.

14. Concluding Notes on the Problems of Transition to a Well-functioning Economy

I

If they are not to be dismissed as merely utopian, the foregoing proposals concerning the principles of decision-making for a well-functioning economy cannot avoid the question of feasibility or 'implementability'. What forces would help or hinder the systemic changes, and how can the transition to the proposed economic system be effected? Further, one of the essential criteria for the evaluation of any new design for the economy is the criterion of durability or stability. Will the new economic system survive in the form in which it is initially established, or will it degenerate into a nightmare as so many utopian experiments have ended?

Although it is not our intention to provide a blueprint for action, we need to face certain implementation problems. There are always transitional difficulties from an actual to a normative system, from 'what is' to 'what ought to be'. It may be useful, therefore, to end this book with a brief discussion of the main transitional problems. We also need to say something about the long-term viability of the new system.

There is no satisfactory theory of transition that would act as a signpost to guide reformers on the road to a well-functioning economy by pointing out costly detours, traps and dead ends. Nevertheless, any transitional process that involves systemic, structural and policy changes, as envisaged here, is bound to face political, psychological and ideological resistance from various groups of citizens, not only from those who believe they will be losers from the changes. Even if there were a universal consensus, there would be still serious technical–administrative problems relating to information requirements, the appropriate speed and logical and chronological sequencing of the proposed reform measures. Such technical problems themselves have political, ethical and psychological dimensions, which cannot be ignored if the transitional process is to proceed smoothly and efficiently.

The following sections discuss in turn: the political and psychological opposition to the proposed changes in the decision-making system, the technical–administrative problems of determining the appropriate speed and sequencing of the reform measures, and the viability and stability of the reformed system.

II

The proposed socially beneficial changes to the decision-making system would most likely be resisted by various groups, including vested interests, ideologues, cynics and others, perhaps the majority, who are either indifferent or who take the view that 'if it is not broken, don't fix it'. We discuss, in turn, each group and suggest how to overcome its opposition to the reforms.

First, we consider the people who are likely to lose from the proposed changes. They include those who currently wield a lot of decision-making authority and control and/or earn enormous incomes that cannot be justified on economic and ethical grounds. The power of these people to oppose reforms rests not only on their own direct power but also on political alliances with many other sections of society. Such people will strongly resist any significant reform of the decision-making system. In particular, they will try to block changes to both the decision-making structure and procedure if the proposed changes are likely to diminish their decision control power over others and/or make them more accountable and their decisions more transparent. They will also resist changes to the incentives' structure that are primarily designed to eliminate arbitrary and unnecessary inequalities of incomes that are the consequence of exploitation, rent-seeking and rent-creating activities. Some workers might resist the proposed changes that target shirking and free-riding. Some groups might even resist changes that make them absolutely better off but relatively worse off than others.

Second, the existing decision-making system is held together not merely by the economic and political power of a minority, but also by ideas accepted in the rest of society. Such ideas include strongly held views as to who should be deciding what and who should be getting what, how the 'public interest' and 'legitimate private interests' are defined and reconciled, and how alternative arrangements are perceived. In other words, ideology plays an important role in the existing arrangements for decision-making. Thus, we would expect both collectivist and neo-liberal ideologues to oppose changes to all or most aspects of the decision-making system, especially to the decision-making structure. Collectivists will probably object to any decentralisation of decisions from the state to the private sector, although they are likely to support some decentralisation of decisions within both sectors. Neo-liberals will resist changes that will increase the degree of centralisation or give more decision-making power to the state. Finally, they would likely oppose changes to the incentives' structure that are aimed at eliminating unnecessary and arbitrary inequalities that have little to do with the efficient working of the economic system, whereas collectivists would support such changes.

Third, cynics and sceptics might not strenuously resist but will not support the proposed reforms. They do not believe in 'social engineering' or in attempts to design better institutions. Following Hayek, they see the existing formal institutions, including the decision-making system, as the product of 'human action', rather than of 'human design'. Hence, the possibility of designing a decision-making system, which purports to lead to a well-functioning economy and a just society, would be regarded as utopian, a self-conceited exercise, that not only will not work but will be counterproductive.

Fourth, as collective action requires its participants neither to incur equitable costs nor to enjoy equal benefits, certain groups will not support the proposed societal reconstruction if they expect to incur more costs or receive fewer benefits than others from the contemplated socio-economic changes. Some may not participate in joint action to change the system for fear of sharing the costs. This is the familiar free-rider problem, which is hard to overcome in organizing a large group to implement Pareto improvements or defend itself against concentrated interest (Olson 1965). Further, some people place little or no value on participation in collective decision-making and would prefer to leave it to others to worry about changing the system. Moreover, people will not support the proposed changes if they are uncertain about the consequences. Finally, in developed market economies, many people, perhaps the majority, may be satisfied with the status quo, even though the distribution of income and wealth is very inequitable and a significant minority of workers are unemployed and poor. Such people would not support the proposed reforms, except in times of crisis when things get bad for them. Indeed, it is usually in hard times that existing 'rules of the game' are most typically altered.

What can be done to overcome the resistance to beneficial changes from the various groups listed above? The normal approach is to compensate potential losers, since the gain is big enough, even after the costs of transition are included. The state on behalf of the winners can negotiate with the losers and try to persuade them to accept the proposed changes. This is not as easy as it seems at first glance. Potential losers are usually concentrated and known, while potential gainers are diffused and relatively unknown. Since people dislike losses more than they like gains, there would be stronger resistance to changes in the decision-making system than support for them. In addition, there is the ethical problem of compensating potential losers who had benefited for years from an unjust system. One of the aims of reforming the decision-making system is precisely to eliminate arbitrary and illegitimate incomes and wealth. Hence, the compensation principle should not apply to these people.

Nevertheless, the problem of vested interests resisting changes that are beneficial to society remains and cannot be solved simply by compensation. The required compensations to persuade people may be too costly for the state budget, or they may exceed the economic benefits. Thus, a government that is committed to reforming the decision-making system is confronted with a democratic–authoritarian dilemma. An authoritarian approach that seeks to impose the reforms on dissenting groups is ruled out in a democratic society and violates the principle of proper decision-making procedures. But attempts to change the rules of decision-making through democratic means are notoriously difficult. Despite what Keynes (1936) has said in the last paragraph of his *General Theory* about 'the power of vested interest is vastly exaggerated compared with the gradual encroachment of ideas', we do not underestimate the tenacity of interest groups to hold on to their privileges and positions of power. They use their privileged positions and wealth to influence and manipulate both public opinion and government, and thereby block the socially beneficial reforms.

Arguably, a good or strong government would not allow itself to become the prisoner of a privileged minority. Such a government has a crucial role in the transition process in transforming the economic system into a better one. It must educate and lead rather than follow the electorate, particularly the large segment, the passive and indifferent citizens who have a built-in bias in favour of the status quo. The possibility of 'good government' is not as remote as it appears in the rent-seeking literature. Dewatripont and Roland (1991, p 292) have shown that a democratic government can win majority approval for its reform proposals 'through the credible threat of future reforms, extract today concessions from the group which will be in the minority tomorrow, and use their votes to hurt another group of voters today'. Alternatively, the government could issue long-term bonds to buy off the losers and tax the gainers to repay, assuming, of course, that there is no problem of identifying losers and gainers. It could also mobilise people's support by enhancing transparency, by education, by allocating the costs of adjustment in an equitable fashion and by promoting financial support for the people adversely affected by the transition.

Collective action directed at improving the status quo is possible and frequently occurs in democratic societies. In such societies where there is open debate and discussion, individuals or groups of individuals can exert political influence to bring about the desired changes. Even if they do not actually use their influence, the belief by the government that they can is itself significant in that it will have an effect on the top decision-makers. If the latter believe that the ordinary citizen would participate in collective action, then they are likely to behave differently from the way they would have behaved in the absence of such a belief. Individuals in a democratic society can and do cooperate with one another to form coalitions or cooperative associations in order to mobilise support for change and thus overcome the resistance of vested interests.

Obviously, it is harder for many people to cooperate with one another than if only a handful are involved.

There are many reasons why individuals would participate in joint action; not least is the sense of injustice, or the idea of working for a better and just society, where by and large people get what they deserve, and in which inequalities in decision-making power, wealth and income are no greater than are strictly warranted by the efficient operation and sustainability of the economic system. In that sense, Keynes's point about the power of ideas in the long run might be right, provided enough time and energy and other resources are mobilised by the more enlightened elements in society to persuade the overwhelming majority of the population to change their attitude and support the implementation of those ideas. A change of attitude leads to a change of policy.

Clearly, democratic changes are hard but should not be regarded as insurmountable obstacles to transition to a well-functioning economy and just society. We should not be either too pessimistic or too optimistic about the possibility of voluntary collective action that proceeds from moral commitment and/or a calculation of self-interest. It is not simply a matter of educating people what their real common interests are or a matter of changing their ideas. In any case, the media and information system have become so complex and controlled by vested interests, it would be difficult indeed to transmit the good ideas to the great bulk of the population over the cacophony and din of advertisements. The ability to make people do what they may not immediately want to do requires a whole set of extrinsic and intrinsic, positive and negative, pecuniary and non-pecuniary incentives. Thus, the implementation of our proposed system, or the transition to a well-functioning economy, requires an effective incentive approach.

III

Apart from the need to take enough time to allow democratic processes to run their course and to persuade opponents and disinterested groups of the merits of the proposed changes, the changes themselves must be introduced gradually to avoid a radical break from the past. The step-by-step approach allows people, especially potential losers, to adjust their habitual ways of thinking and living with minimum economic and psychological costs, and thus reduces their resistance to change. It is, therefore, easier to start with and implement gradualist reform packages. With incremental changes stability and continuity with the past are preserved. Tomorrow will not be markedly different from today or yesterday. But over a sufficiently long period incremental changes are cumulative, and hence a well-functioning economy and a just society will gradually emerge with minimum social and economic costs. Moreover, as Dewatripont and Roland (1991, p 297) have shown: 'gradualism can be an optimal policy for a reform-minded government, in the presence of informational asymmetry, lack of pre-commitment and political constraints'.

Admittedly, there are risks in a gradualist approach to systemic changes. Opponents of the reform package will have ample opportunities to mobilise their resources and form coalitions to derail the reform process. Further, proponents of the reforms and their supporters might grow impatient at the slow pace of changes or lose interest in the entire reform process. However, the alternative strategy of quick transition, the so-called 'shock therapy' or the 'big bang', carries more risks and may lead to disastrous consequences. Witness the enormous human and economic costs of Stalin's rapid collectivisation of agriculture and industrialisation, Mao's 'great leap forward' and 'cultural revolution', and more recently the IMF's 'shock therapy' in the former Soviet Union and Eastern Europe. The history of political and cultural revolutions suggests that the unexpected setbacks and failures were largely the result of hasty decisions that were quickly enforced without concern for the feelings and attitudes of the citizens, who were not psychologically, politically and ideologically prepared for the changes. Institutional changes, including changes in the decision-making rules of society and attitudes, are slow-moving processes.

Accordingly, the proposed changes to the decision-making system should be introduced gradually to prepare the ground and to establish the preconditions for a successful and smooth transition. A gradual approach increases the political acceptability of the reform. Moreover, it is needed to allow the interdependent elements of the reformed decision-making system to mutually adjust to one another, and thus grow together in an organic fashion. Complementarity of reforms requires a gradualist strategy. Needless to say, a gradual step-by-step approach does not justify unnecessary delays in introducing the required changes. There is, in principle, an 'optimal' speed of transition.

The speed of transition depends partly on the initial conditions. If the actual decision-making system is relatively close to the normative system, changes can be introduced more rapidly simply because they are marginal and involve less resistance from opponents. On the other hand, if the current system falls far short of the proposed one, then a longer time is required to effect the transition. Moreover, speed is partly a function of correct sequencing, or the order in which the changes are introduced. A rational sequencing of the reform measures is an essential condition for a smooth and quick transition (Haddad 1995a).

There are, however, conceptual and practical problems with rational sequencing. The interdependence of the decision-making components implies that changes should be introduced simultaneously, as a change in one element will have impacts on the other elements. But, in practice, it may not be feasible on both administrative and political grounds to introduce the required changes all at once, especially if they are more than marginal. Hence, the sequencing of reforms should aim at creating constituencies for further reforms. Further, the decision-making process takes place in time and consists of several distinct phases beginning with the preparation and formulation of decisions and ending with their implementation. Hence, it is sensible to introduce the reform measures in the order, which the decision-making process takes place, in practice, and allow some flexibility when the administrative and political constraints permit the simultaneous introduction of some measures.

The reform of the entire decision-making system along the lines suggested in this book would have the following advantages. It would not only significantly improve the performance of the economic system but would also generate a more equitable and just distribution of wealth and incomes, and hence avoid or minimise the need for imposing a ceiling on personal income and wealth. It allows people to participate in decision-making processes, both inside and outside the workplace, in proportion to the degree they are affected by the decisions. This will lead to a more equitable distribution of decision-making power and genuine economic democracy. Thus, the resulting economic system satisfies the five properties of a well-functioning economic society.

IV

In the last chapter of *The General Theory* Keynes (1936, p 33) wrote: 'The outstanding faults of the economic society in which we live are its failure to provide full employment and its arbitrary and inequitable distribution of wealth and incomes'. Some 65 years later, after an enormous increase in output, scientific discoveries, and technological progress, these faults have remained with us – notwithstanding intermittent attempts by governments to eliminate them. In much of the developed world, the unemployment rate is still high, and more people are being forced to accept part-time work. Even in countries that have lower unemployment rates, such as the USA (if only recently) and Japan, there has been a strong increase in job insecurity, particularly among older male workers. Meanwhile, despite the rapid growth in output and of the welfare sector, inequalities have persisted and even increased particularly over the last two decades. Those who bear the burden of the hardest and most tedious work and who are powerless are the least rewarded, while those who do interesting and prestigious work are highly rewarded. It is hard to imagine that such inequalities are warranted by the efficient working of the economic system. Yet, it is frequently argued that not much can be done about the economic and social inequalities in society; they are the outcome of the working of the economic system.

It is also maintained that what really matters is the provision of equality of opportunity for everyone. But the rhetoric of equality of opportunity is reflected, in practice, less in equality and more in the pursuit of opportunity and greed. Equality of opportunity is both necessary and desirable, but it is not sufficient unless the outcome is fairly equitable. Indeed, the existing enormous inequalities of outcomes reflect inequalities of opportunity. We regard an outcome to be equitable if the existing inequalities are genuinely necessary for the five properties of a well-functioning economy, and only if abject poverty is eliminated.

Although the Keynesian revolution did go a long way towards solving the unemployment problem and, to some extent, the degree of inequality, it seems with hindsight it did not go far enough. It gave a bigger role for the state to manage the economy through monetary and fiscal policies which, for a period of two or three decades after World War II, proved powerful tools to deal with unemployment and, to a lesser extent, both 'arbitrary' and 'inequitable' distribution. However, after this period, Keynesian policies appear to have become counterproductive having led or contributed to the 'stagflation' of the 1970s. They were subsequently abandoned in favour of more *laissez-faire* policies.

What is needed, as this book tried to show, is a comprehensive reform of the entire decision-making system. From our perspective, Keynes focused on the decision-making structure, admittedly the most important component, giving the state greater decision-making authority in macroeconomic decisions. This focus resulted in the transformation of the basically *laissez-faire* economy into a managed economy. However, the other four aspects of the decision-making system, not part of the Keynesian revolution, are necessary conditions for a well-functioning economy and a just society, and hence for solving the unemployment and distribution problems. We believe these problems to be fundamentally the result of a flawed decision-making process, which can be reformed gradually through incremental changes to all components of the decision-making system.

It must be emphasised that our conception of a well-designed decision-making system is not meant to be either definitive or all-embracing. The five chosen principles or components are neither exhaustive nor refined. Human decisions and designs are fallible. However, our aim is to eliminate or, at least, to minimise systemic errors, not human errors. Of course, as the decision-making system is ultimately the product of human decisions, some systemic errors might emerge.

More importantly, our decision-making system is subject to change and (hopefully) improvement with the passage of time. Although we have insisted on the importance of decision-making as the primary determinant of the operation, development and performance of the economic system, changes in the latter will have feedback effects on the decision-making process itself. Choices and decisions are not autonomous or made in a social and economic vacuum. They are partly determined by the economic and social system. Hence, the designer of an 'optimal' economic system must steer a mid-course between the Scylla of 'decisionism' and Charybdies of 'determinism'.

Our decision-making system is not carved in stone. It has an adjustment mechanism and a degree of flexibility built into the decision-making procedures, which are generally democratic and transparent. So when things go wrong and the system needs to be changed, changes will take place according to changing circumstances. Admittedly, the best economic or decision-making system can be hijacked and rendered sub-optimal by incompetent and corrupt decision-makers. Again, our normative decision-making system minimises such a possibility, as the decision-making, information and incentive structures as well as the democratic and transparent procedure will lead to the appointment of the 'right' people to be in charge of the 'right' decisions. Moreover, there are also built-in mechanisms to remove quickly such corrupt and incompetent people.

Finally, our discussion of the decision-making system is incomplete in the sense that it is conducted in general terms and ignores the details. Decisions are made in a world, where details are complicating realities; a world where decisions must realistically fit into a sequence of past decisions and changing attitudes and they must satisfy the constraints imposed by political and ethical considerations. We have given some attention to those issues but not in sufficient detail to satisfy the sceptics and cynics and those who require rigorous proofs. To do so would require tomes and tomes and would far exceed the aim and competence of this author. Our primary aim has been to emphasise the value of the decision-making approach both for the analyst wanting to classify and understand the *modus operandi* of economic systems and for the decision-maker and policy-maker seeking to reach sound decisions and policies. Moreover, our approach points the reformers to the right areas in seeking to improve the current economic system and to establish a more equitable and just society.

References

Alchian A. and Demsetz, H. (1972) 'Production Information Costs and Economic Organization', *The American Economic Review*, **62** (5), pp 77–95.

Anderson, C. (1988) 'Anthropology and Australian Aboriginal Economy', in R.M. Berndt and R. Tonkinson (eds), *Social Anthropology and Australian Aboriginal Studies*, Canberra: Aboriginal Studies Press, pp 125–88.

Andreoni, J. (1988) 'Privately Provided Public Goods: The Limits of Altruism', *Journal of Public Economics*, **35** (1), pp 57–73.

Andreoni, J. (1989) 'Giving with Impure Altruism: Applications to Clarity and Ricardian Equivalence', *Journal of Political Economy*, **97** (6), pp 1447–58.

Andreoni, J. (1990) 'Impure Altruism and Donations to Public Goods: A Theory of Warm Glow Giving', *The Economic Journal*, **100** (401), pp 464–77.

Arrow, K.J. (1951) *Social Choice and Individual Values*, New York: Wiley.

Arrow, K.J. (1962) 'The Economic Implications of Learning By Doing', *Review of Economic Studies*, **29**, pp 153–73.

Arrow, K.J. (1971) *The Limits to Organization*, New York: W.W. Norton & Co.

Arrow, K.J. (1972) 'Gifts and Exchanges', *Philosophy and Public Affairs*, **1** (4), pp 342–62.

Arrow, K.J. (1994) 'Methodological Individualism and Social Knowledge', *American Economic Association: Papers and Proceedings*, **84** (2), pp 1–9.

Balassa, B. (1959) *The Hungarian Experience in Economic Planning*, New Haven: Yale University Press.

Barone, E. (1908) 'The Ministry of Production in the Collective State' in F.A. Hayek (ed), *Collectivist Economic Planning*, London: Routledge & Kegan Paul (1935), pp 247–90.

Barro, R.J. and Gordon, D. (1983) 'A Positive Theory of Monetary Policy in a National Rate Model', *Journal of Political Economy*, **91** (4), pp 589–610.

Baumol, W. and Quandt, R. (1964) 'Rules of Thumb and Optimally Imperfect Decisions', *American Economic Review*, **54**, pp 23–46.

Becker, G.S. (1976) *The Economic Approach to Human Behaviour*, Chicago and London: University of Chicago Press.

Ben-Ner, A. (1988) 'The Life Cycle of Worker-owned Firms: A Theoretical Analysis', *Journal of Economic Behaviour and Organization*, **10** (3), pp 287–313.

Ben-Ner, A., Montias, J. and Neuberger, E. (1993) 'Basic Issues in Organizations: A Comparative Perspective', *Journal of Comparative Economics*, **17** (2), pp

207–42.

Bensusan-Butt, D. (1962) *An Economic Growth: An Essay in Pure Theory,* Oxford: Clarendon.

Bensusan-Butt, D. (1974) 'Political Economy for Aesthetes', *Australian Economic Papers*, **13**, pp 178–87.

Berliner, J. (1976) *The Innovation Decision in Soviet Industry*, Cambridge, Mass.: MIT Press.

Bernardelli, H. (1961) 'The Origins of Modern Economic Theory', *The Economic Record*, **37** (79), pp 320–38.

Bloch, M. (1962) *Feudal Society,* London: Routledge & Kegan Paul.

Blumberg, P. (1968) *Industrial Democracy: The Sociology of Participation*, London: Constable.

Boltho, A. (1971) *Foreign Trade Criteria in Socialist Economies*, Cambridge: Cambridge University Press.

Bonin, J. and Marcus, A. (1979) 'Information Motivation and Control in Decentralised Planning: The Case of Discretionary Marginal Behaviour', *Journal of Comparative Economics*, **3** (3), pp 235–53.

Bornstein, M. (1985) 'Improving the Soviet Economic Mechanism', *Soviet Studies*, **37** (1), pp 1–30.

Boulding, K. (1966) 'The Economics of Knowledge and the Knowledge of Economics', *American Economic Review*, **56**, pp 1–13 (Supplementary).

Brada, J. and Estrin, S. (1990) 'Advances in the Theory and Practice of Indicative Planning', *Journal of Comparative Economics*, **14** (4), pp 523–30.

Brenner, R. (1978) 'Dobb on the Transition from Feudalism to Capitalism', *Cambridge Journal of Economics*, **2** (2), pp 121–40.

Brockway, G. (1984–5) 'Executive Salaries and their Justification', *Journal of Post-Keynesian Economics*, **7** (2), pp 168–76.

Buchanan, J. Tollison, R. and Tulloch, G. (eds) (1980) *Towards a Theory of Rent-seeking Society*, Texas College Studies, A&M University.

Calvo, G.A. (1978) 'On Time Consistency of Optimal Policy in a Monetary Economy', **46** (6), pp 1411–28.

Camacho, A. (1979) 'Performance of Decentralised and Centralised Decision-making Mechanisms over a Class of Lincar Cases', *Journal of Comparative Economics*, **3** (2), pp 91–116.

Casson, M. (1993) 'Cultural Determinants of Economic Performance', *Journal of Comparative Economics*, **17** (2), pp 418–42.

Coase, R. (1937), 'The Nature of the Firm', *Econometrica*, **4** (16), pp 386–405. November.

Collard, D. (1978) *Altruism and Economy*, Oxford: Martin Robertson.

Conlisk, J. (1996) 'Why Bounded Rationality', *Journal of Economic Literature*, **34** (2), pp 669–700.

Coulborn, R. (1965) *Feudalism in History*, Hamden, Connecticut: Archon Books.

Dalton, G. (1971) 'Studies in Economic Anthropology', in G. Dalton (ed), Washington DC, American Anthropological Association, pp 8–24.

Danner, P. (1980) *An Ethics for the Affluent*, Washington, DC: University Press of America.

Davidson, J. (1967) *Samoa Mo Samoa*, Melbourne: Oxford University Press.

Day, R.B. (1988) 'Leon Trotsky on the Dialectics of Democratic Control', in P. Wiles (ed), *The Soviet Economy on the Brink of Reform*, Boston: Unwin Hyman, pp 1–36.

De Long, J. (2000) 'The Triumph of Monetarism', *Journal of Economic Perspectives*, **14** (1), pp 83–94.

Dewatripont, M. and Roland, G. (1991) 'The Virtue of Gradualism and Legitimacy in the Transition to a Market Ecomony', *Economic Journal*, **102** (411), pp 291–300.

Diamond, J. (1997) *Guns, Germs and Steel: the Fates of Human Socities*, New York: W.W. Norton & Co.

Dickinson, H.D. (1933) 'Price Formation in a Socialist Economy', *The Economic Journal*, **43** (170), pp 237–50.

Dilnot, A. (1995) 'The Assessment: The Future of the Welfare State', *Oxford Review of Economic Policy*, (3), pp 1–10.

Dobb, M. (1933) 'Economic Theory and the Problem of a Socialist Economy', *The Economic Journal*, **43** (172), pp 588–98.

Dobb, M. (1960) *An Essay on Economic Growth and Planning*, London: Routledge & Kegan Paul.

Dobb, M. (1963) *Studies in the Theory of Capitalism*, London: Routledge & Kegan Paul.

Domar, E.D. (1989) *Capitalism, Socialism and Serfdom*, Cambridge: Cambridge University Press.

Downs, A. (1967) *Inside Bureaucracy*, Boston: Little, Brown.

Drago, R. (1984–5) 'New Use of an Old Technology: The Growth of Worker Participation', *Journal of Post-Keynesian Economics*, **7** (2), pp 153–67.

Dyker, D. (1983) *The Process of Investment in the Soviet Union*, Cambridge: Cambridge University Press.

Ellman, M. (1973) *Planning Problems in the USSR*, Cambridge: Cambridge University Press.

Elster, J. (1989) 'Social Norms and Economic Theory', *Journal of Economic Perspectives*, **3** (4), pp 89–117.

Elster, J. (1998) 'Emotions and Economic Theory', *Journal of Economic Literature*, **36** (1), pp 47–74.

Estrin, S. and Holmes, P. (1990) 'Indicative Planning in Developed Economies', *Journal of Comparative Economics*, **14** (4), pp 531–54.

Etzioni, A. (1985) 'Encapsulated Competition', *Journal of Post-Keynesian Economics*, **7** (3), pp 287–302.

Etzioni, A. (1987) 'On Thoughtless Rationality (Rules of Thumb)', *Kyklos*, **40** (4), pp 496–514.

Firth, R. (1958) *Human Types: An Introduction to Social Anthropology*, New York: Mentor Books.

Fischer, S. (1980) 'Dynamic Inconsistency, Co-operation and the Benevolent Dissembling Government', *Journal of Economic Dynamic Control*, **2** (1), pp 93–107.

Freeman, R. (1996) 'Working for Nothing', *Working Paper 5435*, National Bureau of Economic Research, Cambridge, MA.

Galbraith, J.K. (1958) *The Affluent Society*, London: Hamish Hamilton Ltd.

Galbraith, J.K. (1967) *The New Industrial State*, London: Hamish Hamilton Ltd.

Gamble, C. (1986) 'Hunter-gatherers and the Origins of the State', in J.A. Hall (ed), *States in History*, Oxford: Basil Blackwell, pp 22–47.

Ganshof, F.L. (1952) *Feudalism*, London: Longman.

Gerschekron, A. (1971) 'Ideology as a System Determinant', in A. Eckstein (ed), *Comparative Economic Systems: Theoretical and Methodological Approaches*, Berkeley: University of California Press.

Gibbons, R. (1998) 'Incentives in Organizations', *Journal of Economic Perspectives*, **12** (4), pp 115–32.

Glassman, R. (1986) *Democracy and Despotism in Primitive Societies*, New York: Associated Faculty Press.

Godlier, M. (1971) 'Salt Currency and the Circulation of Commodities among the Baruya of New Guinea', in G. Dalton (ed), *Studies in Economic Anthropology*, Washington, DC: American Anthropological Association, pp 255–73 .

Granick, D. (1980) 'The Ministry as the Maximising Unit in Soviet Industry', *Journal of Comparative Economics*, **4** (3), pp 255–73.

Greenslade, R. and Schroeder, D. (1977) 'The Bureaucratic Economy', *Soviet Union/Union Sovietique*, **4** (2), pp 314–29.

Gregory, C.A. (1981) 'A Conceptual Analysis of Non-capitalist Gift Economy with Particular Reference to Papua New Guinea', *Cambridge Journal of Economics*, **5** (2), pp 119–35.

Gregory, C.A. (1982) *Gifts and Commodities*, New York: Academic Press.

Grossman, G. (1963) 'Notes for a Theory of the Command Economy', *Soviet Studies*, **15** (2), pp 101–3.

Grossman, G. and Helpman (1994) 'Endogenous Innovation in the Theory of Growth', *Journal of Economic Perspectives*, **8** (1), pp 23–44.

Haddad, L. (1972) 'Wages in the Soviet Union: Problems of Policy', *The Journal of Industrial Relations*, **14** (2), pp 171–83.

Haddad, L. (1975) 'Efficiency and Industrial Democracy', *The Journal of Industrial Relations*, **17** (4), pp 345–55.

Haddad, L. (1980) 'The Soviet Economy: Planning, Policies and Performance', *World Review*, **19** (2), pp 31–46.

Haddad, L. (1991) 'The Role of the State in the Light of Ibn Khaldun's Economics', *The Middle East Business and Economic Review*, **1** (1), pp 54–62.

Haddad, L. (1992) 'From Central Planning to a Market Economy: What are the Questions?', in H. Hendrischke (ed), *Market Reform in the Changing Socialist World*, Centre for Chinese Political Economy, Macquarie University, pp 133–53.

Haddad, L. (1993) 'Ethical Considerations in Formulating National Economic Policy', *Humanomics*, **9** (3), pp 28–46.

Haddad, L. (1994) 'The Disjunction between Decision-making and Information Flows: The Case of the Former Planned Economies', *Working Papers in Economics* No. 200, Department of Economics, University of Sydney.

Haddad, L. (1995) 'The Development of Indigenous Entrepreneurship During the Transitional Period', *Ukrainian Economic Review*, **1** (1–2), pp 118–30.

Haddad, L. (1995a) 'On the Rational Sequencing of Enterprise Reform', *The Journal of Communist Studies and Transition Politics*, **11** (2), pp 91–109.

Haddad, L. (1996) 'Comment, Ethics, Commerce and Government: The Scottish School', in P. Groenewegen (ed), *Economics and Ethics?*, London and New York: Routledge, pp 68–80.

Haddad, L. (1998) 'Economic Dimensions of Human Rights in Transition Economies', *Australian Journal of Human Rights*, **4** (2), pp 107–24.

Harrod, F. (1948) *Towards a Dynamic Economics*, London: Macmillan.

Hayek, F.A. (1935) 'The Present State of the Debate', in *Collectivist Economic Planning*, London: Routledge, pp 201–43.

Hayek, F.A. (1945) 'The Use of Knowledge in Society', *The American Economic Review*, **35** (4), pp 519–30.

Hayek, F.A. (1978) *New Studies in Philosophy, Economics and the History of Ideas*, London: Routledge & Kegan Paul.

Herlihy, D. (ed) (1970) *The History of Feudalism*, London: Macmillan.

Herskovtis, M. (1961) 'Economic Change and Cultural Dynamics', in R. Braibanti and J. Spengler (eds), *Tradition, Values and Socioeconomic Development*, Durham: Duke University Press, pp 114–38.

Hicks, J. (1965) *Capital and Growth*, Oxford: Clarendon Press.

Hicks, J. (1977) *A Theory of Economic History*, Oxford: Oxford University Press.

Hirsch, F. (1976) *Social Limits to Growth*, London: Routledge & Kegan Paul.

Hodgson, G.M. (1982–3) 'Worker Participation and Macroeconomic Efficiency', *Journal of Post-Keynesian Economics*, **5** (2), pp 266–75.

Hodgson, G.M. (1998) 'The Approach of Institutional Economics', *Journal of Economic Literature*, **36,** pp 166–92.

Hodgkinson, V. and Weitzman, M. (1991) *Giving and Volunteering in the United States*, Washington, DC: Independent Sector.

Hoffmann, N.E. (1975) 'Soviet Information Processing: Recent Theory and Experience', *Soviet Union/Union Sovietique*, **2** (1), pp 22–49.

Hurka, T. (1993) *Perfectionism*, Oxford: Oxford University Press.

Hurwicz, L. (1971) 'Centralisation and Decentralisation in Economic Processes', in A. Eckstein (ed), *Comparative Economic Systems*, Berkeley: University of California Press, pp 79–102.

Ibn Khaldun (1958) *The Muqadimmah: An Introduction to History*, translated from the Arabic by Franz Rosenthal in 3 volumes, London: Routledge & Kegan Paul.

Johansen, L. (1979) 'The Bargaining Society and the Inefficiency of Bargaining', *Kyklos*, **32** (3), pp 497–523.

Jorde, T.M. and Teece, D.J. (1990) 'Innovation and Cooperation: Implications for Competition and Antitrust', *Journal of Economic Perspectives*, **4** (3), pp 75–96.

Kaldor, N. (1950) 'The Economic Aspects of Advertising', *Review of Economic Studies*, **18** (1), pp 1–27.

Kennedy, P.W. (1994) 'Information Processing and Organization Design', *Journal of Economic Behaviour and Organization*, **25**, pp 37–51.

Keyes, C. (1983) 'Peasant Strategies in Asian Societies: Moral and Rational Economic Approaches', *Journal of Asian Studies*, **43** (4), pp 753–68.

Keynes, J.M. (1936) *The General Theory of Employment Interest and Money*, London: Macmillan.

Keynes, J.M. (1938) 'My Early Beliefs', in *The Collected Writings of John Maynard Keynes*, Volume X, The Royal Economic Society, Cambridge: Cambridge University, pp 433–450.

King, M. and Rebelo, S. (1990) 'Public Policy and Economic Growth: Developing Neo-classical Implications', *Journal of Political Economy*, **98** (5), pp 126–50.

Kirzner, I.M. (1973) *Competition and Entrepreneurship*, Chicago and London: University of Chicago Press.

Klamer, A. (1989) 'An Accountant among Economists: Conversations with Sir John Hicks', *The Journal of Economic Perspectives*, **3** (4), pp 167–80.

Koopmans, T. and Montias, J. (1971) 'On the Description and Comparison of Economic Systems', in A. Eckstein (ed), *Comparative Economic Systems: Theoretical and Methodological Approaches*, Berkeley: University of California Press, pp 27–78.

Kornai, J. (1971) *Anti-equilibrium*, Amsterdam and London: North Holland Publishing Co.

Kornai, J. (1980) *The Economics of Shortage*, London and Amsterdam: North Holland Publishing Co.

Kovacic, W. and Shapiro, C. (2000) 'Antitrust Policy: A Centenary of Economic and Legal Thinking', *Journal of Economic Perspectives*, **14** (1), pp 43–60.

Lane, D. (1985) *The Soviet Economy and Society*, Oxford: Blackwell.

Lange, O. (1938) *On The Economic Theory of Socialism*, New York: McGraw Hill.

Lazar (1991) 'Labour Economics and the Psychology of Organizations', *Journal of Economic Perspectives*, **5** (2), pp 89–110.

Lenin V.I. (1917) 'The State and Revolution', reprinted in V.I. Lenin, *Selected Works*, Moscow: Foreign Languages Publishing House, **2** (1), pp 220–56.

Lerner, A.P. (1934) 'Economic Theory and Socialist Economy', *Review of Economic Studies*, **2** (1) p 561.

Levy, F. and Truman, E. (1971) 'Toward a Rational Theory of Decentralisation: Another View', *American Political Science Review*, **65** (2), pp 172–79.

Lucas, R.E. (1988) 'On the Mechanics of Economic Development', *Journal of Monetary Economics*, **22** (1), pp 3–42.

Lynch, R.G. (1989) 'Centralisation Redefined', *Journal of Comparative Economics*, **13** (1), pp 1–14.

Malinowski, B. (1922) *Argonauts of the Western Pacific*, London: Routledge.

Marglin, S. (1967) *Public Investment Criteria*, London: George Allen and Unwin.

Marschak, T. (1959) 'Centralisation and Decentralisation in Economic Organizations', *Econometrica*, **27** (July), pp 390–430.

Marx, K. (1875) *Critique of the Gotha Programme*, English translation, New York: International Publishers (1938).

Mead, M. (ed) (1955) *Cultural Patterns and Technical Change*, New York: Mentor Books.

Meade, J. (1989) *Agathopia: The Economics of Partnership*, London: Pergamon and Aberdeen University Press.

Menchik, P. and Weisbrod, B. (1987) 'Voluntary Labour Supply', *Journal of Public Economics*, March, pp 159–83.

Mill, J.S. (1868) *Principles of Political Economy*, London: Longman.

Mill, J.S. (1862) 'Centralisation', in *Collected Works*, (1977) of John Stewart Mill, Volume XXIX, J.M. Robson (ed), Toronto: Toronto University Press.

Miller, J. and Murrell, P. (1981) 'Limitations on the Use of Information – Rewarding Incentives Schemes in Economic Organizations', *Journal of Comparative Economics*, **5** (3), pp 251–72.

Miller, J. and Murrell, P. (1984) 'The Applicability of Information – Rewarding Incentives Schemes in Economic Organizations', *Journal of Comparative Economics*, **8** (1), pp 277–89.

Mirrlees, J.A. (1997) 'Information and Incentives: The Economics of Carrots and Sticks', *The Economic Journal*, **107** (444), pp 1311–29.

Mises, von L. (1935) 'Economic Calculation in the Socialist Commonwealth', in F.A. Hayek (ed), *Collectivist Economic Planning*, London: Routledge & Kegan Paul, pp 87–130.

Montias, J. (1976) *The Structure of Economic Systems*, New Haven and London: Yale University Press.

Morgenstern, D. (1972) 'Thirteen Critical Points in Contemporary Economic Theory', *Journal of Economic Literature*, **10** (4), pp 1163–89.

Morishima, M. (1982) *Why Has Japan 'Succeeded': Western Technology Japanese Ethics*, Cambridge: Cambridge University Press.

Nadiri, M. (1993) 'Innovation and Technological Spillovers', Working Paper Series, Working Paper, No. 4423, NBER, Cambridge, MA, August.

Nash, M. (1966) *Primitive and Peasant Economic Systems*, Scranton, PA: Candler Publishing Co.

Neuberger, E. and Duffy, W. (1976) *Comparative Economic Systems: A Decision-making Approach*, Boston: Allyn and Bacon.

North, D.C. (1990) *Institutions and Institutional Change and Economic Performance*, Cambridge: Cambridge University Press.

Nove, A. (1978) *The Soviet Economic System*, London: George Allen and Unwin Ltd.

Nozick, R. (1974) *Anarchy, State and Utopia*, Oxford: Blackwell.

Olson, M. (1965) *The Logic of Collective Action*, Cambridge, Mass: Harvard University Press.

Pearce, I. (1976) 'Resource Conservation and the Market Mechanism' in D. Pearce and S. Rose (eds), *The Economics of Natural Resources*, London: Macmillan, pp 191–204.

Pettigrew, A. (1974) *The Politics of Organizational Decision-making*, London: Tavistock.

Polanyi, K. (1957) *The Great Transformation: The Political and Economic Origins of Our Time*, Boston: Bacon Press.

Pospisil, L. (1971) *Anthropology of Law: A Comparative Theory*, New York: Harper and Row Publishers.

Powell, R.P. (1977) 'Plan Execution and the Workability of Soviet Planning', *Journal of Comparative Economics*, **1** (1), pp 51–76.

Prash, R.E. (1991) 'The Ethics of Growth in Adam Smith's Wealth of Nations', *History of Political Economy*, **23** (2), pp 337–52.

Priddel, D. and Wheeler, R. (1997) 'Rescue of Bryde's Whale Balaenoptera Edeni Entrapped in the Manning River NSW', *Australian Zoologist*, **30** (3), pp 262–71.

Pryor, F. (1977) *The Origins of the Economy: A Comparative Study of Distributions in Primitive and Peasant Economies*, New York: Academic Press.

Pryor, F. (1980) 'Feudalism as an Economic System', *Journal of Comparative Economics*, **4** (1), pp 56–77.

Putterman, L. (1995) 'Markets, Hierarchies, and Information: On a Paradox in the Economics of Organization', *Journal of Economic Behavior and Organization*, **26,** pp 373–90.

Rabin, M. (1998) 'Psychology and Economics', *Journal of Economic Literature*, **36** (1), 11–46.

Rawls, J. (1971) *A Theory of Justice*, Cambridge, MA: Harvard University Press.

Reischauer, E. (1965) 'Japanese Feudalism', in R. Coulborn (ed), *Feudalism in History*, Hamden, Conneticut: Archon Books, pp 26–48.

Reynolds, H. (1996) *Aboriginal Sovereignty*, Sydney: Allen and Unwin.

Rigby, T.H. (1977) 'Stalinism and the Mono-organizational Society', in Robert C. Tucker (ed), *Stalinism Essays in Historical Interpretation*, New York: Norton, pp 57–76.

Robbins, L. (1932) *An Essay on the Nature and Significance of Economic Science*, London: Macmillan.

Robbins, L. (1934) *The Great Depression*, London: Macmillan.

Roberts, P.C. (1971) *Alienation and the Soviet Economy*, Albuquerque: University of New Mexico Press.

Robinson, Joan (1965) *The Accumulation of Capital*, London: Macmillan.

Robinson, Joan (1970) *Freedom and Necessity*, London: George Allen and Unwin.

Romer, P. (1986) 'Increasing Returns and Long-run Growth', *Journal of Political Economy*, **94** (5), pp 1002–37.

Romer, P. (1990) 'Endogenous Technological Change', *Journal of Political Economy*, **98** (5), pp 71–102.

Rose-Ackerman, S. (1996) 'Altruism Non Profits and Economic Theory', *Journal of Economic Literature*, **34** (June), pp 701–28.

Rosenberg, N. (1976) *Perspective on Technology*, Cambridge: Cambridge University Press.

Rowthorn, R. (1996) 'Ethics and Economics: An Economist's View', in P. Groenewegen (ed), *Economics and Ethics?*, London and New York: Routledge, pp 15–34.

Sah, R.K. (1991) 'Fallibility in Human Organization and Political Systems', *Journal of Economic Perspectives*, **5** (2), pp 67–88.

Sah, R.K. and Stiglitz, J. (1986) 'The Architecture of Economic Systems', *American Economic Review*, **76** (4), pp 716–27.

Sah, R.K. and Stiglitz, J. (1988) 'Committees, Hierarchies and Polyarchies', *The Economic Journal*, **98** (391), pp 451–71.

Sahlins, M.D., (1958) *Social Stratification in Polynesia*, Seattle, WA: University of Washington Press.

Sahlins, M. (1974) *Stone Age Economics*, London: Tavistock.

Schapara, I. (1943) *Nature of Land Tenure in the Bachuland Protectorate*, Lovedale: The Lovedale Press.

Schumpeter, J. (1950) *Capitalism, Socialism and Democracy*, (3rd edn), London: George Allen and Unwin.

Schumpeter, J. (1954) *History of Economic Analysis*, London: Allen and Unwin.

Scitovsky, T. (1976) *The Joyless Economy*, New York and London: Oxford University Press.

Scitovsky, T. (1990) 'The Benefits of Asymmetric Markets', *Journal of Economic Perspectives*, **4** (1), pp 135–48.

Scott, J.M. (1976) *The Moral Economy of the Peasant: Rebellion and Subsistence: Southeast Asia*, New Haven, CT: Yale University Press.

Scott, J.M. (1992) 'Policy Implications of a New View of Economic Growth', *The Economic Journal*, **102** (5), pp 622–32.

Sen, A. (1973) *On Economic Inequality*, Oxford: Clarendon Press.

Sen, A. (1977) 'Rational Fools: A Critique of the Behavioural Foundations of Economic Theory', *Philosophy and Public Affairs*, **6** (Summer), pp 317–44.

Sen, A. (1987) *On Ethics and Economics*, Oxford: Basil Blackwell.

Sen, A. (1992) *Inequality Reexamined*, Cambridge, MA: Harvard University Press.

Sen, A. (1993) 'Money and Value on the Ethics and Economics of Finance', *Economics and Philosophy*, **9** (2), pp 203–27.

Sewell, D. (1996) 'The Dangers of Decentralisation According to Prue' Homme: Some Further Aspects', *The World Bank Reserve Observer*, **11** (1), pp 143–50.

Shackle, G.L.S. (1972) *Epistemics and Economics*, Cambridge: Cambridge University Press.

Sillery, A. (1952) *The Bechuanaland Protectorate*, Capetown and London: Oxford University Press.

Simon, H.A. (1959) 'Rational Decision-making in Business Organizations', *American Economic Review*, **49** (3), pp 252–83.

Simon, H.A. (1965) *Administrative Behaviour* (2nd edn), New York: Free Press.

Simon, H.A. (1983) *Reason in Human Affairs*, Stanford, CA: Stanford University Press.

Simon, H.A. (1991) 'Organizations and Markets', *Journal of Economic Perspectives*, **5** (2), pp 25–44.

Smith, A. (1976) *The Theory of Moral Sentiments*, edited by D.D. Raphael and A.L. Macfie, Oxford: Clarendon Press.

Smith, V. (1975) 'The Primitive Hunter Culture, Pleistocene Extinction, and the Rise of Agriculture', *Journal of Political Economy*, **83** (4), pp 727–55.

Smith, V. and Walker, J. (1993) 'Monetary Rewards and Decision Lost in Experimental Economies', *Economic Inquiry*, **31** (2), pp 245–61.

Solow, R.M. (2000) 'Toward a Macroeconomics of the Median Run', *Journal of Economic Perspectives*, **14** (1), pp 151–8.

Stigler, G.J. (1961) 'The Economics of Information', *The Journal of Political*

Economy, **69** (3), pp 213–25.

Stiglitz, J. (1991) 'Symposium on Organizations and Economics', *Journal of Economic Perspectives*, **5** (2), pp 15–24.

Stiglitz, J. (1998) 'The Private Use of Public Interests: Incentives and Institutions', *The Journal of Economic Perspectives*, **12** (2), pp 3–22.

Stodder, J. (1995) 'The Evolution of Complexity in Primitive Exchange Theory', *Journal of Comparative Economics*, **20** (1), pp 190–210.

Strayer, J. (1965) 'Feudalism in Western Europe', in K. Coulborn (ed), *Feudalism in History*, Hamden Connecticut: Archon Books, pp 15–25.

Sugden, R. (1989) 'Spontaneous Order', *Journal of Economic Perspectives*, **3** (4), pp 85–94.

Sylos-Labini, P. (1962) *Oligarchy and Technical Progress*, Cambridge, MA: Harvard University Press.

Van de Ven, A. (1993) 'The Emergence of an Industrial Structure for Technological Change', *Journal of Comparative Economics*, **17** (2), pp 338–65.

Vanek, J. (ed) (1975) *Self-management: Economic Liberation of Man*, London: Penguin.

Viljoen, S. (1974) *Economic Systems in World History*, London: Longman.

Walras, L. (1954) *Elements of Pure Economics*, translated by William Jaffe, London:Allen and Unwin.

Weitzman, M. (1984) *The Share Economy*, Cambridge, MA: Harvard University Press.

Wicksteed, P.H. (1933) *The Common Sense of Political Economy*, 2 volumes, edited by L. Robbins, London: Routledge & Kegan Paul.

Wiles, P.J.D. (1961) *Price, Cost and Output* Oxford: Basil Blackwell.

Wiles, P.J.D. (1962) *The Political Economy of Communism*, Oxford: Basil Blackwell.

Wilhelm, H. (1985) 'The Soviet Union has an Administered not a Planned Economy', *Soviet Studies*, **37** (1), pp 118–30.

Williamson, O.E. (1981) 'The Modern Corporations: Origins, Evolution, Attributes', *Journal of Economic Literature*, **19** (4), pp 1537–68.

Williamson, O.E. (1985) *The Economic Institutions of Capitalism: Firms, Markets, Relational Contracting* New York and London: Free Press and Macmillan.

Zauberman, A. (1975) *The Mathematical Revolution in Soviet Economies*, London: Oxford University Press.

Zhou, H. (1991) 'Innovation Decision and Reward Structure', *Journal of Comparative Economics*, **15** (4), pp 661–80.

Index

centralised economies 19
centralised information 177–8
centralised information flows 257
centralised–authoritarian economies 41, 61
centralised–command economies 101–2
centralised–democratic economies 41, 61, 102
change 28–9
China 152
climate, and the customary economy 117–18
Coase, R. 56, 64
coercion 96, 101, 148
Collard, D. 95, 107
collective action 269–70
collective decisions 27
command 1, 187
    and the composite economy 192–6
    and decision-making criteria 194
    and decision-making procedures 193
    and decision-making structures 192–3
    and incentives 195
    and information flows 193–4
command economy 136–63
    decision-making procedure 162–3
command model 35–6
command principle 19, 23, 24, 148
    and the composite economy 204–5
competition 1, 169–70, 176, 178–9, 196–200, 199
    and innovation 234
    price and non-price 184
competitive economy 164–86
    cooperation 175
    decision-making criteria 178–80, 185
    decision-making procedure 173–5, 184–5
    decision-making structure 169–73
    evolution 164–9
    incentives 180–83
    information flows 175–8, 185
    motivation structure 185–6
competitive market 4
competitive principle
    in the composite economy 196–200, 205
    and decision-making structures 196
    and information flows 98
    and motivation 199–200

and the valuation problem 198–9
composite economy 7, 187–208
    and command 192–6, 193–4, 195–6
    and the command principle 204–5
    competitive principle in 196–200, 205
    and the cooperative principle 200–204, 205
    custom and convention 188–92, 204
concentration of decision making power 251
concentration of economic power 15–16, 19
conciliation and arbitration 217
confidentiality 44
Conlisk, J. 78, 210, 221
consultation 32, 33, 216
consultative economy 254
consumer sovereignty 170–71, 213
consumption 244–5
consumption decisions 213
cooperation 1, 20, 21, 26–7, 43, 45, 164, 187, 218
    and the competitive economy 175
cooperative principle
    and the composite economy 205
    and decision-making criteria 202
    and decision-making procedures 201
    and decision-making structures 200–201
    and information flows 201–2
    and motivation 203
cooperative societies, structure of information flows 63–4
coordinating mechanisms 1
corn model 146
Coulborn, R. 138, 140, 141
creative efficiency 247
    and decision-making criteria 258–9
    and decision-making procedures 254, 262
    and decision-making structures 250–51, 262
    and incentive structures 260–61
    and information flows 256, 263
creativity 106
criteria continuum 81
    economic systems in 82–5
custom 1